# A HISTORY OF CAERNARVONSHIRE

## 1284-1900

by

## A. H. DODD

CAERNARVONSHIRE HISTORICAL SOCIETY
1968

*Printed by Gee and Son, Denbigh.*

# CONTENTS

# LIST OF ILLUSTRATIONS

# PREFACE

This book has grown out of lectures given to extra-mural classes at Cricieth in the winter of 1964-5 and at Caernarvon in 1965-6, and it has gained much from the knowledge of local topography and tradition which members were able to contribute to the discussions. It is published under the auspices of the Caernarvonshire Historical Society, and its indebtedness to the Society's publications will be evident from a glance at the chapter bibliographies. Less obvious to readers, but equally acceptable to the author, has been the help given in every direction by the Society's Editor, Mr. E. Gwynne Jones, and by his colleagues on the staff of the University College Library, as well as by members of the Editorial Committee. Of the former, I am particularly indebted to the inexhaustible patience of Mrs. A. J. Parry in the thankless task of typing and re-typing successive drafts of the chapters.

The origins of the work have ensured attention to the interests of the general reader; in general, footnotes have been avoided except for the identification of actual quotations, or acknowledgement of sources of information not easily traceable from the chapter bibliographies. These cover the principal works consulted and afford a guide to more detailed works for readers with a more academic approach.

The narrative naturally starts with the formation of the shire by Edward I, since the earlier history of the area has no natural coherence; it is not carried beyond the end of the nineteenth century because since then — leaving out of account any prospective changes in county boundaries — county affairs have become so largely merged in those of the nation as to leave it doubtful whether in contemporary conditions the older concept of 'county history' has any real validity.

I wish to express also my gratitude to the owners of copyrights who have so generously given permission for the reproduction of pictures in their possession. I am indebted to the Comptroller of Her Majesty's Stationery Office for leave to reproduce Plates III, IV, VI, VII and XVI; to the Librarian of the National Library of Wales for the photographs reproduced in Plates, I, II, VIII, IX, X, XI, XIII, XIV and XVIII; to the Vicar and Churchwardens of Ynyscynhaearn for Plate XV and to the Archivist and County Records Committee of Caernarvonshire for Plate XVII. I am especially grateful to Mr. Bryn L. Davies, of the Education Department, U.C.N.W., and Mr. Douglas Williams, of the Normal College, for the folding map which is inserted as a frontispiece. It should be added that the generous financial support given by the Caernarvonshire County Council through its Welsh Church Acts Committee made it possible for the Society to undertake publication.

A. H. DODD.

# I

# THE MAKING OF THE SHIRE

## (1284 - 1536)

THE county of Caernarvon was brought into existence by
King Edward I on his victory in 1284, after a long and bitter
campaign, over Llywelyn ap Gruffydd, the last of the independent princes of Gwynedd and the first titular prince of
Wales. As conqueror, Edward stepped into the shoes of the
dispossessed prince and assumed his rights. This involved a
substantial reorganisation of the conquered territory; indeed
the Statute of Wales, which embodied it, has been called[1]
'the most comprehensive code that any English legislator
issued during the Middle Ages'. The king himself describes
in the preamble to the statute what were his aims and how
he went about the task: after taking advice on the legal
rights and customs of the Welsh rulers, he declares, 'we
have . . . abolished certain of them, some thereof we have
allowed, and some we have corrected; and we have likewise
commanded certain others to be ordained and added
thereto '.

What did this mean in practice? In the first place, he took
over the historic divisions of the land — the *cantref* and the
*cymwd* — and re-grouped them after the English pattern
into shires. His original intention had been to group the
mainland west of the Conway into two shires: one shire
was to have its centre at Conway and to extend from the
river to' the north-eastern limits of Llŷn, with an easterly
spur across the river in the Creuddyn peninsula to secure
control over this important strategic and commercial high-

---

[1] Pollock and Maitland, *History of English Law* (1875), i. 220.

way; the other, with its centre at Cricieth, would have
embraced the rest of the present Caernarvonshire together
with Merioneth north of the river Artro. But different
counsels prevailed before the statute finally took shape, and
instead of two counties of Conwayshire and Criciethshire
(or whatever they might have been called), there emerged
the single shire very much as we know it today, but for minor
adjustments. How long these familiar boundaries will remain
is still in the lap of the gods; but there are some grounds for
doubting whether the king's first plan would not have better
suited the geographical and economic conditions of the age,
for — as this story will repeatedly show — Llŷn and
Eifionydd found their natural contacts across Traeth Mawr
into Ardudwy until better communications eastwards, within
these last two centuries, linked them more effectively with
Arfon and Arllechwedd.

At the head of the shire was the sheriff — for the next two
generations invariably an Englishman. To his court, held
monthly, were summoned all the freemen of the new shire
together with a selection of the 'unfree' villagers who
represented the lower stratum of the conquered population.
And at the head of the three shires of Gwynedd — or North
Wales, as it was now officially called — was the English
administration at Caernarvon. Edward clearly designed this
as a sort of imperial centre; not only did he base the castle
there, as we shall see, on imperial models, but he took pains
to honour the rooted local tradition (arising from mistaken
identity of names) that the father of the Emperor Constantine
had been buried there; similarly he paid homage to the
shrine of Beuno, the patron saint of Gwynedd, and made a
pilgrimage to Bardsey, the Valhalla of its holy men.

The law administered in the new courts, as the preamble
to the Statute of Wales makes clear, was a blend of Welsh
and English law. Edward's main concern was to bring the
criminal code, the mainstay of public order, into conformity
with English standards. In Welsh law crimes of violence
were matters to be avenged by the kindred in accordance
with a fixed scale of penalties. Under the later Welsh princes,

who had done so much to modernise Gwynedd, these hoary customs were already being brought closer to the general practice of more developed states; Edward I carried the matter further and insisted that these crimes be no longer treated as family matters but as breaches of the king's peace. But in Welsh civil law, especially in the methods of holding and inheriting land, he made little change. Subject to gradual erosion by the example of English standards (which came to be preferred by the more substantial folk and had already been allowed to infiltrate by the two Llywelyns), Welsh custom continued to hold its place in the courts long after the Edwardian conquest.

Within the shire, the older Welsh subdivisions and their officials and courts remained, under different names. The *cymwd*, for example, was easily assimilated to its English counterpart the hundred, and attendance at the hundred court, which affected a wider section of the community, touched a familiar chord. Those who attended it found it not very different from the court of the *cymwd*, which like it dealt with local matters and minor offences, with native officials — usually local men of known families — in charge. On the whole, the Caernarvonshire countryman would not find things greatly altered. Except at the very top, there was no displacement of population, no eviction from the soil. The same families tended the same fields, owing similar dues and services (whether to their old overlords or to new-comers), settling their disputes and paying for their offences in familiar ways, except perhaps for greater severity if they resorted to violence; jury service might be new to them, but at least it was done among neighbours. There was no shift in social classes, no basic departure from daily routines; the distinction between free tenure and the more burdensome servile tenure remained as it had been under Welsh laws, save for changes (to be touched on later) which were already creeping in before the conquest and were not directly con- nected with it.

It was different in the towns, but of course these were few in number, and in population no more than in villages. Three of them Edward chose as sites for the ring of castles with which he planned to hold down the conquered territory. He built them on the latest principles of military architecture, using an architect from his wife's home in Savoy, who was to acquire a European reputation. Caernarvon, with its commanding geographical situation, still retained something of the strategic and commercial importance it had acquired in Roman times, and it was here that Edward built his first Snowdonian castle. With its polygonal towers (one of them decorated with the imperial eagle) and its ' banded ' masonry, it reflected — perhaps consciously — the grandeur of the palace at Constantinople where successors of Constantine carried on Roman imperial rule long after Rome itself had fallen to the barbarian. At the mouth of the Conway, hard by the Cistercian foundation whose abbot had been one of Llywelyn's staunchest henchmen, he was able to build on a site of great natural strength, commanding the vital river Conway, as Caernarvon, with its more elaborate defences to compensate for the more vulnerable site, dominated the equally important Straits. He moved the monks out of harm's way up-river, to a new monastery at Maenan on the opposite bank, and looped the boundary of the new shire across the river at this point to include it. At Cricieth — remote, thinly populated and difficult of access, but also of strategic value — he took over and remodelled a castle of Llywelyn's.

Each of these castles had attached to it a borough which was in effect (save in the unwalled borough of Cricieth) an extension of the castle wall to house and protect the civil population necessary to the life of the garrison. The privileges attached to membership of these boroughs were strictly confined to the conquering English. And the same is true of the two later boroughs — Nefyn and Pwllheli — which came into existence some seventy years later, when commerce was beginning to loom larger than defence. Each had been head of an old Welsh *cymwd*, and was well placed for trading; but the Welsh population was debarred from this trade and from the other rights enjoyed by the new English burgesses.

How did the new order work in Caernarvonshire? It would seem that Edward I made a serious and not wholly unsuccessful attempt to deal justly with his new subjects and to win their co-operation and goodwill, so far as was consistent with his rights as conqueror. Of these rights his castles were a living symbol, at least as important psychologically as they were strategically. But friction there was bound to be — cases of local oppression answered by local violence. It was not easy, as the roads then were, to herd men from Llŷn and Eifionydd into the courts at Caernarvon; it might have been easier had Conway and Cricieth been the centres of government, as originally planned. The frequency of fines for non-attendance at court, and the chronic inability of sheriffs to rake in the full quota of dues from their shires, speak for themselves. Edward tried to base his taxation on what had been collected under Llywelyn, but Llywelyn's war taxation had been abnormally heavy and had not been collected without mutterings and mutiny; how much worse when the demands came from utter strangers, unfamiliar with the land and its language, often haughty and over-bearing and always open to suspicion of sharp practice!

Local discontent took on a more serious aspect when, ten years after the conquest, Madog ap Llywelyn, a distant connection of the house of Gwynedd who had been brought up in England and received favours from the crown, returned to Wales and put himself at the head of the scattered malcontents by proclaiming himself Prince of Wales. Roger de Puleston, sheriff of Anglesey and chief revenue officer for North Wales, was hanged by lynch law in front of his own house in Caernarvon, and Edward I had once more to march an army into Caernarvonshire to retrieve from the rebels his seat of government, then to descend on Conway, where for some critical days he was shut up in his own castle; then, having extricated himself from this perilous situation, he went on to relieve Cricieth, which had also been besieged.

The revolt was over, but naturally it was followed by some tightening up of English rule. There is little sign, however, of any policy of revenge and proscription such as was to follow the Glyn Dŵr rising more than a century later. For example, there was still no legal bar to the appointment of Welshmen to local office, and in fact a growing conviction of the hopelessness of revolt against the big battalions drew more and more of them into the king's service, civil or military. It would be an anachronism to think of this or of any of the other Welsh risings before Glyn Dŵr's in terms of modern nationalism. On the one hand Welsh officials could be just as oppressive and just as unpopular as English; on the other hand what the king was bent on imposing was English power, not English culture. The language of law and administration — Latin or Norman French — was just as alien to the Teuton as to the Celt, and the less formal side of public business must needs have been conducted in the popular tongue. Six years after the revolt, in a bid to attract to the English crown the sense of tribal loyalty associated with the title Prince of Wales, rather than leave it vacant for another adventurer like Madog to pick up, Edward I set a lasting precedent by reviving it in favour of his eldest son, Edward of Caernarvon.

In this capacity the new prince acted in some degree as his father's viceroy, and acquired a knowledge of Welsh problems which served him well when he succeeded to the crown as Edward II. For all the bad press he has had from historians, this unlucky king seems to have won the loyalty of the Welsh, and to have leaned on them for support against the turbulence of the barons of the March. He even summoned their representatives, on at least two occasions, to parliament — for the first and last time before the Tudor Acts of Union. The names of those who represented Caernarvon county and boroughs in his last parliament, in 1326, have been preserved. Six men with unimpeachable Welsh names sat for the shire, two Englishmen for each of the boroughs of Caernarvon and Conway; Nefyn and Pwllheli had not yet been granted their charters. It looked as if, amid all the turbulence of the reign and its tragic conclusion, in Wales at least his father's statemanship had been vindicated.

It was during the reign of the third Edward that Welsh

administration deteriorated and Welsh opposition gradually
swelled into something approaching national proportions.
Creçy and Poitiers were glorious victories, but they were also
costly ones to the taxpayer, and the habit was growing of
treating Wales as a sort of milch cow. More and more officials
were non-resident, pocketing the fees and farming out the
work to local hacks who had to recoup themselves at the
taxpayer's expense. Wales had left the English government
at peace for more than half a century since Madog's revolt,
and the crown had grown careless of conciliating its Welsh
subjects. But the government cannot be blamed for the
general misery of the age, which was not peculiar to Wales,
but common to all western Europe. There were repeated and
deadly outbreaks of bubonic plague; the most devastating
of them, familiar in history as the Black Death, carried off
between a half and a third of the population; and the toll
was naturally heaviest among the bondmen with their scanty
fare and their huddled hamlets. As a bond community was
collectively responsible for its dues, the burden fell all the
more heavily on those who remained, and they seized what
chances they could to run away — preferably to the towns,
where they might with luck become wage labourers, filling
the gaps which the plague had brought there too. The vacant
holdings were either seized by the crown and re-sold to
freemen with adjacent lands, or just quietly annexed by
neighbours taking advantage of official slackness.

In other words, the social structure was rapidly breaking
down, and the careful balance of classes prescribed in the
Welsh laws was thrown into confusion. In this atmosphere
the still powerful bardic order began to revert to its primitive
practice of foretelling in cryptic verse the return of the faded
glories of the Welsh people and the humbling of their con-
querors. Such verses circulated orally, not least among
Welshmen who had to all appearance bowed to the yoke
and accepted their conquered status, whether by infiltrating
(as they now did in increasing numbers) into the English
boroughs and acquiring land there on English terms, or by
accepting office under the English crown, or (most frequently

of all) by serving with the English armies in France. Here Welsh soldiers fought under the Prince of Wales — the Black Prince of the history books — in their distinctive linen surcoats of green and white, the colours of the leek. It was the birth time of Welsh national consciousness, and revolt was in the air. A generation after Creçy there arose one more Welsh pretender to the title Prince of Wales, in the person of Owain ap Thomas (better known as Owain Lawgoch), a descendant of the first Llywelyn who, like Madog, had been brought up in England. In the French wars, however, he had fought for England's enemies, and now he enlisted his French master's aid in the cause of Welsh independence. His expedition never got beyond the Channel Islands, but there is some evidence that had he reached Wales he would have rallied support in Anglesey at least, if not in Caernarvonshire.

It was in 1399, some twenty years after this, that the Black Prince's son Richard II, home from Ireland to meet the demands of Henry of Lancaster (newly and rebelliously returned from exile), took refuge in Conway castle with a handful of followers, and on his emergence under promise of safe conduct was seized and made to resign the throne to the usurper under the style of Henry IV. The deposition was bitterly resented in Wales, where the Black Prince's name was still one to conjure with. The general unrest found a champion in yet another Welshman of princely descent but an English upbringing, Owain Glyn Dŵr, and this time Wales really caught fire. Glyn Dŵr had a private quarrel to pursue in his own border lordship: its eddies might never have reached Gwynedd if the waters had not already been troubled there by members of the influential local clan, descended from the first Llywelyn's powerful and favoured seneschal, Ednyfed Fychan, and living on an estate inherited from him at Penmynydd in Anglesey. Kinsmen of Glyn Dŵr, they were not yet anglicised enough to adopt a surname; when they did, it was a name to be made illustrious by England's most successful dynasty, the Tudors. Nor were they the only local malcontents. Alarmed at the prospect of

Gwynedd once more in arms, Henry IV marched his army to Bangor and Caernarvon in 1400 to receive the submissions of some (including the abbots of Maenan and Bardsey and the Rector of Llanllechid) and to wreak his vengeance on the monks of Llanfaes, who failed to submit.

On Good Friday of the following year two of the Penmynydd Tudors took part in a raid which, with help from the town, surprised the Conway garrison and momentarily put the rebels in possession of the castle where Edward I himself had so narrowly escaped disaster a century earlier. Before the end of the year Owain was master of Caernarvonshire and Merioneth, but in November an attack on Caernarvon castle failed, and for the next two years the rebel leader was occupied in other parts of the country. In 1403, however, with the help of ships and men from France (ready as ever to use Wales as a battering ram for her English foes), he was able again to lay siege to Caernarvon, to destroy for good the defences of Cricieth, to burn down the houses of English partisans in Eifionydd — and to receive from his French backers a cargo of wine and spices, landed on the coast of Llŷn.

The next year, 1404, saw a scene immortalised by Shakespeare — the signing at the archdeacon's house at Bangor, by the bishops of Bangor and St. Asaph as intermediaries, of the Tripartite Indenture between Owain, his prisoner Edmund Mortimer (who had married Glyn Dŵr's daughter while in his custody) and the earl of Northumberland, now added to the foes of the house of Lancaster. Under this, Glyn Dŵr was to rule a greatly expanded Wales and Mortimer was to supplant the Lancastrian king on the English throne, but shorn of most of the north, which was to be ruled by Northumberland. Of course nothing came of this. Northumberland's northern campaign in pursuit of the pact was a disastrous failure; forces from Ireland landed in Anglesey and cut Owain off from his friends there; his French allies, after an imposing landing at Milford Haven, cooled off and finally withdrew their troops in 1406. In Caernarvonshire and Merioneth his following was still formidable enough three years later to cause anxiety to the English government, until Harlech, his last stronghold, was captured. Even after that he continued his guerilla operations with a few faithful followers for another seven years, declining all offers of pardon from the crown. Where and how he died no one knows.

His influence, however, was far from dead. For long the bards continued to encourage the belief that he would somehow reappear — until they began to pin their hopes on the Tudor descendants of Ednyfed. Their propaganda was aided and abetted by the savage penal code with which the Welsh people as a whole, irrespective of allegiance, were punished for the panic they had caused across the border; the last remnants of this ominous piece of racial legislation did not disappear till James I's reign. Owain's Anglesey kinsmen faded into insignificance : it was another branch of Ednyfed's stock, headed by Gwilym ap Gruffydd of Penrhyn in Caernarvonshire, that inherited the lion's share of its broad estates, in reward for Gwilym's desertion of Glyn Dŵr when his star began to wane in 1406. On the other hand it was an offshoot of Penmynydd — Owain ap Maredudd ap Tudur, named after the rebel leader — who found service in the English court when the revolt collapsed, took his grandfather's name as a surname, married the widow of Henry V and became the grandfather of Henry VII.

When the Wars of the Roses broke out, hostility to the house of Lancaster had died out in Gwynedd. The rising house of Tudor deserted the Mortimer cause (now represented by the Yorkists) and eventually, through the marriage of Owain Tudor's son to the heiress of Lancaster, became claimants to the English throne itself; it was chiefly in the Marches that the Yorkist cause found Welsh support. Although there was no pitched battle in Caernarvonshire, there was much devastation there, for across the Traeth lay the Lancastrian stronghold of Harlech, which once more became, as in Glyn Dŵr's war, a key point in the struggle, and all Snowdonia was involved in its defence. Owain Tudor's son Jasper, a pillar of the Lancastrian cause in south-

west Wales, swooped from time to time on Caernarvonshire
and Merioneth to rally local partisans such as Dafydd ap
Siencyn, his father's bard, who lived an outlaw's life with
his band in thickly-wooded and thinly-populated Nantconwy. Harlech fell to Welsh Yorkist forces under Sir William
Herbert in 1468, but pride in its epic defence, embodied in
song, became a heritage shared by all Wales.

The Glyn Dŵr wars and the Wars of the Roses added to
the misery of the age, and helped to hasten the dissolution
of medieval Welsh society. But within the shell of the
crumbling social order a new society was beginning to take
shape. Hard as times were for the under-dog, for the bold
and adventurous, the lucky or unscrupulous, they offered
golden opportunities. The seizure, with or without legal
warrant, of vacant ' bond ' holdings or vacant ' burgages ' in
the towns, the purchase of lands ' escheating ' to the crown
through treason or through failure of heirs, encroachments
on the lands of the crown itself when the crown was weak
or ill-served by its officials — all these reached a climax in
the fifteenth century. In addition there were the family
agreements by which many of the local freeholders opted
out of the hampering conditions of ' tribal ' law, and began
building for themselves compact estates after the fashion of
their English neighbours. And finally, in defiance of the
penal statutes Welshmen were worming their way into
public office, on the profits of which they were able to
establish new families. These were the principal elements
out of which the Tudor gentry were fashioned, and Caernarvonshire affords many examples.

In the course of the fifteenth century the Lancashire
family of Bolde grew rich on land and offices in Conway
and Caernarvon. Their possessions eventually passed by
marriage to another immigrant family, the Cheshire
Bulkeleys, and from this nucleus the Bulkeleys extended
their empire into Arllechwedd and Creuddyn and finally
into every corner of Anglesey, which they continued to
dominate till the nineteenth century. But some of the original
local stocks were also rising into prominence. The earliest

home of the family which evolved into the Wynns of Gwydir was in Eifionydd; it is the great Sir John himself who tells us in his history of the house how the deadly feuds that prevailed there drove his ancestors into the upper Conway valley — still the haunt of outlaws, but offering the bait of wide empty lands. Here they first planted themselves on 'bond' lands round Dolwyddelan, and then moved north to more settled regions by acquiring the Coetmor estate of Gwydir, from which they tried to emulate — but never with complete success — the Bulkeley domination of Anglesey. Not far from their original home, rather later in the century, another ancient tribal holding began to expand into what the late Professor Jones Pierce, in his introduction to the calendar of family papers, has called 'the largest accumulation of freehold land in south Caernarvonshire' — the estate of Clenennau, whose owners in the next century took on the surname of Maurice. These and similar families of the 'new gentry' continued to rule Caernarvonshire until the coming of democracy, as the following chapters will show.

## BIBLIOGRAPHY

Brief but authoritative accounts of the principal persons and families mentioned in this and ensuing chapters are to be found in *Y Byw-graffiadur Cymreig* (1953) or in the *Dictionary of Welsh Biography* (1959). J. E. Griffiths, *Pedigrees of Anglesey and Carnarvonshire Families* (1914) is also an invaluable stand-by. There is as yet no satisfactory general history of this period in Welsh history, but the relevant chapters in Vol. I of *Wales through the Ages* (ed. A. J. Roderick, 1959) will be found useful background reading. On the Edwardian settlement of Wales see the work of W. H. Walters under that title (1953; reprinting) and his article 'The making of Caernarvonshire' in *Transactions of Caernarvonshire Historical Society* [*TCHS*], 1942-3. The standard biographies of Owain Glyn Dŵr are by J. E. Lloyd (1931) and by Glanmor Williams (Clarendon Biographies, 1965). On Caernarvonshire rural society in the Middle Ages see articles by T. Jones Pierce in *TCHS* 1939-40 and his introduction to *Clenennau Letters and Papers* (1947). The history of the medieval boroughs is given in E. A. Lewis, *The Mediæval Boroughs of Snowdonia* (1912) and in articles in *TCHS* on Pwllheli (1939-40) and Nefyn (1957) by T. Jones Pierce and on Cricieth (1966) by C. Gresham. Sir John Wynn's *History of the Gwydir Family* (ed. Ballinger, 1927) gives a graphic contemporary picture of Caernarvonshire life in the later Middle Ages. Accounts of the castles are to be found in the official guides of the Ministry of Public Buildings and Works. E. H. Owen and Elfed Thomas, *Atlas Sir Gaernarvon* (1954) covers the whole period in all its aspects.

## II

## TUDOR CAERNARVONSHIRE

THE social collapse of the latter Middle Ages produced two
effects in Caernarvonshire, one positive, the other negative.
The negative effect was the lack of governance made evident
in temporary accounts such as Sir John Wynn's *History of
the Gwydir Family*. It is a fallacy to imagine that conditions
were any better in the principality organised by Edward I
than in the Marches, which he had left under their semi-
independent lords, for, as we have seen, Edward's states-
manlike settlement was undermined by his successors. These
conditions it was the task of the Tudors to remedy, and the
instrument lay to hand in the positive legacy of the troublous
times that had brought them so unexpectedly to the seat of
government; this was the emergence of the gentry, living
on their new compact estates. If their tribal loyalties could
be transferred to the crown, now that it was worn by one
of themselves, and if they could be thus enlisted to co-
operate in the work of government, the situation could be
saved. It was a risk, for the tradition of these gentry was one
of rapacity and turbulence, and this tradition could not be
shrugged off overnight. The genius of the Tudors lay in the
fact that they took the risk and, despite many setbacks,
justified it.

Towards the end of his reign Henry VII granted to the
inhabitants of the principality (as well as of several of the
Welsh marcher lordships which had fallen into his hands)
charters releasing them from some of the more burdensome
conditions imposed during and after the Glyn Dŵr revolt.
The reorganisation of Wales was completed by his son in

two Acts of 1536 and 1542, collectively known to posterity as the Act of Union. The effects were soon apparent. For nearly two hundred years there had been no Welsh sheriff of Caernarvonshire. Among the next sixty-five sheriffs only three English names appear: a Puleston twice, a Peake three times, a Bulkeley four times; and each of these had strong local connections, by marriage or otherwise. The sheriff was still an important local figure, especially after Henry VIII extended representation in parliament to the Welsh shires and boroughs, as we shall see later. Then there was the newer office of lord lieutenant — the premier representative in the shire of the royal dignity. In the North Wales counties this office was normally held by the lord president, the head of the Council of Wales and the Marches, but he was represented locally by the deputy lieutenants, usually one or two for each division of the shire, and these were drawn from the same circle of families as the sheriffs. Their duties could be as important in times of national danger as those of the sheriff were in peaceful times, for it was they who mustered the county militia.

A wider section of the gentry was included in the bench of county justices. It was the admission of Welshmen to this key office that most alarmed some of the king's more cautious advisers, for on the J.P.'s depended the day to day working of government; and although appointment was entirely within the royal discretion, it soon became a normal expectation that as soon as a gentleman attained a certain standing in the shire he would almost automatically be included in the commission of the peace. Then there were the constables of the castles, who were often also *ex officio* mayors of the adjoining boroughs; and below all these, and descending gradually lower in the scale of gentility, came the bailiffs, the collectors and escheators, the high and petty constables, who discharged the less exalted tasks of local administration. All these were drawn from the local gentry, high and low. A broad section of county society was thus harnessed to the work of government.

We might now take a closer look at some of the Caer-

narvonshire families concerned in these tasks, and the way
they set about them. We are fortunate in possessing among
the archives in the National Library two collections of family
papers which throw an exceptionally clear light on this
matter, and summaries of the contents of both collections
can be consulted in the printed Calendars: these are the
Wynn of Gwydir papers and the Clenennau papers. The
ancestors of the Wynns of Gwydir had, like so many of the
old Welsh families, been divided in their loyalties during
the Glyn Dŵr revolt, but the head of the senior branch died
defending Caernarvon castle for the English crown against
the rebel, and in the next generation the heir, Maredudd,
stood foursquare by the Lancastrian cause. It was he who
migrated to Nantconwy a few years after Henry VII's
accession, took a lease of Dolwyddelan from the crown and
then bought the Gwydir estate. From Henry VIII's time on,
Gwydir supplied a succession of sheriffs to the county, as
well as to Denbighshire and Merioneth, and family prestige
reached its peak with the formidable Sir John who lorded
it over family and shire for close on forty years. It is his
correspondence that casts such a vivid light on county affairs
in his day.

Much of it was with his fellow-deputy William Maurice
of Clenennau. The Maurices came of the same clan, but had
remained in Eifionydd — the last of the allied houses of this
area, it has been said, to emerge from the medieval structure
with a consolidated estate. It was also with William Maurice,
as with John Wynn, that the family surname became fixed.
But the emergence of Clenennau to a dominating position in
the shire came later than that of Gwydir, which had begun
providing it with sheriffs fifty years before its kinsmen in the
west. Defence against invasion was inevitably a principal
theme of the correspondence of the two leaders; it was
indeed the consciousness of Caernarvonshire's exposed coast
and the novel danger from enemies oversea that did more
than anything else to raise to broader vistas of national
policy the sights of men whose world had so recently been
bounded by their immediate kin group. In the days when

John Wynn's father was sheriff, France had been the enemy; in 1544 Sir Richard Bulkeley had written to him about the sighting of a French flotilla and seeking his co-operation in the defence of so likely a landing place as ' this poor Isle of Anglesey '. Now it was Spain. In the year before the Armada sailed we find Wynn writing to Maurice urging that each of them, within their respective ' limits ' of the shire (Maurice's being the larger one because he has no towns to protect) should see that beacons were manned, man power mobilised and munitions built up in readiness for the expected crisis; at the same time he deplores their previous ' deffect and neccligence ' in collecting the necessary cash.

The danger did not end with the defeat of the Armada. Twelve years later Sir Richard Bulkeley's son and namesake (a courtier abreast of the latest news) is warning Wynn of the approach of another Spanish fleet, and urging him to have his train-bands ready. Nor was Spain itself the only source of danger; nearer at hand was Ireland, in a chronic state of revolt and a ready landing ground for the enemy. Ireland was the graveyard of many a Caernarvonshire man; and in the Armada year the two deputy lieutenants were warned that since the local levies might have to encounter there not the wild Irish but Spaniards equipped with the latest weapons, they too must lay aside their bows and arrows and learn to handle the new-fangled musket.

Apart from home defence, the two deputy lieutenants were also involved in recruiting for some of the ' reprisals ' against Spain. In 1596, urged by the earl of Pembroke (lord president of Wales), they found fifty Caernarvonshire recruits for the company led by Sir Thomas Gerard (kinsman to Sir John Wynn's Lancashire wife) to join Essex in his assault on Cadiz. Among those who fought there was the soldier poet of Llŷn, Richard Hughes of Cefn Llanfair, near Pwllheli, ' one of her Majesty's footmen extraordinary ' who was later put on the permanent establishment as ' footman in ordinary ' at a salary of £50.

Wynn and Maurice did not find it all plain sailing. Men pressed for the service would appeal to one against the other;

they wrote jointly to Pembroke explaining how Caernarvonshire men, having been 'bred in peace', did not easily
accommodate themselves to military discipline, and would
' venture any imprisonment' to escape the Irish service, and
how hard it was to squeeze the victuals demanded for the
navy from a county which could barely feed itself without
importing grain, or to raise money from the shire when there
was no immediate threat to its safety. Pembroke in turn
significantly had to send his deputies orders for the punish-
ment of men returning from Ireland without leave, and to
remind them that the public service must take precedence
over 'pryvatt quarrells', since 'some men must governe,
some must obey'. The records of the time give only too
clear evidence of the way the new local officials were apt to
abuse their position to promote family feuds — for example
by protecting wrongdoers, by using the militia levies to rid
themselves of an opposing faction, or by lining their pockets
with the proceeds of the money they were commissioned to
collect. If we believed all the wild accusations they brought
against each other in Star Chamber, we should be left
wondering how the county survived such a record of infamy!

There were, of course, many other county families ready
to dispute pre-eminence with Gwydir and Clenennau, but
none of them have left so full a record of their activities.
The descendants of Gwilym ap Gruffydd, now using Griffith
as surname, lived in state in the medieval hall of Penrhyn,
whose vestiges can barely be traced in the cellars of the
nineteenth century 'castle'. The Penrhyn family generally
aimed higher than county politics: for three successive
generations they held the office of chamberlain of North
Wales. A junior branch settled at Plas Mawr in the borough
of Caernarvon — one of those town .seats of the country
gentry which and so often adorned and dominated the
older towns till 'progress' swept them away. Another offshoot lived a stone's throw from Penrhyn at Cochwillan —
now a barn, but still retaining the lovely proportions of the
fifthteenth-century hall, whose builder, William ap Gruffydd,
fought for Henry VII at Bosworth and was rewarded with

the office of sheriff of Caernarvonshire for life. His son, as
so often happened, adopted the father's forename as surname; he acquired under Elizabeth a lease of the extensive
crown manor of Dinorwig, where he contrived to squeeze
out the smaller freeholders and to treat the whole lordship
as a modern estate. To this was added, by some forgotten
transaction, Maenol Bangor, the former 'home' manor of
the bishops of Bangor. Here a younger brother built himself,
towards the end of the reign, a fine house (still standing)
which came to be known by the name of Vaynol, and which
in the following century became the chief family seat.
Naturally the Williamses of Cochwillan and Vaynol frequently held the post of sheriff under Elizabeth and her
early Stuart successors.

Another rising family was that of Thomas. Rice Thomas,
son of a sheriff of Carmarthenshire, got himself made deputy
surveyor of crown lands in North Wales, and in this capacity
was able to lease and soon afterwards to acquire outright
the crown manor of Aber, once a seat of the princes of
Gwynedd. He was promptly placed on the commission of
the peace, and under Elizabeth he served as sheriff both here
and in Anglesey, where he held another crown manor. His
son William, who also held county offices, is better known for
his death on the field of Zutphen in Sir Philip Sidney's company of volunteers. The family had a house in Caernarvon,
where they normally lived until a new mansion (still standing
and inhabited) was built at Aber about the turn of the century. Beyond Caernarvon lay Glynllifon, home of a family,
just learning to use the surname Glynne, which had thriven
by an uncanny instinct for choosing the winning side in the
troubles of the two centuries following the conquest of
Gwynedd — except in the field of culture, where they
remained true to Welsh tradition and went on patronising
the bards (and practising the art themselves) long after it
had ceased to be fashionable. One of them was a commissioner for the royal eisteddfod at Caerwys in 1567. The
family had produced a sheriff for Anglesey, despite the ban
on Welshmen, as far back as the fourteenth century; natur-

ally the Tudors availed themselves of so experienced a family for the same purpose (and others which will appear later) in Caernarvonshire.

In drawing the Caernarvonshire gentry into the public service the Tudors stretched their hand even to distant (but relatively populous) Llŷn. It is a sign of the growing participation of these remoter parts in county affairs that a third of Caernarvonshire's sheriffs during the last twenty years of the century were drawn from Llŷn and Eifionydd, which had supplied not a single one during the first fifty years; and we shall find the same phenomenon in the government of the Church. Some two miles north-west of Pwllheli lay the estate of Bodfel, from which another county family took its name once surnames came into fashion. Until about the middle of the century its record remained undistinguished; then John Wyn ap Hugh took service under the earl of Warwick — soon to achieve notoriety as the duke of Northumberland who virtually ruled England in the later years of Edward VI. He was Warwick's standard bearer when Ket's rebellion was crushed at Mousehold Hill, where (as Sir John Wynn tell us) 'his hors was slaine under him and himself hurt and yett he upheld the great stander of England'. For this he was richly rewarded with both offices and lands, including some of the former lands of the abbey of Bardsey on the island itself and on the mainland of Caernarvonshire. He was accused of using both office and land to promote piracy, with the island as a depôt for his loot and his public position to shield him from prosecution.

Another son of Llŷn who entered the service of the same earl of Warwick was Griffith ap John of Castellmarch (near Aberdaron) — scion of a very ancient family originating south of the Traeth. His grandfather had been appointed to one of the minor offices in the county hierarchy soon after the Act of Union, and his father became sheriff in 1548. Griffith's service with the earl of Warwick, like John Wyn ap Hugh's, brought with it further advancement: in 1549 he was given the influential post of constable of Conway. All this laid a firm foundation for distinguished and lucrative

careers for his sons and grandsons (who took the name of
Jones) in the next century. Also near Aberdaron was the fair
house of Bodwrda, which gave its name to a family closely
akin to the Bodvels. What was the source of the wealth
which enabled this ancient but hitherto inconspicuous family
to qualify for the office of sheriff in 1584, and some forty
years later to rebuild Bodwrda in brick (a rare and long
unique building material for so remote a region) is a matter
of guesswork; one can only observe that, like their kinsmen
of Bodfel, they lived conveniently near the sea! The equally
ancient stock of Griffith of Cefnamwlch, some six miles to
the north, came into its own in the next century, but it too
had supplied a sheriff by 1589. Cefnamwlch lies only a couple
of miles from a sequestered shore; a younger son of the
house, Captain Hugh Griffith, apprenticed to a London
merchant, had for years carried on a profitable privateering
business against Spain, and then extended it to less legitimate
operations, in which his father participated, as well as his
brother-in-law William Jones of Castellmarch, recorder of
Beaumaris and a future judge. There were investigations at
the court of admiralty, but it does not appear that the
dubious gains of the two families were ever disgorged.

There is plenty of evidence of the enrichment of county
society at the top level. One need only cite Gwydir itself
(of which unhappily only the gatehouse remains intact to
bear witness to its former grandeur); or — more happily —
the unspoilt Plas Mawr at Conway. This was built by Robert
Wynn, a younger brother of the master of Gwydir, on profits
made in the service of Sir Philip Hoby, and on the fortune
of his wife, who was a Griffith of Penrhyn. Increasing
numbers were sending their sons to the universities or the
Inns of Court and the English public schools, and making
good matches for them, often across the border. Education,
however, could now be had nearer home, thanks to the
enlightened patronage of some of the newly-enriched local
gentry. Doubts have been cast on the part of Sir John Wynn
of Gwydir in the foundation of the neighbouring school at
Llanrwst, but there can be none on Geoffrey Glyn's claim
to have founded Friars school at Bangor in Mary's reign.

Welsh, of course, had no place in these foundations; but for the masses it was the only language, and even the gentry, if they wrote to each other in English, were generally bilingual at home. Sir John Wynn, when he was negotiating English matches for his sons, was at pains to enquire whether the prospective bride was likely to be willing and able to pick up the language of her adopted country. Nor were the higher reaches of literature neglected. The Welsh of Richard Davies's New Testament or William Morgan's Bible, written as it is by men whose formal education was all in England, bespeaks a strong Welsh literary background in their home environment in the Conway valley. Further up the valley lived Thomas Wiliems of Trefriw, physician and possibly priest, kinsman through his mother to Sir John Wynn of Gwydir (his patron), and author of a Latin-Welsh dictionary which he did not live to publish. In Llŷn the bardic tradition was still very much alive. William Llŷn, who has been called the only bard, in an age of decline, worthy of comparison with the great figures of the preceding generation from whom he learned his craft, ' graduated ' at the Caerwys eisteddfod. Known to contemporaries as ' the bard of Llŷn ', he plied his profession in both North and South Wales, and died at Oswestry. He and his like were welcomed at such houses as Bodwrda and Madrun; Cefnamwlch had its own less distinguished household bard in Morus Dwyfech, whose muse did not range far beyond local themes.

In such a society, with everyone trying to jostle to the top, constant strife and faction were inevitable. A crisis which rent the upper crust of county society for the greater part of two decades arose from the appointment in 1564 of the queen's favourite the earl of Leicester — son of that earl of Warwick who had taken more than one Caernarvonshire man under his wing — was appointed chief ranger of Snowdon Forest. This royal forest, where ' deer ranged freely until late in the eighteenth century '[1] had extended over

[1] F. Emery in *Agrarian Hist. of England and Wales*, iv. (ed. Joan Thirsk, 1967), 139.

CAERNARVON CASTLE AND TOWN, 1750

PLATE I

Vera effigies Clariss:Do<sup>m</sup> Iohannis Wynn de Gwedur in
Com̅ Carnarvon Equitis et Baronetti ˠ.
Obijt primo die Martij 1626. Ætat: 75.

PLATE II

SIR JOHN WYNN OF GWYDIR (1553-1627)

PLATE III

PLAS MAWR, CONWAY

PLATE IV

BODVRDA

much of all three shires of Gwynedd, and the crown's rights there, as in the other royal forests, were hedged round with the most stringent sanctions; but the rising gentry had encroached while the crown was weak, and Leicester caused widespread alarm—notably among the lesser gentry without friends at court — by procuring, some ten years after his appointment, a commission to enquire into their titles. In 1574 a county meeting at Caernarvon drew up a petition appealing to the queen over the earl's head, and taking a stand upon the terms of Henry VII's charter, which the gentry believed to have secured them in their land.

The later tradition that Sir Richard Bulkeley boldly took the lead in withstanding the royal favourite appears to have little foundation. On the contrary the principal gentry generally played safe by runnning with the hare and hunting with the hounds. Outwardly at least Gwydir was hand in glove with Leicester and his chief local agent Elis Pryse of Plas Iolyn, the notorious ' Red Doctor ', who had been Elizabeth's first sheriff of Caernarvonshire. Maurice Wynn, Sir John's father, told the earl of the rising opposition in Eifionydd and Arfon, apologising for the ' savage behaviour ' exhibited, and suggesting he should send officers to ' work terror in the minds of the frowardly bent '. Four years after the county meeting, when Leicester was chancellor and chamberlain of North Wales, matters came to a head there, and several of the gentry of Llŷn and Eifionydd were under lock and key at Ludlow; but by then religion was complicating the issue, for Leicester posed as a champion of the reformed faith, to which the loyalty of some of his opponents was more than doubtful; this is a matter that will concern us in the next chapter. In another ten years Leicester was dead, having achieved little for his pains except to set the three shires — and Denbighshire as well — by the ears. For the moment the threat to the up-and-coming gentry was over.

The schemes of Elizabeth's later favourite, the Earl of Essex, affected Caernarvonshire only marginally. His main Welsh following was on the Devereux estates in south-west Wales, but his steward, Sir Gely Meyrick (whose family came from the north) tried to raise a faction for him there too. He had some success in Denbighshire, where swordsmen who had campaigned with Essex — notably Captain John Salesbury — rallied to him in his treasonable bid for power in 1601. There are slight indications of a similar attempt to infiltrate into the government of Caernarvonshire through Sir William Maurice and one of his predecessors as sheriff, but without much to show for it. After the revolt, however, one of Salesbury's 'footmen', Hugh Lewis, denounced two members of the prominent Conway family of Hookes as implicated. The bailiffs covered themselves by clapping both parties in gaol and reporting to the privy council, which summoned John Hookes to appear before it and held Lewis to bail; but nothing more is heard of the matter.

On conditions outside the gentry class our information is all too scanty. Life was still cheap. Apart from the periodic toll taken by famine and pestilence, the lower orders were frequently involved in the quarrels of their betters, to the peril of life and limb, and murder could still be done with impunity, despite Edwardian and Tudor legislation, if the perpetrator could find a powerful enough protector. Nor was life necessarily more peaceful or secure in the towns. In 1575 the town of Caernarvon had a hot dispute with the then sheriff, Rowland Puleston, on its municipal rights; riots ensued in the streets, and many were thrown into prison — of which faction we can easily guess. Twenty years later the town was in an uproar again, this time over the election of bailiffs. On both occasions a member of the leading town family of Griffith of Plas Mawr (an offshoot, it will be remembered, of Penrhyn) was involved.

There was also a more peaceful and constructive side to the life of Caernarvon. Under Tudor rule trade was increasing, and Caernarvon was a busy port, accommodating ships of from six to twenty tons' burthen, and provided from 1559 with its own customs officials accountable to the head port at Chester. Naturally its trade was predominantly in imports, for Caernarvonshire was dependent on the outside world for its supplies of basic commodities like salt and iron, and in bad years corn had to be imported as well. A little coal came in from the Flintshire pits, or from farther north through Chester; but coal was little in demand save for use the houses of the more prosperous gentry. Chester was in fact ' the shopping centre which catered for the personal, household and occupational requirements '[2] of the whole area, and Caernarvon and Beaumaris were the depôts where ships from Chester (or more rarely from creeks of the Bristol Channel) discharged their cargoes of English and foreign goods for distribution through fairs and markets. In return, Caernarvonshire was able to export some fish and dairy dairy produce, wool, homespun cloth, hides and leather, and above all, roofing slates. This last commodity had long been in local use. Small quarries were opened from time to time to cater for building needs in the immediate neighbourhood; or their produce might even be conveyed coastwise to meet more distant demands, from the roofing of Chester castle in the fourteenth century to that of St. Asaph cathedral in the seventeenth. Some of these quarries were on episcopal lands: it was to Dean Kyffin that in 1570 the bard Siôn Tudor (emulating an earlier bard's plea to an earlier dean) addressed himself in verse with a request for a boatload of slates to mend his leaky roof. There was also some quarrying on Llanllechid common; and small craft could approach the creeks formed by the mouths of the Cegin and the Ogwen — just outside Bangor, but under the jurisdiction of the port of Beaumaris — to carry away the slates quarried on the neighbouring slopes, once they had made their dizzy descent by bridle paths to the sea.

The quarrying was carried out spasmodically by gangs of crofters and commoners as demand rose and fell. Sometimes — as on the Penrhyn estate in 1582 — a token payment by way of royalty was exacted by the slate reeve; sometimes so little value was placed on the slate rocks that it was virtually a ' free-for-all '. It was all very haphazard (as later generations found to their cost), with no specialised tools or skills

[2] E. A. Lewis, *Welsh Port Books*, xxxvii.

and no outlay of capital. Yet a considerable export trade to Ireland had grown up, and for this purpose a rough classification into 'singles' and 'doubles' had been adopted by Elizabeth's reign, 'singles' measuring roughly ten inches by five and selling at 1s. 8d. a thousand, 'doubles' twelve inches by six, at 2s. 8d. a thousand. It appears from surviving port books that between three and four hundred thousand slates were exported to Ireland during the decade after 1583.

Little is known of the trade of Conway at this time, but towards the end of the century Nefyn and Pwllheli are taking an increasing part in Caernarvonshire's trade, especially in fish, with the outside world, and at the same time local shipping is beginning to participate, instead of leaving it all to merchants from outside. Altogether, life in Caernarvonshire under Tudor rule is taking on a more modern aspect.

## BIBLIOGRAPHY

Wynn's *History of the Gwydir Family* and the National Library's calendars of *Wynn (of Gwydir) Papers* (1926) and of *Clenennau Letters and Papers* (1947), are indispensable primary sources. Tudor administration is analysed in W. Ogwen Williams, *Tudor Gwynedd* (1958) and the significance of Henry VII's charters by J. Beverley Smith in 'Crown and Community in the Principality of North Wales in the reign of Henry Tudor' (*Welsh Hist. Rev.*, iii. 1966). The emergence of the county familes, with special reference to Vaynol, is examined in T. Jones Pierce, 'Notes on the history of rural Caernarvonshire in the reign of Elizabeth' (*TCHS* 1940). On the bards of Llŷn see Myrddin Fardd (J. Jones), *Cynfeirdd Lleyn* (1905). Leicester's dealings with the gentry of Gwynedd are described in Penry Williams, *The Council in the Marches of Wales under Elizabeth I* (1958), 237-9. On Sir William Maurice see E. N. Williams in *TCHS* 1963. Disorders in Caernarvon town are referred to in I. ab O. Edwards, *Star Chamber Proceedings relating to Wales* (1929), 31. Details of local export trade may be found in E. A. Lewis, *Welsh Port Books, 1550-1603* (1927), and in D. Thomas, *Hen Longau Sir Gaernarvon* (1952), pennod 2. The primitive slate industry is described by D. Dylan Pritchard in *Quarry Manager's Jnl.*, July and Nov. 1952, and piratical operations in *TCHS* 1960 by Carys Roberts. The recently published Vol. IV of the Cambridge *Agrarian History of England and Wales* (1967) contains in chapters ii, vi and xi valuable data and conclusions on farming, landlordism and rural architecture in Tudor and early Stuart Wales.

# III

# THE REFORMATION

FROM the purely secular angle, the Reformation in Wales is another aspect of the administrative reorganisation which was the theme of the last chapter. The dislocation of civil society in the declining years of the Middle Ages had its counterpart in the Church, and in both the answer of the Tudor monarchy was a blend of tighter control at the centre with the transfer of local control from an alien bureaucracy to families rooted in the soil. On the one hand the crown asserted its supremacy in both Church and State; on the other it replaced alien sheriffs and alien bishops by members of the rising local gentry.

Bangor diocese was roughly coterminous with the ancient Gwynedd; and war and social dislocation had left their mark on the spiritual as well as the secular aspect of the community. The cathedral had suffered during the Glyn Dŵr wars (whether by military action or by mere neglect), and lay partly in ruin till nearly the end of the century. Other ecclesiastical buildings, both public and residential, had suffered a similar fate. Bangor for some years ceased to be the effective head of the see, ordinations and collations being conducted in Anglesey, at Caernarvon, or outside the diocese. A petition from the clergy and laity of Bangor and other adjoining dioceses to Pope Pius II in 1464 paints in lurid (and no doubt exaggerated) colours the conditions under which they lived, with murder, rape and robbery so prevalent as to make it unsafe to venture abroad.

Matters were not helped by the intrusion of political faction into episcopal appointments during both the Glyn

37

Dŵr epoch and the Wars of the Roses. At one time in the fifteenth century there were no fewer than three claimants to the see of Bangor. These bishops rarely visited the diocese. ' The twelve bishops who held the see between the years 1417 and 1541 ', it has been pointed out,[1] ' were Englishmen, almost entirely absentees and holding important appointments in England '. This does not, of course, mean that administration was at a standstill; it was carried on by officials on the spot, and of necessity — since it was not easy to find outsiders willing to take up residence in so disturbed an area — these were increasingly chosen from local families, notably the Glynnes of Glynllifon and the Anglesey Bulkeleys. But these could not bear the same authority, and what they had did not always make for edification or even for the safeguarding of the church's material resources. Richard Kyffin, locally known as ' the black dean ', who held that office from about 1480 to 1502, is represented in contemporary verse (which is anything but hostile in tone) as having built himself a good house out of the offerings at the popular shrine of St. Dwynwen at Llanddwyn (Anglesey) — the opulent rectory bestowed on him in reward for his services in organising local support for Henry of Richmond in his bid for the throne — and to have spent his time there in hunting and in lavish and boisterous entertainment of boon companions. Yet he also took a pride in his cathedral and played his part in its restoration.

The disorders of the age had left their mark on parochial life too. There was much neglect of church fabrics, much non-residence among the clergy. This was partly due to the absence of parsonages in most parishes, partly to the pious but unfortunate practice of ' appropriating ' parish churches to the support of monasteries, which meant that the monks collected the rectorial tithe and appointed to the cure of souls in the parish either a vicar — who would be regularly instituted by the bishop and supported from the ' lesser '

---

[1] A. I. Pryce, *Diocese of Bangor in the Sixteenth Century*, x.

tithes and the people's offerings — or a curate or chaplain, dependent on monastic bounty. Not more than a fifth of the many churches so appropriated in Bangor diocese had vicars; the rest had often to made do with clerical ' sweated labour ' at £5 a year or even less. It has been estimated that only a quarter of the Bangor livings were worth more than £15 a year, for war and pestilence had played havoc with tithes and offerings as well as with manorial dues. No wonder the clergy scrambled for leave to hold several livings together — another fruitful cause for non-residence. And not only the ill-paid parish priests : bishops, deans and archdeacons were often allowed to supplement their stipends by holding livings *in commendam;* for the fixed belief of the age in what Shakespeare called ' degree, priority and place ' as part of the divine order of things made it vital that they should live on a scale compatible with their dignity, even if this meant leaving the work of the parishes to ill-qualified and underpaid curates.

Most of the resident parish clergy were local men whose mother tongue was Welsh. This made for neighbourly relations with their parishioners; but the service was in Latin, and while no doubt most of them could flounder through it without mishap, there is nothing to tell us how much, in the absence of systematic instruction in Latin or in divinity, it conveyed to them or to their congregations. For what was there to attract a scholar to a poverty-stricken Welsh living? Few, in fact, of the Bangor clergy were university men; it is doubtful whether many had even a grammar school education, or stood much above their congregations in theological or any other branch of academic knowledge. One can only hope that few sank to the level of ignorance attributed by Hooper, the ultra-Protestant bishop of Gloucester (a prejudiced witness, it is true, since he would wish to belittle the old order in which they had been brought up): he declared that more than half of those he examined could not repeat the Ten Commandments and nearly a tenth knew nothing of the Lord's Prayer beyond the bare words, while ten of them could not even repeat these!

Sermons were not a normal feature of the pre-Reformation Church service; how conscientiously priests in this diocese discharged the duty of catechising, where knowledge of the common tongue would help them, we have at present no means of knowing, nor has much evidence survived here of the more informal instruction they may have given, such as that embodied in south-eastern Wales in *cwndidau*, or popular verses comparable in manner and purpose with those which Vicar Prichard circulated in central Wales in the next century. Welsh printed books did not yet exist, but there were in circulation manuscripts in Welsh, often compiled by priests for the benefit of their fellow-clergy; these could serve as a sort of pastoral library, containing as they did Gospel and Old Testament stories, prayers and devotions, legends of the saints, and along with these the sort of medical lore (often bordering on magic and witchcraft) which parishioners would expect their parson to use for their benefit. But manuscripts were expensive and beyond the reach of the average working parson.

How far their moral, as distinct from their educational standards rose above those of the laity can only be a matter for guesswork. The one aspect of outward conduct on which a different standard was not only expected but exacted from them by Church law — clerical celibacy — we know to have been honoured at least as much in the breach as in the observance, in this as in the other Welsh dioceses. Tradition is strong and persistent, and clerical celibacy formed no part of the tradition they inherited from the Celtic church. A petition to Thomas Cromwell from the Bangor clergy in 1536 pleaded that a way should be found for them to keep their unofficial wives, if only to make dealings with their parishioners easier. Perhaps they hoped that with all the novelties then being sanctioned and even enjoined by authority they might now find escape from a rule they had always found burdensome. Whatever the shortcomings of the pre-Reformation clergy, there is no sign of popular revolt against them or what they stood for. It was not from the rank and file that the demand for religious reformation came : its origins were academic, and in so far as Caernarvonshire participated in the demand it was from men of the class of the *uchelwyr* or gentry who were up at Oxford during the years of religous ferment which preceded Henry VIII's breach with Rome. Some of these will concern us later.

No account of the diocese would be complete without some reference to its religious houses. There were four of these in Caernarvonshire; all were small, and all had ceased to play any significant part in the life of the country for more than a century. The ancient Celtic monasteries of Bardsey and Beddgelert had since the Norman Conquest been reconstituted as Augustinian houses. Bardsey had property on the Caernarvonshire mainland, including the tithes of Aberdaron and of several other parishes in Llŷn, but its total revenues at the time of the dissolution were estimated at only £58; the number of monks still in residence is unknown. Beddgelert had only three monks; it possessed the tithes of Abererch and Dolwyddelan and a good deal of property scattered around Caernarvonshire and Anglesey, probably including the tolls on the Moel y don ferry. This was a frequented and therefore lucrative passage which took travellers — and, even more important, their horses — from Ireland viâ Anglesey, starting near a house of the prior's in Llanidan parish and landing more or less where Port Dinorwic now stands. But what the total revenues amounted to is not on record. At Bangor was a small Dominican friary much patronised, and perhaps founded, by the Tudors of Penmynydd. Several of them were buried there; so were many other local notables, including a bishop of Bangor who may have been a member of the brotherhood. But for many years now it had housed only a couple of friars, and it may have been already leased out to the Griffiths of Penrhyn, who were not only neighbours, but by the way of being founder's kin.

By far the most important of the Caernarvonshire houses was the Cistercian abbey at Maenan which Edward I had built for the displaced monks of Aberconway. With an income of £162, it now housed eight monks, which was as

many as there had been for a century past. How diligently
they performed their religious offices we have no means of
knowing, but they seem to have abandoned manual work,
leaving this to tenants; and even their tenants no longer kept
the flocks of sheep for which the Cistercians had been famed;
there had been no wool sales since Richard II's day.

Soon after the Wars of the Roses came to an end, recovery
began in the diocese, at least on the material plane. Henry
Deane, the first Tudor appointment to the see, was also
chancellor of Ireland, but at least the passage to and from
his civil post took him frequently through his diocese, and
during his five-year episcopate he began the work of rebuilding the ruined cathedral and of recovering some of the
alienated episcopal property. The election of 1509 of Thomas
Skevington took matters a stage further. True, he was also
abbot of Bealieu in Hampshire, and was said to have left his
Welsh see unvisited for fourteen of the twenty-five years of
his episcopate; but he had an able and militant local deputy
in Dr. William Glynne, a younger son of Glynllifon, whom
he appointed as his chancellor and as archdeacon successively
of Merioneth and Anglesey. The rebuilding of the west tower
and parts of the nave, and the hanging of a peal of three
bells, were undertaken at the bishop's expense; and as soon
as he had finished it, the church at Clynnog was recon-
structed ' in the latest English style ',[2] probably by the same
gang of masons. A magnificent rood screen was added, again
(it would seem) by carpenters who had been employed at
Bangor. The hand of Bishop Skevington is evident here too,
but not necessarily his purse; for there were funds to draw
upon in the long succession of offerings from visitors to the
shrine of St. Beuno, as well as of pilgrims on their way to
Bardsey.

The new spirit that was abroad also inspired some of the
more prominent laity with a desire to leave their mark on

[2] F. H. Crossley in *Arch. Camb.*, 1944, 89.

the parish churches they attended, many of which were now
undergoing repair, by beautifying them in line with what
we might call ' contemporary idiom '. For instance at the
very beginning of the century the parish church at Conway
(all that remained there of the former Cistercian abbey) was
endowed by the constable of the castle, Sir Richard Pole,
with a fine screen. This he appears to have procured at
Ludlow, where he was attendant on Arthur, Prince of Wales.
Forty or fifty years later Clynnog church found another
benefactor in the neighbouring family of Glynllifon, whose
gift of a stained glass window commemorated the family
with the traditional Catholic invocation *orate pro bono statu.*
Neither Bishop Skevington nor his immediate successors,
however, tackled the basic abuses of the Church. More than
a third of his recorded appointments were of absentees with
livings or abbeys across the border or even offices at court.
His chancellor made a corner in some of the more desirable
livings of the diocese, which he was charged with not having
visited for sixteen years.

Skevington died in 1533, leaving injunctions (duly carried
out, as an inquisitive choirboy found years afterwards) that
his heart should be buried under the choir of his beloved
cathedral. His death was followed by two short episcopates
marked only by further alienations of episcopal property. It
may have been now that the bishop's manor, Maenol Bangor,
was disposed of to join the old crown lordship of Dinorwig
in the new estate of Vaynol, vested, as we have seen, in the
Cochwillan family.

These were the years of Henry VIII's quarrel with the see
of Rome, but at first it caused little stir in Bangor diocese.
The king (or his agent Thomas Cromwell) concentrated his
attention in Wales on the diocese of St. David's as the key
point for his new church policy, leaving the other sees to
bishops less committed in their views than William Barlow,
whom he planted at St. David's in 1535. Local interest was
concentrated rather on the long-drawn feud between Sir
Richard Bulkeley and Skevington's right hand man Archdeacon Glynne, warmly backed by his bishop. Basically it

was a struggle for power, through control of the most
enviable post in the Church and the monastic houses,
between what were then the two leading families in the
diocese; but there were wider ramifications. One can detect
echoes of the sentiments which Glyn Dŵr had awakened
and the bards had kept alive; both contestants angled for
the support of the government, which meant first Wolsey
and then Cromwell, and Bulkeley was at pains to represent
the other party as embodying the old familiar tribal turbulence of the Welsh. Neither Wolsey nor Cromwell, of course,
would be aware that Welsh nationalism was wholly alien to
the family traditions either of Glynllifon or of Penrhyn — for
Penrhyn also ranged itself with the anti-Bulkeley faction,
from resentment at Sir Richard's appointment in 1536 as
chamberlain of North Wales, a post held by Edward Griffith's
immediate ancestors for three generations.

These local struggles were now being caught up in issues
of far deeper moment. In 1535 one of the absentee bishop's
officials accused another (a dependent of Bulkeley) of allowing the sale in the diocese of papal indulgences, and caused
them to be seized by the bailiffs of Caernarvon. William
Glynne, who had lost much of his authority in the diocese
since Skevington's death, saw in the incident an opportunity
for regaining it by displaying his zeal against papal abuses;
Bulkeley, who had been one of Wolsey's agents in North
Wales and was now earnestly courting Cromwell, had in
self-defence to play down the whole affair. Matters reached
such a pitch in 1536 that there were riotous affrays in the
cathedral itself, and Bulkeley wanted to see some of the
penal legislation of the post-Glyn Dŵr period revived, at
least to the point of disarming all Welshmen of the three
shires not actually in the king's service. Glynne's death the
following year was followed by a reshuffle of his many bene-
fices, and among those who gained preferment was Sir
Richard's younger brother Arthur; indeed the Bulkeley
faction seemed to be triumphant all along the line, and
opposition to it was momentarily silenced.

Of opposition to the king and his policy there is little sign in any responsible quarter of the shire. A few years earlier, at the time of Henry's marriage with Anne Boleyn, an obscure local priest, William ap Llywelyn, did get himself into trouble by saying what he would like to do to the king if he had him to himself on Snowdon. But when in the following years parsons were called on to subscribe to the oath of supremacy, Bangor diocese provided no known conscientious objectors, though unfortunately there is no surviving list of signatories for Bangor as there is for the other Welsh dioceses. In 1535 an injunction was issued that the clergy must commend the royal supremacy to their flocks by sermons. The bishop of Bangor — John Salcot (alias Capon), who owed his preferment to zeal for the royal divorce — excused himself on the ground of his ignorance of Welsh, but promised that some of his clergy would do something about it. It is hardly likely, in any case, that he would have taken the wearisome journey to Bangor from the monastery near Winchester where he was abbot, merely for this purpose!

Within the next few years came the dissolution of the smaller monasteries and the friaries. Salcot arranged the voluntary surrender of his abbey of Hyde, and was rewarded by promotion from Bangor to Salisbury, to be succeeded by another monkish absentee. Before this, royal commissioners had arrived in Caernarvonshire to report on the state of the diocese, and then of the religious houses. Arthur Bulkeley found the commissioners slack, and told Bishop Salcot so; but the local gentry and clergy seem to have co-operated to the best of their ability, and the three monasteries and the friary which lay within the shire were dissolved without incident. The king took the property into his hands, and either gave it away to favoured courtiers or sold it to specu-lators who generally re-sold it locally, often to men (like Sir Richard Bulkeley at Penmon in Anglesey) who had served the monastery as stewards and so had an inside knowledge of its estates. Bardsey and its mainland possessions, as we have seen, helped to found the fortunes of the Bodvel family; the tithes of Aberdaron, which had belonged to it, eventually passed by a roundabout route to the Owens of Plas Du, of whom more later. The site of Maenan abbey was acquired by the wealthy Denbighshire merchant Sir Richard Clough, from whose family it passed to the Wynnes, owners of the adjacent estate of Melai; the better-known Wynns of Gwydir made a bee-line for Maenan's former tithes of Dolwyddelan. The widely scattered lands of Beddgelert were first assigned as part of the jointure of Anne of Cleves, the 'Flanders mare' who was Henry VIII's wife for six short months; they were later dispersed among a variety of purchasers. The Dominican friary at Bangor had by Mary's reign passed into the hands of Geoffrey Glyn, half-brother to the Marian bishop, who used it for the endowment of Friars school.

Both here and at Maenan the stones of the abbey were plundered for castle repair before the crown disposed of them, but at Maenan enough was left to help in the reconstruction of a medieval hall (incorporated into the existing building) on the monastic site, and it is almost certain that some of the stonework helped in the building of Gwydir. Of Beddgelert nothing remains but those parts of the priory church which have been built (as at Conway) into the parish church. At Bardsey the abbot's lodging was still used as a dwelling house till the early nineteenth century, but the church had fallen into ruins by the seventeenth. That the dissolution helped to consolidate the power and wealth of the local gentry is obvious; whether, as is so often stated, it also helped to bind them to the Reformation is more doubtful. The Wynnes of Melai, for example, like many other purchasers of monastic land, remained staunch in their loyalty to Rome long after their acquisition of Maenan. John Wyn ap Hugh and his son were reputed recusants a quarter of a century after Bardsey came to them; his grandson Roger Gwyn was a missionary priest imprisoned in the Tower under James I on a trumped-up charge of conspiring to kill the king; and it is likely that the eminent Roman Catholic writer and missionary Robert Gwynne was another son of the founder of the Bodvel fortunes. What is certain is that the passing of so much monastic tithe into lay hands increased the pressure of the gentry on the Church and further undermined its independence.

Soon after the dissolution Bangor was given a new bishop in Arthur Bulkeley. The appointment was, of course, a triumph for the Bulkeley faction, but it has other aspects too. Arthur Bulkeley was the first resident bishop for well over a century and the first native bishop (with one brief exception) for more than two; his successors right down to 1716 — again with one exception — were all Welsh. Bangor became once more the effective head of the see, as Bishop Bulkeley's register bears witness. It was the counterpart in the Church of what the appointment of native sheriffs and deputy lieutenants meant in the secular sphere. Bulkeley was also perhaps the first bishop of Bangor to do more than passively acquiesce in the king's religious changes. He carried out his visitations in person, not (as with his absentee predecessors) by deputy, and his queries indicate a new concern for the pastoral aspect of the priestly office, notably in matters like catechising and preaching. As Dr. James puts it in his *Church History*,[3] ' a definite Reformation standard was obviously presupposed '.

Another of Bishop Bulkeley's services to the diocese was his bequest of books to the dean and chapter to form the basis of a cathedral library, and others to the cathedral itself and to friends and relatives and individual members of the chapter. The character of these books throws some light on Bulkeley's theological views and on the progress of the Reformation in the diocese: they include a Latin and an English Bible to remain in the choir and another English Bible ' to be fixed with a Chain in some Part of the Cross-Ile '. Among the private bequests are ' the Old and New Testament compriz'd in five small Volumes, which I bought at my last being in London for private use of Service ', the paraphrases of Erasmus in Latin and in English (the former ' noted with my own Hand '), Josephus, and several of the

[3] p. 108.

Latin Fathers. These last were the principal items in what he left to members of chapter, individually and collectively: from his cathedral clergy at least, the bishop expected a lot! Nor was he neglectful of the cathedral fabric: over £40 — a considerable sum for the times — was spent on the roof and leads of the south side, ' which before was ready to fall ' (an only too familiar predicament!); but most of this came from cathedral funds.

There was a less happy side to his episcopate. A bishop appointed from among the local gentry was always in danger of being too closely tied to them to be able to steer clear of their feuds or to withstand their greed for Church lands. Bulkeley did succeed in recovering some of the property alienated by his predecessor, but at the cost of a lawsuit which had to be paid for by selling (with the consent of the chapter) some of the cathedral plate and vestments; he himself disposed of the tithes of Llandegfan and Beaumaris to his omnipotent kinsman Sir Richard. He is held responsible in fact for a general increase in lay patronage in the diocese. The abnormal number of resignations during his episcopate may have been due to tighter discipline or to changing standards; a sharp decline in ordinations is probably accountable to the uncertainty of the times. But statistics (admittedly incomplete) do suggest a net decline in the number of clergy.

It is unlikely that a man of Bishop Bulkeley's standpoint had much difficulty in accommodating himself to the Protestant doctrines and practices which came in with Edward VI, and which the old king had held at arm's length. On the general attitude of clergy and laity in the diocese we have little evidence. We do not even know whether the two successive English service books of the reign were in fact used in Welsh parishes: if they were, they can have conveyed little to a monoglot congregation. At anyrate there was no popular uprising as in Cornwall, where Cornish-speaking parishes were up in arms against this ' new Christmas game '. One thing which must have helped to reconcile the clergy to the Edwardian revolution is the Act of 1549 which regularised clerical marriages. Nineteen of the clergy of Bangor

diocese are known to have taken advantage of this, since
they were in consequence deprived of their livings in the
next reign; and this is probably not the full total.

On the other hand, what caused deep distress to many,
as the Anglesey poet Sîon Brwynog pathetically recorded in
verse, was the plundering by royal commissioners of altars,
statues, vestments, vessels and stained glass windows as
objects of ' superstition ' — and with the concurrent aim of
easing the contemporary ' balance of payments ' crisis. Perhaps it was as well that Bishop Bulkeley had already
disposed of some of the furnishings of Bangor cathedral for
spot cash; possibly he saw what was coming! Suspicion that
the plundered goods did not always reach their destination
made it harder to bear, and in response to public clamour
commissions were appointed in each shire, responsible to a
central commission under Pembroke, to trace missing goods
and bring defaulters to book; the commissioners were at the
same time instructed on the minimum of church furniture
which must be left to enable the parson to conduct the
services with propriety by Protestant standards. The members of the Caernarvonshire commission included the father
and grandfather of Sir John Wynn of Gwydir, John Wyn ap
Hugh of Bodfel and Rice Thomas of Aber. How much was
recovered and how much medieval craftsmanship lost for
good we shall never know. Caernarvonshire churches were
never very ornate, but even a remote little church like that
of Llanrhychwyn, perched a thousand feet above the Conway
valley and well out of the path of the depredators, has
retained some fifteenth and sixteenth century windows of
yellow stain on clear glass believed to represent (in addition
to the normal subjects) St. Rhychwyn and St. David. But
this was a church where Llywelyn the Great himself may
have worshipped before he built the one at Trefriw, and
perhaps hardly representative of the normal village church.
Only two pre-Reformation chalices are known to have survived in the county. But the commission can in any case
hardly have completed its work in the six weeks before the
young king died.

The reign of Mary is commonly regarded as a period of reaction, but it was also a period of reform. The Council of Trent had now held two sessions and had remedied many of the abuses which helped to provoke the Reformation. But the effects were slow in reaching this diocese. When Arthur Bulkeley died in 1552 the see remained vacant for nearly three years. It was filled at last in 1555 by a man of very different theological outlook from Bulkeley's; he was another Dr. William Glynne, but this time not of the house of Glynllifon. He came of an Anglesey family and had a distinguished career at Cambridge, where he became head of a college and professor of Divinity, until he resigned the latter post, in the fourth year of Edward VI's reign, after publicly championing the doctrine of transubstantiation. In spite of this he was allowed to hold livings in London and in his home parish in Anglesey; but naturally Mary's succession brought him more substantial advancement. He championed the Roman faith in public disputations with the leading Protestant divines, and was employed on a diplomatic mission abroad, from which he returned just before his appointment to Bangor.

The new bishop, as well as being a learned theologian and controversialist, had a strong sense of his pastoral duties, as he showed by regular meetings with his clergy twice a year for instruction and edification — just what they had lacked in the past. He was not a persecutor — there were no burnings in Bangor diocese; but then, of course, there were no heretics to burn, for Protestantism had not begun to take root. The only Caernarvonshire man who is known at this stage to have formed decided Protestant opinions was Richard Davies, son of the curate of Gyffin, near Conway, who imbibed them at Oxford under Henry VIII and held livings in England in the next reign. He was among the five hundred Protestants who fled, unhindered, to the continent on Mary's accession; his career when he returned will concern us later. If his fellow-student Thomas Davies of Caerhûn held the same convictions, they sat on him far more loosely: appointed chancellor of Bangor cathedral at the end of Henry VIII's reign (as well as incumbent of several Bangor and St. Asaph livings while he was still resident at the university), he seems to have found no difficulty in retaining his preferments after papal power had been restored. The only thing the Bangor clergy found hard to swallow was the re-enforced rule of clerical celibacy — enforced, perhaps, more exactingly to conform with the more stringent standards of the Council of Trent. As we have seen, nineteen of the Bangor clergy resigned or were deprived for this reason during the fifteen months following application of this order. But even this was not the upheaval it seemed. It has been suggested that Bishop Glynne was disposed to turn a blind eye on this departure from the strict standards of the Council of Trent because he was himself the son and grandson of priests and had a son of his own, who became an Elizabethan sheriff. The ejected were soon provided with other livings, presumably after making some show of putting away their wives; in fact in some cases it amounted to little more than a general reshuffle for the sake of appearances. Excellent bishop as he was in many ways, Glynne can hardly be taken as a complete embodiment of the reformed Catholicism of Trent.

The bishop predeceased the queen by six months. Mary's chief adviser, Cardinal Pole, recommended as his successor Morys Clynnog, a Caernarvonshire man who had lectured on law at Oxford when Pole was chancellor of the university, and had proceeded to a divinity doctorate and ordination. Pole thought well of him and gave him an important post in his household and several livings, to which his friend Thomas Goldwell, now bishop of St. Asaph, added the rectory of Corwen. The queen accepted the cardinal's recommendation, and Clynnog set off for Rome to obtain consecration and confirmation in his post. To safeguard the interests of the bishopric in the absence of a bishop, Thomas Davies was made 'administrator', with custody of the revenues of the see and power to admit to livings. But while Clynnog was abroad he heard of Queen Mary's death and the succession of her half-sister, Anne Boleyn's daughter;

he heard also that, while declining to revive her father's style of Head of the Church of England, Elizabeth had accepted a substitute almost equally hard to reconcile with loyalty to Rome. He was unwilling to take up his post in these conditions, and a new bishop was appointed, of whom more shortly. Clynnog returned to England in 1560 on a papal mission to ascertain the queen's intentions, but what he heard gave him no satisfaction, and he obtained leave to reside abroad. Seven years later he wrote a strange letter in Welsh to Secretary Cecil thanking him for this unusual clemency; he did not add that he had meanwhile been urging the king of Spain to take steps for the deposition of Cecil's queen!

The bishop appointed in 1559 was Rowland Meyrick. He sprang from Powysian stock which had risen to fame and fortune through the services of Llywelyn ap Heilyn to Henry of Richmond at Bosworth, and had in the next few generations established branches both in Pembrokeshire and in Anglesey, where Llywelyn's son Meurig secured a crown lease of Aberffraw (the ancient seat of the princes of Gwynedd), built himself a house at Bodorgan, and adopted the surname Meyrick. Rowland came of the Pembrokeshire branch. At Oxford, where he became head of a college, he had been contemporary with Richard Davies and the other Welshmen who imbibed Protestant views and became the backbone of the Reformation in Wales. Under Edward VI he had been chancellor of St. David's, and after Elizabeth's accession he and Richard Davies were two of the four visitors sent round the Welsh dioceses to enforce the use of the Elizabethan Prayer Book. This was, of course, in English; it was not until 1567 that the Prayer Book appeared in Welsh, and with it the Salesbury and Davies New Testament. The whole Bible in Welsh, in William Morgan's translation, followed in 1588. In all three of these vital achievements Caernarvonshire men took a major part. Davies had by that time become bishop of St. Davids; the *Epistol* which he wrote as a preface to his New Testament was a manifesto of militant Protestantism. Morgan, born near Penmachno (where his house may still be seen) was a Gwydir tenant who went to Cambridge at a time when it had begun to supplant Oxford as the home of the New Learning and of Protestantism, and had achieved distinction there as a Hebrew scholar. After leaving the university he served in a succession of livings, none of them in his native shire; it was in Denbighshire that he completed his *magnum opus*.

Rowland Meyrick's appointment marks the real beginning of the Reformation in Caernarvonshire, but the progress of Protestant conviction, as distinct from prudential conformity, is difficult if not impossible to trace. Certainly the number of resignations or ejections under Bishop Meyrick was much smaller than that of the married clergy who left vacancies to be filled under Mary. In fact the only Bangor clergyman known to have been deprived of his living for failure to conform was Gruffydd Robert, appointed archdeacon of Anglesey just a month before Queen Mary died, whereupon he too fled to Rome. He was probably yet another of the Caernarvonshire men who had been to Oxford in Henry VIII's reign, but little is known of his origins and early life. A substantial rise in the number of ordinations, and the frequency of ordination services, during Meyrick's episcopate, seem to indicate a readiness among the educated class from whom the clergy were drawn to accept the Elizabethan order. On the wider public it is impossible to venture any generalisation till later in the reign; all we can safely say is that there was no overt revolt. The situation here was probably much the same as in Monmouthshire as it appears in the autobiography of Father Augustine Baker, where he recalls the atmosphere in which his parents halfheartedly practised the conformity from which he later revolted: [4]

> At the first, and for some years after the said change made by Queen Elizabeth the greatest part even of those who in their judgments and affections had befor bin Catholickes, did not well discern any great fault, novelty or difference from the former

[4] Augustine Baker, *Autobiography (Cath. Rec. Soc.* 1933), 16.

religion . . . save only the change of language . . . in the which
difference they conceived nothing of substance or essense to be.
And so easily digested the new religion and accommodated themselves thereto; especially in Wales and in other like places,
remotest from London.

Bishop Meyrick's reports both to the archbishop and to
the government show a full appreciation of the uphill task
before him. There was still much pluralism and non-residence. In 1561 a third of the cathedral clergy were non-
resident and in Caernarvonshire nearly a third of the parish
priests; in other parts of the diocese the proportion was
much lower. Worse still, there were four lay lawyers holding
ecclesiastical preferment in the diocese. Dr. John Gwynne,
uncle to Sir John Wynn of Gwydir, held a prebendal stall
in the cathedral to which his family hung on like grim death,
despite many efforts to dislodge them, for another century,
and even Elis Pryse, the notorious ' Red Doctor ' of Plas
Iolyn, had a Caernarvonshire rectory. That there were only
two licensed preachers in the diocese is not surprising;
Meyrick was certainly taking a rosy view when he named
thirty-two more as ' able to preach and might do good '. The
survival of pre-Reformation practices — vigils, pilgrimages,
telling of beads, resort to shrines, sacred wells, relics and
images — which forms the burden of so many episcopal
returns, does not of necessity argue devotion to the papacy
any more than attendance at Elizabethan Church services
was a guarantee of commitment to what they stood for.
Much of it was a matter of sheer peasant conservatism,
rooted rather in the round of nature than in any theological
conviction.

Another obstacle lay in the crude materialism of many of
the upper gentry, so often castigated by Catholic and Protestant reformers alike. Of this a glaring example is seen
after the death of Bishop Meyrick in 1565, when the earl of
Pembroke — who had already possessed himself of the
handsome revenues of Clynnog — tried to foist on the see
none other than Elis Pryse, who, apart from not being in
orders, did not even (as the church historian Strype mildly

observed in retrospect) have ' a priestly disposition '. Thomas
Pennant, writing still later, goes the whole hog and calls him
' the greatest of our knaves in the period in which he lived '[5]
Such a proposal, even from Pembroke, was hardly likely to
get past Archbishop Parker, some of whose advisers (not
without reason) thought he ought to look outside Wales
because the Welsh ' banded so much together in kindred,
that the Bishop could not do as he would for his alliance
sake '. At last, on the advice of Secretary Cecil, he recommended Nicholas Robinson, who came of an old Conway
family, descended on the female side from the Penmynydd
Tudors, which had acquired estates in Denbighshire and in
Anglesey. Like Meyrick, Robinson was a Cambridge man;
under Edward VI he had taken the Protestant line, but it
was when Pole was archbishop that he took orders. He lived
obscurely at Cambridge until Elizabeth made Parker archbishop, and Parker took him as one of his chaplains. He
came to Bangor diocese in 1562 as archdeacon of Merioneth,
with the reputation of a powerful preacher and a zealous
Protestant, but all his zeal could not conquer the immemorial
habits of the countryside, and his reports as bishop are in
much the same vein as those of his predecessor.

Bishop Robinson, however, had a more serious crisis to
face. The excommunication of Queen Elizabeth by Pope
Pius V in 1570 had violent repercussions both at home and
abroad. Abroad it was the signal for strenuous efforts towards
the reconversion of England, by the despatch of trained
missionaries and the broadcasting of Catholic literature. The
training was mainly centred in Douay, where a seminary
had been established for the purpose in connection with the
university, not long before the excommunication. This was
largely due to the efforts of Owen Lewis, an Oxford graduate
from Anglesey who had gone to Douay university to complete his education rather than submit to Elizabeth's oath
of supremacy. The Welsh connection was long maintained,
starting with a nephew of Bishop Barlow, the protagonist

[5] Strype, *Parker* (1821 ed.), i. 405; Pennant, *Tours* (1883 ed.), iii. 132.

of Protestantism in South Wales. He was soon followed by
Robert Owen of Plas Du, who left his Shropshire rectory
with a permit to study abroad, and never returned to his
cure; and in the next year (under Owen's influence) by
Robert Gwynne of Bodvel. By 1600 a dozen young men from
Bangor diocese had been to Douay to train for the Roman
priesthood, two-thirds of them from Caernarvonshire. They
mostly came from the ranks of the smaller gentry and
yeomen, and as the annual exodus grew in the 'eighties and
'nineties more and more of them had their entire education
at Douay. At least six returned on mission, three of them to
Llŷn; some remained abroad; a few ultimately conformed.
Rome was another centre which drew extensively on Wales
for young aspirants to the priesthood, after the hospice for
English students there had been turned into a seminary and
Morys Clynnog installed as warden through Owen Lewis's
influence with the papacy. This proved not to be a happy
appointment, for the bitter legacy of the Glyn Dŵr period,
forgotten by the Welsh since their own dynasty came to the
throne, still rankled (as we have seen) with the English, even
with students in exile for their faith; moreover tact was never
a strong point with Owen Lewis, which is partly why his
efforts to gain support at Rome for a stream of Catholic
literature in Welsh came to naught, and the task had to be
left (as will appear) to private effort.

At home the excommunication had a double effect: on the
one hand it brought pressure to bear on waverers in religion
to jump down on one side of the fence or the other; on the
other hand it impelled the government to take all the steps
it could to see that they jumped down on the side of the
establishment. 'Matters' as Augustine Baker puts it in the
passage already quoted, 'came to be more discerned and
distinguished concerning religion'. In 1577 John Whitgift,
bishop of Worcester (afterwards archbishop) became vice-
president of the Council of Wales, and as the president,
Sir Henry Sidney, was away in Ireland for most of the time,
carrying out his concurrent duties as lord deputy there, the
bishop was the effective ruler in Wales. Sidney had been

relatively mild in his treatment of Catholic recusants, as one
of them (Robert Owen's brother Hugh) remembered with
gratitude in exile. Whitgift was a strong Calvinist and
bitterly anti-Roman, and he put into practice with energy
the new laws against recusants, and especially against papal
missionaries from abroad, which followed the excommunication.

In the very year of Whitgift's appointment the Council
charged Bishop Robinson and Elis Pryse (who had so coveted
his bishopric) with a commission to examine the activities
of a group of suspected recusants in Llŷn who were also
concerned in the local opposition to the earl of Leicester.
Thomas Owen of Plas Du, who had been sheriff of Caernarvonshire a few years before the bull of excommunication,
was now denounced by some of his neighbours as an
absentee from church. Two of his younger brothers, Hugh
and Robert, refugees abroad on the proceeds of the tithes
of Aberdaron, had been brought up as youths in the service
of the earl of Arundel, now leader of the Romanist faction
in England. It was Arundel who, as lord of Oswestry, had
presented Robert to the border living he deserted in 1570;
Hugh, who remained a layman, had become involved in his
patron's intrigues on behalf of Mary, Queen of Scots, and
had fled to the Spanish Netherlands, where he remained, a
Spanish pensioner and 'intelligencer' on English affairs to
the government at Brussels, till after Gunpowder Plot.
Plas Du was known and denounced as a place of refuge for
missionary priests, who landed at unguarded creeks of the
neighbouring sea coast and were harboured in the roomy
loft still running the length of the house, till they were ready
to continue on their perilous way eastwards, often accompanied by their host. Robert Owen was back in Llŷn in 1576,
with his neighbour and disciple Robert Gwynne, whom he
left to his missionary labours in North Wales while he himself returned to the continent — to die in France over fifty
years later. Of the success of Robert Gwynne's mission,
especially among women, glowing reports were soon reaching Douay. Hugh did not venture back, but he was able for

some years to keep in touch with his home, with his old patron and with fellow recusants in the lordship of Oswestry, with whom Thomas often found refuge in times of stress. Attempts on the part of the government to have Hugh Owen extradited from Flanders under the terms of Henry VII's Magnus Intercursus came to nothing, as did many later efforts.

So the authorities had to be content with what could be done on this side of the water. Several of the Owens' neighbours were in sympathy with them, others were only too ready to join the hue and cry, which had indeed been started by an Oswestry man. Among those most ready to help the commissioners of 1578 with their work was Richard Vaughan of Cors y gedol, who, although his chief estate lay in Merioneth, had acquired by marriage a small property near Pwllheli, on the strength of which (and perhaps of his proven zeal as magistrate against local papists) he was made sheriff in 1578. He it was who had Thomas Owen arrested, tried before quarter sessions and remitted to gaol for trial before the great sessions; Thomas in turn brought counter-actions against Vaughan in the Council of Wales and the Star Chamber. For the next three years the air was thick with accusations and recriminations among the gentry of Llŷn; then it all died down. One by one the recusants and ' fellow-travellers ' conformed, even (it seems) Thomas Owen. His son went to Oxford, not Douay, and acquired a European reputation for Latin epigrams so Protestant in tone as to find a place on the papal Index; it was left to his sister's son Charles Gwyn (of Boduan) to carry on the family tradition by eventually becoming head of the Jesuit mission. Plas Du was sold in the next generation, and the family disappears from Caernarvonshire history.

Between 1598 and the end of the century not a single youth from Caernarvonshire entered Douay, and only two between then and the Civil War. Bishop Robinson was no doubt over-optimistic when he boasted in 1582 that there were not more than half-a-dozen recusants in his diocese, and the sheriff's *nil* return in the following year does not inspire confidence when we recall that the sheriff was John Griffith of Cefnamwlch, himself one of the suspected recusants of Llŷn five years earlier. But equally there can be no doubt that the campaign initiated by Whitgift had had its effect among men of property — those with most to lose. The survival of recusancy in Llŷn depended henceforth on men and women lower in the social scale, unable to provide the necessary support and shelter for priests, and without this the movement was doomed.

The proximity of the bishop and the influence of Gwydir between them helped to keep recusancy at bay in Arfon and Arllechwedd, excepting only the region round Clynnog, where the concourse of pilgrims to St. Beuno's shrine (as with St. Winifred's well at Holywell) ensured the persistence of ancient observances. But Creuddyn was as much off the beaten track as Llŷn, and proved as resistant to change, though here trouble did not boil up until after the crisis in Llŷn had subsided. The principal family in Creuddyn was that of Pugh of Penrhyn Creuddyn, which had also acquired by marriage both estates and powerful connections across the Conway, in Denbighshire, as well as in remoter Lancashire. They even married into the Anglesey Bulkeleys. Early in Elizabeth's reign the then head of the family, Robert ap Hugh, had served Denbighshire as a member of parliament and both Denbighshire and Caernarvonshire as sheriff. He must, then, have shown a minimum of compliance with the queen's religious policy, though both the family's wills and their mural decorations and carvings at Penrhyn (some of which still survive) show where their real sympathies lay. In any case neighbours, many of whom shared these sympathies, were unlikely to cause trouble. It was not until the campaign against recusancy was in full swing in 1584 that Robert ap Hugh's heir, Robert Pugh, together with his wife and ten neighbouring parishioners, were formally reported as recusants by the bishop of St. Asaph, since some of his estates lay in his diocese.

Matters came to a head when the earl of Pembroke began his career as lord president of Wales in 1586 by an intensified drive against recusants. A constant watch was kept for Robert Pugh, but he eluded capture, sometimes by visits to Lancashire or Denbighshire friends, but for some nine months by taking refuge in the Rhiwledyn cave, under the Little Orme. Suitably timbered and furnished, this proved spacious enough to provide both a home and a chapel for a little religious community which at one time is said to have included as many as a dozen priests. In 1587 a local man, obviously outside the recusant circle, stumbled on this hiding place and reported to the nearest magistrate, Sir Thomas Mostyn of Gloddaeth. With a score of stalwarts Mostyn made for the cave, and left his *posse* to lay siege to it all night; but by the morning the occupants had all escaped by some undiscovered exit. On examination it was found to contain not only provisions and arms, but a quantity of leaden type, most of which had been cast into the sea when they fled. It has since come to light that the type had been used for printing Gruffydd Robert's tract *Y Drych Cristian-ogawl*, which purported to have been printed at Milan, but was almost certainly the first book to be printed in Wales. Recent attempts to unearth in the cave relics of its romantic past have failed, but on the facts there can be no serious dispute.

For five years Pugh was a fugitive, for a time at the house of his influential co-religionist Lord Montagu, in Sussex. Then in 1592 he is found at Holyhead, in company with Father William Davies, a Denbighshire alumus of Douay who had been on the English mission for the past seven years and had been a frequent visitor to the Rhiwledyn community; they were arranging for the transport to Ireland of four young Welsh aspirants to the priesthood *en route* for Valladolid, a newly-founded seminary which became popular with Welsh students (including several from Caernarvon-shire) because it could be reached with relative ease viâ Ireland. Davies was captured, and barbarously executed at Beaumaris the following year. Pugh escaped once more. Then attempts were made to embroil him in one of the many plots, bogus and otherwise, hatched among Catholic exiles abroad against Elizabeth; his adhesion was especially desired because of the strong strategic position he would have held in an attempt to raise North Wales, which was part of the plan, and because he was reputed to keep a pinnace. The plot (if it ever existed outside the fertile imagination of an informer or *agent provacateur*) came to nothing, and no charge was made against Pugh, but he was still high on the list of suspects. In the very last year of Elizabeth's reign warrants were issued for his arrest by the Council of Wales. He was then staying with his friend Cadwaladr Wynn of Foelas, just over the Denbighshire border, and through his connivance (magistrate though he was), Pugh once more eluded capture.

What finally happened to him is not known with any certainty; at anyrate he outlived the reign of James I, and it was a tradition in his family that he spent his latter days in peace through the personal intervention of the king. There is no ground for believing that he ever abandoned his faith; nor did his descendants for at least two generations. Several were priests, Catholic controversialists, or soldiers in the cause of the Counter-Reformation; one was confessor to Queen Henrietta Maria, another wrote some very interesting but not very distinguished Welsh verse describing the Rhiwledyn epic. Some will concern us later in this story. It was no doubt the constancy of the Pughs that kept recusancy alive in Creuddyn longer than in any other part of the shire.

*Y Drych Cristianogawl* was not Caernarvonshire's only contribution to the output of literature by means of which the missionary priests sought to bring about the re-conversion of their native shire, especially those who could not be reached by oral preaching. Morys Clynnog wrote a catechism in Welsh, to which Gruffydd Robert contributed a short introduction; and no doubt one of the latter's objects in writing the now classic Welsh grammar which he printed in Milan was to equip his countrymen, who of necessity depended so much on oral transmission and so rarely saw Welsh in writing, for reading these works. Robert Gwynne not only wrote long Welsh letters from overseas with the

same end in view — 'fervent sermons in letter form', they
have been called[6] — before he went on mission; he also translated into Welsh the *Christian Directory* of Robert Parsons.

Caernarvonshire Protestants, however, were by no means
backward in their output of religious literature in Welsh.
Their crowning work was the Welsh Bible, in which, as we
have seen, the county played no small part; but a notable
contribution was the printing in 1595 by Hugh Lewis, vicar
of Llanddeiniolen and later chancellor of the cathedral, of
a Welsh translation of one of the works of that pioneer of
the Protestant Reformation and the English Bible, Miles
Coverdale. And not only parsons, but laymen too were
making their contributions to Welsh religious literature
from the Protestant angle. Even Rowland Puleston, who was
sheriff of the county in 1575 and a descendant of that Roger
de Puleston who had been slain by the Welsh over three
hundred years earlier as an agent of the financial exactions
of Edward I, wrote in 1593 (but never published) a Welsh
book, with a vehemently Protestant introduction, designed
to popularise the contents of the Bible in days before the
complete Welsh translation had appeared, still less been
made available for home reading.

Clearly Protestantism was becoming something more than
an imposed religion. Thirty years of the Welsh Prayer Book
had had their impact, and the impact was greater now that
the houses of the wealthier gentry were ceasing to be available for the mass, and the priests available for celebrating it
were being reduced to a pathetic handful — the process
Archbishop Mathew[7] calls 'encirclement and slow starva-
tion'. Bishop Robinson's work during his eighteen-year
episcopate had perforce been largely negative in character —
the rooting out of 'popish practices'; his two successors,
Hugh Bellott and Richard Vaughan, whose episcopates
jointly covered about the same period of time, were able to

[6] J. M. Cleary, 'The Catholic Resistance in Wales' (*Blackfriars* 1957),
112.
[7] David Mathew, *The Celtic Peoples and Renaissance Europe* (1933), 76.

devote themselves to the more positive task of building up
an educated and devoted ministry in the diocese. Many of
the clergy they placed in Bangor livings were to make
distinguished contributions to English, Latin and Welsh
scholarship, to theology and literature; they included
Edmund Prys, the author of the Welsh metrical Psalms,
some of which are still sung, and Richard Parry, editor of
the revised Welsh Bible of 1620. The results were seen in
the next century.

## BIBLIOGRAPHY

The standard account of the church in Wales before the Reformation is Glanmor Williams, *The Welsh Church from Conquest to
Reformation* (1962). A brief survey of Welsh Church history as a
whole is J. W. James, *A Church History of Wales* (1945). The Reformation in Bangor diocese is dealt with in the introduction to A. Ivor
Pryce, *The Diocese of Bangor in the Sixteenth Century* (1923), and
in Glanmor Williams, ' The Reformation in sixteenth-century Caernarvonshire ' (*TCHS* 1966). The only one of the Caernarvonshire religious
houses to be written up at length is Aberconway, on which see
R. W. Hays, *History of the Abbey of Aberconway* (1963); all that is
known about the Dominican Friary at Bangor is to be found in an
article by Glyn Roberts in the quatercentenary number of *The
Dominican* (Friars School, 1957). Much information on the disposal
of monastic estates can be found by consulting the index to *Records
of the Court of Augmentations relating to Wales and Monmouthshire*
(ed. Lewis and Davies, Bd. of Celtic Studies Hist. and Law Ser. xiii,
1954). Accounts of the monastic buildings will be found in Royal
Commission on Ancient Monuments in Wales and Monmouthshire
[RCAM], *Caernarvonshire*, i and ii. Catholic recusancy in Caernarvonshire is dealt with in E. Gwynne Jones, *Cymru a'r Hen Ffydd* (1951),
and his articles on the Pughs of Penrhyn in *TCHS* 1946, 1957; and
by J. M. Cleary in *Blackfriars*, xxxvii (1957), and in *Checklist of Welsh
Students in the Seminaries* i. 1568-1603 (privately printed, 1958).
For lives of some of the more prominent characters see Glanmor
Williams, *Bywyd ac Amserau'r Esgob Richard Davies* (1953), and
Geraint Bowen, ' Morys Clynnog ' (*TCHS* 1966).

## IV

## PARLIAMENTARY APPRENTICESHIP
### (1541-1629)

HENRY VIII's Act of Union conferred on Caernarvonshire, in common with the other Welsh shires, the right — or, more accurately, the duty — of representation in parliament. It was a novel experience, for Edward II's brief experiment of bringing to Westminster representatives of the three shires of Gwynedd had long since passed out of memory. The aim of this chapter is to find how Caernarvonshire reacted to this new obligation during its period of apprenticeship, from 1541, when (as far as is known) it sent its first elected representatives to the House of Commons, to the last parliament called by Charles I before he embarked on his fatal policy of dispensing with parliament altogether.

I have called representation in parliament a duty rather than a right because that was how it appealed to most people at the time when Wales was made to share it. For one thing it was dangerous; the Wars of the Roses were still within living memory, and parliament had then been a catspaw of the opposing factions, who used it to wreak their vengeance on each other through the process of attainder. Then too it was an expensive luxury. Constituencies were obliged by law to pay their members a fee to cover their journey and their stay in London. It is true that the knights of the shire, the more dignified element in the House, were beginning to forget these fees, which changes in the value of money were reducing to a figure beneath their notice; borough members, on the other hand, still often collected them. It is true also that at the beginning of the century parliaments were still short and rare: Henry VII, for example, called only one session for the last twelve years of his reign, and it lasted only two months; even that was well above average length. But a parliament might stretch to three sessions, and frequent journeys from Caernarvonshire to London and back, with a stay of anything from three to eight weeks, were a heavy tax on all but the more substantial folk who might have personal business there in any case, as well as town houses of their own or their friends' to stay in.

Tudor governments were well aware of this, and they tempered the wind to the shorn lamb when the poor and thinly populated principality was saddled with this new burden. Instead of finding two members for each shire, as in England, Wales was let off with one; and instead of choosing a member for each chartered borough the Welsh shires were allowed to group their boroughs into single constituencies returning one group member; for Merioneth there was no borough member at all. The system was peculiar to Wales, and did not disappear till our own time; in Caernarvonshire, the last survivor, it lasted till 1948. This section of the Act of Union was loosely framed, and the uncertainties it bred complicated many an election dispute.

Three questions naturally arise about parliamentary representation. First, how were elections conducted? Then, what sort of people were elected, and what did their constituents expect of them? Finally, what was their conception of their functions as members, and how did they fulfil their own aims and those of the electors when they got to Westminster? To begin with, the method of election evolved by long usage in England was easily adapted to the Wales that had emerged from the Edwardian conquest. It has been shown in an earlier chapter how in Edward's new shires the freeholders had to meet once a month at the bidding of the sheriff for judicial purposes and any other shire business remitted to them by the king. The sheriff had now to add to his duties the transmission of the royal writ ordering an election, and when the freeholders had made their choice, it was he who had to return the writ endorsed with the member's name. Soon after the Statute of Wales, Edward had enacted another statute, applicable to the whole of the dominions, under which those who held land of a value less than forty shillings a year were exempt from jury service — one of the principal burdens of attendance at the shire court. Over a hundred years later it was laid down that those exempt from jury service could not join in parliamentary elections at the shire court either.

When this law was enacted, forty shillings was still quite a high qualification, but once more changes in the value of money had undermined the intentions of the legislators; by 1540 the forty-shilling freeholders had become small beer. In Wales they were not quite so common because the operation of gavelkind had much reduced the size of holdings here. Forty shillings in 1540 would mean at least £20 today — probably a good deal more; and when we recollect that one of the major-generals Cromwell set over Wales, more than a hundred years after the Act of Union, declared that in Wales it was easier to find fifty gentlemen of £50 a year than five of £100, and that at that time even a gentleman of £500 ranked in England among the smaller gentry, it is easy to appreciate that the forty-shilling men were a minority of the inhabitants of the shire. But in Caernarvonshire they were a minority of a minority. 'Bond' lands were common here, as we have seen — possibly a relic of the inferior status to which the original *Cymry* had reduced the earlier inhabitants of Gwynedd when they conquered the land in the sixth century or thereabouts; and although by this time the holder of bond-lands had long ceased to be in any sense a bondman, and might indeed be a fully-fledged gentleman who during the later Middle Ages had bought up vacant servile holdings, or 'copyholds', as an investment, the lands themselves still carried an inferior status and did not entitle their owner to the vote. Exact estimates of the number of freeholders in Caernarvonshire at any time before electoral rolls were compiled in 1832 are impossible to come by. At that date there were 1,688; judging by the number of votes recorded at various contested elections in the shire, the total in the sixteenth and seventeenth centuries could not have been much more than four to five hundred — perhaps three per cent of the total population of the shire. In this Caernarvonshire and Anglesey were alike; in the more populous county of Denbigh, with its different historical background, the freeholders may have been as many as two thousand, or five per cent of the population.

Three features of modern elections were conspicuously missing from those of the sixteenth and seventeenth centuries: secrecy, election addresses and an electoral roll. The freeholders were asked for their ' voices ' and quite literally that is what they gave. And everyone present knew pretty well who was and who was not a forty-shilling freeholder; it is only late in the next century, as electoral contests grew hotter and membership came to be regarded (for reasons we shall see shortly) as a coveted privilege, that it became worth while for copyholders to try to pass themselves off as freeholders, for the other side to challenge their claims, and for lawyers to be called in or both sides to thresh the matter out — with the resulting long-drawn and ruinously expensive elections that became so familiar a feature of eighteenth-century politics.

In Tudor times there was rarely a contest at all. The gentry prepared to serve would generally have corresponded beforehand to determine which of them should be returned — if indeed the choice was not already predetermined by accepted county precedence. Only in times of acute public tension or family feud (and the two tended to march together) would a poll be necessary. Then the sheriff's call for the freeholder's ' voices ' would generally be answered by a general shout, and it would be up to the sheriff to determine which name was shouted loudest. If acclamation failed to decide it, then the freeholders had to give their individual ' voices '. It need not be emphasised how important a key figure the sheriff was in all this. If — as was usually the case — he was bound to either of the candidates by ties of kindred of friendship, he could be conveniently deaf to cries for the other candidate, refuse a poll and declare his man duly elected; even if there was a poll, his arithmetic need not be correct. In any case, so much were unopposed returns the normal practice that a contested election usually meant a disputed result. The defeated candidate would bring a Star Chamber action against his opponent and perhaps the sheriff as well, alleging unfair practices. Parliament, however, grew jealous of this outside interference in parliamentary concerns, and by the seventeenth century the house of commons had established its claim to decide disputed elections.

Readers of Sir John Neale's works on Elizabethan parliaments will be familiar with these election broils elsewhere. Caernarvonshire did not begin to be disturbed by them until the age of the Stuarts. Initially the electors were glad to leave the burdensome duties of representation to those with administrative experience and broad enough backs to stand both the expense and the political dangers involved in membership of the house of commons, and the smaller gentry had no ambition to challenge their leadership. What the county wanted was someone familiar enough with county affairs and grievances to be able to voice them with some weight at Westminster, for representation was essentially a local matter. When Charles I in 1629 rated the House of Commons for meddling in matters of state, and reminded them that formerly members had concerned themselves only with ' such business as they brought from their countries ', he was just telling the plain truth. As late as his son's reign, it has been pointed out,[1] the idea ' that mere political partisanship should override local and personal obligations seemed monstrous to those who thought themselves entitled to the support of their humbler neighbours '. The deep religious divisions which we have seen to have split Caernarvonshire society in Elizabeth's reign were expressed in the law court, not (as in the Denbighshire election of 1588, for example) at the polls. Even when there was no contest, the candidate nominated liked to be accompanied in triumph

[1] Mrs. Eric George in *Eng. Hist. Rev.* xlv, 1930, 554.

to the polling place. In 1675, to take a late example, Lord
Bulkeley (whose Irish peerage did not debar him from
candidature for Caernarvonshire) writes to ask John Griffith
of Cefnamwlch to escort him from Vaynol, where he is
staying, to Caernarvon on election day, symbolising the
support of the far end of the county.

The freeholder, for his part, marched under the colours of
his hereditary leader to the polls as naturally as in earlier
days — and again when Civil War broke out — he went to
the battlefield. In a Flintshire lease of Elizabeth's day this
obligation is specifically included; there is no sign that any
such reminder was needed in Caernarvonshire. In the Civil
War the Roundhead leader, Sir Thomas Myddelton, thought
it distinctly ungentlemanly for the opposite side to under-
mine the natural loyalty of his Denbighshire tenants by
recruiting among them, and said so in set terms in the manifesto he issued when he invaded the county on behalf of
parliament; his grandson was equally outraged, more than
thirty years later, when a tenant and an agent of his were
bullied into acting for his opponents in the Denbighshire
election of 1679. The only time when friction arose was when
there was uncertainty about precedence in the shire. In the
later sixteenth century the smaller gentry and those most
off the beaten track — as for example in Llŷn and Eifionydd
— began to develop social ambitions which soon found
political expression. Many of them were growing in wealth —
whether by successful marriages or through the law and
public office, or by less reputable means like piracy — and
were parading their new status in imposing new houses like
Bodwrda or Castellmarch; why should they leave the power
and prestige attached to membership of parliament — to say
nothing of the patronage that a member could wield on
behalf of family and friends and the jobs he might net for
himself — to the favoured few? As the sixteenth century
wore on, these *arrivistes* were coming to realise that representation could be a privilege as well as a burden. And the
families who had at first monopolised representation were
now prepared to open their ranks to admit to a share in it

those who were already co-operating with them in the humbler tasks of local government, and often inter-marrying with them.

For Caernarvonshire society did not have the monolithic structure that had come to prevail in Anglesey. There only one family — that of Plas Newydd — could challenge the supremacy of the Bulkeleys, and its interests lay mainly outside the island. In Caernarvonshire gradations of wealth were far more gentle. What the greater gentry — notably the Wynns of Gwydir — would not brook was anything that looked like a bid to dislodge them from their primacy in the shire. Hence the first really stormy election, which took place in 1620. The Wynns were bent, not so much on monopolising representation (Sir John Wynn himself only sat in one parliament) as on holding the strings in their hands; their correspondence for the first half of the seventeenth century reveals these manoeuvrings in election after election. And when in 1620 this primacy was disputed by a Griffith of Cefnamwlch, with widespread backing not only in Llŷn, but from jealous rivals of Gwydir nearer home, like Glynllifon (which had married into Cefnamwlch), Sir John Wynn's fury knew no bounds, and the whole shire was set aflame. Gwydir suffered a severe rebuff — all the more severe when John Griffith in the following year was made constable of Caernarvon castle. Sir John's son and heir Richard, the defeated candidate, eschewed Caernarvonshire politics for twenty years, finding safe seats in English pocket boroughs; when he was canvassed in elections to the Long Parliament he sourly observed that ' for this twenty yeares I had reason to beleeve I was no freeholder . . . for my voice (it seems) was not worth the desiring '.

This struggle brings to light another characteristic of Caernarvonshire society which differentiated it sharply from that of Anglesey — a characteristic arising from the configuration of the land and its historical associations. Anglesey is a natural unit, and had always acted as such before Edward I called it a shire. Caernarvonshire, on the other hand, was an artificial creation of the Act of Union, and to a great extent its older divisions remained the realities of politics. Llŷn, cut off from the rest of the shire for many purposes till communications improved in the nineteenth century, preserved a proud self-consciousness of its own. Morus Dwyfech, household bard to the Griffiths of Cefn-amwlch in Elizabeth's day, had addressed his beloved *cantref* as *trysor penn teirsir a'u porth* — ' chief treasure and stay of three shires '; one cannot readily imagine an Anglesey man apostrophising Malldraeth or Twrcelyn in those terms! It is significant that the Griffiths themselves always added to their signatures ' of Llyn '. And so the election contest of 1620 was in part a reflection of local loyalties as well as of family feuds. As yet there was no politics in it, but that was to come; for these same family and local loyalties were to bedevil the king's cause in Caernarvonshire in the Civil War, as will appear later.

So far we have been dealing only with county elections. The boroughs present a rather more complex problem. The grouping of the Welsh boroughs for parliamentary elections was a novelty in electoral procedure, and there was never any decisive rule about which boroughs were and which were not included in the group. This was a fertile cause of election disputes. In some counties certain ' ancient boroughs ' — the term used in the Act of Union to define those that were to be grouped with the shire town — never exercised the right; possibly never wished to, since it would have made them liable for their quota towards the member's wages. In Caernarvonshire the case was rather different. The ' ancient boroughs ' were those to which Edward I had granted charters for military reasons (Caernarvon, Conway and Cricieth) and the two on which the Black Prince, as Prince of Wales, had later conferred the status in recognition of their mercantile importance (Nefyn and Pwllheli). About the first category there was never any doubt; the writ might be withheld from them for sinister reasons, or the notice of polling sent too late for the voters to reach the poll before it closed, but these would be recognised as legitimate grounds for having the election invalidated.

The position of Nefyn and Pwllheli was shakier. At Pwllheli in 1586, and at Nefyn forty-six years later, crown officers treated these boroughs as crown manors which could be leased by the crown at will, subject only to the freehold rights of resident burgesses; in other words the Black Prince's charters were held not to have conferred on them any corporate rights as boroughs but only individual rights on the existing freeholders and their legal successors. But in both cases there was a powerful group of neighbouring land-owners ready to stand up for the rights of the borough, not on any altruistic ground, but because during the confusion of the later Middle Ages they had bought up ' burgages ' in these boroughs and were prepared to defend their rights to them against the crown itself. As things stood in the seventeenth century, it was only through these gentry that the crown could enforce its orders : it had no civil service, army or police force at its disposal. The upshot was that the boroughs, instead of being, as they were originally designed to be, strongholds of the power of the English crown, acting through a resident English population dependent on it in the midst of a hostile Welsh countrysde, had become mere appanages of the surrounding non-resident Welsh gentry. Cricieth, although one of the original Edwardian boroughs, had never grown into anything more than a village — ' a franchised toune, now clene decayed ', Leland called it in 1537; and after its castle fell into ruin it stood in much the same position as Nefyn and Pwllheli. What these landed patrons of the tiny boroughs valued at the time of the disputes with the crown was, of course, the lands in which they had invested; but they were not unaware of the political power that could be derived from the hold this might give them on the borough machinery, and the future was to show what an important asset these boroughs could become at election time.

We can now consider the way in which parliamentary elections were conducted in the Caernarvonshire boroughs. At the same time that the sheriff summoned the county electors it was his duty to send the authorisation to the mayors or bailiffs of the constituent boroughs, who in turn summoned the electors, by bell or by personal call. At the stated hour the electors for the ' out-boroughs ' proceeded to the county town, Caernarvon, where the election was conducted by the mayor in the same way as the sheriff conducted the county election — and with the same opportunities for gerrymandering. Here, however, there was not a single uniform franchise as with the forty-shilling freeholder in the shire. The voters were the burgesses, and ' burgess ' meant different things in different boroughs. Beaumaris, for example, was a ' corporation borough ', where the vote was vested in twenty-five ' capital burgesses ' named in the charter, and their places were filled, as they fell vacant, by co-optation. So limited a body was easily controlled by the Bulkeleys, whose house lay within the borough walls before Baron Hill was built. It is not surprising that Sir John Wynn, smarting under his electoral rebuff of 1620, plotted to checkmate John Griffith, now constable and mayor, by having the Caernarvon charter remodelled on the lines of that of Beaumaris, dangling before the burgesses the prospect of wider privileges secured at small expense, but no doubt hoping to achieve a control such as the Bulkeleys exercised; but nothing came of it. On the other hand the Caernarvon boroughs, like most of those in Wales, were of the ' freeman borough ' type, where admission to the status of burgess, and therefore to the parliamentary franchise, was by vote of the borough court.

There can be no doubt that the original intention and practice had been that the privileges of burgess-ship should be confined to those actually resident in the borough; that was the whole point of the creation of the Edwardian boroughs. But the process of infiltration during the chaos of the later Middle Ages wore down this limitation, and the victories of the non-resident gentry owning land in Nefyn and Pwllheli over crown officers trying to impose the condition of residence in 1586 and 1632 opened the door wide. ' The status of burgess ', as the late Professor Jones Pierce put it,[2] 'had become divorced from the soil'. At Pwllheli, in Elizabeth's reign, a little under a third of the three hundred inhabitants could claim the status of burgess, and of these, twenty-six were non-resident; early in the next century not more than a third of the sixty self-styled burgesses of Nefyn were resident. It was alleged in the disputed borough election to the Long Parliament, of which we shall be hearing more later, that most of the burgesses who came in from Llŷn were newly created. The device of gaining control of borough elections by getting a body of supporters from outside the borough elected as burgesses — and control of the mayoralty was usually enough for this — had already begun; it reached its climax in the eighteenth century, when the borough electorate in Caernarvonshire was by these means inflated to three times that of the shire.

What were the families that shared, during these formative years, the representation of shire and boroughs, and how did they carry out their duties at Westminster? Naturally enough, when Caernarvonshire was called on to fulfil this novel duty, the freeholders and burgesses turned to the family with the longest political experience in the shire — the Pulestons of Caernarvon, who, as we have seen, had become thoroughly assimilated to the gentry round them and intermarried with them. In the earliest parliaments of which we have record they represented both shire and borough. The house of Gwydir made its first appearance in the capacity of knights of the shire in Edward VI's first parliament and from then until their sensational defeat of 1620, Gwydir represented the shire in seven parliaments. The absence from the lists of the family of Griffith of Penrhyn, which for three generations had held the exalted office of chamberlain of North Wales and had moreover married into the Pulestons, is at first sight surprising; but Edward Griffith died in Dublin in 1541 and his younger brother, who inherited Penrhyn, was possibly not yet old enough; it was not until 1567 that he was pricked as sheriff.

[2] *T.C.H.S.* 1957, 51.

The closely related house of Cochwillan, however, provided
the county member for Elizabeth's first parliament.
Meanwhile other and newer families had begun to appear.
The favour that John Wyn ap Hugh of Bodfel had won
during the primacy of Northumberland in Edward VI's reign
made him a natural choice for the following parliament, and
for the first time brought Llŷn into the parliamentary limelight; indeed for some time the Bodvel family remained the
most powerful in this part of the shire, and the representation fell to it in two of Elizabeth's parliaments; then its local
prestige began to decline — maybe because of its strong links
with the perilous cause of popery. The Griffiths of Cefnamwlch, who had usurped the primacy of Bodvel (and had
indeed been its hereditary rivals since tribal days) were also
for a time suspect in religion, and — what was worse — they
were on bad terms with Gwydir; they did not appear in
parliament till the next century, when they made their
sensational and successful bid against the forces of Gwydir
for the leadership not only of Llŷn, but of the whole shire.
But the Thomases of Caernarvon and Aber were at least
safe: was not Captain William Thomas, married to a niece
of Edward Griffith of Penrhyn and *persona grata* at Gwydir,
to become a co-hero of the Protestant forces at Zutphen with
Sir Philip Sidney? He represented the shire in two of
Elizabeth's parliaments, and we shall meet the family again
in elections to the Long Parliament.

Clenennau first swims into parliamentary waters in 1593,
after the last member — Hugh Gwyn Bodvel — had burned
his fingers by opposition to Leicester and association with
the Llŷn recusant group. Sir John Wynn had procured a
letter from the privy council recommending his brother to
the electors on the ground of the special need in such critical
days of ' persons discreet, sufficient and well-affected '; but
the electors took the bit between their teeth and elected
William Maurice, who was certainly well-affected and had
shown his ' sufficiency ' in his recent co-operation with
Gwydir in county defence and preparedness during the
Armada years — whatever might be said of his ' discretion '.

Glynllifon, like Cefnamwlch, belonged to the group hostile
to Gwydir, and although its principal estate lay in Arfon,
tended to act with the Llŷn faction, having lands also in
Nefyn. William Glynne, nephew of Bishop Skevington's
right-hand man, was high sheriff in 1562 (as his father had
been under Henry VIII), but he never sought parliamentary
honours. He outlived both his son Thomas and his grandson
William (later Sir William), but the latter found his political
feet by entering parliament in 1593 for Anglesey, where he
inherited a small estate through his mother. It was not until
the last parliament of James I that Sir William's son and
namesake at last won the Caernarvonshire seat for Glynllifon. From then till the outbreak of Civil War Cefnamwlch
and Glynllifon play Box and Cox with the county representation; in the end, as will appear, Glynllifon showed its old
capacity for coming out on the winning side.

By the time Elizabeth met her last parliament another
Llŷn family — that of Jones of Castellmarch — was on its
way to eminence. William Jones, the first of the family to
adopt the surname, was a rising lawyer who had married
into the Cefnamwlch family and had represented Beaumaris
in the preceding parliament. He sat for Caernarvonshire in
1601 but in the next reign reverted to Beaumaris; he
remained influential, however, in county elections, and by
1621 even Sir John Wynn was prepared to acknowledge him
as ' prime man ' of the county, for by then he had become
a judge in the Court of Common Pleas.

So much for the shire; what of the boroughs? Here the
choice was by no means as obvious. Petty tradesmen or
borough officials could not be expected to serve; their
resources would hardly rise to the expenses involved, and
they would not carry the weight in parliament which electors
expected of their representatives. There was indeed the
compensation that borough members could still collect their
wages without loss of dignity : in Caernarvonshire we know
that they did so at least as late as the Short Parliament of
1640. But on the other hand boroughs were taxed at a higher
rate than counties, and who would want to court unpopu-

larity among his neighbours in a small community by helping
to make these demands on their pockets on top of his own
expenses (and these amounted to £30 for Conway alone in
1640)? This is where the infiltration of the gentry into the
boroughs has its electoral importance. From the point of
view of the elector, a member of the gentry, resident or
non-resident, was far more likely to make an effective
representative at Westminster than a ' local '; and from the
point of view of the gentry, borough representation was a
convenient means of avoiding the expense of a contest when
another family had claims on the county seat, and was
equally acceptable as a means of enabling the younger
generation to try out its paces before taking over the county.

A striking example, among the resident gentry, was the
family of Griffith of Plas Mawr, Caernarvon (nephews to
Edward Griffith of Penrhyn), who represented the boroughs
in ten parliaments between 1545 and 1614. Another Caernarvon ' gentry ' family of ancient descent was that of Davies.
Griffith Davies, who sat for the boroughs in Edward VI's
last parliament, had moved to Caernarvon from the Conway
valley in Henry VIII's reign; he was a younger brother of
the Thomas Davies whom we have already met as the
' administrator ' of Bangor diocese during the vacancy following the flight of Morys Clynnog, and he had two other
brothers who held the county offices of coroner and escheator
respectively. He himself served twice as sheriff; his son
Maurice had a post at the Caernarvon exchequer and succeeded Griffith as borough member in 1559.

Apart from the resident gentry, however, several of the
more ambitious families of the shire were manoeuvring for
control of neighbouring boroughs from outside. John Griffith
of Cefnamwlch represented the boroughs in James I's first
parliament; by 1640 his son was claiming as life mayor of
Caernarvon to preside over the borough court at the disputed
election of that year — indeed his alleged partiality towards
one of the candidates was one of the grounds of a dispute
that will engage us later. Cefnamwlch also had a stake in
the borough of Nefyn, but here it met with resistance from

a family of relative newcomers to the Caernarvonshire
gentry. It was only towards the end of Elizabeth's reign
that the Wynns of Boduan (or Bodfean), a cadet branch of
Bodvel, began building up an estate both within and without
the borough, acquiring among other windfalls some of the
Beddgelert abbey lands formerly held by Anne of Cleves.
During the dispute between the borough and the crown
agents, referred to earlier in this chapter, Thomas Wynn
championed the borough while John Griffith took the
opposite side; by the eighteenth century the Wynns had
assumed (apparently with no authority at all) the office of
hereditary mayors of the borough. In much the same way
the office of hereditary constable of Cricieth castle — a
meaningless title, now that the castle had long since fallen
into ruin, save that it carried with it the mayoralty of the
borough — had by the seventeenth century been assumed
by a local gentry family which passed it on by hereditary
succession to the Owens of Brogyntyn, heirs also to the estate
of Clenennau, and so gave yet another of the leading families
of the shire an important stake in the borough elections;
but this did not take full effect till the eighteenth century.
In Caernarvon the right of the corporation to enclose the
waste lands of the borough was challenged in 1638 by the
owners of Vaynol and Bodfel, who claimed that the wastes
were the property of the Prince of Wales.

When none of the local gentry were available to fill the
borough seat, resort was had to the ' carpet-bagger '. In
Elizabeth's second parliament the seat was filled by John
Harrington, a courtier who had climbed into royal favour
by marrying Henry VIII's base daughter Audrey and whose
son, the more famous Sir John, was a godson of Queen
Elizabeth herself. Among his rewards was the constableship
of Caernarvon castle, conferred by Edward VI. He had no
other connection with the shire, and even here he discharged
his duties through deputies; but as the constableship carried
with it the mayoralty, he was by this means able to get
himself elected for the boroughs in Elizabeth's first two
parliaments. In the first he opted for Old Sarum, where he

had also been elected; in the second he chose Caernarvon. When John Griffith died in 1609 he was succeeded at a by-election by the clerk of the privy council, another member with no local connections; and in James I's last and his son's second and fourth parliaments the boroughs were represented by judges of the great sessions of Wales. One was Sir Peter Mutton, a Denbighshire gentleman who had previously represented his own shire; the other Edward Littleton, a Shropshireman who, while he sat for Caernarvon boroughs, achieved some notoriety as one of the framers of the Petition of Right.

Another family of distinguished lawyers — but this time with strong local roots — which gave some lustre to the borough seat, was that of Jones of Castellmarch. The founder of the family name and fortunes, Sir William the judge, we have already met. His son Charles, who was recorder of Beaumaris, represented it continuously from 1624 to 1640, while Robert, another son, took over the Caernarvon borough seat in Charles I's first two parliaments, when Littleton was initially elected but chose to serve within his own county. Yet another son, Griffith, played his part later, when he became a prominent figure both in parliament and in county affairs during the Civil War period.

It remains to see how these county and borough members discharged their duties in the House. The earliest appearances of Caernarvonshire members in the official records of the Commons are usually concerned with applications to the Speaker for leave of absence. This, of course, is not surprising in view of their distance from home, nor is it suprising that one of the earliest of such applications should have come from a Wynn of Gwydir in the first two parliaments of Elizabeth, for parliamentary duties always sat lightly on the family; for example, Sir Richard Wynn, the defeated candidate of 1620, told his father, when they were discussing the possible candidature of his brother Owen, that the burden of membership need not be heavy — once sworn in, he could be as casual in attendance as he chose! The first Caernarvonshire member to be recorded as engaged on any constructive

task is William Thomas, who was in 1576 elected to a large
committee concerned with Elizabethan Poor Law of that
year.

William Maurice made an unfortunate first appearance in
the Commons' Journals when as a member for Beaumaris in
1601 his claim for parliamentary privilege in respect of
unruly members of his escort from home, who had got themselves into trouble by entering into a brawl in Shrewsbury,
was disallowed by fellow-members; but he made a braver
showing when he sat for his own shire in the next parliament. Here his great theme, on which he spoke repeatedly
and was elected to several committees, was the union with
Scotland and the answering style of King of Great Britain
(flattering to Welsh sentiment) for James I. It was not a
popular theme, for Scots were still disliked and the proposed
title was prejudiced by recollections of the claims of James's
mother, Mary Queen of Scots, to be 'Queen of Great
Britain'; while Maurice's longwinded references to Welsh
history moved the House only to laughter or boredom.
Attempts were even made to discredit Sir William (as he
now was) by rumour that he had been seen coming from
mass at the Spanish ambassador's. On the other hand his
retort courteous to a scurrilous attack on the Welsh in one
of these debates won the esteem of fellow-members; for the
retort was to support a claim for privilege on the part of the
offending member. Maurice's sister thought the king had not
adequately rewarded his 'godfather', as she playfully called
her brother (a whimsey too often taken literally!). He
certainly was a staunch friend to the establishment. He
stood up for the council of Wales, the royal prerogative and
the Church establishment; he pleaded for generous grants
to the crown; he even declined to join the other Welsh cattle-
breeding counties in attacking the royal right of purveyance,
a feudal survival which sometimes took the form of compulsory purchase of their cattle at arbitary prices. He did
on the other hand attack the Shrewsbury Drapers' Company's
monopoly of the sale of Welsh cloth, which he believed to
be injurious to Wales.

None of the other Caernarvonshire members made such an impression on the House, favourable or unfavourable, as Maurice, unless it were Sir William Jones, who sat on important committees in James's first parliament and made a bold attack in the second on the royal right to impose arbitary duties, or 'impositions', on imports; but this was as member for Beaumaris, then a flourishing port. It was in the same capacity that his son Charles helped Selden to draw up the charges against Buckingham in 1626, and similarly two years later helped Littleton over the preparation of the measure which finally took shape as the Petition of Right. None of the Caernarvonshire members for this period were to be found among the opposition to Charles I. John Griffith, who was earnestly (and in the end successfully) courting Buckingham, defended the royal favourite against the attack in the 1626 parliament; his only part in the Petition of Right parliament was membership of a small committee to which an inocuous bill on bribery was referred. The Caernarvon borough member, Nicholas Griffith of Plas Mawr and Grays Inn, did indeed make some contributions to James's parliaments, mostly on routine legal matters; there is a topical flavour, however, in the argument he put forward in a debate on a bill to put down drunkenness, that to convict on the word of a single witness or the 'view' of a single magistrate gave too wide an opening to 'malice'. The Journal is sparing of Christian names, so it is possible (though unlikely) that some of these speeches of 'Mr. Griffith' were made by John of Cefnamwlch.

It is evident that during the period which had elapsed since the Act of Union the Caernarvonshire electors and those they elected had gained valuable experience, and a few of the latter had been able to make some constructive contribution to debates. Some had been introduced to politics at the Inns of Court, to which increasing numbers of the Caernarvonshire gentry were sending their sons — between twenty-five and thirty before the middle of the seventeenth century, and well over fifty before it finished. They had also begun the habit of sending at least the eldest to the university; Sir John Wynn of Gwydir was sent to Oxford in 1570, John Griffith of Cefnamwlch in 1609, and as many as three of the Bodwrda family to Cambridge about the same time. All this helped to widen their perspective; so did service in great households, which was a liberal education to men like the founders of the families of Castell-march and Bodvel — or for that matter the Owens of Plas Du, whom it led down the opposite path to exile and prefer-ment abroad. But elections as contests between opposing political principals were still far off. The only real issue was still one of precedence in the shire, and the acrimonies of election time still contained a large admixture of tribal feud.

## BIBLIOGRAPHY

On Welsh M.P.'s and elections in general during this period, see A. H. Dodd, 'Wales's parliamentary apprenticeship' (*Transactions Cymmrodorion Soc.*, 1942), 'Wales in the parliaments of Charles I (i)' (*T.C.S.* 1946) and *Studies in Stuart Wales* (1952), v. On Caer-narvonshire in particular, E. Gwynne Jones, 'County politics and electioneering, 1558 - 1625' (*TCHS*, 1929). On the boroughs, Glyn Roberts, 'Parliamentary representation of the Welsh boroughs' (*Bull. of Bd. of Celtic Studies*, iv, 1929), and for the Caer-narvonshire boroughs in particular, authorities listed under chapter I. The *Calendar of Wynn Papers* is indispensable on the subject of this chapter. W. R. Williams, *Parliamentary Representation of the Princi-pality of Wales*, is unreliable, but still useful until the Tudor volume of the official History of Parliament (now near completion) provides us with an adequate biographical dictionary of the Welsh members. On William Maurice and 'Great Britain' see S. T. Bindoff 'The Stuarts and their style' (*Eng. Hist. Rev.* lx, 1945).

# V

## PRELUDE TO CIVIL WAR, (1603-42)

THE causes of the Civil Wars which rent English society in the seventeenth century, and ended in the execution of a king and the declaration of a republic, may be grouped under three headings: religious, constitutional and economic. We have now to consider how far these causes were operative in Caernarvonshire.

We have seen how deeply religious divisions had cut into local society, notably in Llŷn and in Creuddyn. Fears of the return of 'popery' had been roused afresh by Gunpowder Plot, and again by the outbreak of religious war in Europe in 1618 (with the recurrent fear that the monarchy was going to drag England into desertion of the Protestant cause); and it was the Irish Catholic rebellion of 1641 that finally sparked off the war at home. On these issues the Welsh gentry, especially those old enough to remember the Armada, felt strongly, even if their feelings sprang rather from prudential than from theological motives. For Spain was still, in British eyes, the secular arm of the papacy, and the coast of Wales — notably that of Caernarvonshire — lay wide open to Spanish attack. Under these influences, and others more purely religious (which will be considered later), the bulk of those who counted in Wales had come over strongly to the Elizabethan Church settlement, and were prepared to defend it from attacks on either flank — Popish or Puritan.

In 1611 Sir John Wynn of Gwydir was corresponding with his fellow deputy lieutenant Sir William Thomas (son of the Zutphen hero) about the hunt for recusants in their respective 'limits' of the shire, much as he and Maurice had corresponded in more perilous days about beacons and trainbands; but it proved to be like looking for a needle in a haystack. The once flourishing recusant community of Llŷn had lost its patrons and protectors after 1580, as one by one they went over to the establishment. The Plas Du family disappeared from county society after 1614, and the estate passed into other hands. Bodfel had come to terms with Gwydir, and the pact was sealed by the marriage of Sir John Bodvel with Sir John Wynn's favourite daughter Bess. Cefnamwlch and Glynllifon were vying with each other for the patronage of the rising favourite, the duke of Buckingham, as soon as his star same into the ascendant in 1617, in the same way as an earlier Glynne had vied with an earlier Bulkeley for the favour of Wolsey and then Cromwell. Cefnamwlch won, and the prize was succession to Griffith's father-in-law, Sir Richard Trevor, in the office of vice admiral for North Wales, conferred by Buckingham as lord high admiral. This threw Glynllifon into opposition, but the opposition did not express itself in religious dissidence, and when it eventually did, it was on the left rather than the right flank of the establishment — Puritanism rather than Popery — that the Glynnes ranged themselves.

In Llŷn a dwindling remnant clung on to their ancestral faith. Writs were out in 1611 against isolated recusants in Pwllheli, Llanbedrog and Penllech as well as in Clynnog, but the sheriff failed to find them. Eight years later only the Penllech recusant was still ' wanted '; even so the sheriff — a Penllech man himself — was equally unsuccessful. Times were peaceful for the moment, and no one wanted to make trouble for neighbours who kept themselves to themselves. There were still reputed recusants from the same parishes in 1641, when the search was keener because the Long Parliament was in session; but no one could now pretend that this obscure group was any longer a public danger. Almost the last we hear of the Llŷn recusants is some bloodthirsty talk reported of a popish family in Llannor parish, leading to a scuffle in the churchyard; but that was in the heated atmosphere that followed the Civil War.

It was different in Creuddyn. Robert Pugh died a few years after Charles I's accession, but his son followed the family tradition, and under the continuing influence of this stalwart house, recusancy remained a live force in the peninsula: sixty-three recusants are named in 1611, fanning out from Creuddyn proper as far as Gyffin and the site of Colwyn Bay. Thirty years later, despite what was no doubt a much more rigorous search, the number was down to twenty-seven. Yet the strategic possibilities of Creuddyn were not forgotten in those days of scaremongering that immediately preceded the Civil War. Three weeks after the Irish rebellion broke out, Griffith Williams of Conway — nephew and heir of the future Archbishop Williams and deputy vice-admiral to John Griffith — reported to his chief rumours of a plot against Conway on the part of the Creuddyn recusants, inevitably including a Pugh. Search was made, and nothing came of it, but Griffith was convinced that a real danger had been nipped in the bud!

Within the Church itself there was no sign of revolt. Puritanism, whether in its moral or its theological aspect, had as yet made no impression on the county. Sir William Maurice's speeches in defence of the establishment or the borough member's criticisms of the Puritan bill against drunkenness in 1621, probably reflected pretty accurately the feelings of their constituents. The Elizabethan Church order was gaining an assured place in the life of the people, notably during the episcopate of Henry Rowlands, which began towards the end of Elizabeth's reign and covered the first dozen years of James I's. Rowlands, descended from an ancient family, came from a remote Llŷn parish, hard by the birthplace of his predecessor Richard Vaughan, and he received his early education from a local parson. Recusancy was still rampant there when he was born, but his family must have conformed, though he tells us that it was at Oxford he arrived at definite Protestant convictions. He was not an outstanding scholar, but his library included a large collection of Bibles in various editions (including one in Hebrew), Foxe's *Book of Martyrs* and a number of works

of  Protestant  and  Catholic  theology,  all  of  which  were
bequeathed  to  friends  and  neighbours.  He  leaves  the  impression  of  a  man  of  simple  piety  and  warm  charity.  His  chief
memorials  are  the  school  at  Botwnnog  and  the  almshouses
at  Bangor  which  bear  his  name.  His  episcopate  was  marked
by  a  further  raising  of  the  standard  of  the  clergy,  frequent
ordinations  —  and  one  more  attack  on  the  eternal  problem
of  the  cathedral  roof.

The  Church  still  bore  the  scars  of  the  rapacity  let  loose
during  the  Reformation  period.  Those  who  had  benefited  by
it  —  or  their  children  —  resisted  all  efforts  to  make  them
disgorge  their  gains  except  at  the  price  of  a  measure  of
control  which  would  have  undermined  the  independence  of
the  Church.  The  result  was  an  uneasy  compromise,  frequent
clashes  at  both  diocesan  and  parochial  level,  and  the  perpetuation  of  such  abuses  as  pluralism  and  non-residence.
Bishop  Rowlands  himself  had  been  granted  the  rectory  of
his  native  parish  immediately  after  receiving  deacon's  orders,
and  continued  to  hold  it  while  pursuing  his  studies  at  Oxford.
The  fact  that  increasing  numbers  of  the  chief  local  families
—  Glynne  of  Glynllifon,  Griffith  of  Penrhyn,  Hookes  of
Conway,  Williams  of  Vaynol  and  many  more  —  were  educa-
ting  their  children  for  holy  orders  and  finding  them  livings
in  the  diocese  no  doubt  helped  to  stabilise  the  Elizabethan
settlement,  but  it  also  increased  to  a  dangerous  degree  the
dependence  of  the  Church  on  the  gentry,  and  embroiled  it
in  their  feuds.  At  the  same  time  there  is  good  evidence  that
the  clergy,  despite  some  black  sheep,  were  making  a  worthy
contribution  to  the  spiritual  and  intellectual  life  of  the
diocese.  Visitations  by  Rowlands  and  his  successors,  which
seem  to  have  been  pretty  rigorously  carried  out,  revealed
only  a  small  minority  of  defaulters.  Apart  from  the  regular
Sunday  services,  there  was  attention  to  the  instruction  of  the
young  by  catechising,  and  some  of  the  Bangor  clergy  were
continuing  the  production  of  manuals  of  devotion  and
morals  in  homely  Welsh,  to  accompany  the  revision  of
Bishop  Morgan's  Bible  (in  which  Bishop  Richard  Vaughan
participated)  and  its  issue  in  1630  in  a  portable  edition

(*y Beibl bach*) which could be used at home. It was not an age of extensive rebuilding, but many churches were enriched with gifts of plate or other furnishings by the neighbouring gentry wishing, perhaps, to make some amends for the depredations of their fathers.

Bishop Rowlands's successor, Lewes Bayly, was a much more controversial figure. A Carmarthenshire man by birth, he came to the diocese with the reputation of a powerful preacher and an uncomprising Protestant, who had already been a chaplain to Henry, Prince of Wales, and then to the king himself. His published work, *The Practice of Piety,* based on sermons given in one of his English parishes, had a very wide circulation, and remained a standard devotional book among English and (in translation) Welsh readers till the rise of Methodism and Tractarianism. Its tone was strongly Protestant and mildly Puritan, reflecting the Puritanism of the early seventeenth century rather than its more uncompromising successor of Charles I's reign; for Bayly laid as much stress on the sacraments as on preaching, and while strongly sabbatarian in his views, he showed no animus against forms and ceremonies, which he would have left to the discretion of the officiating priest rather than the conscience of the individual worshipper. On the other hand, his outspoken Protestantism, at a time when the king was making a strong bid for the friendship of Spain, got him into trouble in court circles; yet he somehow remained *persona grata* to the king and to Buckingham — possibly because of the strong bond of friendship between him and the late Prince Henry, the king's eldest and favourite son. It was to his supposed courtship of Buckingham that his appointment to Bangor was widely attributed: not very probably, however, for Buckingham had not become all-powerful with the king in 1616, when Bayly was appointed.

It was not Bishop Bayly's theological views that caused trouble in the diocese. He started off hopefully, as so many of his predecessors and successors have done, with an attempt to recover some of the alienated church property. This led to a long and bitter conflict with Sir John Wynn of

Gwydir; but Sir John had influential friends in London, and got the better of it, whereupon the bishop shifted his ground and became his staunch supporter, hoping thus to enlist on behalf of the Church his long purse and his powerful allies among the neighbouring gentry. But the remedy proved worse than the disease, especially as Bayly was incapable of doing things by halves. He threw his whole weight on to the side of the Gwydir faction in the election of 1620, and thereby gained the eternal enmity of the Llŷn faction (the 'baboons', as the bishop politely called them in private), especially Cefnamwlch — as well as of other enemies of Gwydir like the Williamses of Vaynol. This was particularly unfortunate in view of the fact that his own dean was a Griffith of Cefnamwlch. This hampered him at all turns in the administration of the diocese; but he had also exposed another flank, in more exalted circles, by 'disputing malapertly' with the argumentative King James about the Sabbath, on which the king was trying to moderate the excessive zeal of some local magistrates. This landed him for a few months in the Fleet prison.

Fortunately he had a friend at court in Bishop John Williams, now Keeper of the Great Seal (of whom more later), and by his intervention Bayly was restored to favour. But at home his unguarded tongue and his sometimes misplaced humour had gained him many enemies, and they returned to the attack soon after the accession of Charles I. Enlisting the support of M.P.'s bent on bringing his patron, Buckingham, to book, and of a distinguished lawyer whose brother (the registrar of Bangor diocese) was one of those the bishop had offended, they landed him in an impeachment in the Commons at which the wildest charges were brought against him in respect of his conduct as bishop (alongside others that were only too true, like pluralism and nepotism); and witnesses were brought down from the diocese to substantiate them. But once again he was fortunate : the attack on Buckingham was all the House could find time for, and minor matters had to be dropped. So Bishop Bayly ended his days in comparative peace, if in broken health. Despite

these distractions he had kept a vigilant eye on his diocese,
making regular visitations, resisting attempts of lay patrons
to present unsuitable candidates to livings, making proper
provision for sermons and catechising, and himself preaching
every Sunday as long as his health lasted; he also showed
the same zeal as had his predecessor for education, whether
in his choice of clergy, or in his oversight of the grammar
schools at Beaumaris and Bangor, or in the watchful eye
he kept for budding talent among lads in the local schools.
Whether the bishop could preach in Welsh is unknown, but
he certainly had some familiarity with the language and
appreciated its importance as part of the equipment of his
clergy, witness his advance order for a hundred copies of
the Latin and Welsh Dictionary of Davies of Mallwyd — ' a
worthy and necessary piece of work [he observed] which
all our Welsh preachers do much want ' — but which he did
not live to see published.

Bishop Bayly's death in 1630 was followed by two very
short episcopates, uneventful save for two petitions presented
in 1637, one to Archbishop Laud, the other to Bishop
Edmund Griffith (the dean of Bishop Bayly's day). The first,
from the parishioners of Bangor, complained of the bishop's
high-handed action in appointing churchwardens and
empowering them to collect unaccustomed dues towards
the upkeep of the cathedral, hitherto a charge on dean and
chapter funds; the second (and more significant) came from
a dozen parishioners of Beddgelert, aggrieved that the
bishop had entrusted the parish to a young man who could
not preach, and had not mastered ' the distinct and perfect
reading of the Welsh tongue ', whereas for thirty or forty
years (that is, since Henry Rowlands's time) they had been
' edified by a preaching ministry '. They were too late, for
Bishop Griffiths died a few months later. His successor,
William Roberts, was a Denbighshire man and an ardent
disciple of Laud who, as it turned out, was the only Welsh
bishop alive when episcopacy was restored after the Interregnum; so he belongs to a later phase of the story.

There was, then, plenty of ecclesiastical unrest in the

county, but it bore little relation to the deeper religious
issues that were convulsing the country as a whole in the
years before the Civil War. What of the constitutional
issues? It is a fallacy to imagine that Welshmen were not
interested in these controversies or were impelled (as has so
often been alleged) by a ' blind, unreasoning loyalty ' to the
Stuarts. Loyalty there certainly was : the Tudors had inspired
it and the Stuarts reaped the benefit; but it was neither
blind nor unreasoning — nor, for that matter, wholly disinterested! The Wynnes of Gwydir did uncommonly well
out of it. Sir John's eldest son Richard achieved a post in
the household of the Prince of Wales and went with him
and Buckingham to Spain in 1623 on his farcical wooing of
the Infanta — ample compensation for being turned down
by the Caernarvonshire electors two years earlier. In the
same year he tried to secure for himself a favourable lease
of some of the prince's revenues from North Wales, but the
other Welsh M.P.'s (including Thomas Glynne, now sitting
for Caernarvonshire) got wind of it, and after an unfavourable opinion by Sir William Jones — Sir John's personal
lawyer though he was — they succeeded in spiking his guns.
But the loss was soon made good. Two years later the prince
had become King Charles I, and on his marriage with
Henrietta Maria, Sir Richard Wynn became treasurer to her
household, a post he retained until she fled the country on
the eve of Civil War; his brother Henry — ancestor of the
Wynns of Wynnstay — was her solicitor.

Another brother, Owen, who had a post in chancery, was
an invaluable friend at court to his family; it was he, for
example, who pulled the strings to get Richard the grant of
which he was eventually baulked. He was also the chief
purveyor to them of London news; a letter from him (written
in Welsh to avoid prying eyes) gave his father advance
tidings of the Spanish journey while it was still a deadly
secret. Owen in turn was indebted for his advancement to
John Williams of Conway, a scion of Cochwillan who after
a brilliant career at Cambridge attracted the notice of the
king and Buckingham; this resulted in his appointment to

the bishopric of Lincoln and to the custody of the Great Seal, with all the attendant chancery patronage, after Bacon's fall.

These were the fortunate few; but there was a much wider circle of Caernarvonshire society which had been introduced to problems of state by education at the Inns of Court. Apart from those who went there for professional reasons — like the Joneses of Castellmarch, or John Glynne, a younger son of Glynllifon who was rising to eminence at the bar — there were others from houses like Gwydir, Cefn-amwlch, Vaynol, Melai, Bodwrda and perhaps a dozen more of the principal mansions of the shire who went to the Inns of Court mainly to complete their education as country gentlemen or to improve their English; these too were able to take an intelligent interest in constitutional issues, and were sometimes infected with the critical tone of the Inns.

Yet others gained their political education as volunteers in the religious wars on the continent, or as seamen in the merchant service. Hugh Williams of Wîg, near Aber, a brother-in-law of Bishop John Williams, commanded a regiment in the Low Countries in 1622. Rowland Coytmor, a younger son of the house of Coetmor (Llanllechid), like so many younger sons, went in for trade and was among the early adventurers to Virginia and the East Indies; he settled among the merchants and shipowners of Wapping, but his nephew Robert, who entered the service of that great patron of naval and colonial enterprise the earl of Warwick, became important in Caernarvonshire affairs during the Commonwealth. Piers Griffith, heir to Penrhyn, was less fortunate. He too took to the sea, and in 1600 he brought as booty to his home on the Straits a well-laden Spanish ship; but soon afterwards — whether or not, as tradition says, in consequence of more dubious adventures at sea — he was in serious trouble, and eventually had to dispose of the entire estate, which was acquired by John Williams the year after he became Lord Keeper.

To appreciate the reactions of the Caernarvonshire gentry to the policies of the first two Stuarts, we must bear in mind the economy of the shire. It was a hand-to-mouth economy, based principally on the cattle trade, which John Williams aptly called ' the Spanish fleet of Wales, which brings hither the little gold and silver we have '. The drovers' roads, converging from every corner of the shire on Llanrwst or Capel Curig as stages on the way to the English cattle markets or the Midland pastures, were almost the only roads the county had except what had survived of those the Romans made, and pretty well the only communication between its eastern and western sectors. The drovers were the only men who could produce ready cash at short notice, since the landowners generally had theirs locked up in house-building or expensive establishments, or dribbling away in legal fees and mortgage interest. A measure which was unanimously supported by the Welsh M.P.'s in 1621 — indeed their interest was recognised by their election *en bloc* to  the committee on this Bill — was a draft law to limit the importation of Irish cattle, the principal rivals of the Welsh trade. The Bill never got beyond the committee stage, and it did not come up again till the reign of Charles II. Of industry proper there was little save the ordinary household spinning and weaving (which in Caernarvonshire lacked anything like an organised market, such as Shrewsbury afforded to the textiles of Merioneth and Montgomeryshire), some sporadic and superficial quarrying of slates by methods which showed no advance on those in use under the Tudors, and a little prospecting for copper and lead in the Conway valley by the indefatigable Sir John Wynn. His son Maurice, apprenticed to a Hamburg merchant, was optimistic about finding a market there for his father's ores as well as for Welsh woollens, but nothing much came of it.

The financial demands of Charles I, which grew in frequency and peremptoriness as his difficulties increased, bore hard on such an economy. The regular parliamentary subsidy to which Wales became liable when she was given parliamentary representation, had been tempered for the new taxpayer by allowing payments to be spread over a long period; it was also assessed and collected by neighbours.

They might grumble against each other, but they did not rise in wrath against the government as long as James I (always tactful in his dealings with Wales) was on the throne; in fact the Welsh members earned the special thanks of the king when in 1621 they voluntarily renounced on that year's tax their traditional moratorium, in face of the threat to Protestantism involved in the outbreak of the Thirty Years' War. The provision at frequent intervals of levies for Ireland, usually in batches of a hundred (together with the local costs of mobilisation) was another burden on the shire, but since Elizabeth's day it had become familiar if unwelcome routine.

The atmosphere begins to change early in the next reign. Charles I's foreign adventures were expensive, and his inability to come to terms with parliament led him to look round for means of raising ready cash outside its control. In the second year of the reign lists were circulated to the sheriffs of what each taxpayer was expected to contribute by way of ' loan ' to meet the government's immediate needs. Sir William Thomas, appointed collector for Caernarvonshire, was soon engaged in the familiar round of correspondence with Sir John Wynn of Gwydir about the way the obligation was to be shared between the ' upper ' and lower ' parts of the shire. But a plea of poverty — not wholly unjustified, since arrears from some of the earlier subsidies of James I's reign were still hanging over the shire — backed up by friends at court like Owen Wynn, enabled Caernarvonshire to get itself reprieved. Only for a time, however; in 1627 the international situation worsened, and the demand on the shire was repeated. This time Sir William Thomas was associated as collector with Thomas Glynne, John Bodwrda and Henry Bodvel, so that the whole shire should be covered. Gwydir seems to have kept clear of it. The collectors reported that they had ' persuaded ' most of those liable to taxes to lend the sums set down against them, but some had refused, despite their own exemplary conduct in paying on the nail *pour encourager les autres.* Caernarvonshire was in fact blacklisted as one of seven Welsh counties in default.

The 'loans' were by no means the only burden. Soldiers were now being levied for service abroad (Caernarvonshire's quota was thirty-two), and the cost of their equipment and conveyance to the rendezvous had to be borne locally. Shipping was also needed, and a census taken in 1626 showed that Caernarvonshire could produce, in the harbours of Caernarvon, Conway, Pwllheli and Porthdinllaen, seven unarmed merchantmen ranging from six to thirty tons, and not quite twenty seamen to man them. Even before this report had reached the government, orders came that the shire should join with Merioneth in sending to Portsmouth for service against Spain (should the need arise) a thirty-ton barque, manned and victualled, the cost being borne by the coastal districts of the respective shires. There is no record of any protest against this — nor for that matter, of whether the barque ever materialised. It is clear that Caernarvonshire was wrestling with unaccustomed burdens, with nothing to show for them in the way of successes abroad; but whatever recalcitrance there may have been, there is no sign that it was based (as in some of the South Wales shires) on constitutional principle, or that any protest was made at taxation without parliamentary consent.

At any rate, things had now reached such a pass that Charles found himself no longer able to fulfil his commitments without parliamentary grants; hence the parliament of 1628 and the Petition of Right, after which the king struggled on for eleven years without a parliament, raising money by any device his lawyers could think up; for the royal embarrassments would brook no delay. Obviously the first step was to plug the hole in the exchequer by realising any crown assets that could be readily marketed. In Caernarvonshire, for example, there were the ferries over the Conway and the Straits which the crown had acquired, partly by taking over Llywelyn's rights on the conquest of Gwynedd, partly through the dissolution of the monasteries. Up to now they had been farmed out, and brought in a small but regular revenue; now they were alienated to private speculators on long leases for substantial down payments: Conway and Tal y cafn in 1627, Porthaethwy in 1629, Moel y don in 1637. It was in 1632 that Charles I's attempt to claim Nefyn as a royal manor which could be leased out at a profitable rent was met by a noisy opposition in the churchyard, led by Thomas Wynn of Boduan. Then there was the old battle-ground of the royal forest of Snowdon, which had threatened to cause another stir in 1623, and then simmered down until, eleven years later, an unknown projector offered (for a consideration) to make one more assault on encroachments. Nothing came of this until in 1639 the king set up a commission to take evidence at Beaumaris, Caernarvon and Dolgellau, and the usual preparations were made by the threatened gentry for resistance, this time with the legal experience and inside knowledge of Owen Wynn of Gwydir at their disposal. Again no progress was made. Another expedient of 1630 — distraint of knighthood — hit a wider section of the gentry, for it compelled all freeholders of £40 a year to accept the burden of knighthood or compound for it. Twelve of the principal gentry of Caernarvonshire, only five of them knights themselves, were charged with the task of enforcing this, but no opposition is recorded.

In any case these expedients were mere chicken feed. The king's panacea for replenishing his empty exchequer was ship money. In origin this was the ancient prerogative of calling on coastal towns to supply ships, or their cash equivalent, for the king's use in time of national danger. Charles's plan was to put it on a shire basis and to demand it annually in time of peace. This enabled him to compel the sheriffs to bring in their counties' quotas at frequent intervals on demand, and to hold them responsible for all arrears. The normal assessments for subsidy were set aside; everyone was liable save such as had ' no estate above what they get by daily labour '. The three shires of Gwynedd were let off lightly in the first levy of 1635: they paid less than £450 each — not much more than a third what was demanded of Denbighshire, and less than the quota of any of the other Welsh shires. Caernarvonshire's bill went up a little in 1637, but only to £575. With its vulnerable coastline, frequently subject to piratical attack when we were fighting both France and Spain earlier in the reign, Caernarvonshire had everything to gain from ship money, for some of it was spent on building a small fleet for coastal defence, with special attention to the Welsh coast. So the county paid up with commendable promptitude for the first four levies, in contrast with Denbighshire, with its shorter coastline, which was in default on the second levy, or landlocked Montgomeryshire, which fell behind on the third. But on the fifth and final levy in 1639, when the whole country was in default, nearly half the sum due here was never collected.

For by this time the country was staggering under yet another burden. By trying to impose an English liturgy on the Scots, the king had brought on himself a Scottish national rebellion, and this meant more demands for men and for cash to meet the local costs of mobilisation, as well as a further strain on the depleted national exchequer. But once again Caernarvonshire came off easily. Denbigh, Flint and Montgomery were the only North Wales counties included in the levy, because it was found that the force originally planned would cost more than the exchequer could stand, and the poverty of Gwynedd was always recognised. For the country as a whole, however, it was the last straw. In some of the English shires there was much sympathy with the Scots, and even in Denbighshire there was murmuring against the clergy, who were blamed for the so-called ' Bishops' War '. The militia was mustered only with great difficulty, and acquitted itself badly in the field. The king had now no option but to abandon his hope of ruling without parliament.

When parliament met soon after the Easter of 1640, it insisted on discussing grievances before granting the money the king had desperately needed, and it was dismissed after three weeks. Caernarvonshire played a bigger part in this Short Parliament than it had in many a longer one, though not entirely through its own members. The brothers Wynn — Henry, who sat for Merioneth, and Richard, returned by an

THE SOUTH WEST VIEW OF THE CHURCH & PALACE OF BANGOR, IN THE COUNTY OF CAERNARVON

BANGOR CATHEDRAL, 1742

PLATE V

PLATE VI

PENRHYN CREUDDYN

*Painted plaster in S.W. block*

PLATE VII

VAYNOL OLD HALL

ARCHBISHOP JOHN WILLIAMS (1582-1650)

*Portrait in oils. Copy by Miss E. G. Bradley of the painting in Westminster.*

English pocket borough — were both elected to the important committee for privileges; but this was only because, as
high-ranking courtiers, they might prove useful go-betweens.
Henry had also lent money (at the comfortable rate of eight
per cent) 'for the supply of His Majesty's urgent affairs ',
and so had a stake in the country's solvency! Neither took
any significant part in proceedings. John Glynne, elected
for Caernarvon boroughs, had again deserted them for the
borough of Westminster, leaving the Caernarvon electors
unrepresented, since the session was over before a by-
election could be called. It may have been John's standing
at the bar that prompted the later inclusion of his brother
Thomas (sitting for the shire) in the committee of privileges;
on the other hand, it is suggestive that Thomas was also
elected to several committees on such issues as the ecclesiastical courts and sumptuary legislation, on which the Puritan
faction felt strongly. Charles Jones of Castellmarch (still
representing Beaumaris), as chairman of the committee for
privileges, was kept very busy, and at the end of the session
his name appears on what seems to be a note of members
blacklisted by the court for their factiousness. None of the
Welsh members is known to have taken part in the debate
on ship money.

Money or no money, the king must have an army to reassert his authority in Scotland. A fresh levy of men was
ordered, and by the end of May Caernarvonshire had its
hundred-and-twenty ready, with Thomas Wynn of Boduan
as provost marshal. But there were constant changes of
plan, and July came before they were on the march; even
then no directions had come about covering the local costs.
Then early in September a new note of urgency creeps into
Thomas Glynne's letters to his fellow deputy lieutenants;
breaking to them the news that the Scots have crossed the
border and taken Newcastle by surprise, he ejaculates ' God
blesse his Majesty and the kingdome '. Home defence now
became a top priority. Caernarvonshire's county magazine
was bare of powder, and a government warrant was sent to
a mercer in Cheapside to supply it with twenty-four barrels.

By this time government was rapidly breaking down. On the preceding day Charles had been driven in desperation to issue warrants for the election of what turned out to be the Long Parliament. Both Caernarvonshire seats were contested. In the county the contestants were those hardened rivals, Glynllifon and Cefnamwlch, but now for the first time there appear hints of a political undercurrent. John Griffith, the reigning squire of Cefnamwlch, was old and ailing, and rather than face the hurly-burly of a contested county election he secured nomination for Beaumaris borough (which had been left vacant by the death of Charles Jones), leaving the fight for the county seat to his scapegrace heir — yet another John, but ' Prince Griffin ' to his boon companions at Chester. The sheriff, James Brynkir (of Bryncyr in Eifionydd) — who was of kin, on the distaff side, to Cefnamwlch — delayed delivery of the writs till after the ' county day ', leaving both county and boroughs unrepresented when the House met. When fresh writs were issued and Griffith was elected, this was denounced as one of many questionable manoeuvres on the sheriff's part, in a petition referred by the Commons to the committee for privileges. To provide himself with a second string, Thomas Glynne also stood for the boroughs, but again he was unlucky, and again he petitioned against the successful candidate, William Thomas of Aber, who now lived mainly at his new mansion of Coed Alun (later Coed Helen), just outside Caernarvon. In this case the ground of complaint was the failure of the sheriff to give proper notice to the out-boroughs, especially Conway.

Cefnamwlch, as we have seen, had been firmly on the side of the court ever since Buckingham's day; Glynllifon in the Short Parliament, had thrown in its lot with the opposition in the person of John Glynne, and his elder brother Thomas appeared to be veering cautiously in the same direction. If the contest was in any sense political, Caernarvonshire had shown itself clearly on the side of the establishment. The House had so many weighty matters on its hands that four months had passed before the Caernarvonshire petitions were heard. Some ten witnesses appeared, and arrangements were made beforehand to ensure that the committee included members capable of handling monoglot Welsh witnesses. After hearing them, the House voted that both members should be unseated. Old John Griffith (the Beaumaris member) assured the earl of Bridgwater, now President of Wales, that Glynne's smart brother John was deliberately playing for delay in putting this into effect, hoping to pull strings for the appointment of a sheriff favourable to Glynllifon when the election came, and he tried to forestall this by suggesting several names. In any case the House rose for recess before any action was taken, and when it met again the outbreak of rebellion in Ireland overshadowed all other business. The by-election was never held.

This was a very busy parliament, and there were few members not called at one time or another to serve on one of its innumerable committees. Both the Griffiths — father and son — were among these, but the Journal rarely distinguishes them from each other. The elder Griffith, however, was often away ill, so his son must at this stage have been taking his parliamentary duties seriously. But although they both co-operated in the routine work of the House, neither would vote for the Bill of Attainder to dispose of Stafford, the chief agent of the ' Eleven Years' Tyranny ', by summary procedure; in consequence their names appeared, with fifty-six others, on a list of ' Straffordians, betrayers of their country ' posted up in Westminster to hold them up to the obloquy of the mob. Sir Richard Wynn, now sitting for Liverpool, was also (for once) in the unpopular minority. William Thomas, on the other hand, voted against Strafford, and he also contributed to the attack on the clergy in their secular capacity (especially as lords of parliament) three hostile speeches, packed with learned quotations in Latin and Greek; but he made it clear in them, and still more in private letters, that he had no theological bias against bishops or inclination to ' Presbyteriall government, from which ' (he wrote to a friend) ' good lord deliver us '.

A new Caernarvonshire voice heard in the Long Parlia-

ment was that of John Bodvel (or Bodville, as he preferred
to write his name) of Bodfel. He sat for Anglesey — as he
had done in the Short Parliament, but without making his
presence felt — by virtue of a small estate he had there.
Bodvel's father Sir John had left his lands to his wife (Sir
John Wynn's daughter Bess) and her two daughters, for ten
years after his death, with the result that the son, though
now married and twenty-three years old, was still at the time
of the election under the guardianship of his uncle Sir
Richard Wynn. The family mansion was occupied by his
mother, while he lived in Cambridgeshire at the home of
his wife, the sister of a friend he had met as a law student,
and daughter of Sir William Russell, treasurer of the navy.
Like so many Cambridgeshire households, the Russell home
was strongly Puritan. These factors combined to give John
Bodvel a standing in the House out of all relation to his age
and experience. The diary he kept during the first fortnight
of proceedings was incorporated by Sir Symonds d'Ewes in
his own formidable journal; he was one of those who stood
surety for the sum needed to effect a final settlement with
the Scots; and he was included on many of the more important committees appointed to deal with the nation's accumulated grievances.

The House was in one of its most uncomprising ' No
Popery' moods, stimulated by the knowledge that Strafford
had proposed to bring over the well-trained army he had
built up in Ireland as Lord Deputy, either to finish off the
Scots or (as those who brought him to the block believed)
against parliament itself. It had also leaked out that the
king had entrusted with ' some secret service' the powerful
earl of Worcester, who from his castle of Raglan was the
avowed leader and protector of his fellow-recusants in south-
eastern Wales, and that the deputy lieutenants of five South
Wales counties had been given orders to place themselves
at his disposal. The ' secret service' was widely interpreted
as the raising among tenants and dependants of a ' Welsh
popish army' to join forces with Strafford's Irishmen when
they landed. Bodvel, fresh from the Puritan atmosphere of

his wife's home (and before that, of the Inns of Court), was
very ready to believe that the Protestant cause was in danger.
He spoke against the grant of a commission in the 'Bishops'
War' to Worcester's son, and unlike his uncle he voted for
Strafford's attainder. The talk of a 'Welsh popish army'
caused a good deal of stir in Wales, and arrayed against
the government, to an extent unknown in any previous parliament, most of the Welsh members who took any part in
debates. Shortly before the recess, parliament set up in every
shire a commission to disarm recusants. The members of the
Caernarvonshire commission were Thomas Glynne, William
Thomas, Owen Wynn of Gwydir and Thomas Madryn of
Madrun.

The outbreak of the Irish rebellion seemed to justify these
fears. When the House met again in October, 1641, with
this new cloud hanging over it, the main preoccupation was
with measures to defend the country against popish invasion,
and in view of his previous record and the fact that his home
and his constituency were in two shires lying directly in the
path of such an invasion (and on the main route of any army
sent to quell the rebellion), Bodvel was bound to be heavily
involved. The dangers were brought home to Caernarvonshire by the flight from the Irish rebels of the newly
appointed bishop of Ossory, Griffith Williams. He was a
nephew of Archbishop John Williams (as the former bishop
of Lincoln had now become); for seven years he had been
absentee dean of Bangor, and now he was a refugee in his
home at Llanllechid, the still existing Plas Hwfa. In the
heated atmosphere engendered by the situation in Ireland,
control in the Commons fell increasingly into the hands of
the irreconcilables and London into the hands of the mob.
In December the king, as a sop to the moderates, recalled
to his service John Williams, who had been in disgrace since
the beginning of the reign, and made him archbishop of
York (and therefore acting primate, since Laud had been
imprisoned); but the new archbishop was rabbled by the
mob and prevented from taking his seat in the Lords, and
when he rashly protested against the validity of proceedings

in his absence, the Commons responded by an impeachment. Early in 1641 the king fled from these scenes of disorder to seek support in the loyal north. In parliament the main business was to liquidate the Irish rebellion. Unwilling to trust the king with an army which might be used against them, they submitted to him a Bill vesting in themselves control of the armed forces. He naturally refused to surrender this essential attribute of sovereignity, but parliament ignored his veto and proceeded to appoint lords lieutenants and deputy lieutenants in the shires and to empower them to raise the militia. For Caernarvonshire the earl of Pembroke, who had urged the king to accept the Militia Bill, was the chosen lord lieutenant, with John Bodvel and William Thomas as his deputies. For Bodvel, unlike most of his Welsh colleagues, was still actively engaged in the affairs of the House, and although William Thomas had subsided into silence, his attack on the Church hierarchy had not been forgotten, while the two Griffiths were naturally passed over as former ' Straffordians '.

Some months passed in fruitless negotiations with the king before parliament put these plans into operation. Defensive preparations went ahead, but with a subtle change in their direction. The powder ordered in London to replenish the county magazine of Caernarvonshire, as far back as 1640, for defence against a possible Scottish invasion, had never been delivered, or else the order had been countermanded when the crisis passed. At last, in March 1642, it arrived by sea at Chester, with strict orders from parliament that it should be handed to Thomas Glynne, or John Griffith (the county member) ' or such as they should appoint '. But the sheriff, Sir Thomas Cheadle — an Anglesey man, chosen as supposedly neutral to avoid the conflicting claims of Glynllifon and Cefnamwlch — ignored these orders and impounded it, suspecting (with good reason) that by now the ' defence ' parliament had in mind was against the king as much as against the Irish. For in July and August Bodvel and Thomas arrived to exercise their office as deputy lieut-

enants, Bodvel with a stock of arms sufficient to equip twenty
soldiers — ostensibly for the defence of his own house.

The king was at the same time reviving the medieval
method of raising an army by issuing, to such of the county
gentry as were considered trustworthy, commissions of array
empowering them to recruit regiments of foot or troops of
horse within their shire. Denbighshire and Flintshire had
already resolved at a meeting of the two shires to obey the
royal mandate, and Sir Thomas Myddelton, whom parliament had commissioned as its deputy lieutenant there, had
to abandon any attempt to put its orders into force. Sir
Thomas Salusbury, writing to ask Thomas Bulkeley for help
from Anglesey in raising his Denbighshire contingent,
warned him that the Puritans were bragging of a ' great
party' in Caernarvonshire, ' as if they had some design for
the Parliament'. To forestall any such design, Thomas
Cheadle put three suspects under arrest: Thomas Glynne,
John Bodwrda and William Lloyd of Talhenbont (Llanystumdwy), a henchman of Glynllifon. The king's commission of array for Caernarvonshire arrived in early August,
addressed to Cheadle as sheriff with Thomas Bulkeley, Owen
Wynn of Gwydir, Sir William Williams of Vaynol, Griffith
Jones of Castellmarch, Thomas Madryn of Madrun and John
Griffith of Cefnamwlch. The father must have been meant,
sick man as he was; for ' Prince Griffin ' had been expelled
from parliament in June for a ' wicked assault ' on a society
lady, and he spent the rest of the war making a general
nuisance of himself until at last he had to flee to France
with a charge of murder hanging over his head.

There was a widespread air of foreboding abroad. Even
in March Richard Griffith of Llanfair Isgaer (near Caernarvon) had received a letter from a lawyer half-brother in
London saying ' I am affrayd I shall wish my selfe with you
ere long if the times go on as it is suspected it will, but I
hope in god it will be otherwise and we shall have peace '.
This letter also gives us a glimpse of a dissident element
in a lower stratum of county society: the writer applies to
a humble neighbour of Griffiths the newly-coined word

'Roundhead', chaffing him about his addiction 'after his
dayly labour' to that most abstemious of beverages *glasdŵr*,
or milk-and-water. But the atmosphere of the county was
not one in which Bodvel and Thomas could put into effect
the commissions of lieutenancy with which parliament had
entrusted them. Perhaps they shrank from attempting it now
that there was no escaping the fact that it was against the
king rather than the Irish that their commissions were
directed. At anyrate no more is heard of either until they
reappear at Oxford the following year in the 'anti-parlia-
ment' to which the king summoned those M.P.'s who had
deserted their posts at Westminster to join him. Long before
this he had set up his standard at Nottingham and the war
had begun, with Caernarvonshire to all appearance solidly
behind him. The three imprisoned suspects had been
released and had toed the line with the rest; but there were
ominous cross-currents. To some the struggle between Glynllifon and Cefnamwlch (with their respective backers) was
still a more present reality than the struggle between
Cavalier and Roundhead; to many the real enemy was not
the Roundhead but that far more accustomed foe the Irish-
man. These distractions were soon to make themselves felt.


BIBLIOGRAPHY

On religion see A. I. Pryce, introduction to *The Diocese of Bangor
during Three Centuries* (1929); E. G. Jones, *Cymru a'r Hen Ffydd*;
J. Morgan, *Esgob Henry Rowland* (1910); A. H. Dodd, 'Bishop
Lewes Bayly' (*TCHS* 1967). The Welsh political background of the
age is analysed in A. H. Dodd, 'The pattern of politics in Stuart
Wales' (*Trans. Cymmrodorion Soc.*, 1949). Local reactions to Stuart
demands on the county can be traced from the indexes to *Calendars
of State Papers Domestic* and *Acts of the Privy Council* for the period.
Welsh participation in the Short and Long Parliaments is examined
in A. H. Dodd, 'Caernarvonshire elections to the Long Parliament'
(*Bull. of Bd. of Celtic Studies*, xii, 1946 and xiv, 1950), and id., 'Wales
in the parliaments of Charles I (ii)' (*Trans. Cymm. Soc.* 1946-7). On
the life of the gentry in general the *Calendar of Wynn Papers* remains
indispensable.

# VI

## CAERNARVONSHIRE AT WAR
### (1642-9)

AT the end of the last chapter we left the king's commissioners of array in Caernarvonshire raising forces for him, while the two deputy lieutenants entrusted with a similar task for parliament had thrown in the sponge. It soon became clear which of the commissioners were going to put their backs into the job. Owen Wynn claimed, when he was threatened with the decimation tax in 1655 as an ex-Royalist, that he had ' refused to act '. This is, of course, an *ex parte* statement which need not be taken too seriously; but it is unlikely that so shrewd a man engaged himself very actively in the king's affairs until he knew which way the cat was going to jump — especially when his brother Sir Richard continued to sit in the Long Parliament till his death in 1649, characteristically absenting himself from critical divisions. Bulkeley and Cheadle were soon fully employed in Anglesey, and the subsequent conduct of Sir William Williams, his father-in-law Griffith Jones, and Thomas Madryn suggests that they, or some of them, were among those whom the king castigated a few months later as ' some . . . who prefer private ends befor the publique '. This threw the principal burden on John Griffith and John Owen.

John Owen, now forty-two years old, was the great-grandson of Sir William Maurice, but he never showed any trace of the political and theological interests of his ancestor. The only book he is known to have added to the considerable library Sir William had accumulated was a treatise on the art of gunnery, and this was typical of the man. He had gained his military experience (probably on the continent) before he succeeded to the family estate at twenty-six, and soldiering remained the dominant passion of his life, with hunting and hawking to beguile his leisure hours. What more natural that this should be the man chosen by the king to lead two hundred men from the county as a bodyguard to the young Prince of Wales when he accompanied his father on a recruiting tour to the Welsh border in September, and in the following month to raise from the three shires of Gwynedd a regiment of a thousand foot, with the rank of colonel and the administration of the county funds raised for the purpose? And what more natural than that the task should be embraced without a moment's doubt or questioning by this unpolitical knight errant who had been hailed by the bard Hugh Machno, more than a decade earlier, in terms which may be roughly translated as follows? —

> A man of perfect faith and trusty word,
> Of serviceable labours under Charles,
> A generous, wise and trusty man is John,
> A man who is a bulwark to the crown.

John Griffith was too old for service of this sort, but he did not shirk his part. Despite his conviction — as he wrote in a despondent letter six months before war began — that ' the end of the world is not farr of ' (' God prepare us for yt ' was his pious ejaculation), he accompanied the king on his border progress as far as Bridgnorth, returning in mid-October to Chester, where he was quite sure he could do ' beter offices to my Country then I would doe ther ', since ' if this Towne be lost all wales will be noe better then lost '. His prime endeavour was therefore to persuade his neighbours to send all available men and munitions for the defence of this key point. Eventually he made his way to the royal headquarters at Oxford, where he died in July 1643 — five months before the meeting there of the loyal members of parliament. When all allowance has been made for the querulousness of a sick old man, it is clear from his correspondence that he was encountering serious opposition from a section of the Caernarvonshire gentry. Writing to Sir William Williams soon after his arrival in Chester, he deplores the fact that neither the two hundred men nor Owen's regiment of a thousand arrived at Bridgenorth in time to follow the king to Edgehill. Perhaps this was as well, for it is unlikely that such an improvised force would have made any better showing than the raw and largely unarmed levies led there from Denbighshire by William Salusbury. Soon, however, it became apparent that the delays were not wholly fortuitous. Up to the end of September the king's letters to the commissioners of array are full of testimonies to their ' good affections ' in raising men and money for his service; but the tone changes in October. At the end of the month the king tells the commissioners that Owen's regiment, which was due to march immediately, was not only short of its full complement from the county, but was even in danger of disbanding for lack of the promised financial support, and he roundly attributes this dilatoriness on the part of a hitherto loyal county to the ' couldness or disaffection of some particular persons '. ' I am sory ', wrote John Griffith in the following February to one of these ' hinderers ' (probably Griffith Jones of Castellmarch) ' to understand you want fealty . . . And I have very ill lucke when I obey the king to be used like a trajtor by those that take upon them to doe service for the kinge. But if I cannot defend my selfe under the kinges protection and his lawes it is tyme to be patient '. He even hints darkly about warrants drawn out by his enemies ' to seise upon my estate and upon my life '.

The immediate occasion of this outburst was a quarrel that had arisen over the king's design to carry off to Worcester and Shrewsbury four pieces of ordnance intended by the Caernarvonshire commissioners for the defence of the county magazine at Caernarvon and the exposed coast of Llŷn. To a courtier like John Griffith or a quasi-professional soldier like Owen this was a far less alarming prospect than to a coastal squire like Griffith Jones, who was associated with the vice-admiral in the royal directive. In his reply

Jones pointed out to the situation of his own house, with no
defences between it and a stretch of coast 'very subject to
invasion' — as he was to find by experience when eight
years later he was kidnapped in his own house by Royalist
privateers operating from Wexford. The trouble broke out
afresh at the end of August, this time over the proposed
transfer of local ordnance (quite possibly the same pieces) to
Chester. The king had good grounds for stigmatising the
local obstructionists as 'particular person who prefer private
ends befor the publique', but the objectors were not without justification, as appears on many occasions during the
course of the war when the Welsh gentry found their houses
and families exposed to enemy attack after the district had
been stripped of men and munitions for service across the
border.

It must be remembered too that until the king saw the
need for establishing a command on the spot, royal mandates
often took an unconscionable time in reaching Wales from
Oxford, and the only responsible commander for Wales, the
marquess of Hertford, was operating in the south and almost
equally distant. The endorsements on some of the letters
cited show that a month or even six weeks might elapse
between despatch and delivery — unless indeed they were
purposely held back by the first recipient. It was not till
March that control was decentralised by giving Lord Capell
command in North Wales and the adjacent counties, under
the nominal orders of the young Prince of Wales as lieutenant
general, an arrangement superseded early in the following
year by the appointment of Rupert as commander-in-chief
for all Wales and the border, with Byron operating under
him from Chester. But there was more in it than slow
communications; it is clear that there existed in Caernarvonshire a faction which was at best lukewarm in the royal
cause, although at this stage it lacked either the courage or
the conviction to come out squarely on the side of his foes.
It was not only over the county's store of munitions that the
faction pursued its obstructive tactics; in July a 'wilful
declining' of Capell's summons to the standard brought

down a sharp rebuke from the king himself on the commissioners' heads.

The suspects whom Cheadle had arrested on the score of their ' disaffection ' were now back in their posts as magistrates or deputy lieutenants, though they do not appear on the commission of array until later in the war. Glynne and Bodwrda had charge of considerable county funds, and this enabled them to exert a gentle pressure by the simple process of sitting tight on the money bags. Glynne was even given a colonelcy in the royal army in 1644, but he excused himself from service in the field on the ground of his ' weake state of body ' — a plea that may have had some substance, since he died four years later. Jones of Castellmarch, Williams of Vaynol and Madryn of Madrun had been on the commission of array from the beginning, and it was no doubt their policy of ca' canny and their preference of county interests over those of the king that drove successive Royalist commanders to distraction, till in 1645 Byron declared roundly that the king must ' expect no good out of North Wales ' so long as the present commissioners remained in power, and proceeded to weed out as many as he could and to ignore or override the others when he dared.

In spite of all obstructions, Owen had his regiment in the field by the early summer of 1643. He fought under Prince Rupert in operations round Oxford in May, and at the siege of Bristol in July he was (as he wrote to his wife) ' shott thorow the right side of my nose under the leaft heare, all the iuggular vaines and mouth, and did bleed extreamly '; but he was cheered by signal marks of favour from the king, and he was back in the field by September. His son (presumably William) fought with him but — somewhat to the disgust of the seasoned campaigner — he was ill most of the time. Another Caernarvonshire man who held a command under him at Bristol and in his subsequent English campaigns was Hugh Hookes of Conway. He came of a distinguished — and prolific — English family long settled in Conway and experienced in arms (and also, it was said, in piracy), some of whom we have met in connection with

Elizabeth's Essex. The county could afford to lend its best fighting blood to the English campaigns only so long as it was not itself directly threatened. Until such time, the front line of defence for Caernarvonshire, as John Griffith had urged, lay through Chester, and it was for the defence of this city that the man-power of North Wales was chiefly needed.

Early in March 1643, Richard Griffith of Llanfair Isgaer, who had been a captain of militia in the county for the past six years or more, was sent with a Caernarvonshire company to join the garrison there; Colonel Hugh Wynn of Bodysgallen (Creuddyn) had already gone there in January, and he appears to have been in general command of the auxiliaries from Gwynedd. Both were zealous Royalists, fought for the king as long as he had an army in being, and then did further service in Ireland; but both were hampered in their loyal efforts by lukewarmness or divisions in their own camp. Caernarvonshire promised, in addition to its other burdens, to maintain this company, which cost £28 a week; but within six weeks complaints were coming from the officers of the Chester garrison that the county had defaulted and left them £78 out of pocket, and by August Lord Capell was telling the new sheriff (Thomas Madryn) that since the arrears now amounted to £160, Griffith and his men had been left unpaid, and desertions were taking place 'in great numbers'. The trouble continued intermittently throughout the war, but the company held together somehow, in spite of increasing friction latterly between Welsh and English in the garrison.

Summer brought with it the first direct threat to the county. In June 1642 Sir Thomas Myddelton was commissioned by parliament to invade North Wales with a view to depriving the king of the men and materials he was drawing from this source, and the Caernarvonshire commissioners of array were directed to seize him on sight. But it was not till the end of July that his forces were ready, and from then till late in November they were operating with Brereton and Mytton, the Roundhead commanders in Cheshire and

Shropshire respectively, in the border campaign. A minor victory there enabled them to cross the Dee and to over-run Denbighshire and Flintshire. The policy of denuding the Welsh counties of man power and munitions in the interests of the border fortresses now came home to roost, for once the line of the Dee had been crossed, there seemed nothing between the invader and the heart of Snowdonia except the castle of Conway, which was being hastily repaired and manned by Archbishop Williams, a fugitive from his diocese of York to his native town, with no official standing but immense local influence through his descent from Cochwillan and his connection with Gwydir. The castle had been bought from the crown in 1628 by the first Lord Conway (a distant connection of the Conways of Botryddan), and his son had taken preliminary steps towards putting it into repair with the idea of living there; but the decay of the leadwork was found to amount to £130 and of the timber £150, and little had been done before war broke out and Lord Conway was taken prisoner by the Round-heads; so the archbishop had a long and expensive job ahead of him, and the king made over the castle to him and his assigns until his expenses should be repaid. In this outpost of security many of the magnates of North Wales, including the two bishops, now took refuge; others sent their valuables there to be kept in the archbishop's custody. But the crisis soon passed. The landing in the Dee estuary of royal forces from Ireland, now released through the king's armistice with the rebels, cleared north-eastern Wales of the invader within a few weeks; but henceforth more attention was paid to the defences of North Wales, even west of the Conway.

Here it was Archbishop Williams who took the initiative, urging on his Anglesey 'cousins' the vital need for putting the key point of Beaumaris into a proper state of defence, and sometimes crossing to the island himself to supervise the work; procuring from Ormonde in Ireland a stream of supplies and reinforcements now more urgently needed on this side the water; advancing from his own diminished for-tune the initial cost of the munitions, and organising the work of feeding and clothing the men. What royal shipping could be spared was posted to keep an eye on the growing menace from the parliamentary fleet in these waters. One of these vessels, a merchant ship called the *Phoenix*, was wrecked off the Orme early in the war; but the *Swan*, an up-to-date naval vessel of two hundred tons mounting upwards of twenty guns and with a crew of sixty, was by far the most powerful vessel in the area. She had been laid down just before the war, and was commanded by the able Captain John Bartlett who was in general charge of naval operations in the Irish Sea, while Thomas Bartlett (possibly his son) commanded a small armed merchant vessel in the same flotilla. These ships were further reinforced during the winter of 1643-4, and Mr. Aled Eames, who as a 'former naval person' can speak with some authority, maintains that in the early stages of the war the small Parliamentary fleet based on Liverpool was no match for *Swan* and her sister ships, and that by putting the enemy out of action at sea in these waters while this superiority lasted, the Royalists might have given a different twist to the wheel of fortune; but this only made itself evident later on, for at the close of 1643 Royalist power in Gwynedd seemed unchallengeable.

On land, however, the new importance attached to the Welsh theatre of war after this first Roundhead breakthrough was signalised by the appointment of Prince Rupert, early in 1644, to command the whole area and so to give some cohesion to the campaigns in north, south and border. The effect was soon seen in a spurt of energy over the drilling of the trainbands even in Llŷn and Eifionydd, where Thomas Glynne as colonel encountered the usual difficulty of slow communications, scarcity of billets for extended manoeuvres, and shortage of powder, match and bullet — excuses for delay of which he was not slow to avail himself.

All this meant increasing demands on the pockets of the Caernarvonshire gentry, impoverished as they were by the royal embargo on the cattle trade with London, the county's basic industry. In addition to what they had already paid towards putting John Owen's regiment in the field and maintaining Griffith's company at Chester, they had now to meet the needs of their own garrisons and of feeding their auxiliaries, whether on sea or land. Griffith Bodwrda, who was by way of being a minor bard, amused himself in the December of 1643 with an *englyn* which sketches vividly the bustle caused in Aberdaron by the demands of the hungry arrivals from Ireland for fatted beef and mutton and other ' gear ' (*cêr*). Since June the king had been urging the county to follow the example of Shropshire by adopting the principle of a monthly assessment, but the matter hung fire till at the beginning of the following year Charles summoned to Oxford those members of the Long Parliament still loyal to him, largely for the purpose of using their influence to secure better contributions from their constituencies.

The archbishop was there among the spiritual peers, tendering the unpalatable (but by no means unstatesmanlike) advice to come to terms with parliament before the situation was beyond remedy. Bodvel, who had come out openly for the king and taken his place on the Caernarvonshire commission of array by May, attended with the commoners, and so did William Thomas — the first, already custos rotulorum for Anglesey, being rewarded with an honorary Oxford M.A., the second with the post of groom to the queen's privy chamber. Another Caernarvonshire man — Griffith Williams, Bishop Bayly's former *bête noire*, now refugee bishop of Ossory — having attended the king at Edgehill, preached to this ' mungrill parliament ' (as the king ungraciously called it) a sermon which was a vigorous counterblast to those to which members still at Westminster were being treated, and the precursor of a long succession of Royalist tracts and sermons from his pen. When the Houses adjourned in April, the recipients of these honours were expected to justify them by speeding up their counties' war effort. In the absence of ' Prince Griffin,' the knight of the shire, it was Bodvel who was summoned by Rupert, through the sheriff of Caernarvonshire, to attend a council of war in Chester at the end of July 1644, bringing with him warrants for the moneys so

airily voted to the king at Oxford by the representatives of
the North Wales counties who had obeyed the royal summons. Unfortunately the dashing young cavalry leader of
twenty-five who was now in control of Welsh affairs was a
foreigner, who was by temperament a professional soldier
and at his worst in dealing with problems arising out of
economic conditions and territorial loyalties of which he was
wholly ignorant; and his demand for prompt payment from
the six counties was countered by a formidable list of local
grievances.

Two months earlier — as soon as the Oxford Parliament
dispersed — two dozen of the leading gentry of Caernarvonshire had petitioned the king on some of these matters, with
a covering letter to Archbishop Williams asking for his medi-
tation. They declared that having already raised a thousand
men, furnishing half the arms of the infantry and all those
of the cavalry, they were now too impoverished and depopu-
lated (with the Smithfield market closed to them) to carry
on the ordinary tillage and at the same time defend themselves against parliamentary shipping and send help to
Anglesey — still less could they commit themselves to
further burdens. Complaints were also made of the unequal
distribution of assessments, and in particular resentment was
shown against the two returned M.P.'s, who after escaping
the heat and burden of the day at home while they regaled
themselves at Oxford, now arrived on the scene with power
to issue commissions and to levy troops, which enabled them
to over-ride the original commissioners of array and to show
partiality to their own friends and tenants. Among the
twenty-four signatories were naturally old malcontents like
Thomas Glynne, John Bodwrda and William Lloyd, future
turncoats like Sir William Williams and Thomas Madryn,
and hardened fence-sitters like Sir Owen Wynne; but the
names of John Owen and Richard Griffith (both of whom
seem to have been at home at the moment) give some assurance that there was substance in the pleas. Other parts of
North Wales had similar grievances to air, and the upshot
was that before a final figure had been agreed upon for the

North Wales counties, northern Powys was as good as lost to the king, and he himself was on the eve of his decisive defeat at Naseby — which meant that the three shires of Gwynedd had to share between them the promised payment of £1,600 for the next three months.

What had changed the whole situation in the meanwhile was Myddelton's second break-through into Wales, this time along the line of the Severn. He had appeared on the border in May 1644, with reinforcements and an artfully-worded Declaration in which he promised to redress those very grievances on which the Caernarvonshire gentry had just been petitioning the king. His victory at Montgomery in September gave him a permanent foothold in mid-Wales, and for a time it seemed as though the situation of the preceding winter, and the resultant panic, would repeat themselves; but the resistance of Chirk and Ruthin castles gave northern Powys a breathing space and staved off the peril to Gwynedd. Meanwhile Archbishop Williams, cordially recommended by the king to Rupert in spite of his *défaitisme* at Oxford, redoubled his efforts towards strengthening Conway, laying in supplies from Ireland and keeping his neighbours up to scratch. With the enemy established on this side of Offa's Dyke, however, it was no longer enough for those counties still comfortably in the rear of the fighting to do their bit by providing a home guard and a quota for the Chester garrison; they must also take some of the strain from regions in the thick of it, by marching out to meet the enemy in the field before he reached the Conway. The last two Caernarvonshire sheriffs — Thomas Madryn and Robert Jones of Castellmarch — had made little progress towards putting the county on an effective war footing; the situation now called for a man of energy and resource, preferably one with military experience, and for this reason Archbishop Williams (to his later regret) put forward the name of John Owen when sheriffs were pricked in the autumn. But it was without the archbishop's privity (or even Byron's) that the king summoned Owen to Oxford not long before Christmas, made him governor of Conway, and sent him home a knight.

Rumours soon reached Williams of ' high and strange
powers ' under which Owen was claiming to over-ride the
local gentry on the commission of array and Williams himself
at Conway (despite the assurances of the preceding year), by
resort to martial law. Denbighshire had already experienced
some of the fruits of military government, and Williams was
as unwilling to expose the county's depleted stocks of food
to the rapacity of an alien soldiery, whether quartered in
private houses or locked up in garrisons of whose strategic
value he was profoundly sceptical, as he was to play second
fiddle to a backwoods squire. For although in the old electioneering days Owen's family had stood aloof from the
' baboons ' of Llŷn and ranged itself with Gwydir, from the
archbishop's standpoint he was little more than an upstart
soldier of fortune whose personal valour could not outweigh
his limited experience in public affairs. It was but another
example of the friction between civilian and military coun-
sellors that had so often bedevilled the king's plans elsewhere. A bitter blow to the archbishop was the desertion to
Owen of his nephew by marriage, William Hookes of
Conway (brother to Hugh), who had served him in Yorkshire
while he was still in office as archbishop and had been left
in charge at Cawood when his master fled. He had been a
captain of horse in the county militia before the war and
now he was back home, serving on the Caernarvonshire
commission of array. For the moment Owen was needed in
the field, and Williams contented himself with calling his
past services to witness against alehouse gossip to the effect
that he was in disgrace as ' an enemy to the souldiery and a
defender of my nation and kindred '. Meanwhile he carried
on with his self-imposed tasks in and on behalf of Conway.

At sea things were not going well for the king. In January
1644 Parliament despatched a squadron under Captain
Swanley to disrupt communications between Archbishop
Williams at Conway and Ormonde in Ireland, where all
depended on the faithful Bartletts. The defence of North
Wales was gravely hampered by lack of powder and other
stores, which could not now be got in London but could be

spared in Ireland since fighting had ceased there. But with this added strength at sea Parliament was able frequently to intercept stores and despatches or to cause them to be held back. In August Williams persuaded Ormonde to spare him a small craft capable of putting in to Conway and carrying thence to Dublin ' intelligence, pacquetts and otherwise as occasion may serve '; he also made what use he could for the same purpose of such few fishing smacks as could be requisitioned locally. The cost, of course, had to be borne mainly by the archbishop's private purse; fortunately it was a long one. But all depended in the end on the superior weight and gunnery of the *Swan*, which none of the Parliamentary flotilla could look in the face.

Towards the end of January 1645, Byron sent Owen with the posse of his country into Denbighshire with marching orders to meet a renewed threat to the Dee passage at Holt, at the same time tactfully eliciting the archbishop's co-operation and urging in stronger terms than ever the need for Gwynedd itself to be on the alert. By the time the reinforcements arrived in early February, the Roundheads were on the Welsh side of the Dee; but Rupert (who was fully occupied further south) sent his brother Maurice with three or four thousand horse to retrieve the situation, which was putting Chester itself (already blocked up on the English side) in deadly peril; and Maurice promptly commissioned Owen as sergeant major general of foot in North Wales, with orders to co-operate with Sir Edmund Verney in keeping the enemy in check on the Welsh side while he himself relieved Chester from the English approaches. In doing so, he lost Shrewsbury; and by the end of the month the Cheshire Roundheads, reinforced from the midlands, were roaming Denbighshire and Flintshire as freely as they had ever done in 1643, forcing Sir John Owen's men to change their rendezvous almost from hour to hour (with frequent desertions as a natural consequence), repulsing Maurice himself at Holt bridge in early March and at one time penetrating as far as Ruthin. But before March was out Williams was telling Ormonde with some pride how the ' Welsh of the mountains ' (especially his own Caernarvonshire men) had fallen on them and driven them back. Rupert himself had by now arrived on the scene with powerful reinforcements, and for the moment Chester was safe, Holt recaptured, and the Round-heads back on the Cheshire side of the Dee.

Caernarvonshire could breathe again; but it was only a precarious lull. In February the bishop of St. Asaph had decided, after some hesitation, that he could still risk leaving his son at school in Conway, although the town was 'in a ferment' — doubtless owing to the quarrel between Williams and Owen; but the danger from parliamentary shipping was still acute. Only five weeks later Byron warned Owen of a Roundhead stratagem for seizing either Conway or Caernarvon by sea in vessels flying the royal colours. Preparations were accordingly made for organised defence in the castles west of Conway. In March Bodvel was made governor of Caernarvon castle, and the ex-sheriff Robert Jones (who had begun repair work out of his own pocket) of the town; and two months later the defence of Harlech was entrusted to Sir John Owen's brother William. All this cost money which must be found locally. Towards the end of March a meeting of commissioners of array for the five North Wales counties still controlled by the king was held at Chester, and came to a provisional agreement for contributions towards the upkeep of garrisons (including Chester itself) during the next six months. Byron's demands for these contributions grew increasingly peremptory in tone, and it is suggestive that he had to insist that not more than a third of the amount should be passed on by the gentry to their tenants! The principal inhabitants of the county were also made to sign a declaration of loyalty to the crown and repudiation of the rebels and all their illegal engagements without 'any mental reservation or equivocation.'

These were by no means Caernarvonshire's only troubles. No sooner had Owen been released from service in the field than the quarrel between him and the archbishop broke out in deadly earnest, starting with an angry letter to the secretary of state in which Williams virtually called on the king

to choose between him and his would-be supplanter, and
culminating in early May in Owen's violent entry into the
castle and seizure of the archbishop's personal goods and
those deposited with him by his neighbours, coupled with
the exhibiting of nine ' Articles of High Treason ' in which
he attacked the prelate for non-residence and ' intermedd-
ling ' in secular affairs, to the obstruction of the king's
accredited servants and the ' comfort ' of rebels. The king
was too busy with far more urgent matters for the next two
months to intervene between the parties. As soon as Rupert
and Maurice withdrew, the situation round Chester worsened once more, and Charles himself had to advance to the
relief of the city in May; then he left for the campaign in
the midlands which ended disastrously for him at Naseby,
leaving the Roundheads to overrun Denbighshire as far as
the outskirts of Denbigh itself. It was from South Wales,
where Charles had taken refuge after his defeat, that he
wrote to Owen in July enjoining him to be ' very cautious '
about laying ' imputations of soe high a nature ' upon one
who hath given eminent testimonyes of his affections to our
service, and whose power and interest in these parts may
yett be of great use unto us '; he was also to restore to the
owners all private property stored in Conway castle and to
give the archbishop free access to his own effects there.

With the enemy now in control of most of northern Powys,
the Caernarvonshire gentry were becoming more amenable
to the ever-increasing demands on their pockets; even Byron
was pleased with the response to the king's latest appeal
after the stabilising of contributions from the three counties
at the Denbigh meeting in mid-July. Meetings of county
commissioners followed each other in rapid succession —
now at Denbigh, now at Conway or Bangor — and towards
the end of September the king made his last personal appearance in North Wales, after forced marches over the mountains from the south, for a final attempt at the relief of
Chester, which came to grief at Rowton Heath. Charles
retired from the field to Denbigh, where he held what a
diarist in his army called a ' generall rendesvouz ', and sent

for both the archbishop and Owen; but whatever may have been said to ease the tension between them, Owen's commission as governor was renewed and Williams had to swallow the affront. The king then quitted North Wales, but he sent the Herefordshire cavalry leader Sir William Vaughan with a large body of horse to manoeuvre on the Welsh side of Chester in the hope of keeping resistance alive in the city until the arrival of the Irish reinforcements who were confidently expected to land in North Wales as a result of the earl of Glamorgan's negotiations with the Irish rebels, now styling themselves the Confederate Catholics. Byron was shut up in Chester, after the king had opened up the Welsh approaches to the city long enough to admit the entry of badly-needed Welsh supplies and reinforcements; Sir John Owen had from time to time to take the field — for example in August, when he was sent to repel a Roundhead incursion into Merioneth, and again at the beginning of October, when he was once more given the now familiar task of leading the trainbands of Gwynedd to the 'Welsh confines' of Chester to open a way for the entry of supplies; so it was on the archbishop's shoulders that the duty fell of preparing for the reception and victualling of the Irish and at the same time procuring all the backing he could from Gwynedd for Sir William Vaughan's campaign.

These tasks were of vital moment to Caernarvonshire, for apart from the need of keeping Chester out of enemy hands now that it was almost the last avenue of communication with the outside world that remained to the king, the Roundheads were unlikely to cross the Conway in force as long as Vaughan's troop remained at large and all the castles east of the river were still in the king's hand, most of them not even effectively besieged. Yet the cordial co-operation between the experienced politician and the seasoned soldier on which the fate of the county so largely depended was as far off as ever. When at the beginning of November Vaughan was overwhelmed by superior numbers in a battle just outside Denbigh, the small body of foot and the larger company of horse that Williams had scraped together (with the help of Sir William Williams and the newly-knighted borough member, Sir William Thomas) lay inactive at their rendezvous near the modern Colwyn Bay because (so the archbishop alleged) Sir John Owen had spurned them. Still Williams did not lose heart. A month earlier he had sent Roger Mostyn (whose force Byron had discharged from the Chester garrison in a fit of pique) to pick up what men he could in Ireland for immediate service over here, and by mid-December he had an assurance from Ormonde that three thousand foot would be ready to sail before Christmas. He complained bitterly of the way Rupert had denuded the country of men and munitions, and the task of replacing them was not eased when towards the end of 1645 most of Merioneth except Harlech was overrun by the Roundheads, and its resources diverted to Parliament. But the heaviest blow of all was the capture in November of the redoubtable *Swan* — not in a fight at sea, but by a carefully-planned stratagem when most of the crew were ashore. This enabled the Roundheads to man her with their own crew and to put her into immediate service. The balance of power at sea was reversed, and Chester's position was desperate.

When 1646 came, with Chester almost at the end of its tether, Williams urged Ormonde to risk shipping the Irishmen over at once, even if they did not venture beyond the Conway until the king could send an adequate supporting force of horse and foot (which was now gathering in the midlands) to meet them. He was already entertaining and helping to deploy a small band of continental auxiliaries which had recently arrived; but he undertook also to see to the victualling of the Irish during the eight or ten days when the transports were unloading in the Straits and the infantry re-forming. It was only, he explained, because there was no one else on the spot to take the initiative that he assumed it himself, not because he had any official status; in fact (like the king himself earlier on) he complained that his plans were often ' thwarted by private interests for particular ends.' As the month wore on without bringing relief he began to be more sceptical of Irish aid; Mostyn came back with the

merest handful of soldiers, and the archbishop's communications with the garrisons and field forces east of Conway,
not only by sea but also by land, grew more and more precarious, important despatches often falling into enemy
hands. But it was not until the end of January that it became
known that Glamorgan was in disgrace for exceeding his
commission and that his agreement with the Confederates
had been repudiated. With its last hope of reinforcements
now gone, Chester surrendered on honourable terms at the
beginning of February.

Byron, who was allowed to quit the city with the honours
of war, now planned to carry the war into Snowdonia itself.
His military communications were naturally addressed to
Owen as major general, but he was glad to use the archbishop as intermediary with the county commissioners and
gentry on questions affecting the civil population, such as
the billeting and feeding of the soldiers now operating in
the county — those who came with Byron from Chester,
others moving in from Lancashire and Cheshire, and the
Irish and continental auxiliaries who had been looked after
by Williams till they were ready to join in the campaign for
Chester; in all some three hundred foot and four hundred
horse, in addition to the county trainbands and the garrisons
of Conway and Caernarvon. On all such matters Owen was
to consult the archbishop, who was also to have free access
to Conway castle; but Byron, directing operations from
Caernarvon in the capacity of field marshal (Bodvel having
been sent to help in the defence of Anglesey), made it clear
that he would take no orders save from the king himself or
the Prince of Wales.

At the same time Parliament was laying its plans for the
speedy reduction of North Wales before the Irish menace,
which was generally believed to be dormant rather than
dead, could raise its head again. In mid-February Thomas
Mytton, to whom Myddelton had relinquished his command
the preceding summer, was sent to subdue this remaining
Royalist stronghold with the troops already under his command, some seasoned officers now released from the Chester

siege, and Booth's regiment from Lancashire, estimated in all at a thousand foot and nearly as strong a body of horse, to be paid for by £10,000 charged on the excise. Siege was at once laid to the chief castles lying in the invaders' path, and at the beginning of March, Chirk was betrayed to them by the English colonel who held it for the king. Mytton seized the occasion to reconnoitre as far as Llanrwst, and Owen was instructed to deploy his forces for resistance (with particular care for the passes), leaving the defence of Conway castle to his deputy. But the Roundheads drew back, not daring to venture in full strength into the wilds of Snowdonia with so many strong points still in enemy hands to divert man-power and to threaten their rear.

Early in April the fall of Ruthin removed one of these obstacles; Mytton could now push on in force through Llan-sannan and Llanrwst, avoiding the coastal route and leaving the castles that guarded it to be reduced at leisure. With forces so unequally matched (for when all allowance has been made for companies under strength and men detached for siege duty the defence must have been outnumbered by two to one), Byron decided to abandon resistance in the open for concentration at the two strong points of Conway and Caernarvon, provisioning both as fully as possibly, with the archbishop's help, against a prolonged siege. The surrender of Aberystwyth castle soon afterwards released from its garrison another body of Cavaliers who had ' carried them-selves with great fidelity and courage,' and after hastily improving arms for them Byron sent them as a much-needed stiffening to the Conway garrison; ' being Welshmen ', he diplomatically told Owen, ' I thought them fitte for your turn better than any other '. He advised Owen before retiring to the castle to break down Llanrwst bridge and to leave the country as bare as possible of stores likely to be serviceable to the invader — especially those at Gwydir, the largest establishment within range. He had himself made an exten-sive raid in Merioneth early in the month and stocked himself well with Welsh cloth from Dolgellau before Mytton drove him out again. But the very day after Byron sent this

directive, Mytton reached Llanrwst (24 April) and was enter-
tained at Gwydir, giving its owner written 'protection' in
return for his hospitality. Finding the bridge intact, the main
body of Roundheads swarmed across the river and marched
down the opposite bank, but by-passed Conway Castle —
traditionally (and most probably) by cutting across the
mountains by the old Roman road over Bwlch y ddeufaen —
to strike the coast further west, reaching Caernarvon by the
29th. For their immediate job was to occupy what little
remained to the king of the coast where an Irish army might
still land, and that meant reducing Caernarvon and crossing
to Anglesey.

Mytton's first stopping place was Archbishop William's
house at Penrhyn, to which he had retired when Owen shut
himself up in the castle. It was from here that he responded
to Byron's appeal for stores (on the day the Roundheads
reached Llanrwst) by what reads like an olive-branch letter
to Owen, arranging for provisions to be sent to him both
from 'the mountains' and (as soon as he could get over the
'peevishness' of the gentry of the island) from Anglesey,
assuring him of his readiness 'to runne the same fortunes
with you in this dangerous tyme' and subscribing himself
'your affectionate and heartye ffreind and Coozen.' How
soon after this he changed his allegiance — whether indeed
he had not already done so, despite his protestations — it
is impossible now to say. He told Mytton on his summoning
Penrhyn a few days later that he was holding it against
'surprizells' by either side, but to his relatives at Gwydir
he contrasted the Roundhead general's courtesy with the
brusqueness of Byron, while Mytton assured parliament on
the last day of April that the archbishop had now abandoned
'the king's party' and was dissuading the gentry of his
county from the contributions towards its maintenance that
he had so long tried to wring from them. It is even possible
that he was thinking of securing his retreat as early as March,
when a messenger from him was expected by the remnant
of the Lords still sitting at Westminster. He had never
believed in the necessity for the war, energetically as he

played his part in it when it came; he believed in it less when it meant exposing a bare countryside, already sucked dry by war demands, to the tender mercies of rival bands of marauders from outside, each bent on wresting from it the food and pay which so often failed to appear through official channels — especially now that only Caernarvonshire and Anglesey, and a few isolated castles elsewhere, still maintained the king's cause, while Charles himself was no longer accessible, and from 26 April (though this was not yet known) a prisoner in the hands of the Scots.

Early in May Byron, shut up in Caernarvon, made a despairing but unavailing appeal to Ormonde in Ireland to send over three thousand good men to relieve the town, declaring it must otherwise fall within ten days for ' want of all things necessary ', aggravated by the general defection from the king's side of the leading gentry, following the archbishop's example. Parliamentary pamphleteers paid particular tribute to the services of Thomas Glynne and ' Bart Williams ' (Sir William) to the besieging force. By the middle of the month Mytton had secured himself against the victualling of the town on the seaward side by carrying his earthworks down to the Straits and keeping a small fleet of sail there; and now he beat the Cavaliers out of the town and shut them up (save those who managed to escape to Anglesey) in the castle. There Byron held out till early June — over a fortnight longer than his estimate to Ormonde; enemy propaganda (always concerned to exaggerate the strength of the opposing forces) declared there was enough food and ammunition there to stand another three months' siege. On 4 June commissioners from the two sides met and agreed to terms of surrender. Byron and his principal officers were given three months in which to submit to parliament or to go overseas; other ranks were free to return home. A touch of the burlesque was added by a formal document solemnly guaranteeing free quarter to a Lancashire bearward and his bear who had beguiled the tedium of the siege. Thomas Glynne, who had acted as one of Mytton's commissioners, was made governor a couple of days later, and in another week Beaumaris fell, leaving Mytton's hands free for Conway.

Here Owen, during the last days of the siege of Caernarvon, had been busy cattle-raiding over the countryside to provide against a long investment. A raid in the Aber neighbourhood was cut short by the appearance of a strong Roundhead force which retrieved the booty; but Byron's plan of rounding-up the cattle at Gwydir had better success — two hundred head were alleged to have been driven away. Military necessity and the dubious record of Gwydir (for Sir Richard still sat at Westminster and Sir Owen — and later Maurice too — flaunted a 'protection' from Mytton) gave ample excuse for this spoliation, but it naturally caused deep resentment among neighbours, most of all to Archbishop Williams, the doting uncle of Sir Owen's lady. If he had not already made his mind up about the war, this would have been enough to tip the balance. As soon at Caernarvon fell he wrote to friends at Conway advising the town to submit and promising to intercede for favourable terms. But Owen had no thought of weakening, so Williams openly joined the besiegers with his little bodyguard from Penrhyn.

Before June was out, Nantconwy was 'so full of soldiers' that there was 'no going without danger'; and attackers were just as ready as defenders to 'raven and spoyle all the Countrey over'. Three troops of Mytton's horse from Cheshire and Lancashire, kept waiting for their pay, were plundering at large between Trefriw and Penmachno and threatening to raid Dolwyddelan; and Lady Grace Wynn found some of them 'very rude' at Gwydir. This may well have been while Mytton was away from the district discharging his civil duties as sheriff of Shropshire, or superintending the investment of the castles he had left in his rear; at any rate he was back by early August, and holding a council of war at which it was decided to storm the town. Williams attended the council, having offered his services and his local knowledge to Mytton on condition that when the castle fell the goods still deposited there should be restored to their rightful owners. Whether or not, ignoring his cloth and his sixty-three years, he actually donned harness and joined in the attack (as was rumoured at the time), he was certainly wounded, apparently before the actual assault. This took place on 8 August, preceded by a barrage of guns, grenades, stones and bullets and a number of feints which distracted attention from the main attack, with the result that the picked men detailed for it hurled themselves over the walls (despite the fact that their ladders proved too short), overpowered the guards and made themselves masters of the town, with prisoners and booty. Of the former, the Irish were tied back to back, thrown into the sea and (as the parliamentary pamphleteer records with sadistic glee) ' sent by water to their own country.'

In the castle, however, Owen declined Mytton's challenge to surrender and met with flat incredulity his assurance that the king was now with the Scottish army; but he did draft a list of the conditions on which he was prepared to lay down arms. He was quite ready to give Williams satisfaction over the eternal question of the goods deposited in the castle, and (much to his credit) he stipulated that the Irish in the garrison should be given adequate transport home and not treated like those taken in the town. But the demand for back pay for the garrison was made in terms more befitting a conqueror than the leader of a hopelessly lost cause, and naturally Mytton ignored it. Now that the castle was no longer an obstacle to his plan of campaign, he could afford to let the siege take its course, and Owen reap whatever military honour accrued from holding out for four months after the king himself had officially authorised his garrisons to submit, until a time when they had all followed the hint except Harlech (held by his brother) and Holt. On its surrender on 18 November (on terms which, apart from guarantees for the municipal independence of Conway, were concerned solely with questions of military honour), Col. John Carter, a Buckinghamshire man who had served with Brereton in the Chester operations and helped to negotiate the surrender of Caernarvon, was put in charge of the garrison — although according to Archbishop Williams he had taken no part in the siege.

A month later, on the recommendation of Mytton, the Commons agreed to general terms of composition for the Caernarvonshire gentry. All pains and penalties of delinquency were removed from those who had come over to Parliament during the siege of Caernarvon, and Thomas Glynne, already governor of the castle, was given the former Cefnamwlch post of vice admiral of North Wales, with his old subaltern Hugh Hookes as deputy. Glynne was thus the leading man in the shire, with the archbishop in the background as elder statesman. Such high favours to a former commissioner of array were widely attributed to the influence in the House of his lawyer brother, who was now piling up in fees the fortune that enabled him to found a great political family in Flintshire. Naturally there was a good deal of resentment, and Glynne did not enhance his popularity by the dictatorial methods he adopted in raising money for the army (' in greater proportion than the country has been wont to pay ') and clapping defaulters into prison, till in December he had to be sharply brought to heel by the Lord General himself, Thomas Fairfax.

For the aim now was to conciliate ex-enemies, and Mytton had given the Commons a very favourable report on the Caernarvonshire gentry. Accordingly those who had fought for the king, unless there was some special ground for penalising them, were free to live peaceably at home on paying their assessments to parliament, taking the Covenant, and binding themselves not to take up arms again in the same cause. Most of them swallowed these two ' strong pills ', with however wry a face; the archbishop, out of respect for his cloth and his eminent services to parliament, was exempt from ' taking the same physic as the rest of the county '. Sir John Owen's estate had long been earmarked as one of those out of which the expenses of Myddelton's campaigns were to be met, and in May, his ' composition ' was fixed at £771. In the preceding month he had been invited by Rupert to raise a Welsh brigade to serve with him under the king of France, but unable to find transport, he was reluctantly compelled to decline the tempting offer. It is a little surprising in the circumstances that he did not take the same course as Richard Griffith and Wynn of Bodysgallen, and join the army sent by parliament to renew the fight with the Irish Confederates, for here was fighting he could engage in without impairing his loyalty to the king; instead he swallowed the two ' strong pills ' and retired to Clenennau. Bodvel and Sir William Thomas had rendered themselves liable to special penalties as M.P.'s who had ' deserted ' their seats in parliament for the king's quarters, but their cases, as well as those of others among the minor gentry who had taken up arms for the king and not come over to Parliament in 1646, were left to be dealt with at leisure.

So far the war had caused no startling shift in the balance of county politics; rather it had brought about the delayed triumph of which the house of Glynllifon had been baulked in 1640, and this was consolidated by the powerful backing of the wealthiest and most influential lawyer on the victorious side. When new M.P.'s were chosen, however, to replace the deceased John Griffith and William Thomas the ' deserter ', at the begining of 1646, Thomas Glynne did not seek parliamentary honours — probably on account of his age and health. The new knight of the shire was the son of Sir Owen Wynn of Gwydir, who had married a daughter of Sir Thomas Myddelton, and the new burgess the lawyer William Foxwist, sprung from a Cheshire family which had settled in Caernarvon in early Tudor days. Shortly before Conway fell, parliament had replaced Sir John Owen in the office of sheriff by Thomas Williams, brother of Sir William of Vaynol, and in the winter of the next year he in turn gave place to William Lloyd of Talhenbont, one of the trio of ' disaffected ' spirits who had been put under arrest when war broke out. As a further item in the reconstruction of local government, an assessment committee for the county was elected in parliament in June 1647. It included Thomas Glynne with his brothers John and Edmund; Lloyd and Bodwrda, his fellow-suspects of 1642, the latter also with his brother Griffith; Sir William Williams, who had changed sides with him in 1646, and the ex-sheriff Thomas Madryn,

who was probably in the same group; Griffith Jones of
Castellmarch, who had made himself awkward to the king's
party early in the war; the new borough member, and Robert
Coytmor, that younger son of the Coetmor family who had
become secretary to the earl of Warwick, now commanding
the parliamentary fleet; together with Sir Thomas Myddelton
from Denbighshire.

The bias in local government towards the victorious
faction is obvious; yet it was not a wholly unrepresentative
cross-section of county society that was left in power. The
absence of Cefnamwlch is easily understood: the heir,
' Prince Griffin ', was a refugee in France, and etiquette for-
bade his younger brother William (himself a man in middle
life) to supplant him in his lifetime. The heads of the houses
of Bodysgallen and Llanfair Isgaer were away fighting in
Ireland; Bodvel belonged to the Gwydir connection and
Sir William Thomas was closely related to Foxwist, so both
were in a sense represented. Clenennau was naturally out of
the picture, but then Sir John Owen had never concerned
himself greatly with county politics. In general the county
was settling down. The scars of war are quickly healed in a
pastoral society, and the cattle trade was put on its feet again
by the restoration of traffic with the English markets and a
grant of £3,000 by way of compensation to the drovers, procured by the good offices in parliament of the influential
John Glynne. Few of the gentry had as yet been heavily
fined, and the assessments they had paid, first to the king
and then latterly to parliament, though well above the usual
level of taxation, probably did not come to much more than
they would normally have laid out in their pet extravagances
of building and litigation, on which the war had imposed a
temporary brake.

Meanwhile the intruded Roundhead soldiers were gradually being paid off and sent home. In speeding on this work,
smoothing out the difficulties, and resisting (as often before)
the encroachment of the military on the civil arm, the services of Archbishop Williams, who stood so well with parliament, were invaluable. The chief causes of friction were

occasional disorderliness among the men, the cost of disband-
ment to the county, suspicions of graft among some of the
parliamentary officers, and the burning question of how large
a skeleton force was needed for local security. Williams had
full confidence in Mytton, and his opinion is confirmed by
Mytton's own letter to General Cromwell in November,
pleading that Caernarvonshire was 'not a fit county to
accommodate horse', and should be let off with a smaller
quota than its richer neighbours of the £6,000 a month levied
from North Wales for the maintenance of the army of occupation. The archbishop had a very different opinion of
Carter, an able soldier who sometimes acted as Mytton's
deputy, but was blatantly on the make, and soon became the
most unpopular man in North Wales. Williams strove as
hard with the parliamentary authorities against the garris-
oning of Conway and Caernarvon as he had in the same
cause with the king's advisers, for he believed the cost of
their defence, and the resultant disaffection in the surrounding country, was out of all proportion to its military
value; he was confident that the expense of maintaining, as
was proposed, eighty to a hundred men in Caernarvon (with
another hundred at Beaumaris to do virtually the same job)
and 150 at Conway, could never be kept within the limits
of the county's assessments. There was naturally some
murmuring and a rather more serious 'tumult' at Caernarvon, in which Thomas Wynn of Boduan was involved;
but disaffection was disarmed when it became known that
complaints, whether against a stranger like Carter or local
men like Thomas Glynne and his brother, would receive
speedy redress, on the archbishop's representations, from
responsible quarters.

Unhappily for the success of the archbishop's promising
effort at pacifying his county, there were forces outside it
that were spoiling for a fight, and the growing dissensions
among the victors supplied the opportunity. When in March
1648, Byron in the name of the king and the Prince of Wales

renewed Sir John Owen's commission as sergeant major general of North Wales, the prospect was too tempting to be refused. It is true he had sworn never again to take up arms against parliament; but was not 'the maintenance of ... the Privileges of Parliaments, and the Laws and liberty of the subject' one of the prime objects stated in his commission, and was not the parliament that now sat at Westminster notoriously subject to overwhelming pressure from its own army? It is unlikely that Owen debated the matter for long. Locally the moment seemed propitious; the Roundhead cause in the county had been weakened by the deaths of Thomas Glynne and John Bodwrda and the withdrawal of John Glynne from his seat in the House, under pressure from the army, with ten other 'Presbyterian' M.P.'s who stood for a compromise settlement unacceptable to the army. Carter roundly told the Lord General that Glynne and Bodwrda were 'the only faithful men to the Parliament in the country'; but his allegation that the ex-Royalists now entrusted with power, 'instead of endeavouring to quell and appease the insurrections . . . do privately countenance and join in them' with the design 'to destroy the garrisons and Parliament forces here' till 'there will be no living in these parts for any that have been faithful servants to the kingdom' was obviously meant as a counter-attack to the complaints that had gone up from the county against his misconduct.

Owen's original intention had been to raise Merioneth and to lead a force from there to help in the effort on the king's behalf in Pembrokeshire under the ex-Roundheads Laugharne and Poyer. The later attempt of Thomas Wynn of Boduan to saddle Glynllifon with responsibility for diverting his activities to Caernarvonshire must be heavily discounted, as an effort on the part of this ex-Royalist soldier and lifelong intriguer to put himself right with the parliamentary authorities by denouncing his neighbours, and at the same time to pay off ancient family scores. Of Thomas Glynne at least the allegation it patently untrue because he was in his grave before Owen's commission arrived. The story of Owen's campaign in Caernarvonshire has been so fully told by the late Sir Frederick Rees that only the barest recapitulation is needed here. The small guerilla bands collected by him, and used at first for desultory attacks on the parliamentary garrisons, had by the end of May grown (by accretions from other parts of the country) to a force of 150 horse and 120 foot, and Mytton, with only twenty horse and sixty foot, deemed it wise to shut himself up in Caernarvon castle till he could get help from outside. George Twisleton, governor of Denbigh, was busy during May preventing reinforcements from reaching Owen through Merioneth, while Mytton, with the help of the new sheriff and Thomas Madryn, kept the foe at bay by periodic sallies from the castle, in one of which the sheriff was wounded and captured. Twisleton, in response to an S.O.S. from Mytton towards the end of the month, collected all the reinforcements he could from Chester and Conway, amounting in all (with what men he could spare from his own garrison) to some hundred foot and sixty horse; but before they could force their way through to the garrison, the besiegers (who had wind of their approach) engaged them in a running fight which ended on 5 June on the sea-shore at Y Dalar Hir, near Llandygái, with the wounding and capture of Owen and the scattering of his little army, except for about sixty officers and other ranks left in the hands of the enemy. Most of these came from Caernarvonshire and the adjacent counties; the rest from widely scattered districts of England and South Wales. A few stray Royalists still roamed the countryside, after what a Merioneth diarist[1] grandiosely styles the ' battle of Bangor ', until July.

The victors were naturally incensed against the man who had put them to the trouble and expense of reconquering Caernarvonshire, and their wrath was not softened by the news that the wounded sheriff, one of their few tried supporters in the county, had died of rough treatment and neglect on the march from Caernarvon to Llandygái.

---

[1] Penbedw MSS, *Camb. Quarterly Mag.*, i, 1829, 70-2.

Clenennau was plundered; Owen was confined to Denbigh castle and, after an unsuccessful attempt at rescue, removed to London for trial on the triple charge of treason to parliament, violation of his articles of surrender and murder of the sheriff; his servant Morris Griffith (taken with him in the skirmish) was allowed to visit Caernarvon on pass in December, presumably to bring what he needed from home. The Lords having vetoed a resolution of the Commons for banishing him with Laugharne, he was brought to trial soon after the execution of the king himself, before a High Court of Justice set up to try the ringleaders in the second Civil War. A spirited speech in his own defence created a considerable impression, but did not avert the death sentence, from which (with the other prisoners) he appealed to the Commons. On the very day that sentence was pronounced, the loyal Captain Bartlett swooped down from Wexford to the coast of Llŷn, plundered Castellmarch, and carried off the 'well affected' Griffith Jones as a hostage for Sir John Owen's life. Whether under this threat (as some believed), or through the humane intervention of Ireton and others, or simply because the gallant demeanour of this 'poor gentleman of Wales' among the bevy of great peers, with powerful friends, who were his fellow-petitioners, aroused the traditional British sense of sportsmanship (now that righteous indignation had had time to abate), Owen won his reprieve. By July he was free to entertain Evelyn the diarist with a Welsh harpist, and in September he was home at Clenennau — forbidden to travel without a pass and three times put under preventive restraint (in 1651, 1655 and 1658), but otherwise free to put his estate into order (in which he seems to have been protected from the worst excesses of the sequestrators by the goodwill and Myddelton and Mytton) and to amuse himself with his hawks and dogs.

His county, however, had to pay dearly for his exploit. Apart from meeting a fine of £4,000, on top of the usual parliamentary assessments, it was for the next few years under the heel of the officers who had scotched the revolt, and without the championship of Archbishop Williams (now a sick man, and dead by 1650) to fend off military encroach-ments. Carter as governor of Conway, and Madryn, who had swum into favour through his conduct in the revolt and had been given a parliamentary colonelcy on the strength of his pre-war captaincy of militia, became twin tyrants of the county, and indeed of much of North Wales, except when the Protectorate at the height of its power was able to put a curb on their rapacity. Twisleton, who like Carter was rewarded for his services with £1,000 out of Royalist estates, was a less flamboyant character; he married the heiress to Lleuar and eventually settled down on the estate, and on the whole this intrusion from Buckinghamshire seems to have caused no general resentment. If there was no social revolu-tion, no wholesale *pogrom* against the defeated, there were unmistakable signs of what the last Glynne of Lleuar later called 'a kingdom tossed up in a blanket'; and the fate of Caernarvonshire now depended on the extent to which its traditional leaders were able and willing to co-operate with the new order. The alternative was exposed to view in Anglesey, which in the absence of 'collaborators' of any local standing the island was subjected for the next five years to what was in essence military dictatorship from out-side. This was just what Archbishop Williams had dreaded and done his utmost to ward off; it remains to be seen how far his objective was realised after his death. This will appear in the next chapter.

BIBLIOGRAPHY

This chapter is largely reproduced (by permission, which is hereby
gratefully acknowledged) from an article on the same subject contributed by the author to *TCHS* (1953), where full references to sources
are given. This was written, however, before the appearance in the
same journal of the first exposition of the part played by sea power
in the war: Aled Eames, ' Sea Power and Caernarvonshire, 1642-1660 '
(*TCHS*, 1955), of which the main conclusions are incorporated above.
Norman Tucker, *North Wales in the Civil War* (1958) contains Caernarvonshire portraits and other illustrations not to be found elsewhere;
see also his biography of *Sir John Owen* (1963) and shorter accounts
of the Bartletts (' Culverins for Charles ', *TCHS* 1948), Sir John Carter
(id. 1952) and Hugh Wynne of Bodysgallen (id. 1958). The second
Civil War in Caernarvonshire is described in detail in J. F. Rees,
*Studies in Welsh History* (1947), 107-11. On Archbishop Williams,
see B. Dew Roberts *Mitre and Musket* (1938). Particulars of the pre-
war county militia are from Huntington Library (Calif.), MS. EL7443.
The recently published *Calendar of Letters relating to N. Wales*
(Bd. of Celtic Studies, Hist. and Law Ser., xxiii, 1967) contains much
material relevant to this and the two succeeding chapters.

# VII

## THE PURITANS IN POWER
### (1650 - 60)

THE death in 1650 of Archbishop Williams left a great gap
in the life of the county. His descent from Cochwillan and
his alliance with Gwydir gave him automatically a certain
prestige. He had always kept in touch with county affairs
even from a distance, and his correspondence with Sir John
Wynn, to whom he felt a lifelong gratitude for persuading
his father to send him to Cambridge, was voluminous. The
family, and the county generally, found in him a valuable
friend at court. On a visit to Gwydir not long before he
became Lord Keeper he remembered his cloth and preached
to the family, but his services were usually of a more secular
character. The chief posts in his official household were held
by Caernarvonshire men: a Mostyn, a Hookes of Conway,
and at one time two Wynns of Gwydir. Soon after he quitted
office he negotiated in 1627 the purchase of the estate of
Penrhyn, originally meaning to remodel the medieval hall
after the fashion of Gwydir. There is no sign that he ever
carried this out, or indeed ever felt much attracted towards
the old-fashioned house with its faded glories; it was to
Gloddaeth, the Caernarvonshire home of the Mostyns, that
he went to die. But whatever the deficiences of Penrhyn as a
dwelling place, it carried with it all the prestige of an ancient
tribal holding associated with an illustrious family. In the
same year Williams leased from the crown the ferries of
Conway and Tal y cafn and the crown manors — Marle,
Eriannws, Penlassog — which usually went with them. He
did not at first disturb the Pughs of Penrhyn Creuddyn in

137

the tenancy of these properties, which they had enjoyed since Henry VIII's day, but during the war the military importance of the ferries impelled him to take them into his own hand. The whole estate, including Cochwillan, Marle, Eriannws and Penlassog — is said to have covered something like a third of the total area of the shire.

This territorial eminence alone would have made him a power in the land; but in addition he bore with him, even in exile from office, the authority attached to thirty years' experience of public affairs at the centre, five of them in the highest offices in the state and then the Church. The last eight years of his life had been spent among his own people, half of them as the heart and soul of the defence of the county against Roundhead invasion (with no authority save personal prestige and ineffective encouragement from the king), the other half in the rôle of mediator. His shrewd if unheroic counsels and influence were sorely missed. He died a childless bachelor; but for her sex, he would have made his greatly-loved niece Grace, Sir Owen Wynne's wife, his heir, which would have left Gwydir more powerful than ever; as it was, his nephew Griffith succeeded to Penrhyn and its accessories, and founded a new family which remained important in county affairs till the nineteenth century. But Griffith Williams was no leader (the archbishop himself never thought very highly of him), and after the death of Thomas Glynne none of the families which had managed the shire before the war — though most of them were ready to collaborate, even with a republican government— stood in anything like a position of undisputed primacy. This laid their county more open to the demands of its new overlords, the men who had won the war.

The instrument of local government favoured by the victorious Parliament was the county committee. First introduced as a war measure to facilitate the raising of men and money on a shire basis (since that was how the militia worked), it was found too convenient to be dropped in peace time. The members were named for each shire in a parliamentary ordinance, and the aim was to secure a solid backing of proven parliamentary sympathisers, inside and outside the shire, and to add to them representatives of as many of the established county families as were willing to act. The defection of a large section of the county gentry from the king's cause when Archbishop Williams changed sides had made it possible, as we have seen, to include in the earliest county committee a fairly representative cross-section of county society; and as none of this committee had given active support to Sir John Owen, only minor changes were made in subsequent committees up to the Protectorate, except for a strengthening of the military element. This naturally had to be imported, since Caernarvonshire was sadly short of native officers who had actually fought on the Roundhead side. The first and best-hated of these intruders was John Carter, the new governor of Conway, but others followed — chiefly from Montgomeryshire, where the four-year parliamentary occupation had given time for the growth of a fairly strong Roundhead faction within the shire, and Denbighshire, where the long-standing Puritanism of the border rose to the surface once Myddelton had been able to break through to his own people. Unfortunately the disappearance of all records of the Caernarvonshire committees makes it impossible for us to assess the relative shares of this intrusive military element and the native gentry in the actual government of the shire.

The office of sheriff lost much of its practical importance while parliamentary elections were in abeyance, but it was still important from the point of view of morale that so ancient and dignified a post should be held by a man of local eminence rather than a stranger or an obscure partisan. In the year of Archbishop Williams's death his nephew and heir was named sheriff of Caernarvonshire, and in 1652 Sir Owen Wynn of Gwydir. In this phase Caernarvonshire—and indeed Gwynedd generally — stands in marked contrast to the rest of Wales. For it was during the years between the king's execution and the declaration of the Protectorate that the faction which looked for the immediate achievement of the rule of the Saints, as a preparation for the fifth and final monarchy of the world — that of Christ Himself — was gaining the ascendant. Towards the end of 1649 the leader of this faction, Major General Thomas Harrison, was added to all the county committees of Wales, in readiness for the establishment there in the following year of the Commission for the Propagation of the Gospel, over which he presided. The commission's task was to expedite the triumph of Puritanism in what was regarded as one of the ' dark places of the land ' and so a major obstacle to the rule of the Saints. The commissioners, with control of the revenues of the Welsh Church, were given wide powers, exercised through their ' approvers ', over the personnel of the parochial ministry, which they supplemented by a body of itinerant preachers. Naturally the approvers were men of strong Puritan conviction, with a seasoning of Fifth Monarchy men. The commissioners themselves occupied many of the key positions in the government of Wales, including commanders of important garrisons and the sheriffs for most of the Welsh counties between 1650 and 1653. But Caernarvonshire and Anglesey could not boast a single commissioner between them. Nevertheless the work of weeding out parsons unacceptable to the commissioners was well under way within a year of the passing of the Act. The difficulty was to fill their places, and it took some years before even the skeleton of a Puritan parochial ministry had been formed in Caernarvonshire.

The climax of this revolutionary phase came when in 1653 Cromwell drove out the Rump and gave Harrison his head by lending support to what was meant as the first stage in the rule of the Saints — the summoning of the singular assembly known to history as the Barebones Parliament. Constituencies and electoral machinery went by the board; the choice of three members for North Wales and three for the south was made by Harrison and Vavasour Powell — the Boanerges of the Propagation — and communicated early to John Jones, the only Merioneth commissioner (though he had now closer contacts with Wrexham). The men they chose were from Montgomeryshire, Shropshire (again with close

Wrexham contacts) and Cornwall — none from Gwynedd. The only county committee appointed by this 'parliament' was a small body set up to administer in the shires its humanitarian legislation for the relief of poor prisoners. Here again a third of the Welsh members had been commissioners under the Propagation Act. Even Merioneth was now able to put forward a local Puritan in Robert Owen of Dolserau, a cousin of John Jones and later to become one of the Quaker pioneers of Pennsylvania. Not so Caernarvonshire: here the members came for the most part from the range of families that had manned the county committees since they began.

The Barebones experiment broke down after five months; four days later Cromwell was proclaimed Protector, and the revolution was for the time being scotched. The Protectorate, with its promise of stability and its restoration of many time-honoured institutions, brought back into public life several of the older governing families who had no affinities with the religious and political principals on which it was based, but were weary of being 'tossed up in a blanket'; on the other hand, for the same reason many of the mainstays of the Barebones *régime* found themselves now in opposition if not in prison. As this element did not exist in Caernarvonshire, there was no violent jolt here, but the rise of men with a positive attachment to the Protectorate was beginning to challenge the predominance of the older families who were at best reluctant 'collaborators'. It was during this period that the work of the Propagation Commission began to bear fruit here, after Cromwell's reorganisation of the Church under 'Triers', in the slow spread of Puritanism. About a dozen new incumbents satisfactory to the Triers were planted in various parishes of the shire between Cromwell's seizure of power and the Restoration. Most of them are unknown to fame, but there are three who left a sufficient mark to deserve mention. The first, Ellis Rowland, was an Anglesey man. Where he came under Puritan influence is a matter for guesswork: certainly not at Beaumaris grammar school, where he received his early education; possibly at Cambridge, which was rent with strife between Laudians and Puritans during the time he was up there; but over ten years passed between his Cambridge days and his appointment to a Denbighshire living in 1653, and of this period in his life nothing is known. It was four years after this that he was translated to the Caernarvonshire living of Clynnog, with Llanwnda added to it. His wife was a sister of the loyalist Richard Griffith of Llanfair Isgaer, but she was also distantly connected with John Jones, the regicide. The influence of his ministry may perhaps be seen in the fact that worshippers from Clynnog are to be found among the persecuted Dissenters of Caernarvonshire twenty years later.

Henry Maurice, on the other hand, was a man of Llŷn, the second son of Morris ap Griffith of Methlan in Aberdaron parish. He was also a man of some social standing — a nephew of Thomas Wynn of Boduan. Maurice was only eight when the Civil War broke out, and when it was over he went to an Oxford where the Puritans were in the saddle; from there he was called by Cromwell's Triers to take charge of the two adjacent livings of Llannor and Deneio, containing the borough of Pwllheli and within a stone's throw of his uncle's estate. He was there less than a couple of years. During that time he co-operated in the efforts of the great Carmarthenshire Puritan Stephen Hughes towards providing for his fellow North Walians a body of religious literature in an idiom they could understand. Maurice's contribution was to adapt for their use South Wales idioms in the religious rhymes composed before the war by Rhys Prichard for his Llandovery parishioners, and now put for the first time into print under the title *Canwyll y Cymru.* Whether Henry Maurice left any impress on the parishes placed under his charge it is impossible to say. We certainly cannot credit him with the persistence of Dissent after the Restoration in Pwllheli and some ten other parishes of south Caernarvonshire extending for half-a-dozen miles on either side of it; for he himself conformed at the Restoration (to

undergo re-conversion and become a leader of Welsh
Puritanism years afterwards), and on the other hand it is
known that two years before his ministry began there were
already 'frequent meetings of godly persons' at Pwllheli.
It was natural that the men who were trying to fan the
feeble flame of Caernarvonshire Puritanism should turn their
eyes to Caernarvon itself, where their efforts would also
have the forceful backing of the castle garrison. In the same
year that Henry Maurice went to Llannor and Deneio, a John
Williams was sent to replace the existing vicar of Llanbeblig,
himself a nominee of the Propagation Commissioners. The
name is too common to be identified with certainty, but it
is possible he was another of the growing band of Llŷn
Puritans — the John Williams of Ty'n y coed (or Castellmarch Uchaf) who went to Oxford to study medicine at the
end of the war and was, as we shall see, one of the many
Puritan suspects of Llŷn at the time of the Restoration, and
a friend of Henry Maurice in later days. The tradition that,
although unordained, he preached in the Roundhead army
and even served as chaplain to Col. John Jones cannot be
substantiated but is not wholly improbable. Whoever the
incumbent may have been, it does not seem that the Puritan
assault on the citadel of Caernarvon had any immediate success. Until well on in the eighteenth century Dissent
remained a feeble growth there, subject to strong hostility
on the part of the townsfolk, and its few adherents largely
dependent on Pwllheli.

   That Puritanism should have found its earliest Caernarvonshire footholds in the very regions which only two generations back had been strongholds of recusancy, is not easy to
explain. The separateness of Llŷn, and its closer ties with
Ardudwy than with Arfon and Arllechwedd before the days
of the road builders, must always be borne in mind. An
important link between them during the interregnum was
Morgan Llwyd, himself an Ardudwy man who, as an
'approver' under the Propagation Act, travelled extensively
both in Merioneth, where he left behind him devoted followers round Bala and Dolgellau, and also in Llŷn, where

(as he recalls in one of his verses) he ' lost his voice ' through persistent preaching.

Although these little Puritan communities, once they cease to be anonymous (which is not till after the Restoration) are found to be drawn chiefly from the humbler ranks of society — like Richard Griffith's neighbour with his addiction to *glasdŵr* in the days before the war — they were not at this stage without adherents among the minor gentry, who also provided the backbone of the new Puritan ministry. The adherence of Griffith Jones of Castellmarch to the victorious faction was political rather than religious; that of Thomas Madryn appears to have been dictated by little but self-interest and love of power. With Jeffrey Parry, of Rhydolion in the parish of Llanengan, it was a different story. He held the rank of cornet in the Roundhead army, and, like so many of Cromwell's officers, used to preach to his men; detractors jeeringly called him ' a great Heaven-driver in Llyn, and a zealous maintainer of Conventicles '. Where he came under Puritan influences, and what attracted him to the Roundhead army, is unknown; one might, perhaps hazard a guess that (as with John Jones) it was through service in the household of some Puritan magnate. His army career was no doubt in England; it is in 1651 that we first encounter him in Caernarvonshire, as one of the county ' sequestrators ' charged with the task of putting into execution Parliament's policy of meeting some of the costs of the war out of the estates of the vanquished. In typical Puritan fashion he named his son Love-God Parry, and the name (in the truncated and non-committal form of ' Love ') was perpetuated in his family right down the the nineteenth century.

A few miles north of Rhydolion stood Nanhoron Ucha, home of a small but well-connected squire named Edward ap Thomas ap Richard. The family was slower than some of its neighbours in adopting the English fashion of fixed surnames, but Edward's son Richard entered himself at Grays Inn, in the year of the king's execution, as Richard Edwards. As a youth of nineteen he no doubt absorbed some of the Puritan atmosphere of the Inns of Court. His marriage to a

niece of Thomas Wynn of Boduan raised his stature in the
county and at the same time provided another Puritan
connection, for she was a cousin to Henry Maurice. Richard
Edwards's importance in the story of Caernarvonshire Puritanism lies chiefly in the post-Restoration period, but he first
comes into prominence in the county as a member of the
assessment committee of 1657.

This committee has many interesting features. On the one
hand there is an obvious attempt to stabilise the Protectorate
by bringing back into public life members of the old
governing families who had hitherto stood aloof. The most
striking example is the second Viscount Bulkeley of Baron
Hill, who had succeeded to the estate on the death of his
elder brother in a historic duel on Traeth Lafan in 1650,
but had up to now been out of politics; now he appears on
both Anglesey and Caernarvonshire committees. Another is
John Hookes of Conway, son of the William Hookes who had
deserted the service of Archbishop Williams and attached
himself to Sir John Owen to the bitter end. The same tendency is to be seen in the disappearance of the militia
captains imported from Denbighshire and Montgomeryshire,
and in the return to power of moderates who had been on
earlier county committees but had gone to earth during the
' Barebones ' régime. The Protectorate, with its return to
' normalcy ' in so many directions was more to their taste,
and some of them now took up important positions under
Cromwell: John Glynne, his chief justice; Griffith Bodwrda,
established in a legal office through Glynne's influence;
William Foxwist of Caernarvon, a judge of Great Sessions;
Robert Coytmor, secretary to the navy; Maurice Wynn, home
from Hamburg and now receiver general for North Wales.
How much time such men as these were able to devote to
the county committee may be doubted; but as least they
helped to give it both public prestige and local standing.
Still more did the name (it can have been no more) of the
president of Cromwell's council of state, Henry Lawrence.

At the same time it was felt desirable to leaven the secular-
minded element on the committee with some of the few

convinced local Puritans like Richard Edwards and Morris Griffith, Henry Maurice's elder brother[1] (for surnames were still new in this family too, and while one brother took his father's name, the other took his grandfather's). Cornet Jeffrey Parry, an obvious choice, was in bad odour because he had just signed a ' remonstrance ' in which, under the somewhat startling title *A Word for God,* Vavasour Powell and some three hundred other Welsh Puritans denounced the Protectorate as a wordly compromise postponing indefinitely the hoped-for rule of the Saints.

The Protectorate meant also a return to parliamentary government of something like the old familiar pattern. For the first time since 1640 there was a general election. True, there were changes in the franchise, but the most significant of these was the suppression of the borough franchise and a corresponding increase in county representation, which was less liable to manipulation. There were also penal clauses which disfranchised Royalists who had not made their peace with the victorious side. Most of the Caernarvonshire gentry had done so long ago, and their correspondence at election time conveys much the same atmosphere as that of fourteen years back, with one important reservation — that in the background were the parliamentary garrisons ready to pounce in case of ' disorders '. The principal Caernarvonshire gentry who remained political outlaws were Sir John Owen — who, having escaped the gallows, was still living peacefully at Clenennau — and the two M.P.'s who had ' deserted ' their posts, William Thomas and John Bodvel. William Thomas, having come to terms with parliament after paying a fine which entailed the sale of some of his lands, died just after the Protectorate was proclaimed. John Bodvel, who had been more active for the king, got into deeper waters; his Puritan wife, with whom he had quarrelled bitterly, pursued him with relentless hatred; his distant kinsman Thomas Wynn of Boduan, whose mouth was watering for the estate, laid snares for him at every

[1] Wrongly identified in *Studies in Stuart Wales,* 159.

turn. In the end it was the personal intervention of Cromwell, a long-standing friend of Mrs. Bodvel's brother, that saved the estate from outright confiscation by Act of Parliament; Bodvel was also helped by the fact that his wife (against his wishes) had married their daughter to Robert, son of Lord Robartes, a high-ranking and immensely wealthy Cornish Roundhead, and that the bridegroom was a train-bearer to Cromwell at his installation as Protector.

Cromwell's first parliament met six months after this. Caernarvonshire played safe and sent up two men of official standing: Chief Justice Glynne and Colonel Thomas Madryn. The dissolution of this parliament after five months was followed by a widespread outbreak of plots. They extended to northern Powys, but Caernarvonshire was not seriously affected, although as a preventive measure Sir John Owen was confined to Chester gaol — to be released after six months at the intercession (among others) of John Jones. Cromwell's remedy was the brief but unhappy experiment of dividing the country into eleven military districts, each under control of a major general. Wales was under James Berry, a former clerk in a Shropshire ironworks and a man of a humanity and humour rare among his fellow-' commissars'; and the country remained quiet.

The second Protectorate parliament met in 1656 and evolved in the Humble Petition and Advice a new constitution which increased the independence of parliament, reintroduced a second (nominated) House, and would have turned the Protectorate into a hereditary monarchy (a step strongly urged by John Glynne), had Cromwell dared to offend old supporters by complying. The election to this parliament aroused more interest in Caernarvonshire than that of 1654. Colonel Madryn would have liked to be re-elected, but Robert Williams of Penrhyn, great-nephew to the Archbishop, stood against him with support from his father, from Edward Williams of Wîg (the sheriff to whose lot it had fallen to proclaim Cromwell as Protector), Robert Coytmor, and above all Chief Justice Glynne, who canvassed on his behalf all the leading men of the shire. Madryn had to accept

defeat — another victory for the old families over what
Dr. Richards[2] calls the 'military middle class' which had
ruled Wales during the Propagation era.

The chief justice was himself re-elected to the other
county seat, but as he had also been returned for Flintshire
(where he was now a considerable landowner through his
acquisition of the confiscated estates of the Royalist earl of
Derby), he opted for that seat, and recommended the Caernarvonshire electors to choose in his place Henry Lawrence,
which they duly did. Parliament in return appointed
Lawrence on to the Caernarvonshire assessment committee,
as we have already seen. John Glynne seems to have
'managed' the Caernarvonshire election to this parliament
in much the same way as the duke of Newcastle managed
eighteenth-century English elections. But Sir Owen Wynne
cannily declined to act as his local agent, on the specious
plea that he had not 'attended public assemblies in the
county' since the beginning of the war (this despite his
having been sheriff four years earlier!), and so was 'a
stranger to persons of quality there'; instead he persuaded
Edward Williams of Wîg to take over the distasteful job.
What a contrast from the electioneering zeal of his father,
the great Sir John!

Anglesey, until the Protectorate was on its last legs and
the Restoration in sight, consistently borrowed its parliamentary representatives from Caernarvonshire, failing to find
any native islander willing to act. In 1654 its members were
William Foxwist and George Twisleton, and in 1656 Twisleton's place was taken by Griffith Bodwrda, who although a
placeman was by no means a rubber stamp. His speeches,
which were frequent, are those of a man of culture, wit and
humanity, notably one in which he demolished the argu-
ments for persecution in a House thirsting for the blood of
James Nayler, the crazy Quaker 'Messiah'. He approved the
constitutional changes of the Humble Petition and Advice,
even the provision that the Protector should name his suc-

[2] *The Puritan Movement in Wales,* 94.

cessor, but put in a plea for greater financial control in the hands of parliament. The Protector's foreign policy was expensive, and soon the House had to appoint another set of county assessment committees. This time an even wider range of the Caernarvonshire gentry was included. Now that Prince Griffin was dead, his far more respectable younger brother William, who inherited, came on to the committee; so did Thomas Glynne's brother Edmund, the new master of Glynllifon; so both houses which had contested the county seat for the Long Parliament were back in politics. William Griffith even offered himself as sheriff in 1657, but was passed over in favour of Robert Williams of Penrhyn. William Glynne of Lleuar, Twisleton's father-in-law, was another member; in short, virtually all the old governing families were back.

The second Protectorate parliament came to an abrupt end in 1658, and preparations were in hand for summoning a third, with the prospect of something more nearly approaching government by consent, when Oliver died, passing on the reins of government to the son whom he had so unwisely nominated as his successor. At first all went smoothly. In Caernarvonshire a congratulatory address to the new Protector, urging him to continue his father's religious policy, was sent up with nineteen signatures, headed by that of Thomas Madryn. Ominously enough the rest were mostly unknown men or newcomers like Ellis Rowland and two of his fellow-ministers.

Early in 1659 Richard Cromwell ordered a general election, in which the borough franchise was restored and the county representation correspondingly decreased. In Anglesey this simply meant that Griffith Bodwrda switched over to the borough, leaving the shire to Colonel Twisleton; and it was no doubt Twisleton's influence as a military officer that procured the election for Caernarvonshire of his father-in-law William Glynne of Lleuar, leaving the restored borough representation to Robert Williams of Penrhyn, whose father — the sheriff of 1657 — was now flaunting a baronetcy conferred by the Protector. The election was not a quiet one. Richard Wynn of Gwydir, Sir Owen's son (and the preceding year's sheriff), reported how as he came from Caernarvon town hall after the polling he saw Sir Griffith Williams at the stair head and below him a ' great crowd ', with one sword drawn; more swords were drawn when Wynn tried to restore order, but the trouble, whatever it was, apparently simmered down. In the country at large, however, there was such lack of security that the drovers had again ceased to ply their trade, and there was ' no safety in sending money by Chester or Shrewsbury '.

Caernarvonshire's new member dutifully took his seat and kept Gwydir posted, as his predecessors had been wont to do, with the latest parliamentary news; but he did not relish his position. This was the occasion of his rueful outburst ' When a kingdom is tossed in a blanket, happy are those who are out of it '. He might have felt even more uneasy had he known what was happening in the background, where army officers were intriguing to get back their old power in alliance with the left-wing Puritans and doctrinaire republicans who had always hated the Protectorate. By early May they had got their way and had jockeyed both Protector and parliament out of power. But they were not ready to set up an open military dictatorship, still less would their republican allies have stood for it; so to give an appearance of legality they recalled the Rump, which after all had never been legally dissolved. For Caernarvonshire this meant Richard Wynn of Gwydir, and for the boroughs William Foxwist, both of them ' recruiters ' elected at the end of the war to fill the seats of the deceased Prince Griffin and the ' deserter ' William Thomas respectively. By July the air was so thick with rumours of plots and of intrigues between old Royalists, at home and abroad, and disgruntled ex-Round-heads and Cromwellians, that it was felt necessary to appoint new and more reliable militia committees. This time separate provision was made for each of the South Wales counties, but those of North Wales were lumped together under a single committee, on which Caernarvonshire was very thinly repre-

sented. The old county families who had so recently re-
entered politics — the 'neuters' as the faithful called them
— retired back into their lairs; the Wynns of Gwydir were
represented only by Maurice. Cromwellian officials like
Foxwist, Bodwrda and Coytmor are all left out, in company
with so old and influential a Roundhead swordsman as
Sir John Carter, whose knighthood, conferred by Oliver,
would hardly impress the new ruling powers. Jeffrey Parry,
having signed the anti-Cromwellian *Word for God* was
acceptable, and Madryn and Twisleton were too useful to
be dropped since they were ready to toe the line.

The new militia committees were appointed none too
soon; early next month the threatened risings broke out in
various parts of the country. The only one which at all
directly threatened North Wales was that headed by the
Cheshire ex-Roundhead Sir George Booth, in which many
of his fellow-Roundheads from north-east Wales took part,
including Thomas Myddelton. The heir to Gwydir, Richard
Wynn, came under suspicion of complicity, and spent part
of the autumn of 1659 in Caernarvon gaol. The whole episode
was over in three weeks, thanks to the promptitude of the
measures taken and the military skill of General Lambert,
who now began to think of himself as cast in the rôle of
another Cromwell, and even copied him to the extent of
once more turning out the Rump by military force. But there
were far too many would-be Cromwells, and the one with
the trump cards was General Monk, in command of the
crack regiment stationed in Scotland; when at the beginning
of 1660 he crossed his Rubicon — the Coldstream — into
England (thereby immortalising its name in the British
army), the die was cast.

Meanwhile in Caernarvonshire the sequestrators had got
busy with the estates of those who had backed Sir George
Booth. Madryn, at the head of them, became once more, as
he had been before Cromwell's rise to power, the local tyrant
who had to be 'courted' — and 'handsomely' at that — by
those whose estates were in danger. Richard Wynn was
home on parole in October, and by November he had a

certificate from Madryn and his fellow-commissioners for
sequestration — Richard Edwards, who had served as cornet
of horse under Lambert at the battle which quelled the
rising, together with Jeffrey Parry and two others — that the
estate was clear. At the same time the much more serious
case of Sir John Owen was under consideration. Released
from a three-weeks' incarceration in Beaumaris castle for his
part in an obscure rising the preceding year, he had served
in arms under Booth at the express invitation of the exiled
royal family. But before his fate could be decided, the wheel
of fortune had taken several more turns. A week before
Monk crossed his Rubicon, a splinter group of officers, in
collusion with the republicans, once again recalled the
Rump, and since cash was urgently needed if any sort of
government was to be carried on, new county assessment
committees were set up in January 1660. The most striking
changes in Caernarvonshire are the return of Sir Owen
Wynn and his son and of Griffith Bodwrda, and the dropping
of Thomas Madryn, who at long last seems to have failed to
adjust himself quickly enough to the new situation.

In the following month Monk reached London and prevailed on the Rump to readmit those members who had been
' purged ' at the end of 1648 to clear the way for the king's
trial and execution. This of course meant that it was only a
matter of time till the monarchy was restored; but in North
Wales those who had identified themselves with the rule of
the Saints made one last desperate bid to stave off this final
disaster. It was pointed out to Monk in February that the
principal strong points of North Wales — Beaumaris, Caernarvon, Conway, Denbigh and Powis castles — were still
in the hands of men of ' unsound and desperate principle '.
The report was not wide of the mark, for four of the five had
been signatories of the *Word for God*, and indeed the whole
strategy of the Saints at this crisis breathes of Vavasour
Powell. The governors of Powis and Caernarvon castles were
ardent disciples of his from Montgomeryshire; the command
of the six-county militia as organised to meet the threat from
Booth was vested in a third. Members of Morgan Llwyd's

Wrexham congregation ruled at Denbigh and Conway; Beaumaris was assigned to his intimate friend Colonel John Jones, and when Jones was whisked off to Ireland his place was taken by his kinsman Robert Owen of Dolserau, one of those products of Llwyd's evangelism in Merioneth who ultimately turned Quaker.

It was a bold and well-planned manoeuvre, but it missed fire. In March the restored Long Parliament appointed fresh militia committees in the shires to prepare the way for the Restoration. The six shires of North Wales were again treated as a unit, and their joint militia placed under the command of Sir Thomas Myddelton's son, since the father was in his place in parliament. Glynllifon was trebly represented on the committee, Penrhyn by Sir Griffith Williams and his son, and flanking them the heads of the houses of Lleuar and Melai — but not of Gwydir, which was unaccountably (but only temporarily) under eclipse. An active Royalist like Richard Griffith of Llanfair Isgaer sat cheek by jowl with a quondam ' hinderer ' of the royal cause like Griffith Jones of Castellmarch; placemen like John Glynne, William Foxwist and Griffith Bodwrda stood ready to take office under any government that would restore stability.

Four days after appointing this committee the Long Parliament dissolved itself, after ordering elections to what came to be known as the Convention Parliament. As in 1656, John Glynne was for the moment the key man in county affairs — a monarchist who, having failed in his attempt to convert the Protectorate into a new monarchy, now turned to the old as the only practical alternative. He sat for the shire, and his son William for the boroughs. Griffith Bodwrda, again representing Beaumaris, was one of the delegation which went over to Holland to invite the exiled prince home. For the tiny remnant of irreconcileables the game was up. Writs were out for the arrest of Robert Owen and half-a-dozen of his fellow-commissioners for the 1659 militia; Vavasour Powell and John Jones were already under lock and key; and on the very day the Convention Parliament met, Sir Griffith Williams and his son Robert were sitting as magistrates with Edmund Glynne of Glynllifon and Griffith Jones of Castellmarch to hear evidence that on the preceding day ' Thomas Madryn of Madryn (called Colonel Thomas Madryn)' had been seen leaving Madrun on horseback, apparently unarmed but with a servant, two ' foot men ' and two other companions, one of whom was his kinsman by marriage Jeffrey Parry of Rhydolion. They went through Pwllheli and across the Traeth into Merioneth, after which the story peters out. In little more than a month Charles II had come into his own, and Caernarvon gaol was full to bursting point with suspects whose fate will concern us in the next chapter.

So ended twenty years of being ' tossed in a blanket '. What marks did it leave on the county? Physically very few. There had been no great pitched battles, and the two sieges of Caernarvon and Conway had inflicted only minor damage. But it was during these years that the castles were last used in warfare, and it was from now on that they degenerated into romantic ruins — not through gunfire, but through neglect and abuse. Orders were issued by Monk to Sir John Carter for the dismantling of Caernarvon castle shortly before the king's return, and after the Restoration Carter was associated in the same task with Griffith Bodwrda and William Griffith. Fortunately for posterity neither order was carried out; probably the expense was too great. Conway was restored to its pre-war owner, Lord Conway, who proceeded to strip it of timber, lead and iron for his Irish property, meeting local protests with the bland assurance that the material was needed for the king's service. Once stripped in this way, the building soon fell into the ruinous state in which it remained until the nineteenth century. The membership of the last Commonwealth committee brings home to us how readily county society had slipped back into its old pattern. True, there were social changes at work, the effects of which will be noticed later, but these were only marginally connected with the Puritan Revolution.

Finally, how deep an impress did the Propagation make on the county? So far as it was an attempt to provide it with a Puritan parochial ministry, it had failed even before the Restoration reversed the stream. A Welsh-speaking ministry satisfying the demands of the Propagators or of Cromwell's Triers simply could not be found in sufficient numbers to go round, and they were left with the choice of either leaving parishes vacant (as tended to happen in the earlier days), or creating a new pluralism by grouping several parishes under a single incumbent — a frequent resort — or accepting candidates who from the strict Puritan standpoint were sub-standard theologically, academically or morally. A commentary on the first course is a petition signed by Sir Owen Wynn and Sir Thomas Myddelton in 1652 and claiming to represent 'many thousands' in the six shires of North Wales. This tells of vacant livings and lapse of the sacraments in many parishes since the Propagation Act. As to pluralism, for Henry Maurice to hold together the livings of Llannor and Deneio was no great matter — the churches are only some two-and-a-half miles apart and they had usually been treated as a unit; but if, as seems likely, he held Cricieth concurrently with them, that meant another eight miles, which did not help towards an effective ministry. Clynnog and Llanwnda, Ellis Rowland's parishes, were almost as far apart. That a certain measure of 'dilution' was accepted under the Protectorate is suggested by the frequency with which candidates rejected by the Propagation approvers were accepted or reinstated by Cromwell's Triers — not to mention the readiness of most of the Caernarvonshire incumbents to conform to the Prayer Book and episcopal rule after 1660. It is indeed likely that although the Prayer Book had technically been illegal since 1645 its use, if only from memory, survived at least in remote parishes much as in an earlier age 'popish' practices had escaped the vigilance of Tudor governments.

About the effects of the itinerant ministry it is less easy to speak with confidence. Clearly it made an appreciable impact, witness the survival of pockets of Dissent — small but very persistent — into the age of persecution. Negatively the impact is seen in the way Puritanism long remained associated in local memory with subversive politics and bullying militia captains — an association it took the early Methodists many years to live down. On the other hand it may be that the spiritual excitement to which the itinerants appealed in their open-air preaching to mass audiences aroused an appetite which was not satisfied again until Methodism came. There are certainly links, even if hidden links, between the age of the Propagation and the age of the Methodist revival. This is a question which will be considered later on.

Episcopacy, of course, had been banished with the Prayer Book in the course of the Civil War. William Roberts, the last of the pre-war bishops of Bangor and the only member of the Welsh episcopate to survive the war, lived in seclusion in his native Denbighshire during most of the period. The dean and chapter were dissolved, the episcopal manors confiscated; Colonel John Jones entered into negotiations for that of Gogarth — as an investment only, since he professed himself 'not much in love with such interest as holds up any burthensome power over the people'. What happened to the cathedral is uncertain; we cannot be sure how far the repairs that had to be undertaken after the Restoration, like those made necessary after the Glyn Dŵr revolt, were due to wanton damage, how far to mere neglect; and the allegation that the cathedral was used for stabling horses during the siege of Caernarvon is so much common form that it can be accepted only with considerable reserve. There was certainly a vicar of Bangor : he was there by 1652, probably by 1647, and the adjacent parish of Pentir was later added to his charge. He remained there till the Restoration, when he was transferred to Llanddeiniolen. And he must surely have held his services, with or without the Prayer Book, in the cathedral, since no other church appears to have existed in the city since early in the sixteenth century.

The dissolution of the cathedral chapter had other effects, for both the endowed grammar schools of the county were

under its government. Botwnnog school had ceased to exist
by 1656, and a petition was sent to the Council of State by
' Henry Morris ' (almost certainly the Henry Maurice who
was two years later presented to the livings of Llannor and
Deneio) that the endowments should be transferred to
Pwllheli, where the ' frequent meeting of godly persons . . .
would have a good influence on the youth of the place '. The
plea was reinforced by a trustee of the school, Henry Bodvel,
on the quite different but undeniable ground of the remoteness and inaccessibility of Botwnnog. Cromwell issued orders
for the removal of the school as suggested, but they never
appear to have been carried out, and after the Restoration it
was revived in its old situation, with the local rectors as
headmasters.

Friars school was fortunate in its headmaster, the Thomas
Meredith whom we have met as vicar of Bangor through all
the troubles. Meredith may not have been a man of strong
principle, but he was certainly a man of energy and drive.
The abolition of dean and chapter had deprived the school
of any legal means of recovering its rents, which had fallen
badly into arrears during the war. In the interval of peace
before the second Civil War broke out, Meredith, fortified
with a document signed by the all-powerful Thomas Madryn,
Sir William Williams of Vaynol and his brother, Thomas
Glynne and John Bodwrda, set off for London to represent
the ' distressed condition ' of the school and to seek a remedy,
invoking the aid of John Glynne, then recorder of London.
In consequence, a report on the school was presented to
parliament, and it was agreed that the dean and chapter in
their private capacities should continue to act as ' wardens
and governours of the said schoole '. So Friars remained in
being right through the ' distracted and Bedlam times '.

This was exceptionally generous treatment, in which one
cannot but suspect the hand of John Glynne. He had not
then fallen out of favour with the dominant faction, as he
was to do shortly afterwards on account of his opposition to
the trial of the king. Generally the old grammar schools were
frowned upon because of their episcopal associations, and

one of the purposes to which the Propagation Commission devoted the funds in its hands was the setting up of a grammar school under Puritan auspices in every market town of Wales. It is believed that over sixty of these schools were in fact established, but only forty can be identified, and half of these had petered out before the Restoration swept the rest away. One was in Caernarvon; nothing is known of it beyond the fact that the headmaster, Rowland Lloyd, had a salary of £15—£5 less than the headmaster of Friars received — and that it lasted only three years. The whole project was an interesting experiment in state education, not to be repeated till the nineteenth century; but like the rest of the work of the Propagation in Wales, it left nothing behind it but a memory and (for some) an inspiration.

## BIBLIOGRAPHY

The standard authority on Welsh Puritanism is T. Richards (*Puritan Movement in Wales*, 1920, *Religious Developments in Wales*, 1923). On the county committees see A. H. Dodd, ' Nerth y Committee ', in *Studies in Stuart Wales*. On John Bodvel see id. in *TCHS* 1945; on Friars school see Barber and Lewis, *History of Friars School* (1901) and W. Ogwen Williams in *The Dominican*, 1957, 27-50; and on the Propagation schools, T. Shankland in *Seren Gomer*, 1901, 326-8. The closing years of the Commonwealth in North Wales are described by A. H. Dodd in ' The background of the Welsh Quaker migration to Pennsylvania ' (*Jnl. of Merioneth Hist. and Rec. Soc.*, iii, 1958).

# VIII

## CAVALIER CAERNARVONSHIRE
### (1660-88)

ONCE the monarchy was back, the restoration of the old machinery of government, central and local, soon followed. So much of it had been left intact, with only the personnel transformed, and even here no drastic 'purge' was called for, since all but a few of those who had supported the late government had during the concluding months of anarchy come to see in the recall of the Stuarts the only escape from another and much more meaningless civil war. The Act of Indemnity and Oblivion, passed three months after the king's return, may have caused heartburnings to loyal Cavaliers who saw in it oblivion for loyalists and indemnity for traitors; but it materially helped to settle the country by reassuring all who took the oaths of allegiance and supremacy by a fixed date — and few were so rash as to decline — that unless specifically excepted in the Act they would not be called in question for past treasons. Apart from the county machinery, the municipal corporations were brought into line by an Act of 1663 invalidating all elections since 1648; the only Caernarvonshire borough where there is any record of this process is Nefyn.

Naturally the fear of renewed activity by the armed Saints continued to lurk in the background, and early in 1661 there broke out in London what has been called[1] 'a frenzied burst of religious mania' on the part of some thirty London fanatics goaded to revolt by the final collapse of their hopes

---

[1] Craik, *Life of Clarendon* (1911), ii, 118.

of the Saints' millenium. In normal times this would have excited little notice outside London, but seen against the only too recent past it created widespread panic, and was thought a serious enough menace to warrant the retention of Monk's regiment as the Coldstream Guards. The effects were soon felt in Caernarvonshire. On instructions from the privy council conveyed by the earl of Carbery (now lord president of Wales) the deputy lieutenants met at Caernarvon, and instituted a search for arms in the houses of all political suspects. Full enquiries were made into any rumours of seditious talk, even among illiterate labourers of Llŷn who were unable to sign their depositions; and the militia was kept under arms. It is significant that most of the suspects came from Llŷn and Eifionydd; altogether about a couple of dozen from these parts, many of them known later in the reign as haunters of conventicles, were found to possess one, two or even three cases of pistols — a fact that helps to explain the long-lasting suspicions of Dissent in the shire. Thomas Madryn soon cleared himself, and five years later was trusted with the office of sheriff; but nineteen political prisoners were in Caernarvon goal by the beginning of 1661. They included Richard Edwards of Nanhoron and Jeffrey Parry of Rhydolion, together with his corporal, Owen Jones, and a Gruffydd Jones of Clynnog of whom nothing is known but that he signed the congratulatory address to Richard Cromwell mentioned in the last chapter. Even Edmund Glynne of Glynllifon was questioned about disrespectful words he was alleged to have used about the Prayer Book. John Williams of Ty'n y coed was apparently out of the county, but a watchful eye was kept on his correspondence with Edwards and other local ' incendiaryes '.

What disturbed the authorities was that both Edwards and Williams had been in touch with Vavasour Powell, now in a London prison under suspicion of collusion with the London insurgents. However, the two Caernarvonshire suspects and most of their fellow-prisoners took the oaths of supremacy and allegiance so as to avail themselves of the Act of Oblivion. A search of Jeffrey Parry's house apparently produced nothing incriminating, nor did the arms he was believed to have hidden in a gorse patch come to light; Edwards remained in prison till about the middle of February, when representations from some of the local gentry (like Thomas Wynn of Boduan) — who strongly dissociated themselves from his principles but badly needed his legal services — procured his liberation on bail. Two years later evidence was produced that he and John Williams had again been in touch with Vavasour Powell in London, and both were clapped in prison there on orders from the government. There was, however, some doubt whether the evidence had not been faked, and the enquiry extended to Llŷn, where some of their old associates were called in to identify handwriting. In the end the prisoners were given the benefit of the doubt and freed again after ten weeks' confinement. Both returned to Llŷn to resume, the one his legal, the other his medical practice. But in 1665, for some reason which has not yet come to light, Edwards forfeited his recogisances and fled to Ireland; his house was searched once more, but with no result. After that, both characters fade out of the picture till 1672, when we shall meet them again in circumstances which make it clear that their principles had remained unchanged.

Side by side with the restoration of the monarchy went that of the Church; indeed the two were parts of the same process, carried out largely by the same agencies. But in the Church there was more to restore because more had been destroyed; bishops, deans and chapters gone, church fabrics neglected or damaged, far more extensive changes in personnel at the parochial level, and in Wales parishes themselves partly superseded by the itinerant system. But Bishop William Roberts was still alive and back in his see, and locally the basic structure had remained; the parish was in being, even if churchwardens were neglectful or non-existent, and Cromwell himself[2] had resisted as 'treacherous'

[2] Carlyle, *Cromwell* (ed. Lomas, 1904), ii. 538.

attempts by some of the Puritan extremists to eliminate tithes, which he called ' the root of visible Profession '. In Caernarvonshire the ejection of ' intruded ' ministers was much more a legal than a theological matter; it was for lack of legal title, or the possession of better title by another, that most of the nominees of the Propagation or the Triers were ejected — not for their refusal to conform to episcopacy and the Prayer Book. And the process proved a long and complex — sometimes a riotous one, because of the number of counter-claims.

Ellis Rowland at Clynnog is a case in point. Within three months of the king's return, the restored bishop instituted, on the nomination of the legal patron (the earl of Pembroke) a new vicar. But Ellis Rowland continued to hold services there until in December some of his own parishioners locked him out of church while his supplanter officiated. Undeterred by an attempt to connect him with the January ' plot ' by having him arrested and searched for arms, he actually brought a suit before the magistrates at Caernarvon in the following summer against his assailants, assuring them that he was ' conformable '; the magistrates in turn (impressed no doubt by his ' county ' connections) referred the matter to the bishop and ordered that meanwhile he should be left in peaceful possession. The bishop, whose definition of ' conformable ' would be more exacting than that of Rowland, rejected his plea, but seems to have made another appointment, if not two in succession; at any rate Rowland had to retire discomfited. It was also in 1661 that Henry Maurice had to make way at Cricieth for the pre-war incumbent; but this was a simpler matter : Maurice conformed and was given another living. For the time, Caernarvonshire Puritanism had to go underground, but we shall meet it again.

The more positive side of restoring the Church was also proceeding. The major tasks facing Bishop Roberts during the five remaining years of his episcopate were the restoration of the cathedral fabric and services, the reconstitution of the cathedral chapter, and in general the reassertion of episcopal authority throughout the diocese. Substantial progress had been made in all these directions before he died in 1665. Episcopal lands were restored (by Act of Parliament) and episcopal rights zealously safeguarded; much work was done towards remedying two decades of neglect of the cathedral fabric, and the bishop left in his will a further £100 towards restoring the choir. Griffith Williams, bishop of Ossory, who had been appointed absentee dean when his predecessor, Edmund Griffith, succeeeded to the bishopric, now recovered his post, but as he returned at once to his Irish see, Bangor was again left virtually without a dean. Other places in the cathedral chapter, however, were filled in the course of 1660. The new archdeacon of Merioneth, appointed within a couple of months of the Restoration, was Robert Morgan, a zealous churchman from Montgomeryshire who had been Bishop Roberts's chaplain before the war, and who now succeeded to the see on his death. Under the Long Parliament Morgan had been turned out of his livings, but he secured himself by purchasing the tithes of Llanddyfnan in Anglesey, where he remained till the Restoration, helping to draw up the county's declaration for the king in 1648, and in 1656 boldly preaching a funeral sermon in which he denounced the 'new and phantastick revelations' of the Saints.

In Robert Morgan the diocese found a man of character and courage, a stickler for episcopal rights who was prepared to stand up to the ever-recurrent attempt of the house of Gwydir to thrust unsuitable incumbents into livings in the diocese, and a zealous preacher in both English and Welsh. With the episcopate of Humphrey Lloyd, who succeeded in 1674, the work of restoration in the Church may be said to have been completed. He had been turned out of his vicarage of Ruabon under the Propagation, and the war had prevented him from taking up his appointment as chaplain to John Williams, archbishop of York. After the Restoration, having failed to dislodge Griffith Williams from the deanery of Bangor, he was given that of St. Asaph. Both there and later in his episcopate of Bangor he showed the utmost tenacity in defending the rights of the Church; but his

greatest achievement was to obtain for the first time by Act
of Parliament (in 1685) an earmarked revenue for the upkeep
of the cathedral fabric.

Meanwhile the re-establishment of the old civil *régime* in
the shire was proceeding apace. The 'establishment' as it
emerged at the Restoration consisted in three elements. First
there were the consistent loyalists who had stuck to their
principles at least to the point, shortly before the death of
Oliver, when the prospect of a Stuart restoration seemed to
have receded into dreamland and the most likely outcome
was the perpetuation of a new Cromwellian monarchy with
many familiar landmarks restored. The most consistent and
conspicuous loyalist was Sir John Owen, who stood high in
the county hierarchy till his death in 1666; and next to him
William Griffith of Cefnamwlch, who had not sought public
office during the Interregnum till 1657, and after the Restoration became, both in county affairs and (as will appear later)
in parliament, one of the staunchest pillars of monarchy and
Church. The Wynnes of Melai might also be added to this
list; Richard Griffith's record under the Protectorate was
more dubious, and he wondered whether he ought to 'sue
out a particular pardon' at the Restoration. He might perhaps more appropriately be classed with the 'collaborators'
who had taken no part in the revolution which abolished the
monarchy and episcopate and set up a republic, but were
prepared to co-operate fully once it became a *fait accompli*.
The most obvious examples are the Wynns of Gwydir, and
behind them were arrayed a fairly solid phalanx of the
country gentry.

Finally there were those who had risen to power as supporters of the new order, whether among the minor houses
like Madryn and Bodwrda, which had provided the county
with sheriffs since Elizabeth's day but never before risen to
parliamentary honours, or from outside the county, like
George Twisleton, who came in with the victorious army,
married the heiress of Lleuar, and a few months before the
Restoration inherited the estate through her on the death
of the last of the Glynnes, thus founding a new county

family. These soon made their peace with the restored monarchy; as a Merioneth Quaker, writing a quarter of a century later from his new home in Pennsylvania scornfully (and perhaps a little unfairly) put it, 'they . . . rather than run the hazard of their estate . . . take these oaths . . . which when they were in power they judge it really to be the marke of the beast that war'd against the Lamb'. Bodwrda, more flagrant than most of them, bought himself into favour by turning vulgar informer on the regicides, and finished up in a comfortable Irish job. Otherwise they dropped out of public life like Jeffrey Parry, and as Richard Edwards would have done had not his legal services been so much in demand; as it was he had to wait till after the Revolution of 1688 to attain to the office of sheriff. To the same general category belongs the new branch of Glynllifon now settled at Hawarden through the legal eminence of John Glynne. It was in this branch that the time-honoured Glynllifon nimbleness in jumping down on the right side of the fence was best displayed. After doubly representing Caernarvonshire in the Convention parliament, the Glynnes of Hawarden naturally transferred their interest to Flintshire politics; the parent branch faded into insignificance until, towards the end of the century (as will appear later) it was absorbed by the still nimbler house of Boduan and once more rose to a dominant place in the shire.

Such were the men who for the next generation manned the county bench and provided its sheriffs, and from among whom it found its representatives at Westminster. Until his death in 1674 Sir Richard Wynn was member for the shire, as he had been from the by-election of 1647 till the Protectorate. As with most of his family, his parliamentary duties were treated lightly. Almost the only committee in which he took part was on a measure which had been unsuccessfully backed by the Welsh M.P.'s forty years earlier — a Bill to restrain the importation of Irish cattle; this time the long struggle ended in victory. Far more effective was his borough colleague in the long-lived first parliament of the reign — the so-called Cavalier Parliament — William Griffith of Cefn-

amwlch. With him county politics at Westminster retained
something of the pre-war flavour of critical interest in public
affairs. Griffith sat on numerous committees, and he showed
in the House the same zeal against Dissenters in general, and
Quakers in particular, as characterised his conduct as magistrate and deputy lieutenant at home, where he was the chief
assailant of Richard Edwards in 1661. He was also vigilant
on local affairs. In 1663 he promoted a Bill to transfer the
Great Sessions from Conway to Caernarvon as more central.
John Wynne of Melai, who naturally found Conway more
convenient (but did not become member for Denbighshire
till the following year) told Sir Richard Wynn he feared the
Bill was going to go through; actually it never got past the
Lords; the transfer, in fact, did not take place till about 1793.

In general, however, the sense of a special Welsh ' interest '
in the House was fading away, either because members were
becoming less parochial in their outlook, or because the
sense of nationhood was at a low ebb, as it certainly was in
this period. Only rarely were Welsh members elected *en
masse,* as they had been in the past, to committees of
special concern to Wales. Even the sub-committee in
charge of the proviso in the Act of Uniformity for translating
the revised Prayer Book into Welsh had only one Welsh
member. Towards 1668 the whole tone of politics begins to
change. The honeymoon period of the king's return is over,
and new controversies begin to embitter relations both
between king and parliament and between rival groups in
the House. This, combined with the narrowing range of
membership, helped to throw politics into the hands of the
professional politician and what we may call by anticipation
the party organiser; the independent country member is
pushed more and more into the background. This naturally
had its reflection in Wales generally and particularly in a
poor and backward area like Gwynedd, unable, like some
of the more advanced regions of Powys or Morgannwg, to
participate in what was becoming a heavily-weighted
scramble for power and place. A suggestive contrast has

been drawn[3] between the pre-war members, 'conscious of their stake in the country and confident in their expanding acres ', whose 'traditional loyalty to the throne had from time to time been tempered by a will to criticise what they regarded as abuses, and a readiness to voice their grievances ', and those after the Restoration who 'were conscious only of their needs ' and ' could have confidence only in their wits '. From this point the parliamentary history of the shire ceases for the best part of a century to be of interest to posterity — as indeed it did to contemporaries at home.

It is time now to consider some of the new controversies that so changed the climate of politics. They concerned religion and foreign policy, both centring in the king's dealings with his cousin Louis XIV of France — in English eyes the embodiment of popery and arbitrary government. Suspicions of the character of these dealings, and fears for the Protestant establishment, grew apace from 1670 onwards, and opposition in the House of Commons developed into something more nearly approaching party organisation, with party labels, than had ever been known before — largely in response to a tighter organisation of the king's supporters, who were adroitly held together by the rewards and punishments at the disposal of his ministers. Public knowledge that the king's own brother and heir presumptive, the duke of York, was himself a papist, sharpened the opposition, and led to a movement for his exclusion from the throne or at least the drastic whittling down of his powers in the event of his succession.

Neither side showed much scruple in its campaigns. The opposition, or Country Party (eventually dubbed Whigs) did not shrink from appealing to the 'no popery' sentiments which never lay far below the surface, by endorsing wild rumours of a 'popish plot' which brought scores of innocent

[3] D. M. Elis-Williams, 'The Activities of Welsh Members of Parliament, 1660 to 1688' (see Bibliography), 43-4.

Catholic priests and laymen to the block in 1678. The king,
apart from gross deception of both parliament and ministers,
began his campaign for undermining both the Protestant
establishment and the legislative authority of parliament by
conceding to Catholic and Protestant Dissenters a measure
of freedom of worship embodied in a comprehensive Indulgence (congenial to his own native tolerance) which was in
effect a license to break the law. From the dissolution of the
Cavalier Parliament in 1678 through the three short parliaments that followed, party strife grew ever more acute, in
House and country alike, until the political atmosphere
recalled only too vividly the days of the Long Parliament of
Charles I. But Charles's son — a far subtler strategist — out-
manoeuvred the opposition, regained public opinion, and for
the last four years of his reign dispensed with parliament,
living in the main on his French cousin's bounty. Before
holding his last parliament (in loyal Oxford instead of tur-
bulent London), he had undertaken a comprehensive purge
of local government, especially the bench and the militia
(sheriffs were changed annually in any case) with a view to
disarming the opposition. In Wales the task was entrusted
to the new president, the marquess of Worcester (soon to be
rewarded with the dukedom of Beaufort); he got rid of
twenty-seven potential trouble-makers in the thirteen shires.

How did the Caernarvonshire gentry react to all this? In
parliament the shire was represented, from Sir Richard
Wynn's death in 1675, by Viscount Bulkeley and then his
brother Thomas. The Bulkeleys were firm adherents of the
court party; indeed a third brother, Henry, was master of
the king's household and eventually went into exile with
James II. In the boroughs it was different. William Griffith,
uncertain of his support in the coming election, had begun
canvassing the out-boroughs of Llŷn and Eifionydd (in itself
a significant symptom) a fortnight before the Cavalier Parliament was dissolved, but as it turned out, the electors chose
in his stead Thomas Mostyn, son and heir of the great Flintshire baronet Sir Roger but living during his father's lifetime
on the family's Caernarvonshire estate of Gloddaeth. He too

was a staunch loyalist; his father had been one of Charles I's most devoted Welsh supporters, and the son claimed — no doubt justly — to be 'free from a disloyall thought, much more word or action'. Yet like so many of the Welsh Cavalier squires he was a firm Protestant (despite his marriage into a Cheshire recusant house), and he could not but be disturbed by the current threat to the Protestant establishment. While opposing Exclusion in the parliament of 1679, he ventured to suggest certain safeguards for the Church in the event of a popish succession. This did not endear him to the court, and he had also put himself wrong with Worcester by offering unpalatable advice to the marquess's recusant sister, Lady Powis (the future governess of the Old Pretender) about keeping her hands off the Protestant establishment in Montgomeryshire. So he was dismissed from his deputy lieutenancy and his militia commission — a bitter blow, not lightened by the fact that his companion in disgrace was (of all people!) Griffith Bodwrda, whose death in Dublin the preceding year had apparently not come to Worcester's notice. There were three replacements: Sir Robert Owen, Sir John's grandson; William Glynne, the borough member in the Convention; and an otherwise unknown Randolph Wynne. William Griffith of Cefnamwlch, who was already in office, was a safe loyalist and so was left undisturbed.

In spite of it all, the Caernarvonshire electors sent Mostyn back to Westminster in 1681. Sir Robert Owen had a tougher fight in Merioneth; he was a strong court party man (or Tory, to use the new nickname), high in the favour of the king and Worcester and — unswerving Anglican though he was — a supporter of the duke of York. This told against him with those whom a friend of his dubbed the 'young and ignorant', who were defying all precedent by allowing politics to sway them against 'an honest worthy Gent'. The very number of contests, the sheaf of disputed results that came before the House in the years following 1678, and the whole tone of the correspondence of the gentry at election time, speak volumes for the heated atmosphere which prevailed all over the country once the 'no popery' scare had been raised. Happily the scare was too remote here to find vent in a blood-bath such as that which disgraced parts of South Wales at the height of the 'popish plot' panic; the total of recusants in the shire was reckoned in 1676 at forty-two, thirty of them (inevitably) in Creuddyn, where some at least of the Pughs of Penrhyn still adhered to their ancestral faith — a very different matter from the 540 of Monmouthshire, where the panic was severest and cruellest.

Of greater significance to religion in the shire were the effects of the Indulgence, which brought Dissent into the open. That it had persisted underground is made clear by the readiness with which advantage was taken of the Indulgence to license houses for Dissenting worship in 1672. One was the home of Ellis Rowland, who after his ejection lived in Caernarvon, and in 1666 had been busy distributing there a Welsh translation of one of Baxter's works. Another was Ty'n y coed, the home of John Williams (described here as 'Congregational teacher'); he procured a second licence for the same purpose for Bodfel House. This house, as will be shown later, had passed after the death of John Bodvel to his son-in-law Robert Robartes, whose father, a member of Charles II's privy council, had been a consistent supporter of toleration. No fewer than three houses in the parish of Llangybi were registered, two belonging to the brothers Rowland (describing themselves as 'yeomen'), who remained among the principal props of Dissent in the neighbourhood in the ensuing days of persecution; for the Indulgence was withdrawn under parliamentary pressure within a year.

It may be doubted whether the Indulgence alone would have produced this mild but significant upsurge of Dissent in Llŷn and Eifionydd had it not been accompanied by a resurgence of the itinerant evangelism of the Propagation period. In 1671 Henry Maurice, who since 1660 had ministered in a succession of English parishes as a respectable conformist, suddenly renounced his orders and in the following year, not long after the issue of the Declaration but before advantage had been taken of it in Caernarvonshire, he set out on a missionary tour of North Wales. He was usually refused the use of the parish church, but preached sometimes in the churchyard (as at Llanarmon), more often in the houses of sympathisers, mainly at Pwllheli. He also stayed with Richard Edwards at Nanhoron, with John Williams at Ty'n y coed (reproaching him for his long neglect of preaching) and with some of his own relatives. Maurice then left for South Wales, the scene of his main missionary activities for the rest of his life; but four years later he persuaded the distinguished South Wales Presbyterian and controversialist James Owen to undertake a preaching tour in the north. By now John Williams was dead, and the leadership of Caernarvonshire Dissent had passed from Llŷn to Eifionydd in general and Llangybi in particular. Pwllheli, as a busy market town, was too much in the public eye now that persecution had been resumed, whereas Llangybi, it has been pointed out,[4] must then have been 'a desolate uncleared land of marsh and brushwood'. Yet as it turned out, James Owen's congregation at Llangybi included two spies (as well as three genuine worshippers) from Clynnog, who informed the authorities and brought the law down on their companions. The congregation fled; there was a scuffle and some 'effusion of blood', and the help of the militia was sought.

After that we hear no more of the matter, but subsequent encounters with the law, right up to the Toleration Act, give evidence of the continued existence of a scattered body of Dissenters in south Caernarvonshire, drawing its adherents from a coastal strip extending from Cricieth to Llanengan and as far north as Clynnog — in fact a typical early ' gathered church ', after the pattern first set at Llanfaches in 1638, ignoring parish boundaries and meeting at any convenient central spot where shelter could be found. According to a census taken in 1676 there were only just over sixty avowed

---

[4] Richards. *Wales under the Penal Code,* 24.

Dissenters in the whole shire, including seven from Caernarvon; not many more than the total of Catholic recusants, but with this difference: the recusants were a dwindling remnant, spiritually starved for lack of available priests, whereas the Dissenters escaped this disability by their literal acceptance of the Lutheran doctrine of 'the priesthood of all believers'.

The Caernarvonshire Dissenters had revealed themselves as men of the church militant. In Merioneth many of the disciples of Morgan Llwyd, after the last attempt to bring about the rule of the Saints by force had broken down, turned to the more peaceable doctrines of George Fox, and Quakerism became a force in the religious life of the shire. Fox himself had preached in Caernarvon ('the City like a Castle') in 1657, arriving, as Wesley was so often to do in later years, from Dolgellau; but he made little impression. Only after the Restoration are we given a brief and tantalisingly blurred glimpse of Quakerism in Caernarvonshire, and then it appears — as might be expected — in that corner of Llŷn which had seen the rise of earlier branches of left-wing Puritanism, and in close association with the Quakerism of Merioneth. In 1672 a Quaker tract — in English, surprisingly — was published by one Evan Jones, of Llanengan; a few years later we learn of a group of eight Quakers from the same parish, one of whom — John Roberts — became acquainted with Fox's disciples in Bala and Dolgellau, found a wife among them, and in 1683 joined in their emigration to Pennsylvania, where he became a magistrate and a member of the legislative assembly. A few comrades from Llŷn went with him. Shortly afterwards another Quaker meeting, this time a little north of Aberdaron, was pounced on, and the dozen worshippers taken before the nearest magistrate, Hugh Bodwrda, and fined. They came from a range of adjacent parishes stretching to Llanbedrog, and appear to have been mainly humble folk, except for one man of substance who had joined them from Dolgellau. This is almost all we know of Caernarvonshire Friends, but it was probably they who inspired a group of ten from the same neighbourhood in their refusal to pay Church rates in 1679; one is definitely described as a Quaker, but none of the names figure in the other prosecutions.

Another of the developments of the Commonwealth period to which the Restoration had put a stop was also revived during these years of strange contrasts. The supposed spiritual ignorance of the Welsh was still a matter of concern to English Puritans, the more so since the collapse of the Propagation grammar schools, and in 1674 Thomas Gouge, an ejected London minister, with the help of some wealthy Puritan merchants and the support of a few distinguished Anglican parsons of what we should call the ' Broad Church ' school, founded the Welsh Trust to carry on this work by the setting up of schools and the dissemination of religious literature. The schools were to be conducted in English, because even the work of the Welsh itinerants in the Propagation era had never quite convinced their English brethren that ' the more speedie attaining of our English tongue ', as a Puritan writer had put it fifty years earlier, was not a necessary basis for reclaiming ' the ignorant country of Wales ' and others in the same darkness from ' their exceeding ignorance of our holy God and of all true and good learning '. The schools were to be for boys and girls; all were to be taught to read, and the boys to write and ' cast accompts ' as well; and the parish was expected to provide supervision and half of the local costs. On books the policy was more liberal, thanks to the presence at the time in London of Stephen Hughes, who had also been ejected from his living and had resumed his work of translating religious classics into Welsh. The Trust had begun operations in Caernarvonshire by 1675, despite the coolness of Bishop Humphrey Lloyd, who like many other staunch Anglicans feared the children might be brought up with what Judge Jeffreys called ' the twang of fanaticism in their noses '. All the same, the vicars of Conway and Caernarvon sponsored schools under the Trust in their respective parishes, the former with thirty-six pupils (but only half that number in 1678), the latter with twenty. Similar schools at Llanllechid

and Llandygái, each with twelve children, had as manager
Sir Robert Williams of Penrhyn.

The free distribution of Bibles was another activity.
Mercers' shops (where books were generally sold) were ransacked everywhere for Welsh Bibles, but only 32 copies of
the whole Bible and 479 New Testaments could be found;
so a new edition of eight thousand was printed and distributed, along with translations of such works as Bishop
Bayly's *Practice of Piety* and Richard Allestree's *Whole Duty
of Man*. Nearly two hundred books went to the four places
where schools were opened, and over two hundred more to
parishes in Uwchgwyrfai and Eifonydd (Llanllyfni, Llanwnda, Cricieth and Llanystumdwy) where these could not
be set up. From about 1680, however, the work languished;
subscribers fell off, especially after Gouge's death in 1681;
parishes withdrew their co-operation; above all, the use
made of Dissent by the country party in the political storms
of the following years gave the Trust a bad name. But it
had pointed the way for future, more lasting experiments in
the same direction, which will concern us later.

Charles II died in 1685, and after all the Exclusion fury
his brother succeeded not only peacefully, but with acclaim.
The story of how he forfeited this initial popularity belongs
to general history, and need not be repeated here. In James's
one and only parliament Caernarvonshire was still represented by Thomas Bulkeley; the borough member was his
son-in-law John Griffith of Cefnamwlch, son of the county
member in the Cavalier Parliament, but he appears to have
died in the course of the session. Both were silent spectators
of the breach between king and parliament which began
within six months of the opening of session and provoked
the king a week later into a succession of prorogations lasting
until the Houses were finally dissolved in the summer of
1687, when preparations were begun for summoning a new
parliament. But the king was determined that this should
be a submissive one, and with that end in view he set about

a purge of local government designed to get rid not only of avowed opponents of royal policy but of all who would not pledge themselves to positive co-operation, and to replace them on the one hand by his own co-religionists, on the other by Dissenters bound to him (he fondly imagined) by favours rendered, and ready to join him in bringing low the Church which had persecuted them.

A month or so after the dissolution of parliament he set the machinery going, first by calling in the charters of boroughs so as to have them remodelled on lines which would give the right bias in their government; then by ordering the lords lieutenant in the shire to question magistrates and deputy lientenants on their readiness to promote the return to parliament of men who would support there the policy the king was now pursuing on his own authority — the undermining of Anglican supremacy by the removal of religious tests for office and by an Indulgence for worshipping outside the establishment; finally the compilation for each shire of lists of Dissenters suitable to fill gaps in the bench of magistrates. For Caernarvonshire none of this amounted to much. There is no record of interference with borough charters except at Conway, where matters never got beyond the initial steps. The only Dissenter who could be suggested for the magistracy was Richard Edwards, and in the end he had to wait for promotion till after the Revolution. No other Dissenter in the shire could attain to the £100 qualification for office; the ' preaching cornet ' was dead, and his son, who now called himself Love Parry, was a loyal Anglican who had served as sheriff under Charles II and was no friend to any Indulgence for those of his father's faith. And when in the autumn of 1687 the duke of Beaufort, as lord lieutenant of all the shires of Wales, summoned to Ludlow the key men from each of them — three hundred in all — fewer than half turned up, and those who did showed scant enthusiasm for the royal design.

The parliament planned for the end of 1687 never met, and in the following year events moved rapidly towards a crisis: the trial and acquittal of the seven bishops (including

Lloyd of St. Asaph but not Lloyd of Bangor); the birth of an heir, threatening the perpetuation of a Catholic monarchy; finally in November the landing of William of Orange on the invitation of a group of malcontents. Even before he had landed, three offers reached Beaufort from Caernarvonshire and Merioneth of help in raising local forces to resist the invasion. That the contemporary Pugh of Penrhyn, who shared the king's religion (and in the end died fighting for him in Ireland) should have been one is not surprising; but Sir Robert Owen, who volunteered to raise five hundred men, had been consistently snubbed by the king: he had been refused his grandfather's office of vice-admiral of North Wales, and had only belatedly scraped in as sheriff of Merioneth after another appointment had been cancelled. And Thomas Mostyn, the third volunteer, still felt the humiliation he had suffered under Charles II. But the king, after massing an army near London and bringing reinforcements in from Ireland, decided in the end on flight, having already declined the offers of the Gwynedd loyalists.

With the king's flight in December the maintenance of law and order became the most urgent issue. The Irish soldiers the king had brought over awakened memories of how Charles I had resorted to the same expedient, and when the country was left with no certain government, panic rumours of Irish invasion spread from London to the remotest parts. Sir Robert Owen, so far from raising a regiment for the king, had his work cut out to keep order in Merioneth, where a mob in Dolgellau seized arms, broke open the prison, and declared that neither gaoler nor sheriff could any longer claim authority. In Caernarvonshire Creuddyn was as usual looked on as the danger spot. Shortly before Christmas the resident magistrates, Thomas Mostyn and Robert Wynne of Berthddu, left to their own resources, sent out scouts to ascertain the truth about the Irish, and resolved to await their report before ' raising the country ' or taking any further measures beyond the precaution of disarming local recusants. A search of Penrhyn Creuddyn for this purpose produced only the arms of a single foot soldier (for

SIR JOHN OWEN OF CLENENNAU (1600-1666)

PLATE X

CONWAY CASTLE, 1749

PENMAEN-MAWR, 1750

PLATE XI

PLATE XII

BISHOP HUMPHREY HUMPHREYS (1642-1712)

which Pugh was liable) and one other sword, but the constable and his men took occasion to deface the private chapel which Pugh had recently repaired. Elections to the long-delayed parliament (now a Convention only, since there was no king to call it) followed in January, when the last Sir William Williams of Vaynol was elected for the shire and Sir Robert Owen — who would also have liked the county seat but entered the field too late — contented himself with the boroughs. The Convention declared William and Mary joint sovereigns, and Caernarvonshire took it all quietly. The Bloodless Revolution was over.

On the other hand, a far more vital revolution had been imperceptibly changing the face of the local society during the years between the restoration of Charles II and the 'abdication' of his brother. This was the slow concentration of wealth into the hands of a narrowing group of families, and the corresponding depression of those below them in the social scale. The tendency was nation wide, and in some regions the Civil War was at least a contributory factor. The richer Cavaliers were able to escape the worst effects of parliamentary sequestrations by feeing a good lawyer like John Glynne (who made a handsome fortune that way) and often to recoup their losses in the king's service by exploiting the minerals on their estates (like the Mostyns in Flintshire) or by compensation in the form of pensions and sinecures — one of the factors which helped to turn post-Restoration politics into a scramble for jobs. Smaller men to whom this course was not open for lack of capital were often permanently impoverished.

This did not happen on any appreciable scale in Caernarvonshire because of the general defection to Parliament in 1646. Sir John Owen, the most heavily penalised, could well afford his fine, for he had inherited the great fortune made by his father, John Owen of Bodsilin, in the service of Sir Francis Walsingham, while his mother was heiress to the most important estate in western Caernarvonshire; and the Restoration had come just in time to save his remaining fortune from the penalties of joining Booth's revolt. On the other hand the Thomases of Aber and Coed Alun never recovered the position they had held in county society before the war; they ceased to rank among the 'parliamentary families', and not till nearly the end of the century did any of them again fill the office of sheriff. This, however, is attributable less to the war (for William Thomas's fine had been reduced by the sequestrators on the ground of his already 'low condition') than to a ruinously expensive election and perhaps the shouldering of public office by him and his forbears oftener than their resources could stand. John Bodvel was hit hard by parliamentary exactions, but the family fortunes were secured by his daughter's wealthy marriage.

It does not appear, then, that any of the Caernarvonshire gentry were substantially reduced in fortune by losses in he king's service, so for the causes of this growing gulf between greater and lesser gentry we must look beyond the Civil War into economic factors common to the whole country, and still imperfectly understood. In those days of pre-scientific agriculture on the one hand, and on the other of growing luxury in every direction, it was becoming increasingly difficult to live as a gentleman from landowning only, without some of those extraneous aids which only the wealthy could command : lucrative matches, good jobs under government, overseas investments and the like. The smaller gentry, eager to follow suit, fell to mortgaging their slenderer resources till, too often, they lost their freeholds and sank into the class of tenant farmers — hence, in part, the number of farmhouses dotted round the county which bear unmistakeable marks of old gentry residences.

A Welsh victim of this process in 1675 spoke of himself as 'swallowed up by the great Leviathan of our laws and lands' — a telling phrase, for the land legislation of the Restoration period, with its facilities for entails and family settlements, undoubtedly helped to widen the gulf. Landlordism was becoming big business and as such addicted to the seventeenth-century equivalent of 'take-over bids', but with the marriage market rather than the stock market as its chief agency. The more sinister side of this is illustrated in the activities of Thomas Wynn of Boduan, the kinsman and evil genius of John Bodvel. It will be remembered how when the Bodvel estate was in jeopardy at the end of the Civil War, Wynn schemed to seize the prize for his branch of the family, but was thwarted by Cromwell. He had not shot his last bolt. When a second son was born to Bodvel's daughter, the colonel and his wife were reconciled, and Bodvel willed the estate to this grandson, whom he planned to have brought up as a Caernarvonshire gentleman, speaking the language and living on the estate. But Wynne got his kinsman once more into his clutches at a time when he was desperately sick in mind and body, cajoled him into substituting a will making his own son heir to the estate and the family name — and would have succeeded had not the Robartes purse been long enough to stand a chancery suit and a private Act revoking the second will. So Bodfel House passed to the colonel's grandson; but the second part of his plan remained unfulfilled. When Lord Robartes (whom Charles II had made earl of Radnor) died in 1685, the estate and title passed unexpectedly to Bodvel's son-in-law through the early death of both his father and his elder brother. The Caernarvonshire estate became a mere minnow beside this Triton. Instead of the marriage with the heiress of Gwydir which had been proposed for the young grandson, he found his partner in England; Bodfel House was let to tenants, and the only surviving link with Caernarvonshire was the colonel's former governorship of Caernarvon castle (carrying with it the titular mayoralty of the borough), which remained as a sinecure in the family till late in the century. A more successful take-over bid — crucial in the history of the shire — by Wynn's grandson will be dealt with in a later chapter.

A much more important Caernarvonshire house came under 'remote control' from England when Mary Wynn, the heiress of Gwydir whose hand had been sought for the

heir of Bodvel, married instead (in 1678) a Lincolnshire
magnate, Lord Willoughby de Eresby, later duke of Ancaster.
The house became more of a museum of curios than a
family mansion, until — much reduced in size — it was let
out to tenants in the eighteenth century and eventually
gutted by fire. Clenennau was already going the same way.
After the death of Sir John Owen in 1666, the family resided
chiefly on their far more accessible Shropshire property of
Brogyntyn or even at Glyn Cywarch in Merioneth, with
occasional visits to Clenennau during the next quarter of a
century,[5] during which it was doubtless in the hands of a
steward or bailiff; then the block Sir John had added to the
original fifteenth-century hall was adapted as a farmhouse
and the rest of the extensive group of buildings fell into
decay.

In this decline of stately homes into humdrum farmhouses
the effects of the concentration of wealth are most obvious
to the eye. The age of the Tudors had seen the proliferation
of manor houses as junior branches of the family hived off
for themselves; the process is now brought into reverse. We
are apt to lay all this at the door of modern taxation; actually
it had begun even before the Restoration. When the last of
the Owens of Plas Du had to sell out in 1617, Sir Thomas
Myddelton bought it (and doubtless let it to tenants) as a
speculation. John Williams considered taking it off his hands
when he was bishop of Lincoln; Sir John Wynn (who also
nibbled at it) was advised that even at a cut price a place
so much 'in a corner and out of the world' was a bad
bargain. About the middle of the century it was possibly the
birthplace of a future bishop of Bangor, John Evans; but his
origins are obscure and his family certainly did not rank
among the great gentry of Caernarvonshire. Similarly with
the medieval hall of Cochwillan: the Williamses preferred
the newer Elizabethan mansion of Vaynol, and sold the old
place in 1620 to the earl of Pembroke; and when John

---

[5] RCAM *Caernarvonshire*, ii. 67 says Sir John was the last of the family
to live there, but a letter in the Brogyntyn collection (NLW, 1549) shows
his grandson there in 1689.

Williams bought it back into the family a few years later, the use he made of it is probably indicated in the name by which it has gone locally in quite recent time: 'Archbishop Williams's barn'. At Llanfairfechan, where the Bulkeleys were principal (almost sole) landowners, the *plas* from which they had edged out the old local family of Roberts was similarly let to tenants when Thomas (later Viscount) Bulkeley unexpectedly inherited Baron Hill from his nephew in 1640.

Whether the abandoned mansion was let to tenants or left in the hands of a bailiff or steward to keep it going for rare family visits, the ultimate effect was the same: superfluous wings abandoned, allowed to decay and eventually demolished, and the reduced status of the house reflected in its diminished size. The effect of the concentration of wealth is seen also in the changing character of farmhouses. It has recently been pointed out[6] that those which the small squires of Tudor and early Stuart days built for themselves often showed a loving attention to the detail of internal craftsmanship which we miss in their successors built for the occupation of tenant farmers.

Apart from these visible traces, there were important political aspects to this concentration of wealth. Membership of parliament, for example, was becoming more expensive as sessions grew longer and more frequent, and so provided an excuse for long seasons in town; fewer and fewer could afford it. During the hundred-and-twenty years from the Act of Union to the Restoration sixteen families shared the representation of Caernarvonshire, and sixteen (some of them the same) the boroughs; during the following century the numbers dwindled to five and eight respectively. An election like that of 1620, when a group of smaller squires was able successfully to challenge an attempted monopoly of representation, was no longer thinkable. And this little county oligarchy found itself increasingly linked to the English families with which it associated, whose tastes it

[6] P. Smith in *Agrarian Hist. of England and Wales* (see above, ch. i), iv, 773.

shared and into which it so often married, rather than with its neighbours at home. It is chiefly during this period that the greater gentry ceased to speak Welsh, and the survival of the language (as more than a *patois* of the market place) came to depend on the small squire, yeoman and farmer to whom ' town ' meant the nearest market place and ' education ' the local grammar school. A few — like Sir John Owen's son Robert, patron of the most notable of the many Royalist rhymesters of Wales, Huw Morus, — still clung to the custom of retaining a household bard; others, like Thomas Mostyn of Gloddaeth, were assiduous collectors of Welsh poetry; but what had been common in the earlier part of the century was now exceptional, even in Gwynedd, where it had survived longest.

The Restoration restored much, but there was much that could never be restored. As so often happens after revolutions, dreams of a return to the ' good old days ' proved to be largely an illusion; life in Caernarvonshire grew more and more unlike what it had been before the Civil War.

### BIBLIOGRAPHY

Part II of Richards, *Religious Developments in Wales* (see chap. vii. above) is useful on secular as well as religious aspects of the Restoration; see also A. H. Dodd, ' Caernarvonshire and the Restoration ' (*TCHS* 1950). The standard accounts of the rise of Dissent are in Richards, *Wales under the Penal Code* (1925), *Wales under the Indulgence* (1928), ' Richard Edwards of Nanhoron ' (*TCHS* 1947), ' Henry Maurice (*Cofiadur* 1928); see also W. Gilbert Williams, ' John Williams, Ty'n y coed ' (id.), and Bob Owen, ' Independents in Caernarvonshire ' (*TCHS*, 1945). The Welsh M.P.'s of the period are fully dealt with in D. M. Elis-Williams, ' The activities of the Welsh Members of Parliament, 1660-1688 ' (MS. thesis, U.C.N.W. Library). On Welsh politics of the period generally, see A. H. Dodd, *Studies in Stuart Wales*, 177-234, and ' Tuning the Welsh Bench, 1680 ' (*Nat. Lib. of Wales Jnl.*, vi. 1950); and T. Richards, ' Declarasiwn 1687 ' (Cymdeithas Hanes Bedyddwyr Cymru, *Trafodion* 1924). On the Welsh Trust, M. G. Jones in *Bull. of Bd. of Celtic Studies* (ix. 1938), and J. Cornish, *Life of Firmin* (1780), 31-6. General social conditions in Wales during the period are discussed in A. H. Dodd, ' The landed gentry after 1600 ' (*Wales through the Ages*, ed. Roderick, ii. 1960, 78-85).

# IX

# POLITICAL AND ECONOMIC
# STAGNATION (1688-1780)

## A. POLITICAL AFFAIRS

FOR nearly a century after the Revolution of 1688 Caernarvonshire was politically and economically stagnant. To thread our way through the politics of the age, it is necessary first to take a glance at the dwindling group of county families which shared political power in the shire and its boroughs; for the consolidation of estates that had been so marked a feature of the age of the Restoration was continuing and even accelerating. Almost every one of the families that had dominated Caernarvonshire under the Tudors and Stuarts was affected by the process, usually through failure of male heirs. Hyde Hall the topographer has a simple but sweeping explanation for this: the women were sober; the men drank themselves into an early grave! Look first at Penrhyn, the premier family of early Tudor days: already mutilated to meet the needs of Sir Griffith Williams's six sons, the estate passed in 1684 to co-heiresses who married into England, and until, nearly a century later, the ' moieties ' (including Cochwillan) were reunited through marriage and purchase, Penrhyn faded out of the political scene.

It has already been shown how in 1678 Gwydir, for default of male heirs, became an appanage of a great Lincolnshire house. But the baronetcy conferred by James I could not be transmitted through females; it was continued in a junior branch, founded by the first Sir John's younger son Henry, who settled (on profits made at the bar) at Rhiwgoch in Merioneth, and so gave the family an important footing in the neighbouring shire. As Henry's son John, later the fifth baronet, could not inherit Gwydir, his father arranged for him a marriage to the heiress of a Denbighshire estate of which he said, when he went to spy out the land soon after the Restoration, that for situation he had ' not seen its equal in Wales '; this was Watstay, now renamed Wynnstay. He did not think so highly of the house, but the new owner soon set to work remoulding it nearer to his heart's desire. Sir John lived to be ninety-one. Naturally his main interests were in Denbighshire and Merioneth, but from the age of seventy to that of eighty-six (when he was totally blind) he represented successively Caernarvon boroughs and county in parliament. He died childless, but he willed his estate (and his family name) to a distant kinsman, Watkin Williams, grandson of the Sir William who had been Charles II's speaker and James II's solicitor general. Watkin Williams was heir in his own right to another baronetcy and a vast complex of territories in most of the shires of North Wales, and Wynnstay became, so to speak, the Tory headquarters for the whole area during the next century and a half.

William Griffith of Cefnamwlch died in the year of the Revolution, but not before he had dug the family in politically and socially by marrying his son to a daughter of Baron Hill. A succession of early deaths in the family, however, put it out of politics for a quarter of a century. At Castellmarch, on the death of Griffith Jones (the victim of the ' kidnapping ' of 1650 who lived to promote the Restoration), another line ended in co-heiresses. A strong bid was made by Vaynol for absorbing the estate by a double marriage of Sir William Williams (the Cromwellian sheriff) and his younger brother, to the two heiresses. And Castellmarch did indeed become a farm on the Vaynol estate; but Vaynol itself soon ceased to rank, for several generations, among the governing houses of Caernarvonshire. The last baronet — another Sir William Williams — died childless in 1696, having made an eccentric will (drawn up, it was said, by a shady lawyer when the baronet was in his cups), leaving the whole estate to the crown after providing life interests for some west country acquaintances of his: a noted duellist who had recently fought with his fellow M.P. Thomas Bulkeley in Hyde Park, and his two sons. William III granted the reversion of the estate to John Smith, a Whig politician in office, and it was on his descendants the Assheton Smiths, that it eventually devolved. But they did not come to live at Vaynol for century or more. Fortunately the interim occupants, whoever they may have been, did not find the house of unmanageable size, and it was left intact even after the Assheton Smiths had built themselves a more modern mansion.

Bodwrda was another of the old Caernarvonshire families that lost its separate identity through the failure of male heirs towards the end of the seventeenth century; in this case the estate was absorbed by marriage into the Coytmor inheritance at the eastern end of the shire. But the days of the Coytmors as a county family were also numbered: before the middle of the next century this estate too had devolved on a heiress, who married into the Pughs of Penrhyn Creuddyn. Her husband sold Bodwrda to the still flourishing Edwardses of Nanhoron. To round off the story of this thinning down of the old families it should be added here that her son, the last of the Pughs of Penrhyn (no longer a recusant family), having reasserted the dignity of his ancient house by serving as sheriff in 1776, sold Penrhyn Creuddyn and died childless. The Madrun inheritance had suffered this fate at a much earlier date. Colonel Thomas Madryn's son and namesake died childless in 1688, and his younger brother, who then inherited, sold the estate to an Anglesey lawyer, Owen Hughes, whose legendary wealth gave him the nickname ' Yr Arian Mawr '. It also enabled Hughes to buy a way into the county families of both Anglesey and Caernarvonshire for the children of his two sisters (for he had none of his own), thereby putting several of these impoverished gentry families on to their feet. It was

by these means that Madrun, in the second half of the
eighteenth century, eventually came into the hands of the
great-grandson of Jeffrey Parry of Rhydolion; by a strange
freak the ghosts of two of the leading figures of the Puritan
period in Caernarvonshire — the colonel and the preaching
cornet — were reunited in an environment far removed from
that in which in their lifetime they had laid down the law
to Caernarvonshire!

In Anglesey the operations of Owen Hughes had important political overtones; on Caernarvonshire their effects
were mainly social, for none of the families who benefited
were, at this stage at least, in the political hierarchy of the
shire. But a transaction, about the turn of the century, which
brought about the union of the houses of Glynllifon and
Boduan, profoundly affected Caernarvonshire politics for the
rest of the century. Glynllifon, it will be remembered, had
been a power in the shire from the earliest day of its formation. Boduan was a newer arrival, and had not yet attained
to parliamentary stature; but the Wynns had been steadily
building up an empire of their own in Llŷn since Elizabeth's
time, and although Thomas Wynn's assault on Bodfel had
missed fire, the family ambitions had not been damped. The
line of Glynllifon, like so many other Caernarvonshire houses
at this time, ended in an heiress, and when Thomas Wynn's
grandson and namesake secured her hand in marriage, a
formidable combination of forces in east and west Caernarvonshire was created. Boduan was abandoned and Glynllifon became the home of the Wynns. The political effects
of this were soon apparent.

Up to this point the Bulkeleys had continued to dominate
the political field, though here of course it was a limited
monarchy they exercised, not a virtual dictatorship as in
Anglesey. Their Caernarvonshire possessions were considerable, and they had extended their sway in 1678 by the purchase from the declining Thomas family of some of their
Aber properties (to link up with their wide estate in Llanfairfechan) and eventually of the manor itself. Of the five
families remaining in the county hierarchy, Vaynol, Cefn-

amwlch and Mostyn were all tied by marriage to Baron Hill,
and with Thomas Mostyn's succession to the Flintshire estate
and baronetcy in 1690 his main interests, like those of
Brogyntyn and Wynnstay, now lay outside the shire —
though all three were ready to throw their weight into
county affairs when occasion demanded. In these circumstances it was not difficult for Baron Hill to arrive in 1708 at
a gentleman's agreement with the other Caernarvonshire
houses for distributing between them both county and
borough seats without the expense of a contest. The viscount
invariably took the Anglesey county seat for himself, leaving
Thomas Bulkeley to take his turn for the two Caernarvonshire seats, county and borough alike, with the other families
in the 'ring'. There was no political obstacle. Baron Hill,
Brogyntyn, Cefnamwlch and Wynnstay were firmly Tory;
Thomas Mostyn's brief Whig period under Charles II and
James II had been due simply to the strength of his religious
convictions, and when those controversies were settled by
the Revolution of 1688 he soon returned to the family's
traditional Toryism. Vaynol politics seem to have been more
elastic; at anyrate there was nothing in them to provoke a
contest with the other county families.

The labels Whig and Tory, however, had lost much of
their original meaning with the Revolution. Although
James II in the end exasperated both parties, the Tories
with their addiction to Divine Right could only accept the
Revolution as at best a necessary evil, whereas the Whigs
gloried in it. So the traditional rôles of the two parties were
to some extent reversed, the Whigs becoming more of a
court party while the Tories voiced the country opposition.
This was brought to the test in 1696 when a plot came to
light involving the assassination of William III and the
restoration of James II by an army from France. Both parties
officially condemned it, but the Whigs cashed in on the
crisis by their scheme for an Association (following Elizabethan precedents) for the protection of the king and
vengeance on his enemies, and all loyal members of both
Houses were expected to sign their assent to it. The Tories

were placed in a dilemma by a form of words implying recognition of William III as a *de jure* as well as *de facto* monarch. Lord Bulkeley apparently refused at first and then relented; Sir Robert Owen stayed away and never signed. Sir William Williams of Vaynol had no such scruples; his signature to the Association must have been one of the last things he wrote.

Four years later the death of the only surviving child of the Princess Anne, who stood next to the throne, raised the whole question of the succession after her death, and the Act of Settlement vested it in the house of Hanover. It was another blow to Divine Right, and from now on disgruntled Tories were constantly tempted to intrigue with the exiled Stuart court. The reign of Queen Anne, of course, as that of a legitimate monarch, brought the Tories back to their natural rôle of a court party; but James II was now dead, and even responsible Tory leaders were beginning to vie with one another for the favour of his son the Pretender rather than face the bleak prospect of a Hanoverian succession. By 1710 the fourth Viscount Bulkeley was locally reputed a Jacobite, and correspondence which came to light long after his death revealed that in fact before the end of Anne's reign and right through the Jacobite rebellion of 1715 against George I, he had been in close and active touch with Jacobite circles which nourished the illusory hope that the Old Pretender was about to jump the barrier to his succession by renouncing his father's religion. Sir Robert Owen is not known to have engaged actively in any Jacobite intrigue, but his family was long reckoned with that wing of Toryism.

The question of succession to the throne was closely linked with that of succession to the parliamentary seat. As early as 1698, in the third viscount's day, opposition to the Bulkeley monopoly of power had begun to show its head in Anglesey, backed by the bottomless purse of Hughes ' Yr Arian Mawr ', who had obtained the mayoralty of Newborough and revived its long abandoned claims to participate in the borough election. Hughes was elected, and Bulkeley prestige suffered accordingly. The success was not repeated, but the fourth viscount, who was personally unpopular, encountered opposition in both borough and county at every election from 1708 (when the first recorded contest for the Anglesey seat took place) to the end of the reign. The opposition used the Whig label, and made no scruple of trading on the viscount's Jacobite leanings to discredit him with the government whenever the Whigs were in power, in the hope of undermining his authority in the island by having him stripped of the many public offices he held. Alarmed by this assault on his ancestral citadel, Bulkeley was now bent on securing the Caernarvonshire outworks, and this was what prompted the pact with his fellow-members of the county hierarchy in 1708 about the future devolution of the two parliamentary seats. The old hands were amenable enough, but Thomas Wynn flatly refused to play ball.

Wynn's first operations were in the boroughs — naturally enough: he knew all about borough machinery, for it was round the borough of Nefyn that the family had originally built its empire in west Caernarvonshire. As mayor of Nefyn he had the power to admit new burgesses, and between 1707 and 1713 he exercised this power on a massive scale by admitting no fewer than 689, most of them non-residents. This meant a thirty-fold increase in the voting list in six years, and it was the beginning of a process which reached its culmination in the later years of the century, bringing the voting strength of the boroughs to a figure far exceeding that of the shire, where it remained under five hundred till after the Reform Bill. But of course there were four other boroughs to manipulate. Cricieth was hopeless, since it remained under the control of Brogyntyn, which never budged from its high Tory principles. Pwllheli was easier; the ruling house there was that of Vaughan of Cors y gedol, all-powerful at the moment in Merioneth and possessing important interests in Caernarvonshire; and Thomas Wynn's mother was a Vaughan. Her brother followed Wynn's lead, and Pwllheli's burgess roll shot up from thirty-six to two hundred and ten. At Conway the office of constable (united by charter with that of mayor) had since Elizabeth's time been only occasionally filled, and it had therefore ceased to have any connection with the government of the town. The office had in fact been vacant since 1679. This made control more difficult, but Brogyntyn was believed to be extending its influence there by cultivating some of the more important local families.

There remained Caernarvon. Here too the office of constable (a life appointment by the crown) carried with it that of mayor, but normally the mayors left matters of internal government, including the admission of burgesses, to the two bailiffs who were elected annually. From 1709 there was a struggle between the partisans of Bulkeley and those of Wynne to get their respective nominees put in as bailiffs, with alternating success. Then the office of constable, which had been held by John Bodvel's grandson the second earl of Radnor, fell vacant, and Thomas Wynn saw a chance of snatching in this way a useful fragment of that Bodvel inheritance which his grandfather had so narrowly missed; but Bulkeley, with the great advantage of a Tory government in power, secured the appointment for himself — too late, however, to help him in the crucial elections of 1713, the last of Queen Anne's reign, for which the stage was now set.

These elections were crucial for the country because the Queen's precarious health gave immediate urgency to the question of succession; they were crucial for Caernarvonshire because they were to determine the leadership of the shire for the next fifty years. For the first time since the Long Parliament, both seats were contested. In the boroughs any preparations the Bulkeley (or Tory) faction may have made at Caernarvon, Conway and Cricieth were a mere fleabite compared with Wynn's mass creations at Nefyn, and his uncle's at Pwllheli, of voters committed to the Whig ' ticket ', and he sailed triumphantly in over the head of Sir Robert Owen's son William, the new heir of Brogyntyn. But his supreme triumph was in the shire. Here William Griffith of Cefnamwlch, who, having just reached his majority, had been designated next in rotation for the boroughs in the

agreement of 1708, was bribed by Wynn to desert the
Bulkeley caucus by the more attractive prospect of being
returned for the shire; and although Sir Roger Mostyn offered
himself as arranged, Wynn's assiduous canvassing, especially among Bulkeley's enemies and Owen Hughes's *protégés*
in Caernarvonshire, easily carried the day. In both constituencies the defeated candidate petitioned — another echo of
1640 — but once again the petitions were never discussed.
In the next year the first of the Hanoverians was securely on
the throne.

The house of Glynllifon, having backed the right horse,
was equally firmly in control of Caernarvonshire. From 1713
until 1790 the boroughs were continuously represented by
Glynllifon, except at a by-election in 1754, when, owing to
the death of the family representative shortly after the
general election, its close ally Robert Wynn of Bodysgallen
temporarily took over the seat. The only contest in all that
span of time came nine years after the initial victory; in 1722
William Price of Rhiwlas in Merioneth was put up as candidate by the Baron Hill family (to which both his mother and
his wife belonged) in the hope of shoring up the family
interest, which was going through a bad patch in Anglesey
as well as in Caernarvonshire. But only in the Brogyntyn
stronghold of Cricieth was he able to secure a majority, by
the now fashionable device of wholesale admission of non-
resident burgesses. The number of voters in the five boroughs
had now shot up to over 1,500, more than ninety per cent
of them non-resident, and the poll took four days to complete.
Glynllifon won by a handsome majority; Price petitioned
against the result, but again without success. The county
representation likewise remained in the hands of Glynllifon's
allies of Cefnamwlch for a quarter of a century, after which
the family was unable to supply a candidate of suitable age.
For two elections in the 'forties (in one of which the seat
was contested for the first time since the Protectorate), Sir
John Wynn of Glynllifon, in his own words, ' made a com-
pliment' of the seat (at the chief minister's request) to a
neighbouring squire, a *protégé* of Owen Hughes who had

already tilted against the Bulkeleys in Anglesey; then Glynllifon took over, and continued to represent the shire till
George III's reign.

Here was monopoly of power with a vengeance! It was
not much more than a century since the attempt at a far
more modest monopoly by the Wynns of Gwydir had been
scotched by a coalition from other parts of the shire. But the
narrowing down of the county hierarchy which made this
now impossible was only a pale reflection of the concentration of power and wealth on the national plane. The
Revolution of 1688 had put the country in the hands of
what Disraeli dubbed a 'Venetian oligarchy'; the Whig
triumph of 1714 had pared this down still further by exclud-
ing from power for fifty years the Tories, whose leaders,
intoxicated by their sweeping victory in 1711, had over-
played their hand and underestimated the attachment of
public sentiment to the Protestant succession. Henceforth all
public appointments were controlled by a clique of Whig
families who saw to it that the plums went to their friends;
by these means they were able to control the electoral
machinery and to secure the return to the Commons of a
comfortable majority of 'yes-men'. The triumph of Glynllifon displays the whole process in miniature. In the year
after Thomas Wynn's first election for the boroughs he was
made equerry to the Prince of Wales, who in turn gave him
his coveted post of constable of Caernarvon. In this capacity
he broke with precedent by personally presiding over the
borough court; he could thus supervise the admission of
burgesses instead of leaving this to the annually-elected
bailiffs. For example, in expectation of a contest in 1754 his
son John (who succeeded him as constable) admitted 267 new
burgesses, nearly all of them non-residents from the Glynllifon estate. This consolidated the family hold on the
boroughs, for the Brogyntyn opposition at Cricieth could
now be ignored, and at Conway the influence of Wynn's
confederates the Kyffins of Maenan neutralised that of the
Bulkeleys (who were burgesses there) and of their allies the
Coytmors. It should in fairness be added that Caernarvon

made many material gains from the Wynn mayoralty —
notably the new town hall built in 1767.

It was on the national level, however, that the richest
prizes were secured. In 1724 Wynn was rewarded with the
highly-paid sinecure of clerk of the green cloth, and eighteen
years later a baronetcy. It was reckoned that the income from
his various government jobs amounted to £1,300 a year.
His son Sir John secured the post of deputy treasurer of
Chelsea Hospital (worth £800 a year), but surrendered it at
the government's request in order to re-enter parliament in
1754; compensation was found (though never enough to
satisfy his clamours) in such offices as surveyor general of
mines in North Wales. Conversely Lord Bulkeley from 1714
had to pay for his consistent Toryism and his flirtation with
the Jacobites by losing all public offices — chamberlain and
vice admiral of North Wales, constable of Beaumaris and
Caernarvon castles, and so on. Financially, of course, these
losses meant little to a family like that of Baron Hill; what
mattered was the temporary overshadowing of the age-long
influence of the house, partially in Anglesey and almost completely in Caernarvonshire; and the occurrence in the family
of a long minority lasting more than twenty years from 1752
prolonged these conditions.

Glynllifon, to to it justice, kept its part of the bargain by
supporting its paymaster through thick and thin. The first
Sir Thomas voted dutifully for all the Whig measures
designed to secure the Hanoverian succession, followed his
patron the Prince of Wales into opposition in 1718, and
returned to the orthodox Whig fold when Walpole brought
about a reconciliation of the prince with his father. He then
supported Walpole consistently to the end of his ministry
and its successors till his own death just before the middle
of the century. His Cefnamwlch allies were equally conformable. But by mid-century not a shred remained of what
political meaning there had ever been in the party labels
inherited from the days of Charles II. Up to 1715, or a little
later, politics still had at least one aspect everyone could
understand — the Protestant succession, to which the mass

of the country was attached, as one writer put it,[1] by 'the memory of James II's reign and the history of Mary Tudor's '. During the 'twenties and 'thirties Jacobitism became no more than an excuse for convivial gatherings and noisy toasts, and even the landing of the Young Pretender in 1745 and his march into the midlands, whatever panic it may have caused in London or on the Welsh border, meant little or nothing in Caernarvonshire. And so politics went dead. It is true that there were more voters going to the poll than ever before, but to the imported non-resident burgesses elections meant no more than a round of free drinks and free meals, and to the small freeholder the chance of some job in the ministry's gift. We find Sir John Wynn of Glynllifon, for example, pressing the minister of the day for the office of postmaster of Conway for one of his supporters, and urging that the crown living of Aberffraw be bestowed in such a way as 'to promote the Whig interest in North Wales ', of which he regarded himself (not without reason) as the mainstay.

The storms of George III's early years, when he was struggling to free himself from dependence on the great Whig families, hardly produced an answering ripple on the surface of Caernarvonshire politics. Sir John Wynn's son Thomas began the reign with an ostentatious display of loyalty by founding the 'Society or Garrison of Fort Williamsburg' (the toy fort he built in his park and named after William III, the patron saint of all good Whigs). The 'Garrison ', with its complementary 'Sisterhood ', its fantastic rules, rituals and uniforms, was a retort to the older Jacobite clubs, but with George III's coronation day instead of the Pretender's birthday as the occasion for loyal toasts. Wynn also held a colonelcy in the county militia, which in 1762 was belatedly embodied under an Act passed five years earlier when French invasion was feared; under Wynn's direction it worked in close concert with his ' Garrison '.

An attempt by a Kyffin of Maenan, in the first election of the reign, to rally opposition to the Glynllifon ascendancy

[1] Herbert Paul, *Queen Anne* (1912), 149.

(which the family had initially supported) came to nothing, but the mere threat was enough to drive Sir John Wynn to the safety of the borough seat, leaving the shire to his son Thomas. By the next septennial election, in 1768, opposition had grown. The houses of Mostyn and Brogyntyn were no longer prepared to let the county seat go by default, especially as Thomas Wynn was less popular than his father; and they found powerful backers outside the shire in Wynnstay and in the Anglesey house of Plas Newydd. Here the Baylys, having married into the noble and wealthy Staffordshire family of Paget, with every prospect of succession to the lands and title, saw themselves now playing a more decisive rôle in the politics both of the island, and of the Caernarvonshire mainland, than that of stopgap to the Bulkeleys. Sir John Wynne, now nearing seventy, retired from the fray, handing over the safe borough seat to his younger son Glyn. The opposition candidate, William Wynne of Wern (Penmorfa), had recently enhanced his importance by acquiring the Bryncir estate and some lucrative properties in Merioneth; but he was new to Caernarvonshire politics and lacked a following, and Glynllifon, with the backing of its old allies of Cefnamwlch, once more carried the day.

The real challenge came in 1774. The long minority which had proved such a setback to Baron Hill had now come to an end, and the seventh Viscount Bulkeley was determined to reassert the family influence in both shires. This time the opposition to Glynllifon was able to put up a candidate with all the prestige of one of the premier estates of the shire as well as two other properties in England. Thomas Assheton of Ashley in Cheshire had just succeeded to the Smith inheritance in Hampshire, Cheshire and Caernarvonshire, and added the family surname to his own. In 1774 he was made sheriff of Caernarvonshire, but he died in office, having already made preparations for the candidature of his son for the county seat. The county rallied strongly to the newcomer, even Cefnamwlch and the absentee bishop, and he won the seat handsomely. A petition from Sir Thomas Wynn (who had followed his father in the estate and title in 1773), with the usual allegations of bribery, intimidation and a biased sheriff, failed to cut any ice: the Glynllifon monopoly in the shire was broken at last, though Glyn Wynn was able to cling on to the boroughs for another decade. Sir Thomas was consoled with the title of Lord Newborough (in the Irish peerage) and a pocket borough in Cornwall; and Vaynol had once more become politically important.

The election also had repercussions at Westminster. The Glynllifon interest had consistently supported each of the short-lived ministries which George III successively called to power; but in 1770 the king discovered a minister after his own heart in Lord North. North however, found the Commons restive in face of public events, and Assheton Smith, in contrast with his predecessors in the Caernarvonshire seat, voted consistently with the opposition. This did not indicate any revolutionary change in the climate of county politics; on the contrary, there were complaints that Assheton Smith was too much out of touch with his constituents. In fact it does not appear that as yet he paid more than passing visits to Vaynol, which as late as 1792 is described by a local topographer as ' once the mansion of conviviality and mirth, now the neglected seat of A. Smith, Esq.'[2] But during Lord North's ministry there arose issues, both local and national, which did at last begin to rouse the shire out of its political apathy. These questions came to a head during the years 1778-82, and can best be dealt with in a later chapter, for they open up a new phase in the political history of the shire.


B.   ECONOMIC AFFAIRS

IF politics were dead in early Georgian Caernarvonshire, there was not much more vigour in its economic life, with the limited exception of slate quarrying. Cattle rearing was the basic industry — so much so that even sturdy loyalists

---

[2] [Nicholas Owen], *Caernarvonshire*, 58.

had petitioned Charles I for a restoration of the trade with London when parliamentary control cut them off from this profitable market. Yet Bakewell's experiments in stock breeding in Derbyshire, about the middle of the next century, had little impact on cattle breeders here, whose only specific for the trade was the exclusion of Irish cattle — a measure eventually passed, it will be remembered, with the support of the county member in the Cavalier Parliament. By the end of the eighteenth century Llŷn and Eifionydd were exporting about 1,500 yearlings and 4,500 two-year old cattle annually, a trade which brought in well over £40,000; but in other parts of the shire the cattle were thought to have 'nothing to recommend them except extreme hardiness and consequent cheapness of rearing'.[1]

Tillage was in no better shape. Farm accounts of the early eighteenth century from Plas Brondanw (actually in Merioneth, but typical of the country round the Traeth) reveal conditions which are almost medieval: oxen regularly used for ploughing, and shared among a group of neighbouring farms. In Eifionydd the state of agriculture some fifty years later is described in the following letter[2] written in 1812 but embodying half-a-century's recollections by a local squire whose family had been settled in the neighbourhood for many generations:

> No ground was then fallowed, no pease, grass, turnips or potatoes raised, no cattle fattened and little grain sold. Oats and barley were alternately sown, and during seven months of the year the best soil was ravaged by flocks of sheep, a certain number of which were annually sold and carried off to be fed in richer pastures . . . When seed time was finished, the plough and harrow were laid aside till autumn, and the sole employment of the farmer consisted in weeding his corn fields and in digging and conveying home peat, turf and heath for winter fuel. The produce of a farm . . . was barely sufficient to pay the trifling rent and the servants' wages and to procure his family a scanty subsistence.

[1] W. Davies, *Agriculture of N. Wales* (1810), 312.
[2] Robert Jones, Ynysgain, Cricieth (1767-1840) in *North Wales Gazette*, 9 July, 1812.

It cannot all have been as bad as this. The late David Thomas has shown from custom house records[3] that, contrary to general belief, Caernarvon by the third decade of the eighteenth century was able to send occasional cargoes of wheat, barley or oats to Chester, Liverpool and sometimes London. In the course of 1740 as many as twenty-eight grain ships sailed from the port for Liverpool, and in the preceding year Porthdinllaen even sent one to Lisbon. But this was most exceptional; Llŷn and Eifionydd remained normally dependent on corn imports for at least another twenty years, and their mariners rarely looked beyond the coasting trade. Conway (less surprisingly) was sending some grain to Dublin by the 1780's. But the fact that corn was exported did not necessarily imply a surplus in the county. Good prices were to be had in the growing cities across Offa's Dyke, and farmers were naturally tempted to cash in on this demand rather than rely on the more sluggish home market. This would account for incidents like those at Pwllheli in 1751 and Caernarvon in 1766, when hungry mobs stormed the port, bent on preventing vessels from sailing with provisions they were so short of at home. Potatoes were also a regular import, even in the Conway valley, till past the middle of the century; but at least this shows they were being consumed (which was itself a novelty); and if some of them (as Mr. Thomas suggests) were seed potatoes, a beginning may have been made of growing them at home. The fact remains, however, that even at the end of the eighteenth century Caernarvonshire grew less than half as much grain as Anglesey, and there the total was under 60,000 quarters a year.

Afforestation was also neglected. ' Instead of planting upon land that will bear neither grass nor corn ', commented a traveller[4] towards the end of the century, ' . . . the great proprietors . . . seem emulous which shall the speediest and

[3] *Hen Longau Sir Gaernarfon,* pen. 6.
[4] J. Evans, *Letters written during a Tour through North Wales in the year 1798* (1804), 205.

most effectually divest of timber his respective domain '. Of course, they had good reason for this. The use of charcoal for smelting (which persisted into the second half of the eighteenth century) and the consequent denuding of the English forests, meant that handsome profits were to be made by exporting timber; indeed it long remained the principal export of Conway. But the soil had to suffer for it. One of the few good things the Hon. John Byng has to say about Gwydir in 1793[5] is that the absentee owner ' has not destroyed the timber around the house '.

Yet elsewhere this was an age when the ' wind of change ' in agriculture was blowing strongly enough to justify the term ' Agrarian Revolution '. And not only in remote English shires : Caernarvonshire landlords and farmers had only to look across the Straits for an object lesson. Nearly thirty years before the appearance of Jethro Tull's treatise which began a revolution in tillage in the 'thirties, Henry Rowlands, vicar of Llanidan, wrote (but did not publish) a work on the principles of agriculture in which he was able to embody not only up-to-date theories of soil science but factual accounts of the fruitful experiments of his neighbours; and nearly twenty years before Walpole's brother-in-law retired from politics to earn the nickname of ' Turnip Townshend ', Edward Wynne was applying to his estate at Bodewryd — at the opposite end of the island — the advanced methods of agriculture he learned during his spells of residence in Herefordshire as chancellor of the diocese. This he did to such good purpose that he was already cultivating turnips in 1714, and by 1737 — only seven years after Townshend set the example — the crop was taking twenty-six days to hoe. Why was Caernarvonshire left behind? The answer probably lies not so much in lack of capital as in lack of leadership. So many of the great estates to which the local gentry and farmers had been accustomed to look for this had passed to non-resident owners. Lord Willoughby de Eresby, who owned Gwydir, might hold the honorific office

[5] *Torrington Diaries* (ed. C. B. Andrews, 1936), iii. 277.

of custos rotulorum in 1714, Sir William Yonge, one of the co-heirs of Penrhyn, in 1739 (having previously emulated his Tudor predecessors at Penrhyn by holding the offices of chancellor and chamberlain of North Wales); but their practical interests lay elsewhere. William Smith, son of the man into whose lap the Vaynol estate had so unexpectedly fallen, was made sheriff of Anglesey in 1759 and of Caernarvonshire ten years later; but so far as is known his visits to the two shires were confined to formal occasions. The Wynns of Glynllifon, for their part, found politics more paying than turnips, and as yet contributed little to agricultural advance beyond the introduction of some superior strains of cattle from England. The ' prostration of agricultural improvement '[6] in their Llŷn estates was adversely commented on even in the early nineteenth century.

In coastal regions small-scale tillage was often combined with fishing, as, for example, at Nefyn, where in 1747 nearly five thousand barrels were exported, a small pier being built for the purpose. The industry was less well organised at Pwllheli, but at Conway the ancient mussel fishery, which produced a small quantity of excellent pearls, continued to flourish, and even in the early nineteenth century — after a period of decline — still employed forty hands. The expansion of the fishing industry, however, was hampered by its seasonal character and by lack of adequate protective measures to reduce the heavy losses by poaching. There was equally little sign of progress in the textile and extractive industries. The manufacture of woollens remained on the primitive domestic plane described in an earlier chapter, supplying little but home needs. There was some expansion (though again only for local purposes) in linen manufacture, the flax being grown locally and dressed by domestic labour at Conway, Caernarvon and Pwllheli. The heavy industries hardly existed in the shire. An iron furnace at Eglwysbach, on the Denbighshire side of the Conway, added to Conway's export trade

---

[6] Hyde Hall, *Description of Caernarvonshire*, 1809-11 (ed. E. Gwynne Jones, 1952), 286.

small quantities of pig iron shipped to Liverpool, Chester and elsewhere during the third quarter of the eighteenth century, but when the furnace was advertised for sale in 1779 the vendors offered the significant inducement that it might be ' converted into malt houses '.

In mining the tale is the same everywhere: a period of activity, then the capital gives out, or else the water floods in and the prospectors are without the resources necessary to drain the mine. The mines in the Conway valley opened up by Sir John Wynn in James I's day made no progress until they were taken over by a Macclesfield firm in the eighteenth century. The same firm was responsible for reviving two other early mining projects in the county. A lead mine at Penrhyn Du (on the sea coast in Llanengan parish, remote from any dwelling) had been first developed soon after the Restoration by Lord Herbert of Cherbury (who owned the land), but was then abandoned for a century — doubtless owing to difficulties of transport as well as flooding by the sea. A revealing letter written by Lord Herbert's agent in 1668 reports that the ' best works ' have already been drowned out, but eighty tons of ore have been shipped and sold at £420, and more remains in the storehouse awaiting the ship's return. Meanwhile the whole of the £420 is needed for meeting eighteen months' wages, debts incurred for stores in the works and provisions for the workmen — a clear indication of the small scale on which such works were then conducted even when they had the capital of a wealthy land-lord behind them. The other abandoned project successfully revived from Macclesfield in the 1760's was a copper mine opened at Llanberis some twenty years earlier by a local prospector named Sîon John Robert, who was reputed to have made £300 in six weeks (or in other versions three months) — and then apparently to have retired on his gains. The two oldest copper mines in the shire are those of Llandudno and of Drws y coed in the Nantlle valley — both claiming (with some plausibility) a Roman origin. The Llan-

dudno mine was working up to about the middle of the
eighteenth century, and then was drowned out and abandoned till the nineteenth, while Drws y coed had been
revived and forsaken again before Pennant visited it in 1773.

In slate quarrying the obstacle to expansion was not
flooding, but lack of adequate tools, transport and organisation. Yet the eighteenth-century growth of towns and cities
could not but stimulate so essential an industry, and one in
which Caernarvonshire enjoyed such natural advantages.
The slate industry had remained almost static in the seventeenth century, but early in the eighteenth adventurers were
working on Cilgwyn common. This is reputedly the scene
of the earliest quarrying in the shire, but working had been
spasmodic here, as everywhere else, and sales limited to the
immediate neighbourhood. But now the quarrymen began to
look farther afield; Caernarvon was only six miles away, and
although the way was rocky, it could be negotiated by
sledges; at anyrate exports of slate — mainly to Ireland, and
mainly from Cilgwyn — become from now on a regular and
increasing item in Caernarvon's trade, with an agent on the
spot to supervise sales. Other loads were carried coastwise
to Chester, occasionally to Liverpool, and more rarely to
South Wales, mostly in locally-owned ships. By 1721 exports
had extended to Dunkirk and Rotterdam, and in the next
decade the total had risen to more than two million slates
in the course of a year — at least five times the total exports
from the whole shire in Elizabeth's reign. The quarrymen
still worked in small, self-employing groups, and enjoyed the
great advantage of paying no rent, so that once costs of
transport had been met, what they made by sales was clear
profit.

Similar conditions existed in another area which in due
course helped to swell the exports of Caernarvon. Since the
beginning of the century there had been no resident owner
at Vaynol, and in the parishes of Llanberis and Llanddeiniolen, most of which lay within the estate, the waste lands
of the manor had been freely used by the inhabitants as a
source of slates for roofing their houses as well as peat and

brushwood for warming them. In this way the slopes to the east of Llyn Padarn became what has been called[7] a ' mosaic ' of shallow quarries, each *bargen* known by the name of the man who started working it — somewhat in the fashion of a gold-digger's ' claim ' in Klondyke or California. By the middle of the century these primitive arrangements were beginning to change, in response to the growing demand for slates in distant towns and cities, into something more like an organised business. Partnerships of from two to a dozen were formed to extend the working of these old ' claims ', and the slates, instead of being exclusively used on the spot, were ferried across the lake and carried by cart or sledge along the rocky roads westwards to Caernarvon or eastwards to Moel y don for wider distribution by sea. By 1772 five such partnerships were working little quarries above Llyn Padarn and three more above Llyn Peris, and a trickle of quarrymen was coming in from farther afield — Llanllyfni, Conway, even Anglesey and Denbighshire — to join the ' locals '. They were helped by the use of blasting powder, of which their knowledge no doubt came from the more experienced quarrymen of the Bangor area. All this was bringing new life to a parish where, less than a century earlier, ' neither miller, nor fuller, [nor] any other tradesman but one tailor '[8] was to be found.

As we have seen, the quarries that found their outlet near Bangor had a longer history than any except, perhaps, Cilgwyn; and although the Penrhyn estate, like Vaynol, lacked a resident owner, its agents had long exercised some sort of supervision over quarrying on the estate. Yet here too production remained static till well past the middle of the eighteenth century. In the first six months of 1740 there were no recorded overseas exports, and those carried coast-wise amounted to less than a million slates. Caernarvon, as a long-established port with a harbour of sorts and a customs house, could command sea-going vessels on the spot; Bangor

---

[7] D. Dylan Pritchard in *Quarry Manager's Jnl.*, Nov. 1944.
[8] Quoted F. Emery, in *Agrarian Hist. of England and Wales*, iv. 116-7.

had nothing but fishing smacks, and masters of vessels from outside were not disposed to go for slates to the creeks at Abercegin or Aberogwen when they could find both slates and loading facilities at Caernarvon.

In the days before 1684, when there were still Williamses at Penrhyn, no one had taken the slate industry seriously, but at least the owners lived on the estate and knew every inch of it. Sir Robert Williams, the second baronet (people recalled sixty years later) used annually to walk his bounds, rocks and all, and ' no man durst as much as turn a sheep on Llandegai mountain nor take any other liberty whatsoever without his consent '.[9] It was different now that Penrhyn was inhabited by tenants or agents, while the estate was shared by owners one of whom divided his time between Devon and London, and the other lived in Cheshire — each managing the estate by remote control and sharing the rents and profits equally. Regular reports were received from the agents, it is true; Sir William Yonge, the Devonian co-heir, held honorary posts in Caernarvonshire as well as an active one in the government, and in 1754 his wife came to the aid of the school Dean John Jones had founded at Llandygái with a consignment of books. But all this was no substitute for a resident proprietor. During the fifty years after Sir Robert Williams's death the boundaries of the estate and the extent of its owners' rights over the slate rocks fell into confusion under negligent agents, and were in dispute with the crown, the bishop and the commoners in Llandygái and Llanllechid.

A ' new broom ' appointed as agent in 1736 found the total profit to the estate from the sale of slates less than £100, but he himself presented no accounts for the next seven years, during which production fell catastrophically and old hands were turning to other jobs. A few improvements, such as an extension of classification by size, were introduced; but the agent wanted to go much further: his aim was to take from

---

[9] Agent's report, 1736, quoted *Quarry Manager's Jnl.*, July 1942.

the crown a lease of Cilgwyn and the adjacent commons so as to control production there and cut out competition. In this he believed Sir John Wynn of Glynllifon might join him; but nothing came of it. In 1746, on the contrary, Wynn took out on his own account crown leases over a wide area of mining and quarrying land; but he still charged only a token royalty, his aim being prestige rather than systematic exploitation; so Caernarvon could still undersell Penrhyn. For this reason the agent appointed the same year at Penrhyn adopted the plan of reducing both prices and royalties, and even suggested that the owners should for a period of years forego all thought of profit in the hope of recapturing the market. When Lewis Morris published in 1748 his survey of Welsh ports, he credited Caernarvon with sales amounting to four million slates a year, but he did not consider Bangor slates worthy of mention. Even twenty years later a traveller visiting Bangor could find no seagoing traffic there except fishing boats.

A few years before this, however, developments occurred at Penrhyn which were in the end to transform not only the quarrying industry, but the whole economy of the shire. In 1765 General Hugh Warburton, the Cheshire joint owner, married his daughter and heiress to the son of John Pennant, an immensely rich West Indian sugar planter now returned to England. Pennant came of an ancient Flintshire family, of the stock from which sprang Thomas Pennant, the naturalist and antiquary. His grandfather had gone out to Jamaica in the seventeenth century, and John returned to England with a comfortable fortune already swollen by marriage with the daughter of a wealthy fellow-planter and by inheritance from his elder brother, who had also come home and risen to be lord mayor of London. Having secured the reversion to the Warburton 'moiety', John Pennant started negotiations for the puchase of the other half. The final disentangling of this property was not achieved until his son's day, but already in 1768 he was sufficiently in control of the Yonge 'moiety' to grant twenty-one year leases, jointly with Warburton, both of the hall and demesne to their existing occupant, and of quarrying rights on the rock face to fifty-four local adventurers; these were to form themselves into 'Sets or Companies' of five or more to quarry and dress the slates in their respective 'bargains', paying fixed rents instead of variable royalties, and to convey them to Abercegin ready for shipment. The lessors undertook to appoint a salaried slate reeve who should be responsible for marketing, keeping quarterly accounts and dividing the proceeds among the partnerships. Even so, output continued to fall, and was actually smaller in 1782 than in 1738. But in the former year, after John Pennant's death, his son Richard took the working of the quarries into his own hand, and a new chapter opened, which must be dealt with later.

Meanwhile quarrying, even in the areas where production had expanded to meet urban demands from England and Ireland, remained crude, primitive and wasteful, using methods which were a positive hindrance to future development. A grim light is thrown on conditions in these seemingly flourishing regions by the part quarrymen played in the recurrent food riots at Caernarvon in the middle years of the century. In 1752 a mob of quarrymen from Cilgwyn and Rhostryfan swarmed into the town to raid the grain granaries there, and in the ensuing armed scuffle with the authorities two men were killed. Cilgwyn men were also to the fore in the riots of 1766 to which reference was made earlier. Hunger was never very far below the surface while agriculture and industry remained undeveloped; and they could never develop so long as the local gentry most capable of infusing capital and enterprise into them diverted these into other channels, while outside capital was held at bay by the formidable barriers to internal communication which must be removed before results could be achieved.

Here indeed we have one of the chief causes of economic backwardness. The only *made* roads in the shire were those the Romans had made, and these had been steadily deteriorating over the centuries, where they did not lie buried and forgotten. Road repair remained the job of the parish, and it lay at the mercy of the able-bodied parishioners mustered once a year for six days under an equally reluctant and unskilled surveyor of highways. In any case Roman roads stopped short at Caernarvon. West of this there was little but mud tracks used by the drovers, affording some sort of gangway for horsemen (but scarcely for wheeled traffic) from the farthest parts of Llŷn to Llanystumdwy and Penmorfa, and then by the much-trodden ways across the Traeth into Merioneth; or again the ancient pilgrim routes to Bardsey, converging on Aberdaron by the northerly approach from Clynnog (itself a place of pilgrimage) and the southerly through Abererch and Pistyll. There were also a few cross-country tracks and bridle-paths threading their way north and south through the mountain passes, like the ' horse path . . . worked in the rudest manner into steps' which Pennant had to use through Nant Ffrancon in 1773, or the more frequented but ill-kept road from Caernarvon to Bedd-gelert which the Post Office employed for the mails to Ardudwy. From Beddgelert to the crossing of the Traeth, according to an earlier traveller, was ' all stone steps '.[10]

Fastidious travellers of Pennant's day saw in Caernarvon the last outpost of civilisation and the return from Snow-donia as a re-entry into ' Day-light and the polite World '. Pennant himself has little to say for Llŷn, with its mud-walled and chimneyless thatched cottages, warmed only by such wretched fuel makeshifts as furze and dried dung; for the slates of Arfon and Arllechwedd could no more be entrusted to its bumpy roads than the coal of Denbighshire and Flintshire, save only such cartloads as neighbouring gentry might bring for their own use from Pwllheli. Pennant blamed preoccupation with the herring fishery rather than the state of the roads for the backwardness of Llŷn, but locally this was strenuously denied.[11] Whatever the cause,

[10] J. Kelsall (1722), quoted R. T. Jenkins, *TCHS* 1940, 75.
[11] J. Cradock, *Account of . . . North Wales* (1777), 65, cf. Pennant, *Tours* (1883 ed.), ii. 374-5, Hyde Hall, 33, 261; D. Thomas, *Hen Longau*, 34.

regions which in Tudor days had perhaps provided a living
for more families per acre than any other part of the shire
now gave all the appearance of a stagnant backwater.

Even over the more manageable terrain farther east, with
stretches of Roman road which at least provided a firm foundation and better gradients, wheeled traffic, other than the
cumbrous farm wagon lumbering its way to market, was far
from common. Almost the only occasions calling for more
extensive travel on wheels were the progresses of the king's
deputies on their way to and from Ireland and of the assize
judges on circuit. Of the difficulties of the former we have
an example from James I's reign when the judge, then staying
with Sir Roger Mostyn at his Flintshire home, was proposing
to bring his coach up from there to Gloddaeth (since his
lady could not sit a horse) and then on to Gwydir. Sir Roger
writes to ask Sir John Wynn to get his men to repair the
way from Llanddulas 'both above and under' Penmaenrhos
in readiness for it, 'so that if they may not take the one way
they may be sure of the other'. He is even unsure whether
the coach can tackle the rough and heavily wooded track
above the right bank of the Conway to Gwydir, while the
tides make it doubtful whether Sir John's boat can make it
by river. The intention apparently is to make his way from
Gwydir to Conway for the assizes by the more frequented
road alongside the left bank — a roundabout way, but at
least avoiding the perils of Conway ferry. Sixty years after
this, the second earl of Clarendon in travelling to take up his
post as lord lieutenant of Ireland claimed to have 'introduced a new way of travelling' when he was able to take
his luggage by coach over Penmaenmawr instead of having
to load the dismembered vehicle in sections on to his horses
and reassemble it the other side; but the human cargo stuck
to the relative security of horseback and litter!

These were among the few occasions when a coach
appeared in Caernarvonshire before 1740. The first 'resident'
coach was that used by Sir Nicholas Bayly of Plas Newydd
in Anglesey for travel between his Caernarvonshire proper-

ties, after he succeeded to the estate in 1741. Hyde Hall[12]
records a description given him by an ' aged informant ' of
the sensation caused by this ' portentous exhibition ': ' the
plough was deserted, the wheel stood still, and the spade
was thrown down, until curiosity had been gratified by sight,
or still more by the touch, of the massive fabric '.

If internal communications were bad, there were also
serious obstacles in the way of the main approaches to the
shire from without. Mention has just been made of Penmaenmawr, ' over which ', as Sir John Wynn commented in
Charles I's day,[13] ' yf either man or beaste shoulde fall, both
sea and rocke, rocke and sea, woulde strive and contend
whether of bothe should doe hym the greatest mischief '.
The original trackway over this formidable mass is attributed
in a persistent tradition to the sixth-century St. Seiriol, who
had, in addition to his principal cell on Ynys Seiriol (the
so-called ' Puffin Island ') a wayside shrine on Penmaenmawr,
of which the ruins were still visible in Pennant's day. ' And
this way ', to quote Sir John Wynn again, ' is ever sythence
kepte and repayred by a heremyte, who hath nothing for
his labour and service therein but the charity of well disposed people and passengers '. The services of a guide — the
successor of Sir John's ' heremyte ' — could still be hired at
an inn on the shore below in 1771, but forty years later the
guides were a memory and the inn a dilapidated ruin. We
have seen that by the time of the second earl of Clarendon
it was just possible to take goods by coach over the headland;
this was the result of improvements made some time after the
Restoration, of which nothing is known.

It was again the needs of travel to Ireland that prompted
a second and a third attempt to rob this part of the journey
of some of its terrors — both of them on the initiative of the
Bulkeley family, the principal landowners of the neighbourhood. Proposals made by the third viscount to the Irish
government about 1703 were put into effect by 1720; and a

---

[12] *Description*, 37.
[13] *An Ancient Survey of Pen Maen Mawr*, ed. Halliwell, 1859 (repr 1906),
21.

much more far-reaching scheme initiated by the seventh viscount in 1772, providing a carriage road all the way from Conway through the Sychnant and down to the coast again, was completed under the supervision of a skilled professional engineer, with help from both the English and the Irish parliaments — a work which in contemporary opinion,[14] ' effected what was before thought beyond the reach of art to remedy ', and which ' perhaps equals anything of the kind in Europe '. Yet we shall see that the old complaints about Penmaenmawr continue to be echoed in the nineteenth century; and although it was thought safe in 1776 to run a regular coach service using the new road, and nine years later to entrust the royal mails to it by a ' flying post chaise ', the alternative route across the sands at the base of the rock at low tide, which had till then been the official mail route, was still in use and marked on maps for another thirty years.

Even before reaching Penmaenmawr, the traveller entering Caernarvonshire from the east had to encounter the currents and sandbanks of the Conway ferry, a source of frequent delays and not without its toll of casualties. It was still in the hands of Archbishop Williams's heirs, but in the division of the Penrhyn estate in 1663 the other ferry higher up the river at Tal y cafn passed to another branch of the family. It generally carried local traffic only, but travellers sometimes used it to avoid the twin perils of Penmaenmawr and Conway ferry; for they could then take the old Roman road across Bwlch y ddeufaen and drop down at Aber. The Roundheads, we have seen, used this route for their conquest of Caernarvonshire; it was good enough for pedestrians or horsemen, but hardly catered for coaches!

The traveller through Caernarvonshire to or from Ireland had also to cross the Straits by ferry. There were six of these in all, but those at the two ends — Abermenai (the old Newborough ferry) and Porthesgob (the property of the bishops of Bangor, connecting Bangor with the island) —

---

[14] Pennant, *Tours,* iii.. 108; Defoe, *Tour* (1778 ed.), ii. 324.

were of very limited local use. Beaumaris had been granted
by Edward I a lease of the crown ferry from his new borough
to the edge of Traeth Lafan, which could be crossed to Aber
at low tide. Here the danger lay in the ever-present risk of
being overtaken by the tide; guide posts fixed in the sand
from time to time usually had a short life, but in 1817 the
same Lord Bulkeley who had set on foot the latest improvements on Penmaenmawr fixed a warning bell in the tower of
Aber church. Despite the inconveniences, the Irish mails
were generally carried this way until the eighteenth century.
Caernarvon, less lucky than Beaumaris, was not endowed
with a ferry when the borough was created, and the Tal y
foel ferry, which came into use later, was never widely
patronised owing to uncertainties of tide and wind. The older
Moel y don ferry, although a few miles outside the town (at
the modern Port Dinorwic), became Caernarvon's chief
highway of trade with Anglesey, since it could carry horses
and market produce; and inhabitants of that part of the
island, remote from market towns, did most of their shopping at Caernarvon. John Wesley often used what he called
'Baildon' or 'Baldon' ferry on his frequent journeys to
Ireland; but the most frequented crossing from Tudor times
onward was the Porthaethwy ferry, just beyond Bangor but
generally known as 'Bangor ferry'. Early in the eighteenth
century it superseded the Beaumaris crossing as the official
mail route, and it continued to operate until it was put out of
commission by Telford's bridge.

The other principal gateway into Caernarvonshire was
from Merioneth, the route generally taken by travellers from
South Wales or those who entered Wales by the Severn
valley and travelled north through Bala and Dolgellau. Here
the obstacle to be encountered was the crossing of Traeth
Mawr. Before Madocks built his embankment, Penmorfa was
what its name implies, the head of a treacherous tidal marsh,
across which the traveller, unless very familiar with it, was
well advised to hire a guide. John Wesley, who knew it from
frequent use, saw no need for this at all until one March
night in 1756 he reached the sands after dark, and was glad

to accept the company of an 'honest Welshman' who knew no word of English! As long as these impediments persisted, it is not surprising that the trade of Caernarvonshire remained mainly local, and its industry and agriculture in consequence undeveloped; for the navigable stretches of its rivers were short, and the capacity of the undeveloped harbours of Caernarvon, Conway or Pwllheli to handle sea-going traffic strictly limited. Once more the need for an enlightened outlay of capital becomes apparent.

It was from outside the county that the first moves came. Penmaenmawr is a case in point; but there are others. The eighteenth century was the great age of turnpike trusts. These were bodies, consisting of the principal local gentry, entrusted by Act of Parliament for a period of (generally) twenty-one years with control of the roads in a defined area. During that period they were to put the roads into such trim that they could henceforth be satisfactorily maintained (it was hoped) by the parishes. To meet their expenses they were empowered to levy tolls on all passing vehicles at gates erected at suitable intervals. They could also employ a paid surveyor and under his direction widen, straighten or divert the roads and generally undertake such improvements as were beyond parish resources. The Acts could be, and in fact nearly always were, renewed if the task could not be completed in time. By the middle of the century these trusts had made their first appearance on the North Wales border. One set up in 1759 to cover a wide area of Denbighshire and Flintshire included a short stretch of road on the Caernarvonshire side of the Conway, from the Tal y cafn ferry to Conway itself. Six years later there followed the Anglesey turnpike, covering the road from Porthaethwy through Llangefni to Holyhead.

Caernarvonshire now constituted an awkward gap in the turnpike system, and it was remembered in the early nineteenth century that the man who set on foot the agitation to get this gap filled was the landlord of the White Lion, Chester, who had lost several horses on the Caernarvonshire roads. A few years later he despatched from his inn the first coach to tackle the new Penmaenmawr road and then to proceed through Caernarvonshire to Holyhead, along turnpike roads right through Caernarvonshire and Anglesey. For in 1769 the first Caernarvonshire Turnpike Act was passed, with trustees numbering something like a hundred and fifty — which must have included everyone in the shire with the requisite property qualification. The Old Carnarvonshire Turnpike, as it came to be called, did not stop short at Bangor ferry, but included also the road from Bangor through Caernarvon to Pwllheli. Forty years later this beginning was looked back upon[15] as having first ' roused the long dormant spirit of local amelioration ', since ' itinerant trade ', instead of terminating at Caernarvon, was extended into Eifionydd by a ' tolerable carriage road having been taken in the most eligible direction for a distance of twenty miles '. Unfortunately no early records of the trust survive, so we are left in ignorance of the progress of the work or what it involved. As far as Clynnog there was probably not much to do, for according to Pennant the parishes had kept the old pilgrim road in good repair; how much new work the continuation south across the peninsula entailed is not on record. What is clear is that, both within and without the shire, isolation was beginning to break down.

[15] J. Evans, *North Wales* in *Beauties of England and Wales* (1812), 342.

## BIBLIOGRAPHY

A.

County politics of the age are described in P.D.G. Thomas, ' The parliamentary representation of Caernarvonshire in the eighteenth century' (*TCHS* 1958-9), 'Anglesey politics 1689-1727' (*Trans. Anglesey Antiquarian Soc.* [*TAAS*] 1962, 'Jacobitism in Wales' (*Welsh Hist. Rev.* i. 3, 1962), and his biographical articles in *Hist. of Parliament*: *The Commons 1754-90*, ed. Namier and Brooks (1964), ii. 29, iii. 668-9; Glyn Roberts, ' The Glynnes and the Wynns of Glynllifon ' (*TCHS* 1948). Signatures to the Association of 1696 are given in A. Browning, *Thomas Osborne, Earl of Danby* (1904), ii. 212.

B.

Conditions in agriculture, industry and transport before the machine age are briefly described in chap. i of A. H. Dodd, *The Industrial Revolution in N. Wales* (1951). A sample of agrarian conditions appears in W. M. Richards, ' Some aspects of the Industrial Revolution in south-east Caernarvonshire ' (*TCHS* 1942-3); on contemporary conditions in Anglesey cf. H. Rowland, ' Idea Agriculturae ' (*TAAS* 1934-6), and Francis Jones, ' A squire in Anglesey ' (*id.* 1940). The slate industry during the period is described by D. Dylan Pritchard in *Quarry Manager's Jnl.*, July, Sept., Nov., 1942, Feb., 1945, and by E. Gwynne Jones in ' Hanes bore chwarel Dinorwig ' (*Lleufer*, v., 1949). On seaborne trade generally, D. Thomas, *Hen Longau Sir Gaernarfon* (1952), pen. 3-6. The vicissitudes of the Penrhyn estate can be traced from the family papers deposited in U.C.N.W. Library, Bangor. For examples of early coaching see *Cal. of Wynn Papers* 1223, 1475; S. W. Singer, *Correspondence of Henry Hyde, Earl of Clarendon* (1828), i. 196-201. On the roads, R. T. Pritchard, ' The post road in Caernarvonshire ' and ' Caernarvonshire Turnpike Trust ' (*TCHS* 1952, 1956), and H. L. North, *The Seven Roads across Penmaenmawr*, 1935. The ferries are exhaustively dealt with in H. R. Davies, *The Conway and the Menai Ferries* (1942), briefly summarised in review in *TCHS* 1942-3; the *Journals* of John Wesley are also a source of information on this subject.

# X

## RELIGIOUS AND EDUCATIONAL
## MOVEMENTS (1688-1780)

THE stagnation which was so evident in the political and economic life of Caernarvonshire under the later Stuarts and the early Georges did not extend to the two closely related fields of religion and education. Hitherto we have been dealing with a limited class — the gentry who had managed county affairs since the Acts of Union. We have watched the lesser gentry being gradually edged out of the governing establishment; those below them in the social scale — farmers, shopkeepers, peasants, labourers — have hardly come into the picture at all, so scant are the records (even the identifiable dwellings) they have left behind them. Now we begin to come face to face with a movement which brings these forgotten men into the limelight, and eventually equips them for leadership as the traditional leaders abdicate or are passed by. It was the first stage in a long-drawn revolution which on the one hand saved the national tongue from degenerating into a *patois,* but on the other hand exposed the national culture to the ever-present peril of turning in on itself, in default of the wider cultural contacts which aristocratic patronage can bring.

All this lay in the future; what was immediately evident was a more dynamic leadership in religious life which, had not the intrusion of the political factor cut it short, might have given a different twist to the county's history. The Revolution of 1688 inaugurated what proved to be one of the most fruitful periods in the life of the diocese. In the following year began the episcopate of Humphrey Hum-

phreys. Descended from an old Caernarvonshire family, educated at Friars school before he went to Oxford, and married
to the daughter of one of his predecessors in the see, Robert
Morgan, he had already served in the diocese as vicar of
Cricieth and as dean during the epicopate of Humphrey
Lloyd. Humphreys was a distinguished Welsh scholar and
patron of Welsh literature. In the first visitation of the
diocese in 1690 he made history by issuing his visitation
queries in Welsh. And these visitations of his were no mere
formality. Bishop Humphreys kept in close touch with his
clergy, and in turn encouraged them to hold frequent con-
ferences with each other. He was a warm supporter of the
Revolution (was not his wife related to one of the Seven
Bishops?), but he did not, like Bishop Bayly, enter into the
hurly-burly of politics, except on one occasion when he tried
(unsuccessfully) to prevent the election for Beaumaris of
Sir William Williams, the prosecutor of the Seven Bishops,
on the ground that he was an enemy to the Church. His
greatest work, however, was for education. When the Society
for the Promotion of Christian Knowledge was founded in
1699 he was one of its firmest friends, and he elicited the
help of his clergy in its activities, especially in the translation and distribution of religious literature, in which Bangor
diocesan clergy played a prominent part. For the S.P.C.K.
revived the work of the Welsh Trust, but under more hope-
ful auspices, since its principal backing came not from a
group of charitable Londoners but from the episcopate and
clergy at home; and in the schools it set up, although its
educational curriculum was a little less ambitious than that
of the Trust, it did have the wisdom to provide for teaching
through the medium of Welsh.

   With some difficulty, the bishop persuaded the treasurer
of the cathedral, John Jones, to fill the vacant place of dean.
John Jones, of the Anglesey family of Plas Gwyn, was
incumbent of several Anglesey parishes, where (before taking
up his residence at the deanery) he was actively engaged in
the work of the S.P.C.K. from its inception, serving as local
correspondent for Anglesey, holding meetings with the local

clergy to canvass their co-operation, and setting up at his own expense several elementary schools. On moving to Bangor he continued the work by founding schools at Aber, Llanllechid, Gyffin and Bangor itself, with from ten to twelve pupils in each school. He provided for the continuance of the work by leaving in his will legacies of £100 to each of them ' for the instruction of poor children for ever to read the Bible and the Common Prayer Book in Welsh and be taught the catechism of the Church of England in Welsh '. The great obstacle, the dean found, was the poverty of the children : ' of late ', he wrote in 1699, ' their poverty is so great that they cannot allow themselves time to learn '; and later, in 1716, he explains the situation more at large :

> It is impossible in those parts to fix the poor Children constantly and regularly at school, because they must go for ever and anon to beg for victuals, there being no poor rates settled in these parts, it is the constant method to relieve the poor at their doors, and the houses of the several Parishes being scattered about at considerable distances from each other increases the difficulty the poor children labour under, and in harvest the poor parents take them out of School, and declare they had rather they should not be taught at all then [than] be debarred of the use and service of them.

It is very depressing picture of life in Caernarvonshire in the early eighteenth century — and a striking commentary on the backward condition of agriculture and industry to which reference was made earlier on.

In addition to the setting up of schools and the widespread distribution of religious literature, the S.P.C.K. tried to encourage the clergy to keep up their own reading by establishing parochial libraries. Two of these are known to have been started in Caernarvonshire — at Pwllheli and at Eglwys Rhos. Nor were Dean Jones's educational services confined to the S.P.C.K. As governor of Friars school he kept a vigilant eye on school buildings and endowments, and there may be significance in the fact that the first mention of a school library comes in his period of office. It was altogether one of the most flourishing periods in the history of the school; but this was partly due to a bequest by a son of Llŷn (Thomas Jones) who was a customs house officer in London, which made it possible to add to the usual classical curriculum the teaching and writing and arithmetic; this appealed to parents wishing to give their children a 'modern education'. In this context mention should also be made of a substantial legacy left in trust by the vicar of Llanystumdwy in 1695 to Griffith Vaughan of Cors y gedol, for the establishment of a school in in one of the three shires of Gwynedd. A petition signed by over a score of responsible burgesses put forward the claims of Pwllheli to benefit by this endowment on the ground of the remoteness of Llŷn and Eifionydd from any 'free school';[1] Botwnnog was already losing its character as a grammar school. Pwllheli's plea succeeded; the history of its grammar school will be followed up later.

Bishop Humphreys (to his own regret) was translated to Hereford in 1701, and succeeded by John Evans, another Caernarvonshire man. By this time, unhappily, the intrusion of party politics into episcopal appointments had already begun; Bishop Evans was nominated by a Whig ministry; and fell foul of the Tory faction, especially in Anglesey, where some of his clergy aligned themselves, unchecked, with the gathering revolt against Baron Hill. But John Jones was still dean till his death in 1727, and his educational work still had official support. John Evans is best remembered, however, as the last bishop to reside in the diocese for nearly sixty years, and the last Welsh-speaking bishop for still longer. The eleven bishops who held office during these years treated Bangor as a stepping-stone to higher things; only one of them stuck to it for the rest of his life. This proved a severe setback to the quickening of religious life in the diocese, marked by an increase of communicants in almost every parish, which had begun in Humphrey Humphreys's episcopate. Energetic functionaries could to some extent fill the gap, as they had done in similar conditions two centuries earlier; it is true also that the bulk of the clergy were resident

[1] U.C.N.W. Mostyn MSS. 422-3.

in their parishes, at home in the language of their parishioners and alive to their regular duties. What was now lacking was the fellowship and understanding between bishop and clergy and among the clergy themselves which Humphrey Humphreys and John Jones had successfully fostered and which communicated itself to their flocks. It is against this background that we must consider the second stage of the religious and educational revival, which will be dealt with later.

Meanwhile, however, something should be said about religious bodies outside the establishment. On the dwindling recusant community there is little to add to what has already been said. In a sense the lengthy *cywydd* in which Gwilym Pue (as he liked to spell his name) commemorated, not long before the Revolution, the century-old exploits of his grandfather Robert Pugh and his companions of the Rhiwledyn cave, may be looked on as the swan song of Catholic recusancy in Creuddyn, which in turn was its last Caernarvonshire refuge. Many years were to pass before Roman Catholicism again became a significant factor in the life of the shire.

To Protestant Dissenters, on the other hand, the Revolution brought a substantial measure of legalised freedom of worship. Some of the houses which had been licensed for their worship during the brief period of Charles II's Indulgence, and had since been used occasionally for the same purpose whenever they could escape the vigilance of the authorities, now gave them more permanent shelter. Richard Edwards remained a pillar of local Nonconformity till his death in 1704, and one of its meeting places (which he probably attended) was within a stone's throw of Nanhoron and on the estate. Ellis Rowland precariously held together the tiny remnant of Dissent in and around Caernarvon during the days of persecution, and in later and easier years he kept a 'private grammar school' there. Whatever his earlier sufferings, he was in comfortable circumstances when he died in 1693: for the last fifteen years he and his wife had held the Llanfair Isgaer estate in trust for the infant heir. From 1689 too the Dissenters of Pwllheli and neighbourhood

had had a regular minister in Daniel Phillips, a Carmarthenshire man and a pupil of Stephen Hughes. He had preached
there occasionally since 1684, had married the widow of
Henry Maurice, and lived in her house at Pwllheli, which
became a sort of manse for four successive ministers, until in
1741 (or possibly earlier) the congregation built its own
chapel — the first in Caernarvonshire.

In accordance with the usual practice of the early Dissenters, Phillips exercised a general pastoral oversight over all
the Dissenters of the shire, and the few who were to be found
in Anglesey, and for this purpose he received small grants
from central funds established by the Dissenting denominations from 1690. Worshippers in Llangybi and Llangian
parishes — at Ty Helyg (later Capel Helyg) in the former
and Lôn Dywyll in the latter — looked to Pwllheli as their
mother church, going there for important occasions like
reception into the Church (the Independent counterpart of
confirmation) and receiving periodic visits from the minister.
The Caernarvon congregation was in much the same position.
A handful of Independents had been meeting there since the
Toleration Act; twenty years later there were a dozen adherents — yeomen, craftsmen and shopkeepers, with just one
who styled himself ' gentleman '. It remained a static group:
even in 1791, when the first chapel was built, it had to
accommodate only fifteen regular worshippers. Our last
glimpse of Quakerism in Caernarvonshire is a meeting at
Penmachno in 1731, addressed by a Pennsylvania Quaker (of
Bala origin) on tour from Merioneth to Ireland in an effort
to revive the waning cause.

East of Caernarvon Dissent did not exist. It remained on
the whole localised in the regions where it had first grown
up in the days of the Propagation; a return made in 1749
shows much the same distribution as the census taken by
Archbishop Sheldon more than seventy years earlier. Its
adherents formed small, closed communities, generally
marrying within their own circle, and too thankful for their
recent relief from penal laws to draw attention to themselves
by proselytising among their neighbours. To a very limited

extent they were able also to educate their own young. By the will of Dr. Daniel Williams, a Wrexham Presbyterian minister who died in 1716, a substantial part of his fortune of £50,000 was devoted to the educational needs of his fellow-Dissenters, including the establishment of seven free schools in North Wales, of which (after legal difficulties had been smoothed out) one was fixed at Caernarvon and one at Pwllheli; Conway, influenced by its vicar, refused one. The Dr. Williams foundation, of course, did not provide buildings; the schoolroom was generally the chapel, and the minister rather than the place was the determining factor in the allocation of grants.

The second phase of the revival was in a real sense an offshoot of the first, for Griffith Jones, its central figure in the early stages, had thrown himself whole-heartedly into the educational activities of the S.P.C.K. in Carmarthenshire from within a decade of its foundation; his work was supported generously from its funds and he himself owed his living of Llanddowror to one of its founders, Philipps of Picton. But his deep concern at the spiritual ignorance and moral decline he believed to have infected the country since the Restoration would not allow him to await the slow impact of the printed word on a largely illiterate public, or the rise of a new generation of whom a handful only would have learned their letters in the scattered ' Charity schools '. So he determined to address himself directly to those already grown up as well as to the children, and in order to reach the largest number in the shortest time he devised schools which should open in the winter months when farm work was slack — thus minimising one of Dean John Jones's difficulties — and move on elsewhere as soon as the pupils had been grounded in Christian principles (based on the Bible and the Church catechism) and trained to read on from here for themselves. Children were to be taught in the day time, and adults — who in fact constituted two-thirds of his pupils — in the evening.

But Griffith Jones was bent on appealing to the heart as

well as the head. A powerful and stirring preacher, he revived the itinerant evangelism which had been under a cloud since the days of the Propagation, 'going about preaching', as his bishop complained, 'on week days in Churches, Churchyards, and sometimes on the mountains to hundreds of auditors'. The Circulating schools were his special contribution to the revival, but his itinerant evangelism was taken up from 1735 in Cardiganshire by Daniel Rowland, a clergyman profoundly influenced by Griffith Jones, and in Breconshire by Howel Harris, a schoolmaster stirred to evangelism by a sermon in his own parish church. A couple of years later they joined forces, set out on preaching tours of widening scope, and began organising their converts into 'Societies' to which the new nickname 'Methodist' began to be applied. From the outset there was acute division in both Anglican and Dissenting circles about this revival of field preaching with its appeal to mass emotion, so alien to the spirit of the age.

In Caernarvonshire the earlier and more sedate phase of the revival had almost been confined to Arfon and Arllechwedd — naturally enough, since it centred in the cathedral. The second and more 'enthusiastic' phase, like the seventeenth-century Puritanism with which it had so much in common, first struck root in Eifionydd and Llŷn. Early in 1741 Howel Harris for the first time extended his activities to North Wales, through the invitation of Lewis Rees, a Montgomeryshire minister who belonged to the wing of Dissent which welcomed the new 'enthusiasm'. Harris then continued his journey through Bala and Trawsfynydd and so across the Traeth to Penmorfa and Llangybi. It was a route John Wesley was often to follow a few years later; but Wesley after crossing the Traeth always headed northwards for Caernarvon because his objective was Ireland; why did Howel Harris turn west into Eifionydd and Llŷn? Many different accounts have come down to us, but in one point all are agreed. The invitation came from William Pritchard, a substantial farmer of Glasfryn Fawr in Llangybi parish. Local tradition represents Pritchard as an easy-going churchman who was awakened to religious zeal by chancing to pass one night under the window of one of the 'country' members of the Pwllheli congregation when family worship was in progress. It made a deep impression; he began to find his vicar's sermons 'unscriptural' and to set his heart on a visit from one of Griffith Jones's schoolmasters and from one of the South Wales revivalists.

The former aim was fulfilled first. It happened that a Circulating school at Llanuwchllyn in Merioneth had just run its course, and the teacher, Jenkin Morgan, went on to Glasfryn, where, after the use of the church had been refused, William Pritchard accommodated it — children and adults — in his farm kitchen. It was Jenkin Morgan who went to Bala to escort Howel Harris to Glasfryn. Harris preached to the Llangybi Dissenters and during the next five days travelled through Llŷn as far south as Llangian and as far north as Nefyn and Porthdinllaen, preaching where he could find hearers, sometimes making contact with existing groups of Dissenters, whom he always tried to woo back into the Church. Then he returned to Glasfryn and back into Merioneth. He met with a good deal of popular hostility, and with obstruction from the civil and ecclesiastical authorities — notably from Chancellor John Owen, vicar of Llannor and Deneio, who virtually ruled the diocese in the absence of the bishop, and showed an animus against both Methodists and Dissenters which could certainly have been moderated had his bishop (the more tolerant Zachary Pearce) been on the spot to check him. Pritchard and Morgan were both victims: the one lost his farm, the other was arrested as a vagabond on his way south. Pritchard was also cited before the Church court, where his slighting comments on the vicar's sermons were brought up against him; the case was carried up to Great Sessions, and dragged on for two years, but he was a man of sufficient means to afford a good lawyer, with whose help he won his case. It is not surprising to learn that the parish clerk at Llannor — William Roberts, a personal friend of the chancellor — wrote in 1745 an *anterliwt* which was a venomous satire on the Methodists.

This hostility is easily understood. Country memories are
long, and the nicknames for the new preachers which sprang
readily to the lips were those which recalled the rule of the
Saints: they were the new *pengryniaid,* or Roundheads;
they were dubbed Cradocks, after the name of one of the
agents of the Propagation who (as it happened) had worked
entirely outside Caernarvonshire. After all, it was only eighty
years since the houses of local Puritans had been ransacked
for arms, and cases of pistols produced; not much more than
thirty since Richard Edwards died, a man who had served
under General Lambert and had lain in prison under suspicion of plotting against the Restoration monarchy. To the
Church authorities the new itinerants were men who, like
their seventeenth-century predecessors, undermined Church
discipline by ignoring parish boundaries and spurning the
ministrations of those clergy to whose lives or teachings they
took exception. The lay authorities were equally suspicious
of the men who tramped the highways, collected crowds
and so invited breaches of the peace; and the man in the
street, then as always, resented interference with his pleasures.

Harris, however, was not to be deterred by an initially
unfriendly reception. During the next dozen years he made
further preaching tours of Llŷn and Eifionydd, sometimes
accompanied by other Methodist leaders from the south, and
followed by helpers sent to consolidate his work and to
organise his converts. A reply to the bishop's visitation
queries in 1749 from a Merioneth parish contains the significant comment that the parish had become ' a great thorough-
fare through which are frequently seen troops of Methodists
passing and repassing on their way from South Wales to
Caernarvonshire '. Less than a year after Harris's first tour
of Llŷn there were prosecutions in the bishop's court for the
holding of ' conventicles' (doubtless Methodist Societies) in
the neighbourhood of Llanbedrog, and in 1747 charges were
brought against inhabitants of Llangian and Llanengan for
assembling to hear a ' presumptuous strolling person ' in
whom we may probably recognise a Methodist ' exhorter '.

In that year there were four Societies in Llŷn, with nearly thirty members, almost equally divided between men and women. In local tradition the terror caused by a partial eclipse of the sun is said to have come to the aid of the Methodist exhortations. A visit by Howel Harris to Waunfawr about the same time was a first step in bringing the Methodist gospel into Arfon. Here again his contacts seem to have been a group of Caernarvon Independents who had taken refuge there from the hostile atmosphere of the county town; but his advice to them was to return to the Church in the hope of leavening it with their spiritual zeal. Before long the local *seiadau* were able to keep going under their own leaders with only occasional visits from the southern evangelists. As early as 1748 a farm hand at Cefnamwlch is said to have undertaken a general oversight of converts in this neighbourhood; soon afterwards his place was taken by another disciple of Harris, a carpenter named Charles Mark who turned farmer and in 1752 built, as an annex to his farm of Ty Mawr (in Bryncroes parish) a tiny thatched meeting house believed to be the first building in the shire devoted entirely to Methodist worship. It became the Mecca of Methodists over a wide area, and Mark remained a pillar of the cause till his death in 1795. A report to the bishop in 1776 roundly declares that half the parishioners of Bryncroes are Methodists.

In 1746, on a visit from South Wales by Peter Williams, the Caernarvonshire Methodists made their first convert in the higher reaches of county society — no longer a mere *gwas,* but the mistress of Cefnamwlch herself. She was the wife of the William Griffith whose father had thrice represented the shire in parliament: an important man socially, but by all accounts rarely sober and often violent at home. When Harris revisited the district two years later she accompanied him to the Methodist Assemblies down south, and eventually (her husband having refused to have her back) remained there till her last illness, becoming a cause of bitter dissension among the Methodist leaders. This and other internal troubles, doctrinal and otherwise, proved a serious

set-back to the movement and a brake on its missionary
activities. So it was in the main local zeal, with occasional
backing from South Wales, that carried Methodism deeper
into Eifionydd and Arfon in the 1750's, when two new
Societies were formed — one at Brynengan (in Llanystumdwy parish), one just outside Clynnog. Both were regions
where seventeenth-century Puritanism had left some mark,
and this may have helped to prepare the ground for the new
preachers. It may be remembered that Llangybi had
remained one of the chief Puritan centres in the shire after
the Restoration, and that the worshippers who met there in
secret included elements from Clynnog, where Ellis Rowland
had ministered in the days of the Propagation. In 1718 — not
much more than forty years after the forcible dispersion of
the 'conventicle' addressed by James Owen — Richard
Nanney had become vicar of Clynnog, where he remained
for nearly half a century. He was an Oxford man, sprung
from the ancient Merioneth family and himself a squire in
a small way; but from early in his incumbency he was also
a staunch supporter of the Griffith Jones schools in his area,
and before it ended he was filling the old pilgrim church
with congregations drawn from far and wide and roused to
a high pitch of spiritual excitement by his fervent evangelism.

By the 'sixties and 'seventies Methodism was making its
first contacts with the industrial as distinct from the agricultural elements in the shire: first among the quarrymen of
Llanllyfni, then farther east among those of Llanberis, where
a father and son working one of the early 'bargains' in the
quarry (and credited with the introduction of gunpowder
there) began organising quarry services during the lunch
break. About the same time Societies were forming in those
parts of the shire in closest contact with Merioneth: the
hinterland of the Traeth on one side and Nantconwy on
the other. The spread of the movement owed at least as
much to random personal contacts as to planned evangelism.
The removal of an earnest Methodist farmer to a farm in
another part of the shire — it might be after eviction by a
landlord or steward who banned the use of the farm premises

for Methodist meetings — was often the first step in the
penetration of a new area; persecution was liable to defeat
its own ends.

The zeal of the Methodists also began to infect the old
Dissenters. Here ' Dissenter ' had come for practical purposes
to mean ' Independent ', as the use of the term *Sentar* in
colloquial Welsh itself suggests. The Presbyterian groups of
the seventeenth century did not long survive the restoration
of the episcopal order in the Church in 1660, and Presbyter-
ianism is no more heard of in the shire until the Methodists
themselves were driven to adopt a Presbyterian order after
separating from the Church. The Baptists had never taken
root in Gwynedd. So some who had been awakened by the
revival but were scared away from Methodism by its continued attachment to the Church (despite official rebuffs to
' enthusiasm ') gravitated towards the Independents, though
not on any significant scale until the next century. An ironical
result of the persecutions of William Pritchard and Jenkin
Morgan is that both of them renounced their Anglican
allegiance, turned to the Independents, and carried their
new faith into Anglesey, succeeding, if slowly, where the
Propagation and the Roundhead army had so signally failed
in the preceding century. For help he turned to Lewis Rees
and a ministerial colleague from Montgomeryshire who
shared his crusading enthusiasm.

Two incidents connected with their journey to Anglesey
in 1744 help to explain on the one hand the reluctance of
many of the old Dissenters to associate themselves with the
new ' enthusiasm ', and on the other hand the popular hostility towards the revival of itinerant evangelism. William
Edwards, the seventy-year-old master of Dr. Williams's
school at Caernarvon (who appears also to have had pastoral
oversight of the Pwllheli church), told the Dr. Williams
trustees how he had been roused at dead of night by the
vicar of Llanbeblig, with a mob at his heels, summoning him
to appear before the bishop's court. The charge was occasioned by his having contacted the two Montgomeryshire
missioners to direct them on their way to Anglesey; for the

Toleration Act covered only Dissenting worship in licensed chapels, not irregular itinerant preaching. Edwards could not, like William Pritchard, afford the cost of defending his suit in court, and wrote for advice. The result is unknown, but the appearance of the two ministers near Penmynydd (where Pritchard was now farming) opened a second act in the drama. Word had gone round that two *rowndiaid* were expected, and a small crowd gathered; local tradition records that when Edmund Prys's translation of the 121st Psalm ('Disgwyliaf o'r mynyddoedd draw') was announced, all eyes turned towards the Caernarvonshire hills in expectation of another armed invasion from across the Straits such as their grandfathers had experienced, and the timid took refuge behind a neighbouring dyke!

The stirrings of the revival had been strongly felt among the Baptists of South Wales, where the cause had struck strong roots in the age of the Propagation. In 1776, with the aid of a grant from central funds, a small band of Baptist missioners set out to evangelise the north. They took the familiar route through Dolgellau and Penmorfa, and after a successful preaching tour in Anglesey returned to Llŷn, preached at Pwllheli and Nefyn and then extended their mission to the Conway valley. In both regions they left a nucleus of disciples. Their gospel was essentially the same as that of the Methodist missioners, and at first they had the co-operation of both them and the existing Dissenting bodies, and sometimes the hospitality of their chapels. But their insistence on the rite of adult baptism by immersion as the outward and visible sign of conversion soon separated them off, and by the 'eighties they too were building their own chapels and so contributing to what was to become so characteristic a feature of the rural landscape of the shire. Meanwhile their open-air baptisms in streams or tarns often drew even larger crowds than the field preaching of the Methodists.

It was during this same period when Methodist effort was halted by internal stresses that yet another strand was added to the variegated web of religious life in the area. Arriving from Germany shortly before the rise of Methodism (which they profoundly influenced), the United Brethren, or Moravians as they were generally known here, had established several centres of worship and community life in England and one in Pembrokeshire. In 1771 David Mathias, a Pembrokeshire Moravian, obtained leave from his fellow-Brethren to carry into the heart of Snowdonia the Moravian gospel, which differed from that of the Methodists in that its stress was mystical rather than doctrinal or moral, and its methods those of personal contacts rather than field preaching to the masses. At Caernarvon Mathias had to run for his life from a mob pelting him with stones and dirt (a not unusual experience in those days for revivalists in that unruly town), but he found a warmer welcome in the hills, and with Drws y coed as resident centre he established a number of small Societies meeting in farmhouses in Nantlle, Beddgelert and as far as Cricieth, with one under the friendly roof of John Morgan, the penurious but hospitable curate of Llanberis. The mission only lasted five years, and an attempted come-back in the early 1790's, with a now much more subdued Caernarvon as centre, found the Methodists back on the crest of the wave, and achieved little. It was a brief episode, and left no visible mark behind it, but it made its contribution to the general atmosphere of religious revival that was soon to sweep the county. For example, it was his contact with the Moravian mission that turned John Morgan into a powerful evangelistic preacher, drawing to Llanberis church congregations some of whom travelled as much as twelve to fifteen miles to sit at his feet.

The educational revival continued alongside the religious revival, and followed much the same path. After Jenkin Morgan's Circulating school had run its course at Glasfryn in 1741, the movement was extended westwards to the farther parts of Llŷn, where two schools had been set up by the end of the following year; then eastwards into Arfon, and finally by 1750 into Arllechwedd, with the establishment

of a school in Llandygái. By 1761 a total of eighty-five
Circulating schools — the largest number in any county of
North Wales — had been set up in Caernarvonshire. This
does not, of course, mean that they all ran concurrently; in
fact more often than not a school returned to the same parish
several times within a year or two. The number attending
in a single session was usually thirty to forty, sometimes sixty
to seventy. The teachers were mostly local curates, sometimes parish clerks. The education provided was rudimentary
in comparison with what was given in the S.P.C.K. schools,
still more when compared with the curriculum in those of
the Welsh Trust. On the other hand it reached a far wider
public. There can be no doubt that the bounds of literacy
were greatly extended, and this in turn gave an impetus to
the religious revival, for Methodist strategy called for a
nucleus of literate lay helpers to consolidate the work of the
leaders, and the Circulating schools provided just that
nucleus.

A striking example — though hardly a typical one — is
that remarkable man Robert Jones of Rhoslan. He started
with the initial advantage of a literate mother well versed in
the Welsh Bible and Prayer Book, but his formal schooling
was confined to six weeks in a Circulating school in his own
parish of Llanystumdwy when he was a lad of seventeen and
a working carpenter. That would be about 1763. Four years
later he was instrumental in reviving the schools in his district after Griffith Jones's death. He himself taught in seven
of them between 1766 and 1778, and in the latter year he
published an elementary guide to reading Welsh specifically
aimed at the unlettered. He became an influential figure in
the Methodist movement, and ended by writing its early
history in what has become a Welsh prose classic — *Drych
yr Amseroedd*. Education in the shire was certainly not
stagnant; nor of course were the folk arts of the countryside.
It was in the early eighteenth century, and in the sequestered
parish of Ynyscynhaearn, that David Owen the harpist is
believed to have composed what remains one of the loveliest
of Welsh songs, *Dafydd y Garreg Wen*, and its livelier com-

panion *Codiad yr ehedydd;* and from farther west in a later
generation came Thomas Jones, the blind harpist of Pwllheli,
who fought at Trafalgar, performed on both flute and clarinet
(whether at convivial gatherings or in Llanystumdwy
church), and became father of a bard of local repute. But
the general poverty which Dean Jones had found so hampering remained a depressing influence; our next task will
be to examine some of the means by which the county was
drawn out of the economic backwardness which lay at the
root of this.

## BIBLIOGRAPHY

On Humphrey Humphreys and John Jones see E. G. Wright in
*TAAS* 1949, 1952. Conditions in the church generally are described in
A. I. Pryce, *Diocese of Bangor during Three Centuries,* xxxviii-xlvi,
and in J. W. James, *Welsh Church History,* chs. 12 and 13. The
S.P.C.K. schools and Dr. Williams's schools are listed and described
in T. Shankland, ' Sir John Philipps and the Charity-school movement
in Wales ' (*Trans. Cymmrodorion Soc.* 1906), Griffith Jones's schools
by R. T. Jenkins in *Bull. of Bd. of Celtic Studies,* v. 1931, 354-79. On
Caernarvonshire Dissent during the period see Rees and Thomas,
*Hanes Eglwysi Annibynol Cymru* (1873), ii. 450-60, iii. 156-8, 234-45,
Bob Owen in *Cofiadur* xx (1950), and *Cal. of Letters relating to N.
Wales* (see above, ch. vi), pp. 15, 19; on the rise of Methodism,
W. Gilbert Williams in *Cylchgrawn Cymdeithas Hanes M.C.* xxxvii
(1952), and O. D. Williams (ed.), *Ty Mawr, Llŷn: Daucanmlwyddiant*
(1948); on the Baptist mission to Caernarvonshire Joshua Thomas,
*Hanes y Bedyddwyr yn mhlith y Cymru,* ed. B. Davies (1885), 580-2;
on the Moravians R. T. Jenkins, *The Moravian Brethren in N. Wales,*
(1938), vi-xi, and on the decline of Quakerism, id., in *TCHS* 1940,
75-6.

# XI

# ECONOMIC EXPANSION
## (1780-1900)

THE crucial turning point in the economic development of Caernarvonshire came when, after John Pennant's death in 1781, his son Richard (raised to the Irish peerage two years later as Baron Penrhyn) secured at last control over the undivided Penrhyn inheritance. He had already commissioned the distinguished architect Samuel Wyatt to draw up plans for the extension of the hall, and as soon as the work was completed he went to live there. In this way one of the historic estates of the shire fell into the hands of a man resident on the estate, amply provided with capital to develop it, and fortified by three generations of business experience on the grand scale. There could have been no more timely shot in the arm for Caernarvonshire's stagnant industries, communications and agriculture. The effects were felt in all three fields, and once the vogue of 'improvement' had set in it soon spread to other estates and other parts of the shire.

## A.   AGRICULTURE

Let us look first at agriculture. Much of the Penrhyn estate is wind-swept and subject to high rainfall, and by way of protection the new owner resorted on an extensive scale to the fashionable pursuit of afforestation; from the time he acquired control of the estate he planted an annual average of something like thirty-five thousand trees, reaching a total of about six hundred thousand by 1797. His farming improve-

ments were chiefly in the direction of stock-breeding, better
farmhouses and the adoption of leases which, while laying
down conditions of cultivation governed by the best contemporary practice, also provided compensation to the tenant
for any improvements he might make. An obituary notice in
the local press[1] on his death in 1808 describes him — no
doubt with justice — as having been responsible for 'greater
advances towards improvement than during several preceding centuries'.

His example gave just the spur that was needed to bring
the Agrarian Revolution belatedly to Caernarvonshire, and
to turn its landlords into what Arthur Young called 'spirited
proprietors' vying with each other as 'improvers'. In 1816
Thomas Love Peacock, later the friend and benefactor of
Shelley, having recently spent a couple of years in North
Wales, published in *Headlong Hall* the first of those fictional
satires on contemporary society on which his fame chiefly
depends. The scene is laid in Llanberis; Squire Headlong's
father, descended from a long line of barbarous and tur-
bulent ap Rhaiaders, had 'troubled himself about nothing
but the cellars, and suffered everything else to go to rack
and ruin'; but the son stands for the new fashion in landlordism, and Headlong Hall under his régime becomes a
rendezvous for others who have caught the spirit of the age,
and who express it in the table talk, recorded with whimsical
solemnity, which forms the main content of the book.
Leaving the realm of fiction, we find much the same contrast
drawn a few years earlier in Hyde Hall's *Description of
Caernarvonshire*, in which he speaks[2] of the 'great improvements introduced . . . within the last thirty years'. 'At that
time', he says (referring to Llŷn in the period round 1780)
'a farm becoming vacant hung like a dead weight in the
landlord's hands; while at present the suspicion of a vacancy,
however remote or slight, occasions application after application in despite of raised rents, denial of leases, and absence
of all lures and promises'. In both the fictional and the

---

[1] *North Wales Gazette*, 26 Jan. 1808.
[2] P. 293.

factual account the contrast is no doubt exaggerated, for Hall never saw Caernarvonshire before about 1795 or Peacock before 1810; it must be borne in mind too that the former wrote at the height of the Napoleonic war, the effects of which on farming will concern us later. But the spirit of change is evident in many directions.

A slight but significant symptom is the formation of a county agricultural society. These had long been common elsewhere: Breconshire had one (thanks to Howel Harris) as early as 1755; Anglesey's 'Antient Druids', who also aimed at fostering agriculture, were in existence by the 1780's; Denbighshire and Montgomeryshire followed in the 1790's, Merioneth at the turn of the century; Caernarvonshire not till 1807. These agricultural societies organised ploughing matches and sheep-shearing competitions, introduced new agricultural implements, distributed seeds and brought in men skilled in special branches of husbandry; they offered premiums to farmers for success in particular crops, to farm servants for faithful service, to cottagers for bringing up large families without coming on the parish. Sometimes they organised new fairs, or petitions to parliament on the needs of agriculture, or agitations on the state of the roads. The local press also helped. In 1808 the *North Wales Gazette* began publication at Bangor. In its early years about a quarter of the contents consisted in contributions on agricultural topics.

It has been shown how the Asshetons of Ashley, on succeeding in 1774 to the estate and name of the Hampshire Smiths, began to interest themselves in their Caernarvonshire property of Vaynol as a political asset. Soon afterwards the economic possibilities of this 'tract of bogs and rocks' (as their ancestor had called it) thrust themselves on their notice, and from 1778 they thought it worth while to let their farms on long leases with restrictive clauses, designed to give greater security to the tenant and to encourage him to better husbandry. But many of the tenants lost heart and left for America before the leases ran out; weary of waiting for better times at home, they thought they saw a quicker road to prosperity in the prospect of freehold and fertile land in the freer conditions of the new republic. Hyde Hall sees an exception to the prevailing spirit of improvement in the 'wretched appearance' of the parish of Llanddeiniolen where the home estate of the Assheton Smiths lay, but with a hint that the recent advent of 'new occupiers' might herald a better day. But the more obvious possibilities of Vaynol lay in the direction of industry rather than of agriculture, and the family did not emerge as agricultural pioneers (notably in the field of cattle breeding) until long after they had taken up permanent residence on their Caernarvonshire estate. In Llŷn and Eifionydd the initiative was taken by the Edwardses of Nanhoron. After Richard Edwards's death they had abandoned religious and political dissidence and stuck firmly to the practice of the law, which enabled them to extend their estates (to the old domain of Bodwrda, for example) and to farm them on enlightened and profitable lines. Throughout the area there was a greatly improved yield of wheat, better attention to pastures, and increased planting of potatoes. From about 1780 exports of corn from Pwllheli, which had been rare till past the middle of the century, became substantial and frequent.

One of the great obstacles to 'improvement' was the exis-tence of common and waste lands. The movement for enclosing and allotting these had long been under way, and it reached the highlands of Gwynedd in the 1790's. It was a general assumption that communal property of any sort provided no spur to productive energy, while 'the magic of property', in the classic phrase of Arthur Young — referring of course to individual property — 'turns sand into gold'. Here in Snowdonia there was no question of consolidating arable strips in the village fields to give better scope for enterprise and experiment, as in the English midlands or in the rich river valleys of Powys. Up to now, as we have seen in connection with the slate industry, neither private landowners nor the agents of the crown (which was lord of so many Snowdonian manors) had placed much value on these rocky wastes, many of which had been treated as a sort of no-man's land. But the tendency to overstock the available sheep walks, and the increased value to be expected of enclosed lands, were powerful inducements to follow the popular fashion of applying to parliament for a private Enclosure Act, which would encounter little opposition in a parliament of landlords and would be administered by commissioners, named in the Act, drawn mainly from the dependent class of land agents. The outbreak in 1793 of a war with France destined to last twenty-two years was a further argument in favour of a far more intensive use of our land resources. On the other hand, in the words of the Land Report of 1896:[3]

> It would be idle to suppose that the main motives of the Welsh landowners who eagerly sought the facilities given by Parliament was to extend the margin of cultivation. They saw . . . that the movement gave them the opportunity of acquiring the sheep-walks and pasture lands till then unenclosed as their own in severalty under the title of an Act of Parliament, while the prospect of costs gave the family solicitors of the Principality a sufficient inducement to use their best endeavours to secure the passing of an Inclosure Act wherever a waste was extensive enough.

The outstanding problem with which the enclosure commissioners had to cope in this area was that of the squatters who had settled on waste land with no legal title but with the connivance or even encouragement of the local authorities. These squatter settlements were now beginning to wear a different look in their eyes, and Ireland was held up as an awful warning of the effects of indiscriminate squatting on common lands. The cottagers, however, had other views. The very earliest parliamentary enclosure in Caernarvonshire, under an Act of 1802, was that of the extensive crown common of Rhoshirwaun, covering two or three thousand acres extending over three parishes in the far west of Llŷn, on which scores of fishermen over the years had been permitted to ' squat '. When it was proposed to sell their holdings and cottages over their heads if the encroachments had

been made within the past twenty years, the squatters offered
forcible resistance, especially when they found that they
were going to lose the turbary which had hitherto supplied
them with free fuel. Hyde Hall, who was on the spot at the
time collecting information for his *Description of Caernarvonshire* thought that the ' opportune arrival of a party
of dragoons sent for to England for the purpose ' had put an
end to resistance, but the Act could not be finally put into
operation till 1814.

Four years after the Rhoshirwaun enclosure started on its
stormy course, a similar Act, promoted by Assheton Smith
of Vaynol and Rice Thomas of Coed Helen, dealt with the
common lands of Llanddeiniolen. Alarmed by the resistance
at Rhoshirwaun, the gentry of the shire had held a meeting
at Caernarvon in 1808 at which they resolved to take all
necessary measures to enforce the Enclosure Acts and to
bring to justice any who resisted them. Opposition at Llanddeiniolen was accordingly met by the reading of the Riot
Act and the issue of warrants for the arrest of six of the
rioters — four men and two women. Within three weeks
three of them were in Caernarvon gaol; one, named Ellis
Evan Siôn Foulk, fled to Merthyr, the contemporary Cave of
Adullam, and returned when the storm had blown over, to
become father of Ellis Evans, a highly respected Calvinistic
Methodist minister. What happened to the rest is unknown;
let us hope they benefited by the general amnesty by which
the jubilee of George III was celebrated in 1810. Out of more
than three thousand enclosed (and used mainly as a grouse
moor by Assheton Smith), less than a hundred were reserved
as common for the cottagers, and long before the end of the
century the greater part of this had been quietly annexed
to the Vaynol estate; the cottagers, being either tenants or
employees of the estate, had no remedy. It is hard not to
sympathise with Ellis Evan Siôn Foulk, Mary Werglodd
Coch and their companions in crime ! Even Hyde Hall, a
firm friend of improvement, was by no means convinced that
enclosure was the answer to the backwardness of cultivation
in this area.

Another area of four thousand acres west of Pwllheli, and including Carn Fadrun and Mynydd Mynytho, was the subject of an Act of 1808, under which once again the cottagers lost their customary right of cutting turf for fuel. Hyde Hall, who was here also during the progress of the enclosure, foresaw wholesale depopulation of the district for lack of fuel unless some remedy were found, and referred gloomily to the ' general spread of this misery through Llyn '. The old trouble about ' encroachment ' of cottagers on the wastes came to a head again in what was probably the most extensive of the Caernarvonshire enclosures, covering anything up to ten thousand acres in the north of Llŷn and Arfon from Nefyn to Llanllyfni, under the terms of an Act passed in 1812. Once again there were riots among the cottagers whose ' encroachments ' were to be sold on the ground that they were less than twenty years old. This time two men were sentenced to death (the exact charge against them is not clear), but for one the sentence was commuted to penal servitude.

In one case, however, resistance to enclosure proved successful. This was a late measure, and it was defeated partly because with the end of the war a mood of disenchantment with the effects of enclosure set in, partly because its chief promoter, the second Lord Newborough, was not (as will appear later) very popular among his fellow-gentry. Application was made in 1826 for a Bill to enclose the common lands of Llandwrog and Llanwnda. This would have included the village of Rhostryfan, consisting of 140 houses put up by Cilgwyn quarrymen after working hours (often by moonlight), after clearing the ground themselves — and all under the direct encouragement of the parish vestry twenty years earlier. Some seven hundred men, women and children living rent free were all thus threatened with eviction. But the Rhostryfan victims were luckier than those of Llanddeiniolen. A group of London Welshmen took up their cause. Griffith Davies, the eminent mathematician whose actuarial skill was making him a figure in the world of insurance, was an old Cilgwyn quarryman; John Lloyd, the Anglesey schoolmaster-bard, is said to have coached the children of the duke of Wellington; these and others like them stirred up an agitation in the London Welsh societies. Between them they gained the ear of Colonel Hughes of Kinmel (later Lord Dinorben), the wealthy co-owner of the Anglesey copper mines, who had sat in parliament for Wallingford since 1802. It was he who led the opposition in the House to the Enclosure Bill, and succeeded in killing it. Rhostryfan showed its gratitude by brewing a special cask of ale for consumption at a triumphal dinner for its London friends.

Municipal as well as manorial commons were affected by the movement. Caernarvon was well enough organised to deal with its own common lands; a marshy tract known as Morfa Seiont was drained and enclosed by the corporation in 1781 — probably the first formal enclosure in the shire; a more leisurely division of two other stretches of moorland common began soon after Waterloo and took over a dozen years to complete. Conway retained most of its extensive borough lands (which included those acquired from the abbey in 1284) as corporate property, or else leased them for building and other purposes; an enclosure project of about 1822, which would have divided up some two hundred acres of ' fertile sandy loam ' held by the corporation and reserved for the use of the commoners at trifling rents, came to nothing. Nefyn and Pwllheli were less fortunate; their tiny corporations had neither the influence nor the skill to safeguard their municipal commons when these were included in Acts covering a much wider area. The bailiffs of Nefyn, it appears, were bluffed into signing away three or four hundred acres of common used by the inhabitants as a sheep run, while Pwllheli corporation received (under another Act but with the same commissioner) a few square yards of barren rock in exchange for lands worth about £500 a year. On the other hand, the drainage schemes carried out under the Act made possible the improvement of Pwllheli harbour. Cricieth had its borough lands nibbled away to vanishing point, without any formal enclosure, in the 1840's, because (as a lawyer found)[4] the burgesses were 'quite in the dark' as to their rights and privileges.

The General Enclosure Act of 1845 established a standard proceedure for enclosure, minimising the need for a separate (and expensive) Act of Parliament for each individual case. By this time ten Enclosure Acts had been passed for Caernarvonshire, bringing down the proportion of common and waste lands in the shire from a third to an eighth. The General Act also included safeguards for the interests of the commoners, but it did not wholly put an end to disputes, even riotous disputes, about common rights. An enclosure project in the Conway valley, in the neighbourhood of Caerhûn, sponsored by Lord Penrhyn, Lord Newborough and Sir R. Williams Bulkeley in 1858, taxed right up to the limit — and beyond it — the resources of the new county police force founded two years earlier, for there were not enough policemen available to cope with a situation where fences were pulled down as fast as they were put up! It took more than ten years for the trouble to simmer down.

There was, of course, a more constructive side to enclosure. Between 1815 and 1843 the value of land in Caernarvonshire went up more than forty per cent — higher than in any other North Wales shire except Anglesey. Naturally road-making (which will be dealt with later) was an important contributory factor, but the drainage works carried out under several Enclosure Acts must not be left out of account. The draining and enclosure of Penmorfa marsh had been achieved under a private agreement by W. G. Oakley of Tan y bwlch during the closing years of the eighteenth century, that of Morfa Dinas Dinlle under an Act of 1806. Three thousand acres were said to have been reclaimed from the sea between Aberdaron and Pwllheli under the Act of 1811. But the crowning achievement was the reclamation of Traeth Mawr by W. A. Madocks.

This was an old project. Sir John Wynn of Gwydir had broached it two hundred years earlier, and the duke of

[4] Quoted C. Gresham in *TCHS* 1966, 35.

Ancaster, one of his successors in the ownership of Gwydir, had revived the idea in 1770; but no one had yet been prepared to face the formidable capital outlay it involved. Madocks was no wealthy capitalist or projector, but a Denbighshire gentleman of modest fortune, trained for the bar (since he was a younger son), but unable to find in the law an outlet for his abounding energy and soaring imagination. It was the age of Romanticism, when love of rugged nature came into its own; and since war so often made the Alps inaccessible, substitutes were found at home in the Lake District and Snowdonia. But Madocks was not content to visit; he wanted to *live* among the mountains, and in 1798 — just before Wordsworth settled at Grasmere — he bought a small property nestling at the foot of the mountains on the Caernarvonshire side of the Traeth and set about 'improving' it by turning the converted farmhouse of Tan yr allt into a modest country place where he could stage the house parties he delighted in, and by rescuing the adjoining land from submergence at high tide. This he had achieved by 1800, employing some two hundred 'locals' (at a time of general poverty), with no more elaborate equipment than spades and wheelbarrows, to build a two-mile dyke varying from eleven to twenty feet high. In the next season he was able to grow crops on at least part of the thousand acres reclaimed. But this was only a beginning. Visitors to the Lakes, however wild the scenery, could at least approach by passable roads, but the natural approach to Madock's paradise, from the Merioneth side, was still barred by what remained to less intrepid travellers than Wesley a formidable stretch of treacherous sand. Madocks was a realist as well as a romantic, convinced that the pleasures of wild nature could be enhanced by a modicum of civilised amenities. Moreover the recent Act of Union with Ireland had made the improvement of communications with Dublin a matter of urgency, and Madocks saw here a means of linking his local plans with the wider issue of transport through North Wales generally and Caernarvonshire in particular. These more far-reaching enterprises can best be dealt with in their proper context later on.

The high corn prices prevailing during the French wars had been a powerful spur to agricultural improvements, especially those like enclosure and drainage involving a high capital expenditure in expectation of a corresponding return. Even at the time, some local observers feared that high wheat prices were stimulating the extension to unsuitable soils of a crop which would never pay its way in normal times. With the conclusion of peace the market collapsed, and a long depression ensued. In place of the critical and informative discussions of agricultural topics which had enlivened the local press in the war years, there appeared a depressing sequence of notices of sales of farms or stock under distress, of compassionate reductions of rent, of farming bankruptcies and sluggish fairs. Wheat cultivation was already on the down grade in the 'twenties, and some land was going out of tillage altogether. The small farmer doggedly hung on in hopes of better times, but from the middle of the century the census begins to show a declining population in most of the purely rural areas. Naturally there were some permanent gains: drainage and reclamation, better farm implements, a lasting increase in the cultivation of green crops and root crops, and in consequence more fattening of stock on the farm instead of driving the cattle by the drovers' roads to the lowland pastures for others to fatten and sell. But the buoyancy and optimism of the early years of the century never recurred, and by mid-century grain imports were again the order of the day and grain exports dwindling.

Towards the end of the century the sporadic efforts at agricultural education which had been made by enlightened landlords during the boom period were taken up by public institutions. In 1888 the newly opened University College of North Wales set up a department of agriculture — the first in the kingdom — and this was followed by the establishment of a county advisory scheme in co-operation with the government and the county authority, and by the purchase of an experimental farm. But the Royal Commission on Land in North Wales, reporting six years later, gives in general a depressing picture of agriculture in Caernarvonshire. The testimony of one witness, Mr. Pugh Jones of Ynysgain (Cricieth), is of interest because eighty years earlier his grandfather had written to the local paper a letter, quoted in an earlier chapter, contrasting the bad farming of his youth with the improved practices that were gaining ground when he wrote. The grandson's report is a fitting pendant to this section :

> Formerly one-half of the land was under cultivation, but of late years, whilst of root crops as much again are raised as in the old times, the farmers, except in certain corn-growing districts, now rely upon the pastures and meadows . . . The low price of grain, the high prices at which unfattened cattle and sheep sold for years, and the increasing cost of labour have been the causes of the change.

Llŷn and Eifionydd, of course, had always been primarily grazing regions, and were not so much affected by fluctuating grain prices; but the witness declared he did not know half-a-dozen farms in the shire where wheat was raised, and the production even of oats and barley had gone down. Sheep, with their smaller demands on labour and on soil fertility, had correspondingly increased, but even here there were still complaints of over-stocking of the mountain pastures, and although dairy produce remained an important export, there was much local criticism of the quality of the goods — a point on which great stress was laid in the schemes for agricultural education referred to above. In Caernarvonshire the Agrarian Revolution had been nipped in the bud.


### B.   Mining and Quarrying

It has been shown in an earlier chaper how during the third quarter of the eighteenth century English capitalists, notably the firm of Roe of Macclesfield, began to interest themselves in some of the abandoned copper mines of Caernarvonshire. The expansion of the copper industry in England and in

South Wales, and then the long period of war which began with our quarrel with America and lasted, with only short intervals, till Waterloo, created an almost unlimited demand for copper ores, especially for the navy, which played so vital a part in both the great wars of the age. In leasing the mine of Penrhyn Du to Roe of Macclesfield in 1764, Sir Nicholas Bayly insisted that they should also take in hand the hitherto unsuccessful workings on their Anglesey property on Mynydd Parys. This proved to be, at its height, the most productive copper mine in the world; but the lessees also continued to operate Penrhyn Du as a subsidiary enterprise, and they combatted the menace of flooding, which had called a halt to work there a century earlier, by installing a Boulton and Watt engine in 1782. But the output proved disappointing, and when three years later their Anglesey lease ran out, Roe and Company transferred their activities to Llanberis. Before the end of the eighteenth century from eighty to a hundred men and boys were employed there, and the ore proved very productive through the first half of the nineteenth century, in the hands of a Nantwich company which took over from Roe of Macclesfield. From 1824 an eight-mile tramway carried the ores to the new quay at Port Dinorwic for export.

The Drws y coed mine was successfully worked from the Napoleonic War until near the end of the last century, yielding 200 tons of pure copper in 1879 and 140 two years later. Indeed it helped to absorb the unemployed from Amlwch when Mynydd Parys declined about 1840, including a number of women who had the local reputation of making bad wives because they had never learned to cook! At Aberglaslyn and again at Bron y gadair (near Madocks's embankment) successful mining enterprises were stimulated by war demand; the former, after closing down in 1808, was revived after the war and remained productive till the 'thirties; the latter was drowned out, despite the installation of a steam pump, in 1844. Two mines were in operation at Llandudno during the French wars, one of them worked by a Liverpool company, the other by small partnerships of

independent miners. By 1833 the annual output was estimated at three thousand tons, giving employment to 120
men. But the sea water, the old enemy of the Llandudno
mines, rushed in once more in the 'sixties; the mines were
abandoned, and the population moved down seawards to
cope with the growing throng of summer visitors.

Mining in Caernarvonshire never reached such dimensions
as to create a specialised mining population, as at Amlwch.
In these country mines, work was liable to be interrupted
(as at Drws y coed) at hay harvest, and many of the miners
(as at Llanberis) also had small holdings cultivated by their
wives when work in the mines was brisk, or eked out their
livelihood by fishing (as at Llandudno). The total number of
copper miners in the shire reached its peak in 1851, when
there were over three hundred; by 1891 it had sunk, under
the stress of foreign competition, to fourteen. But the
industry did for a time swell the volume of the county's
exports. The ore, after being crushed on the spot by a
stamping mill, was taken to the most convenient local quay
for shipment to Swansea, or occasionally to English smelting
works. Nearly a thousand tons were shipped from Caernarvon in 1844. A single firm at St. Helens paid nearly
£50,000 for Llandudno ores shipped from Conway in
1810-12, and thirty years later, when the bulk went to
Swansea, shipments of these ores from Conway amounted to
seven thousand tons. Even Pwllheli was exporting a little
copper ore to Swansea — presumably from Bron y gadair —
in 1808; sixteen years later exporters of ore from here and
Aberglaslyn were able to use Madock's new harbour, which
was both nearer and more commodious.


Far more extensive, and far more lasting, were the developments which took place during those years in the slate
industry. No sooner was Richard Pennant in control of the
Penrhyn estate than he set to work making its slate resources
a paying proposition. He called in the fifty-four leases his
father had granted on the rock face, and took the working

into his own hand as a single undertaking. About the same time he leased from the crown and the bishop of Bangor lands adjacent to his own, thus laying the whole quarrying area open to systematic exploitation. He was able to find locally a slate reeve of unusual ability and intelligence in William Williams, an Anglesey ex-weaver who had moved in literary circles in the island and, after apprenticeship to a lawyer, had been employed as land surveyor on various Caernarvonshire and Denbighshire estates. For ten years he kept the quarry books with a system and accuracy unknown before, and established excellent relations with the quarry-men; and when in 1802 he was pensioned off at sixty-four he spent his remaining fifteen years in literary work, in which he achieved some distinction.

Penrhyn was equally wise in other appointments. As agent for the whole estate he chose Benjamin Wyatt, the archi-tect's brother, himself no mean architect; indeed the houses he designed for tenants and employees set a new standard for the whole neighbourhood. Wyatt was also responsible in 1790 for planning the development of the quay at Abercegin (now named Port Penrhyn) into a port which could eventu-ally accommodate ocean-going vessels, and for turning the bridle paths leading to it from the quarry into cart roads along which over a hundred carts, hired from neighbouring farms (for the Penrhyn estate when Pennant took over could only supply four) carried the daily output. In the quarry itself, nine years later, he found a competent manager in Wyatt's brother-in-law James Greenfield, who showed great skill both in planning future developments (and repairing the ill-effects of past mismanagement) in an enterprise of unpre-cedented scale, and in deploying the expanding labour force.

Before the wars with France broke out, over a dozen ship-loads, on an average, were being conveyed coastwise every month, mainly for Liverpool, but a few for Scotland and the north, and a few for London and the south. Most of them had been bought by ships' captains on speculation, but already some vessels were being sent on the personal responsibility of Lord Penrhyn or through his agents and managers. Ireland accounted for about half as many. In all, well over three million slates a year were being sold — four or five times as many as were recorded half a century earlier. And this was only a beginning.

The example was not lost on Vaynol. In 1787 the solicitor to the estate joined with a fellow attorney and a third partner to take a twenty-one year lease of the whole quarrying area from Assheton Smith. They kept on the existing gangs of quarrymen — as many as were willing to work in the new conditions — and made themselves responsible for paying some thirty or forty men and transporting and marketing the slates. The Dinorwic Slate Company, as it called itself, was not a wealthy concern, and it was all it could do to meet all these obligations. The old quarrymen were reluctant to sacrifice their independence, and for ten or a dozen years a few hung on to their ' claims ' or tried to establish new ones in place of those the company had taken over. The new partners, for their part, were aghast at having to meet a wage bill of £130 on the quarterly day of settlement — but woe betide them if the cash was not forthcoming! As for transport, the partners considered making an inclined plane from quarry-face to lakeside, but were no doubt deterred by the expense, and ten years after they began operations the slates were still brought down the steep slopes in sledges, with one horse to pull and another behind to act as brake. By these primitive means of transport two thousand slates could be carried in a day by sledge and rather less than two thousand on horseback. By 1791 exports from what may now be called the Dinorwic quarry through Caernarvon had reached two and a half million in the year — more than half of the port's total trade in slates.

At Cilgwyn, too, the haphazard working of earlier days was giving place to a more systematic order. The extensive Glynllifon lease of quarrying lands in this area from the crown, to which reference was made in an earlier chapter, came to an end in 1773, but for reasons of prestige (without any active participation) the family hung on as tenants-at-will of the crown, charging only nominal royalties to the independent quarrymen and treating them to a supper on the proceeds, until in 1790 the crown agents reasserted crown claims by putting up the quarrying rights to auction. As a result, the Cilgwyn and Cefn Du Slate Company, consisting of a lawyer, a merchant and two landowners, was formed in 1800. It leased from the crown a wide area extending into Merioneth, and bought a sloop to convey its exports. The independent quarrymen put up a tough fight, and there were many riotous scenes, even after the company had established its claims by a successful lawsuit in 1805. A further stretch of crown common west of Llyn Padarn, and so within much easier reach of Caernarvon, was exploited by groups of working quarrymen on license from the crown from about 1809, but this quarry (Hafodlas) remained a small concern. By 1786 the slate rocks of Nantconwy were also being worked on a sufficient scale to build up a cargo of twenty thousand slates in that year for export from Conway; they were probably quarried by Llanrhychwyn and Llyn Crafnant, and manhandled down the steep slopes to Trefriw for conveyance down-river to the port.

In slate quarrying the outbreak of war in 1793, so far from creating a fresh demand (as with copper), drastically curtailed what existed by the brake it put on building operations. Employment at Penrhyn was reduced in the course of five years from about five hundred to a hundred and twenty, and exports from Port Penrhyn were nearly halved during the two years following 1794. A further blow to the industry was the imposition of the war tax of twenty per cent (eventually increased to nearly forty) on slates carried coastwise. Like most of its kind, the tax operated very unevenly. Penrhyn and Dinorwic between them produced nearly sixty per cent of the total output for North Wales, and the greater part of this went coastwise to Liverpool or Chester for distribution to the English industrial towns, largely by canal; some of the smaller quarries which still dealt principally with Ireland were at first not affected, but by 1797 the Irish market too had gone dead. A meeting at Caernarvon in 1794 drew up a petition against the tax, which was losing the quarries some of their most important English markets; two years later it was an issue at the county election. But it lingered on for nearly forty years, in spite of renewed agitation after the war.

All this helped to accentuate the distress of the war years, ×
to which of course many other factors contributed. Once more there were corn riots, or near-riots, at Caernarvon in 1800 and the following year. Lord Penrhyn, rather than dissipate his labour force, used the lean years to advantage by enlarging Port Penrhyn to accommodate ships of greater tonnage and constructing an iron tramway to carry horse-drawn loads of slate from quarry face to quay — thus at once alleviating distress and preparing to meet the expected post-war boom. Agriculture gained in the long run by the release of the horses for farm work, but farmers long missed the subsidiary source of income. It was also during these years that Greenfield began to organise the series of terraces in the quarry which facilitated future working and virtually created a new landscape. Vaynol, as usual, followed suit. There too better roads were built, and the quay at Felin Heli (the landing place of Moel y don ferry) was enlarged in 1793 to receive the produce; thirty years later it was renamed Port Dinorwic, and soon afterwards it was connected with the quarry, like Port Penrhyn, by a tramway — a great economy, since the cost of transport had hitherto exceeded the cost of quarrying.

When the Peace of Amiens was signed in 1801, the ' spirit of building ' began to revive, and there was a corresponding recovery in the slate industry. This survived the renewal of war, especially after Trafalgar had made the seas safer for shipping. Lord Penrhyn's agents were busy signing on new hands, till the number reached three hundred again. A hundred tons a day were being taken to Port Penrhyn by the new tramway, and in 1804, 229 ships sailed from the harbour, most of them coastwise despite the slate duty; in fact 45 slate ships made for London alone from the Caernarvonshire ports in 1808, and the London demand was soon greater than the quarries could satisfy. With the spread of schools, writing slates were in great demand, and Penrhyn acquired a monopoly in this branch of manufacture, which consumed some three thousand feet of timber a year. Others were exported unframed. Even during the war there was a brisk trade with Holland and the West Indies — mainly through Liverpool, and so subject to coastal duty; but in 1809 a load of slates for Boston, Massachusetts, left direct from Port Penrhyn. The port itself was flanked by works which turned out not only writing slates but chimney pieces and tombstones, and kept another batch of men in employ.

When Assheton Smith's lease to the Dinorwic Slate Company ran out in 1809, a new partnership was formed in which the owner — now fully awake to the possibilities of the industry — himself took a hand with his solicitor, adding as third partner a Lancashire prospector named William Turner, who was already beginning to make a success of one of the Ffestiniog quarries, and whose family was henceforth to be intimately associated with quarrying and many other enterprises in both shires. The passing and ruthless enforcement of the Llanddeiniolen Enclosure Act strengthened Smith's hands against any surviving opposition from the independent quarrymen, and at last the projected incline was carried into effect. But unlike Penrhyn, who had had a dozen years of peace in which to establish himself, Smith had to contend with hampering war conditions from the outset. It was not till 1820 that he ventured to take the entire working of the quarry into his own hands.

Many smaller quarries also contributed their quota to the county's war-time trade in slates. Two new quays were opened at Trefriw before 1809 to accommodate slates from Dolwyddelan and Crafnant for conveyance by boat to Conway, and some little improvement was made in the shocking roads of the former parish to facilitate transport from the quarry. Quarrying had begun on Moel y gêst, in the south-eastern corner of the shire, about 1780, and the slates were loaded at high tide on boats at a quay on the Dwyryd for re-loading into sea-going vessels at the mouth of the Traeth; nearly seventy of these vessels set out with

cargoes of slates from here and the developing quarries of
the Ffestiniog area in 1811-12. Even the small quarries on
Llanllechid common had from 1812 their own quay at Hirael
on the Bangor sea-front, though this was soon afterwards
absorbed by Penrhyn. The Cilgwyn Company's boat sometimes avoided Caernarvon by sailing from Foryd Bay, at the
south-western entrance to the Straits. But this concern did
not flourish. It had leased a large number of small quarries
with a view to keeping interlopers at bay, and many of them
proved a dead weight; Cilgwyn itself was the only one that
paid, and even here the net profits during the years 1806-12
did not reach £3,000.

In many industries the conclusion of peace in 1815
brought with it a devastating slump; not so quarrying, for
here there were formidable arrears of building to make up.
Lord Penrhyn died childless during the war, his widow (who
carried on the quarry) soon after it, and the property passed
to a Jamaican connection of the Pennants, who added to his
family name of Dawkins that of Pennant. It was he who in
1827 pulled down the old mansion (so recently extended by
Lord Penrhyn) to build the pretentious pseudo-Norman
' castle ' that took its place. He and Assheton Smith were
far-sighted enough to avoid a war of prices by agreeing, as
soon as Dawkins Pennant took over, to a common price list,
and between them they dominated the industry. Smith now
had as many as eight to ten vessels at a time loading at his
enlarged port, carrying between them an average of fifty tons
a day, and profits had reached a peak of over eighty per
cent on outlay (including cost of carriage to the port). By
1820 the labour force at Dinorwic had risen to about two
hundred, but at Penrhyn it was nearer nine hundred, output
not far short of twenty-five thousand tons (as well as over
a million slates sold by tale and eight hundred crates of
writing slates), and profits more than £7,000 — an increase
of over tenfold in the first, well over twentyfold in the
second, and over eightyfold in the third, since the first Lord
Penrhyn began operations. Cilgwyn was not so happily
placed; output began to decline in 1822, and a bad fall of

rock the following year made matters worse, till at last the company had to go into liquidation in 1830. This did not prevent the continued development of quarrying in this area — as indeed everywhere in the shire where slate could be worked in marketable quantities. The opening in 1824 of Madock's new harbour at Portmadoc provided an outlet, far outstripping in capacity and convenience the little creeks of the Traeth which had hitherto been in use, for both the slates of Merioneth (which were now coming into serious production) and those of south-western Caernarvonshire.

In all the parishes where quarrying was a principal occupation population doubled, trebled, and in one case (Llanllechid) nearly quadrupled itself between 1801 and 1841; and little of this increase came from outside the shire, for nearly ninety per cent of the inhabitants in 1841 were Caernarvonshire-born. In the whole county, population rose during the decade following the repeal of the slate duty by twenty-two per cent to over eighty thousand — almost twice as high a rate of increase as in any other North Wales county.

What is striking is the creation of new industrial villages. An outstanding example is Bethesda. When Lord Penrhyn started quarrying in earnest he built in Llandygái a model village for his workmen in which (as his kinsman Thomas Pennant noted with pride) 'no corrupting alehouse' was permitted. That was all very well for the small labour force with which he began, but as numbers expanded, something bigger was needed. The new Irish road planned (as we shall see) by Telford opened up in 1818 a new tract of wild and desolate country below the quarry but on the opposite bank of the river, in the parish of Llanllechid and outside the Penrhyn estate. The land was owned by one or two substantial yeomen farmers of the parish who, unlike Lord Penrhyn, were ready to sell or lease it in building lots without playing the benevolent despot over the occupants, and without any prejudice against the erection on it of either chapels or 'corrupting alehouses'.

In 1820 a small group consisting mainly of quarrymen, who had for the past few years been meeting for worship

wherever they could find friendly farmers to house them
(with occasional visits from Independent ministers of Bangor
and Caernarvon), erected there a small Independent chapel
and named it Bethesda. There was already an alehouse there,
and a cluster of quarrymen's cottages and further chapels
soon followed. Within a decade the new village came to be
known collectively as Bethesda. It is a sign of the rapid
growth of population that Bethesda chapel had to be
enlarged and rebuilt in 1830 and again in 1840; the population of the village a quarter of a century after this was reckoned at five to six thousand — over four times as many as the
whole parish contained in 1801. Robert Roberts ('y sgolor
mawr '),[5] who went there to teach in 1853, found the houses
' plain ugly buildings, nearly all of one story and containing
no more than two rooms ', but ' wonderfully clean and well
and comfortably furnished '. Bethesda was in many respects
a prototype of Caernarvonshire's quarry villages, whenever
the quarrymen settled near the quarry, round their chapel
and away from any existing village; hence those Hebrew
names — Bethel, Ebenezer, Carmel, Saron, Nebo — with
which the map of Caernarvonshire is so freely strewn, to the
unending mystification and merriment of visitors! They have
been, perhaps, the most important legacy of the Industrial
Revolution in Caernarvonshire, for they created an entirely
new type of social community, with a vigorous culture and
sturdy independence unsuspected by those who see only the
drab exterior — as Dawkins Pennant himself found with
surprise when for the first time he interviewed his own
quarrymen in 1865.

To return to the post-Napoleonic period : the potentialities
of slate had come to be appreciated far outside Caernarvonshire by 1825, which was a year of widespread speculation
in both mines and quarries. Merioneth, a comparatively
virgin field, suffered from this wave of speculation more than
Caernarvonshire, where the two biggest concerns were under

[5] J. H. Davies (ed.) *Life and Opinion of Robert Roberts* (1923), xvii.

single proprietorship and so offered no bait to the specu-
lator. Even here there was a goodly crop of lawsuits concerning some of the smaller quarries; but the strike of 150
Penrhyn men in that year had quite other causes. The system
of remuneration there was a fossilized survival of the days
when separate contracts were made with separate groups for
their several workings, with settlement of accounts at long
intervals. The result was wide disparities of earnings and
frequent complaints of favouritism and shady practices,
especially after the retirement of William Williams and the
death of James Greenfield. The men had no organisation,
and the strike was soon over, but at least a few of the more
crying grievances were remedied and a new overseer
appointed.

Whatever dislocation was caused by the inevitable slump
that followed the boom, the industry was soon back on its
feet, especially after the removal of the slate duty in 1831,
which inaugurated forty years of unprecedented prosperity,
interrupted only by a spell of short time and reduced wages
during the Hungry Forties. Dinorwic by 1856 was making
for its owners a clear profit of £30,000; six years later, over
three times as much. Even Conway, one of the minor slate
ports, had to enlage its quay in 1835 to accommodate the
growing export of slates from Dolwyddelan and Crafnant,
which during the three following years produced between
them nearly five thousand tons, mostly sent by boat to
Conway for export, but some direct to Liverpool or Runcorn
from the quay at Trefriw.

The 'sixties were years of intense trade union activity in
the country at large, and inevitably the quarrymen caught
the infection, especially as they now had a firm champion
in W. J. Parry of Coetmor Hall, Bethesda, a quarryman's
son who had raised himself to a comfortable professional
standing. The first attempt of the Penrhyn men to form a
union, in 1865, was a disastrous failure, for on the threat of
dismissal the great majority abandoned the union, and the
eighty who stood out were within the next few years found
to be 'redundant'. A second attempt in 1874 — a time of

booming trade, with profits soaring and demand outstripping supply — fared better. Parry succeeded in forming a union to cover all the principal quarries of North Wales, with himself as secretary; and attempts on the part of the owners at Dinorwic, Penrhyn and one of the smaller Llanberis quarries to nip it in the bud by 'locking out' all who refused to renounce it revealed a new solidarity among the quarry-men which forced the owners to recognise it as a negotiating instrument, subject to some modification of the rules. At Penrhyn the dispute terminated in a new price list and a change of overseers which kept the peace for a dozen prosperous years.

From 1879, however, trade began to slump and the union to weaken. The proprietor of Penrhyn (Dawkins Pennant's son-in-law and heir, for whom the lapsed family peerage had been revived) kept the agreement in letter and in spirit; his son succeeded to the estate in 1886 determined to smash the union, which had been further weakened by a prolonged and bitter but profitless strike at Dinorwic, the preceding year. Labour relations rapidly degenerated into what would in modern jargon be called a 'cold war', reaching its climax in 1896 in a lock-out lasting nearly a year. The basic issue was Penrhyn's reiterated declaration 'I decline altogether to sanction the interference of anybody (corporate or indi-vidual) between employer and employed in the working of the quarry' — and this included the Board of Trade, whose new conciliation machinery he rejected. An uneasy truce was patched up in 1897, but three years later hostilities broke out again on the same issue in a strike lasting three whole years, till sheer hunger broke up the solidarity of the quarrymen. It was an epic, not to say tragic, struggle which shook the whole of Wales as well as the Welsh community in America, and was further embittered by sectarian and political undertones. It also helped to ruin the quarry indus-try, already weakened by foreign competition and the discovery of cheaper roofing materials, and destined within the next half-century to meet its Waterloo in two world wars. In the course of the preceding century, however, the industry had immeasurably enriched the social and cultural life of the whole shire and given a new dignity and articulateness to its working population.

No account of quarrying in Caernarvonshire would be complete without at least a passing reference to another if far less extensive branch of the same industry — the quarrying of stones. The growing English towns were in as urgent need of stones for paving their streets as of slates for roofing their houses, and to some small extent the demand was met by cargoes from Caernarvon and Conway during the first half of the eighteenth century. The business naturally increased as population grew; in 1808 as many as forty shiploads left Conway for Liverpool, and five more for Chester. This was nearly twenty years before work began seriously on what was long the main source of supply — Penmaenmawr mountain. Here too the stone was brought down the rock in sledges until an incline was made; by the 1870's some sixty to seventy thousand tons a year were being quarried, and the contour made familiar in earlier prints was being substantially modified.

By this time, however, a further source of supply had been found on Yr Eifl. It was opened by Samuel Holland, a Liverpool man (cousin, incidentally, to Mrs. Gaskell the novelist), whose father had invested in many mining and quarrying enterprises in North Wales. Among other things, he had quarried at Cefn Du in its early days, and his firm became selling agents for Penrhyn, a post retained by his manager, Samuel Worthington, long after Holland had relinquished it for other interests. In 1821 he brought his son to manage a quarry he had opened at Ffestiniog, and it was in this neighbourhood that the younger Holland spent the rest of his life. But when railway communications with Ireland were under discussion early in Victoria's reign, and the projectors could find no ready answer to the problem of carrying the railway over the Straits, Holland threw in his lot with those who were for by-passing this difficulty by

substituting Porthdinllaen for Holyhead as the packet
station. This would obviously mean a great demand for
suitable stone for enlarging the harbour at Porthdinllaen,
and Holland with this end in view made trials on Yr Eifl,
which proved eminently satisfactory; so he opened a quarry
there, with an incline and a quay below, and the hamlet
which grew up around it came to be known as Pentre Trevor,
after the name of his foreman, Trevor Jones. The advocates
of Porthdinllaen, as we shall see more fully later on, lost the
day, but the quarry carried on, mainly to meet the demands
of Manchester. The setts were trimmed at Nefyn and
Llanaelhaiarn, and sixty-seven loads were exported in
1854-5; employment in the stone quarries in the county rose
from under five hundred in 1861 to over two thousand ten
years later. But that level was not maintained, and in comparison with the industry in the coastal districts of Denbighshire, still more with Caernarvonshire's own slate quarries,
stone quarrying has remained a minor item in the county's
economy.

## C. WOOLLENS

  It has been pointed out earlier that in Caernarvonshire the
woollen industry had never achieved the degree of organisation it reached in Montgomeryshire or Merioneth. In Caernarvonshire weaving and spinning, like slate quarrying
before Richard Pennant took it in hand, like copper mining
till well on in the nineteenth century, had never been a specialised occupation, but rather spare-time work carried on by
the small farmer or labourer when farm work was slack and
by his family all the year round. The prevalence of the
industry is attested by the frequent appearance of the name
*pandy* on the map; for the fulling mill was the only form of
machinery in use before the nineteenth century, unless we
dignify by that name the home-made spinning wheel which
was a standard piece of furniture in any self-respecting
household. Fulling mills were often to be found on the larger
farms, worked, it might be, by the water wheel that ground

the corn. How soon they were introduced into Caernarvonshire is not known. There were certainly several in the neighbourhood of Caernarvon by the end of the seventeenth century; it was probably one of these that Lewis Morris designated a ' woollen mill ' in his *Plans of Harbours* in 1748. Here the local weaver brought his *brethyn cartref,* or homespun cloth, for fulling, much as the farmer brought his corn for grinding, paying the appropriate toll. Caernarvonshire's local product was known as *brethyn Sir Fôn,* because Anglesey was its chief market outside the county; and very little went farther afield.

All processes other than fulling were performed by hand until the nineteenth century. As usual, Wales lagged behind the more developed English textile regions. More than a quarter of a century after Hargreaves invented the spinning jenny, and almost a decade after it had come into general use in the English woollen industry, spinning was still done on the wheel everywhere except in a few Montgomeryshire towns; and that was at a time when in England the jenny itself was being rapidly ousted by the water frame. This in turn was superseded in England before it reached Wales at all, and the mule did not establish itself here for sixty years after Crompton's patent in 1779. Naturally it was in the flannel district of Montgomeryshire, the most advanced textile region of Wales, that machinery was first adopted; it made its appearance about the time of the French Revolution. Merioneth was much later in adapting itself to machine production, but the weaving of the local ' web ' cloth and the knitting of stockings — both by hand, of course — had grown apace during the century, with organised markets at Bala and Dolgellau; and for a time, both before and after the war with America until the French war finally ruined it, Barmouth served as depôt for a thriving export trade to Europe and the West Indies. This meant an ever-increasing demand for woollen yarn, and Caernarvonshire wools were of the requisite fineness to provide the warp for the loom. Another link was thus developed between Caernarvonshire and its southern neighbour.

The earliest introduction of machinery in the textile industry of Caernarvonshire, however, had a more ambitious aim than to act as a feeder to Merioneth. As with the slate industry, the man with the capital and enterprise to set it going came from outside the county. The thousand acres reclaimed from the sea by Madocks near Tan yr allt were not all used for agriculture; as will be shown later, his wider scheme included also the new town of Tremadoc, built on the reclaimed land and equipped, among other amenities, with an up-to-date woollen factory. This was built in the year of Trafalgar, and was the first of its kind in North Wales outside Montgomeryshire. Associated with him in the enterprise was his neighbour Gwyllym Lloyd Wardle, son of a Flintshire landowner, who had served as colonel of militia in Ireland but had been refused a commission in the regulars. Wardle was married to a younger daughter of Madrun, and about 1800 he had bought the neighbouring estate of Wern (Penmorfa), once the property of that William Wynne whom we met in an earlier chapter as unsuccessful candidate in 1768 (against Glynllifon) for the county seat. Wardle, who was sheriff of Anglesey in 1802 and of Caernarvonshire the year after, now became a member of Madocks's little circle. The third partner was an otherwise unknown army clothier in London.

As with all his projects, Madocks paid the closest attention to detail in setting up his five-storey factory. He secured an abundant supply of water power by damming a stream high up in the hills above Tan yr allt; he was even at pains to procure samples of the sort of cloth required by the army. The brunt was borne by John Williams, the untrained factotum whom he discovered and put in charge of his many projects. When completed, the factory had several carding engines (delivered by sea) — with plenty of room for more — and sixty handlooms; and the finished goods could be sent by sea from within a mile of the factory door. A house for the manager and six cottages for the workmen were attached to it. Ships of up to two hundred tons burthen could approach the shore, and an abundance of excellent wool was to be had on the sheep runs above.

Madocks and Wardle were both politicians of the Left, unsparing critics of the government in parliament, where both sat for English boroughs — Madocks from 1802, Wardle five years later. What more natural than that sinister rumours should arise about those ship-loads of cloth seen leaving the near-by quay for an unknown destination? In time, circumstantial stories grew up of a cargo actually captured on its way to France, and of other smuggling escapades on Wardle's part. The stories have never been verified or even investigated; there seems every reason, on the contrary, to believe that the army cloth from Tremadoc went to Wellington's men in the Peninsula. On the other hand, Wardle's attacks in parliament on the army contractors (his firm's potential competitors) had an ugly look. But he reached the height of his notoriety when in 1809 he raised his sights and attacked the duke of York himself, commander-in-chief of the armed forces, on the score of the brisk traffic in army commissions at the house of his mistress, Mary Ann Clarke, a stonemason's wife whom he had set up in an expensive establishment. The duke now felt bound to resign his command. For a few months Wardle was fêted everywhere as the super-patriot — till it was discovered that Mrs. Clarke, jilted by the duke, had transferred her affections to his critic and briefed him for the attack out of feminine spite! Wardle's deflation was rapid. He lost his seat in parliament and (as his credit declined) much of his fortune, and ultimately took refuge in Italy. The factory was disposed of in 1810, and again five years later, but it went on producing cloth under a succession of owners and tenants until late in the century.

So promising a venture (and the valuation the owners put on the undertaking in 1810 was £3,500) could not but find imitators — though on a much smaller scale — as long as the demand for army cloth remained at its peak. When the Aberglaslyn copper mine temporarily closed down at the beginning of the Peninsular War, the ore-crushing mill was offered as suitable premises for a carding mill or woollen manufactory. Then or later the suggestion seems to have been taken up, if these were the premises occupied by a man describing himself as 'flannel manufacturer, wool carder and spinner' at Beddgelert twenty years later. The Penmachno mill, which has gone on producing till our own day, was in existence by 1809, when George Nicholson the artist drew it; naturally the drawing tells us nothing of what went on inside. We know a little more about the Tryfan factory, south of Caernarvon, which was offered to let in 1814. This contained two carding machines, but all the other processes were performed by hand, for the remaining contents were three looms and three spinning wheels. The sale also included a fulling mill and dyehouse ('if required'), and four adjoining workmen's cottages. But the manufacturer was among the crop of bankrupts of the black year 1817; despite the small scale of the factory, however, he was a man of some substance, owning also lands, houses, farms and a tannery; and the concern was carried on for at least another nine years. By this time the spinning wheels had been replaced by three water frames — the first known use of this invention in Caernarvonshire. Jennies were at work at two little mills at Llanrûg and Llanwnda by 1810; these too were in production for another thirty years. It is not until after the Napoleonic war ended that we first hear of a factory on the Glynllifon estate at Dolgarrog, which was sold by auction in 1818. It then contained, in addition to two carding engines, three jennies and an unspecified number of looms, as well as a newly-erected fulling mill and dye house, a foreman's house and six rooms for the accommodation of the workmen and their looms; and it was still at work thirty years later.

If the copper mines of Caernarvonshire did not bring into existence anything we could dignify by the name of a mining community, still less did the woollen mills create a factory-minded population. With the exception of Madocks's mill, it does not appear that any of these early concerns employed more than half-a-dozen hands. A statistician's estimate in 1835[6] put the number of 'manufacturing labourers' in the

[6] Ure, *Philosophy of Manufactures*, 77.

shire at 143, with a round hundred in 'domestic woollens and flannels', as compared with between six and seven thousand agricultural labourers; and the figures collected at the next census give much the same picture.

Small mills, relying on the conservatism of local custom, were still sometimes opened in the second half of the century, when Merioneth webs were being driven out of the market and even the Montgomeryshire flannel manufacturers had their backs to the wall. But abundant water power, Caernarvonshire's one great asset, was too slow and too erratic to stand up to mass production, especially after weaving itself fell a victim to mechanisation. The Trefriw mill, which started its career towards mid-century, still flourishes, after switching over from water power to electricity. In 1881 there were twenty-four independent weavers left in the county, and ninety-three others engaged in textiles in one way or another; and the total remained static at a little under a hundred for the rest of the century. In England, and even in the more advanced textile counties of Wales, the decline and fall of the hand-loom weaver was a long-drawn and harrowing process. Caernarvonshire was spared this by the absence in pre-factory days of anything like a specialised group of textile workers. In the numerous government reports on the industry which appeared in the 'thirties and 'forties, and in the factory inspectors' reports following the Factory Act of 1833, Caernarvonshire is never mentioned, so insignificant is its textile industry. It was in the sphere of agriculture that the loss of subsidiary earnings from spinning and weaving must have been most acutely felt, but of this, of course, we have no statistical evidence.

It was fortunate for the handicraftsman that the demand for teachers in the new schools and preachers in the new chapels appeared just about the time when he was being displaced by machinery, and the country textile industry as a whole by the 'dark satanic mills' of Lancashire and Yorkshire. Many who took up these professions were ex-weavers or of weaving stock; for in Wales handloom weaving never became, as in parts of England, 'the refuge of the surplus numbers from nearly all other trades ', or ' a receptacle for the destitute from all other classes '.[7] On the contrary, weavers here tended to be intelligent men with a taste for reading. John Elias, who so long dominated the Calvinistic Methodist body of Anglesey and Caernarvonshire, was the son and grandson of weavers from Abererch, and owed his early education to his grandfather; Robert Dafydd of Llanengan, another early Methodist preacher, was also a weaver's son, and so was Eben Fardd (Ebenezer Thomas), a pioneer elementary school teacher and one of the more reputable bards of the century, who followed his father's trade till about 1822. Dafydd Ddu Eryri (David Thomas) worked as a weaver at Waunfawr till he took up teaching as a private venture in 1787. Gwilym Llŷn (William Rowlands) went to school before starting to work on his father's loom about 1820, and stuck to the trade another ten years before entering the Wesleyan ministry and making his name as a Welsh writer and biblographer. Bishop Owen of St. David's, born in Llŷn in 1854, was like John Elias (with whom he had little else in common!) a son and grandson of weavers.

Other examples could be added of teachers drawn from the same source : a Dissenting school founded at Conway in 1846 had as its master an ex-farmer and weaver who had been teaching for ten years and now kept a grocer's shop to supplement his income; the master of the British school founded at Llanengan the preceding year had turned to teaching from spinning in 1841 — a factory spinner, no doubt, since hand spinning was not a man's job. He now commanded a salary of £35 a year — at least twice as much as he would have earned at the mill; but he had first to put in six months' training at Borough Road. Neither the country factory nor the handloom weaver has ever quite died out, but their operations are confined to specialised products in a limited market. Madocks's dream of a Caernarvonshire industry which would capture the market through its control, within a small compass, of raw material, power, machinery

[7] *Rept. on Handloom Weavers* (1840, x), 40; Lipson, *Woollen and Worsted Industries* (1921), 201.

and shipping proved as illusory as Maurice Wynn's hope, two centuries earlier, of blazing a trail for his county's products in the ports of Germany. But if textiles did not create a great industry in the shire, they greatly enriched its social pattern.

## D.   COMMUNICATIONS

In the story of the development of Caernarvonshire's road system three names stand out: Lord Penrhyn, W. A. Madocks and Thomas Telford. Penrhyn's new road from quarry to port was in 1800 extended all the way to Capel Curig, where he built an inn with accommodation for sixty and stocked it with coal brought overland from Ruabon; this in itself bespoke a revolution in road transport as well as in the amenities of what had been a wild and secluded spot. Even more important, however, was the fact that the road, although it was found ' rough and precipitous ' and was soon superseded by a turnpike varying the route, was the first step in opening a new gateway into the county from the east. Madocks did the same for communications from the south. In 1807 he procured an Act empowering him to drain the whole of Traeth Mawr by an embankment across its mouth a mile and a half long; Benjamin Wyatt was appointed commissioner under the Act; Madocks, who was destined to spend about £160,000 on the scheme, was to have all the sands and fifth of the marshlands reclaimed. It was, on the face of it, an enterprise far beyond his resources in cash or in expert assistance. He planned it himself, and the details of construction, and of the recruitment, lodging and supervision of as many as three hundred labourers, were left to the indefatigable John Williams, while a growing slice of Madock's own time and energy was taken up with fending off creditors. Yet the work was completed in 1811, and celebrated by a whole week of banquets, balls and races, with the inevitable ox roasted whole on the embankment.

   Less than a fortnight later, a conspiracy of wind and tide brought about a deadly breach in the embankment. The speed with which neighbours — rich and poor, 'natives' and 'colonists' — rallied round to repair the breach, contributing according to their means gangs of men, teams of horses, loads of material, persuasive speeches (like Shelley's at Beaumaris), or just the labour of their own two hands, speaks volumes for the affection inspired by these two strangers and for the extent of local pride in the achievement. But it took three years to make the dyke secure, and the hole in Madock's fortune was never repaired. For in the meanwhile he had invested liberally in his new village (or 'borough', as he preferred to call it) of Tremadoc, built on the land previously reclaimed near Tan yr allt. Once more Madocks was his own architect and town-planner, and Williams his clerk of works; but he was fortunate to have built it at a time when (as his recent biographer puts it),[8] 'the indigenous tradition of sound design meant that the local builder converted the haziest of plans into a sturdily proportioned straightforward building'. Madocks and Williams also between them helped to make it the home of an equally well-proportioned community; it had its Calvinistic Methodist chapel as well as its church; Twm o'r Nant, last of the purveyors of Welsh traditional drama, worked as a stonemason on the embankment, and his portrait hung at Tan yr allt; an eisteddfod was, symbolically, part of the celebrations that marked (too prematurely) the completion of the work.

Fifty years later, when Robert Roberts, 'y sgolor mawr', kept school there, the first inspiration had faded : he found[9] 'the little aristocratic Saxon colony . . . so supremely contemptuous of the Welsh people among whom they lived, so intolerably condescending or arrogant, and such Philistines!' The arrival of Tremadoc and its younger neighbour Portmadoc did in the end completely transform the life of what had been a waterlogged, isolated and completely Welsh tract of country, where no English service book was to be found in either of the parish churches that served it, and

[8] Beazley, *Madocks*, 86.
[9] *Life and Opinions*, 325.

even certificates of banns of marriage were printed in Welsh. The influx of a new floating population greatly complicated the task of parish overseers and churchwardens accustomed to dealing with more stable conditions. Gradually all parish business was moved to Tremadoc, and the long heart-breaking task of keeping the tiny but historic church of Ynyscynhaearn repaired and accessible was abandoned.

Tremadoc, however, was designed as something more than a pleasing composition or the home of a balanced community; it was part of what we should today call a regional plan. Thirty years earlier the revival of a long-standing scheme for making Porthdinllaen instead of Holyhead the packet station for Ireland had inspired an energetic Montgomeryshire vicar to equip the roads through his extensive parish with milestones in readiness for its part in the design. Nothing came of it then, but the union with Ireland in 1801 brought it back into practical politics, and Madocks was quick to see its relevance to his own schemes. Tremadoc's inn would obviously be an important posting station on the way; Madocks's neighbour Jones Parry of Madrun built another at Chwilog, on the site of the dilapidated mansion of a defunct junior branch of Clenennau, to serve as half-way house between Tremadoc and Porthdinllaen. Another neighbour, Wardle of Wern, chaired a meeting of local gentry at Pwllheli in 1802 to promote a Turnpike Act connecting the proposed new packet station with Merioneth through Pwllheli and Cricieth and across the Traeth; and a few weeks later a further meeting petitioned for yet another turnpike linking the projected new highway with the Capel Curig turnpike, through Beddgelert and Nant Gwynant. Thanks to these efforts, an extremely comprehensive Turn-pike Act was secured under which a network of cross-country roads was completed in the course of the next six years. A road through Llanberis pass connecting up with these others had to wait till 1829-30, but by this time the roads of Llŷn and Eifionydd, excepting only the extreme tip of the peninsula, had caught up with if not surpassed those in the

eastern part of the shire. Pwllheli market in 1809 was found[10]
' more plentiful and more reasonable than any in the county '
— a striking commentary on the effects of easier communications.

A major highway like the Irish road was another matter,
for this was a question of national policy which could only
be settled in parliament. In 1808 the General Post Office, on
the advice of ' Pontifex Maximus ' Telford (as his friend
Southey called him), decided to entrust its mails to the new
Capel Curig road. While the issue was still in the balance,
the Chester local press pooh-poohed the new route as
impracticable; as soon as it was adopted the landlord of the
Capel Curig hotel was able to retort with rosy pictures of
the ' sudden turn . . . in course of travelling ' and reminders
about occasions when the old route had been snowed up for
days. But there could be no disputing a saving of twenty-two
miles and the avoidance of Penmaenmawr, which still had
its terrors for the timid in the shape of landslides and falls
of rocks after frost. The Post Office, however, was loud in
its complaints of the constant delays and frequent accidents
on the Welsh part of the road to Ireland, and Irish M.P.'s
who had to make the journey to Westminster agitated in the
same sense in the House. In response to these complaints,
the first of a succession of parliamentary committees was
appointed in 1810 to examine the whole question.

At the outset the issue was prejudged against Porthdinllaen by the committee's recommendation of improvements
in Holyhead harbour; fortunately the new roads to Porthdinllaen were already in being! The committee also concluded that local turnpike trusts had neither the funds nor
the skilled assistance to cope with a national highway. So
Telford was commissioned to make a complete survey of the
road, and on his report, as soon as the French war was over,
a parliamentary grant was voted towards the improvements
he urged, and vested in a body of parliamentary commissioners. Work was pressed forward as a means of relieving

[10] Hyde Hall, *Description*, 283.

distress caused by the post-war slump and the local effects of enclosure — as for example round Capel Curig, where Dawkins Pennant testified that the cottagers were in dire straits for lack of fuel since their customary right of digging peat had been curtailed. It was also hinted that this was a good time for procuring cheap labour! In 1819 a new turnpike trust, with funds at its disposal, was set up by Act of Parliament to supersede the existing trusts along the Welsh section of the Irish road.

During the next ten years the road from the Denbighshire border to Bangor Ferry was put into shape under Telford's supervision by widening, straightening, levelling, re-surfacing and where necessary diverting it, and many new bridges were built along its course. The culminating achievement was the suspension bridge which in 1827 superseded Bangor ferry — the third attempt to solve the formidable engineering problems involved. Previous plans in 1783-5 for an embankment and wooden drawbridge, and in 1801 for a cast-iron bridge of three arches, had been defeated chiefly by opposition from Caernarvon, with the powerful backing of Assheton Smith — a champion of Porthdinllaen who carried his opposition to Telford's road to the bitter end. The building of the new bridge involved the purchase of the ferry rights from the successor to the patentee who had received the grant from Charles I.

Naturally travel slackened on the older coastal route, but some of the parliamentary grant was applied to improving this too; so Telford added one more to the long succession of roads over Penmaenmawr, and built another suspension bridge to put an end once and for all to the dangers and annoyances of Conway ferry. This had since 1788 passed from the ownership of Archbishop Williams's heirs to that of Thomas Williams, the Anglesey 'copper king', whose son in turn sold it to the bridge commissioners. The new bridge also put an end to the project, sanctioned in the Turnpike Act of 1777, for using the old Roman road over Bwlch y ddeufaen as a turnpike so as to avoid the ferry. It appears from excavation that work had begun at both ends of the track but never reached the middle.

Better roads brought with them the era of public transport, which in Caernarvonshire may be said to have dawned in the last quarter of the eighteenth century, when rival coaches to Holyhead were put on the road by Chester and Shrewsbury innkeepers, and another competitor established a line of post-horses along the Welsh part of the road, by means of which he was able to offer the services of a chaise and pair at ninepence a mile and a four-horse post coach at 1s. 3d. a mile. By 1810 post chaises were to be had at Conway, Bangor Ferry, Capel Curig, Beddgelert, Tremadoc and Pwllheli. Conveyance of goods, as Lord Clarendon had found in 1685, was easier; by the middle of the eighteenth century wagons between Chester and Holyhead seem to have been fairly frequent, if irregular. In 1780 a group of Caernarvon tradesmen appointed two regular carriers to Bangor and Chester, and soon afterwards two partners in Chester and Holyhead set up a weekly wagon service for goods between their respective towns. Ten years after this there were two wagons each travelling fortnightly, and a third irregularly, from Chester to Pwllheli. Traffic with Shrewsbury lagged behind, because until Lord Penrhyn opened up a new way the route was tiresomely roundabout. It is said that before 1770 all the goods traffic between Shrewsbury and Bangor amounted to a weekly cartload; but when the Capel Curig road was made, the Holyhead partner in the Chester wagon was able to extend his service to the new route.

A great stimulus to coaching in Caernarvonshire was the decision of the Post Office in 1785 to adopt Palmer's newly invented mail coach for the conveyance of the Irish mails, which now travelled by the new coach through Conway and Penmaenmawr, until thirteen years later the Capel Curig route was officially substituted. The mail coach, which had the advantage of being much better sprung than its predecessors, found a host of imitators among private proprietors, and coach travel in every direction became a feature of daily life, while once or twice a week the carrier set out with his loads for distribution far and wide from Bangor, Caernarvon and Pwllheli.

Of course there long remained gaps in the system, dictated mainly by geography. When young Samuel Holland set out from Liverpool to join his father at Ffestiniog in 1821, he was advised at Llanrwst that after Dolwyddelan the road petered out into an obscure footpath over the mountain into Merioneth; so he slept the night (so far as the rats at the inn would allow) at Penmachno, and reached Ffestiniog with the help of a pony and a guide the following morning. Even a dozen years later there was no carriage road from this part of the shire into Merioneth : the traveller had to choose between Madocks's embankment farther west and a long *détour* eastwards. On the other hand the roads still left under parish control were faring a little better now, and the old bugbear of statute labour was disappearing. For years the Post Office tried to bring the poor and thinly populated parishes of North Wales up to scratch by the antiquated procedure of 'presenting' an ill-kept piece of road (such as that from Caernarvon to Beddgelert in 1777) at Quarter Sessions, with a view to the imposition of a collective fine which could go towards more professional repair. The attempt was abandoned after a mass indictment of over twenty Denbighshire and Flintshire townships in 1809; sixteen years later Bangor parish vestry substituted a parochial rate for statute labour, and in 1827 this policy was adopted throughout the shire — eight years before this out-dated survival was swept away by the new Highways Act. Turnpike gates lasted much longer : they did not disappear in Caernarvonshire until 1890 — twenty or thirty years after Denbighshire got rid of hers; in Anglesey they remained for another five years — the last survivors of all.

Just as the roads were getting into trim, there arrived what a road enthusiast called the 'calamity' of railways, which postponed further development (save for some improvements in administration) until the coming of the motor car. The earliest Caernarvonshire railways were the horse tramroads to Port Penrhyn and Port Dinorwic. It was in 1848 that the little Nantlle narrow-gauge led the way in steam locomotion in the shire. Meanwhile another tramway had been built to convey the produce of the Ffestiniog quarries to Portmadoc harbour. It had been part of Madock's original plan when he made the harbour, but unluckily the scheme ran into the rivalry of speculators like N. M. Rothschild as well as the opposition of local farmers who were still making good money by hiring their teams for slate transport; and the railway was not in operation until 1836, after Madock's death, when Samuel Holland took over the plan and successfully carried it through. Passenger carriages were added in the 'sixties, when it was turned over to steam traction; the Penrhyn tramway underwent the latter change in 1874. A far more important issue was the conveyance of the Irish mails by steam locomotion instead of stage coach. Inevitably Porthdinllaen reared its head once more, and in 1837 the Irish railway engineer C. B. Vignoles reported in its favour, with a railway leading to it through mid-Wales and Dolgellau; but the alternative scheme of George Stephenson, taking the railway along the North Wales coast, was the one that carried the day — a route, objected Vignoles, ' bounded by the sea on one hand and by almost inaccessible hills on the other, having no connexion or means of connexion but with the places it may actually pass ', instead of ' affording access . . . to the very heart of North Wales ', as his would have done.

The Chester and Holyhead line was opened in 1848, the problem of bridging the Straits being eventually solved by the brilliant inspiraton of a tubular bridge; four years later the line was extended to Caernarvon, and then in 1874 to Ffestiniog. It only remained to connect Caernarvonshire up with what Vignoles called ' the very heart of North Wales ', and this was done when in 1867 the Cambrian line linked Caernarvon with Pwllheli and Pwllheli with Barmouth. This extension once more projected Porthdinllaen into the limelight. This time its claims were urged by Colonel Love Jones Parry, whose grandfather had built the inn at Chwilog with the same end in view more than sixty years earlier, and who had himself just won a sensational victory as Liberal candidate in the county election of 1868. But too much public money had now been spent on Holyhead for the claim of any rival packet station to be considered. Unfortunately progress on the railways too often spelt retrogression on the roads. The trustees of the Ffestiniog-Maentwrog turnpike reckoned that their securities had gone down fifty per cent within four years of the completion of the quarry railway. On Penmaenmawr mountain, towards the middle years of the century, the road collapsed, whether through quarrying or tunnelling or merely by the cumulative action of heavy frost; but no record of the disaster can be found. It caused no stir because by this time no one used the road except the occasional pedestrian. The railway had found the answer (at great expense) to this intractable transport problem), and the twentieth-century road builders followed the lead of the railway engineers by going round and under instead of over the headland.

When Vignoles criticised the route chosen for the Irish mail trains as 'bounded by the sea on one hand and by almost inaccessible hills on the other', he did not foresee the future economic importance of this narrow coastal strip, when once the railway began to attract to it a swarm of summer visitors and a resident population dependent on them — till more than half the inhabitants of Snowdonia came to be concentrated along a ribbon of land covering less than an eighth of its total area. In North Wales the vogue of sea-bathing had begun before the end of the eighteenth century, but the visitors were the 'gentry and clergy' who used the stage coach or came in their own gigs, bringing their servants with them. Bangor and Caernarvon were catering for this type of *clientèle* by the early nineteenth century; at Caernarvon the Pagets of Plas Newydd, during their period as mayors from 1785 onwards (and again after the steamboat began to visit it in the 1820's), helped by the provision of bathing facilities in the summer and 'assemblies' and visits of theatrical companies from Chester in the winter.

But it was the railway that attracted to the seaside a wider public, first from the business and professional classes, then (with cheap excursion fares in the 'seventies) from the better-paid artisans; and with them a resident landlady population.

Llandudno is a case in point. An enclosure award of 1843 had allotted to the Mostyns of Gloddaeth the bulk of the common lands up to the north shore, and this made possible systematic planning by a single owner as soon as the railway came within reach. From 1849 the land was leased in building lots subject to stringent conditions, and in less than a decade, after a branch line had extended the railway to the town itself, it was already ' rising into favour as a salubrious and picturesque bathing-place ',[11] with accommodation for some eight thousand visitors, and an Improvement Commission set up by Act of Parliament. Penmaenmawr, which until the railway reached it had been just a quarrying village as Llandudno was a mining one, was by the 'sixties offering its summer visitors the use of ' bathing boxes ' on the shore. At Llanfairfechan the break-up of the Bulkeley estate in 1856, followed by the building of a railway station in 1860 (through pressure from its new squire, the retired Lancashire cotton man John Platt), began the transformation of a poor and thinly-populated parish of small farmers into yet another of the north coast resorts. So too with the Cambrian line. At Pwllheli the drainage brought about by enclosure in 1816 had improved not only harbour but foreshore, and was followed during the next dozen years by some activity in building to accommodate holiday-makers; but once the railway reached it, this accommodation was soon outstripped by demand, and new areas on the sea front were developed. At Cricieth the speculative builder arrived with the railway, and what had been described[12] just before the railway came as ' a small insignificant place consisting of only a few straggling cottages along the sea shore ' developed into another thriving resort.

[11] Hicklin, *Excursions in N. Wales* (1856), 147.
[12] Black's *Picturesque Guide to N. Wales* (1866), 156.

Yet another effect of the railway — helped by the spread of anglicised elementary education — was the penetration of the English language into hitherto monoglot Welsh areas. The Anglican Church had always catered for English-speaking worshippers — sometimes too exclusively so; but in Caernarvonshire the early Nonconformist chapels had all been Welsh-speaking. From the middle of the century the various denominations began to extend their chapel-building activities to meet the needs of English-speaking congregations.

Developments in inland communication were matched at sea. Before the outbreak of the French war, Caernarvon had nearly 250 vessels engaged in the slate trade alone, and its commerce had extended across the Atlantic; by the Peace of Amiens over a thousand foreign and nearly two thousand coasting vessels were reported ' cleared out ' of the port. The need for a more commodious and approachable harbour was becoming urgent, and in 1793 an Act of Parliament was procured for the purpose. The war must have held up operations, for nothing had been done sixteen years later, when a second Act provided for the setting up of a harbour trust with something of the character of a turnpike trust : it was authorised to undertake extensive improvements and to meet the cost by a port tax on tea and coal. Under this Act some £400 or £500 were spent in blasting dangerous rocks at the Swillies and more in constructing new quays. It was on these grounds that Caernarvon had opposed the schemes brought forward in 1786 and in 1800 for crossing the Straits by means of bridges which local merchants believed (not without reason) would obstruct shipping; only with the utmost difficulty were they persuaded that the objections did not apply to Telford's plan. Reference has already been made to the improvements in Pwllheli harbour resulting from enclosure. The work begun at Porthdinllaen, which came to a dead end when the packet station project was abandoned, would have changed the fortunes of its neighbour Nefyn; as it was, neither developed into more than fishing ports with a population stagnant except in the summer season; and since the railway never reached it, Nefyn had to wait for the arrival of the motor car to come into favour even as a health resort. Conway made do with things as they were until increasing trade in slates called for additional berths in the 'thirties.

The most notable addition to sea-going communications in the period was of course the new harbour of Portmadoc. Madocks had a port in mind as part of his regional development scheme from the outset, but its actual location was determined by the accident of a deep pool formed when the waters of the Glaslyn were diverted in the course of draining the Traeth. Parliamentary authority was obtained in 1821; three years later the quay was ready to receive shipping, and a few houses had grown up around it. By mid-century it housed a population of between two and three thousand. Even before the quarry railway was built, Portmadoc was already exporting between eleven and twelve thousand tons of slate annually, thanks largely to the staunch support the scheme received from Samuel Holland. Before long, the average annual shipments came to five or six times this total. When the quarry railway came, and especially after it was turned over to steam, Portmadoc became the principal depôt for the export of slates to the continent, and also an important shipbuilding centre, usurping the primacy hitherto held by Pwllheli.

This was a craft that had been carried on on the shores of the Traeth before ever the port was built, but it soon became the mainstay of Portmadoc. By 1856 there were six ship-building firms employing a hundred carpenters and smiths, and twenty years later the Portmadoc shipyards began to specialise in the building of three-masted schooners for the Newfoundland trade. The vessels indeed traded all over the world; they were largely manned by local crews who had deserted the plough for the tiller. Their exploits were remembered in songs and shanties sung afloat and ashore, in which outlandish names from across the globe took their place with homelier settings such as that of the familiar *Fflat Huw*

*Puw,* commemorating a local craft that plied the neighbouring coasts for years with coal and timber till she foundered
in 1858.

The late David Thomas compiled in an appendix to his
*Hen Longau Sir Gaernarfon* a list of over twelve hundred
ships, of tonnage ranging from seven to four hundred, built in
the ports and creeks of Caernarvonshire from the time registration began in the last quarter of the eighteenth century.
Pwllheli, with over four hundred to its credit, shows the
largest total, but from the time Portmadoc came into existence it built half as many ships again as did Pwllheli during
the same period. Caernarvon's quota is over two hundred,
those of Conway and Nefyn over a hundred each; even tiny
creeks like Aberdaron and Abersoch, Llanbedrog and Llanaelhaearn, Edern and Clynnog, and river ports like Trefriw,
added their mites. The ships were owned in shares, after the
same pattern as fishing boats, and the shareholders were
often farmers from the neighbouring countryside, so the
industry played a far bigger part in the county's economy
than the numbers of active participants would suggest. In
the heyday of shipbuilding, in the third quarter of the last
century, the new Company Acts tempted speculators into
forming limited companies for the purpose, in which quarrymen often invested their small savings; but they came at an
unlucky time, for the industry had already reached its peak,
and in the days of decline that followed, one after another
of the new companies foundered.

The decline of the ports began even before that of the
slate industry on which they so largely depended, for the
railway could offer rapid and smooth transport to far more
commodious English ports. Decline began in the decade
1870-80, when the number of ships registered as belonging
to the ports of Beaumaris and Caernarvon, with their sub-
ordinate 'creeks', suddenly dropped from 238, with a tonnage of nearly forty thousand, to under a hundred, totalling
less than twelve thousand tons. Steam had been applied to
navigation earlier than to land transport. From the time that
it was successfully used on the Dublin packets in 1819 it

rapidly became an accepted feature of voyages round the Caernarvonshire coasts. Two years later the *Cambria* steam packet was launched at Liverpool, and began making regular trips to the Dee estuary at Bagillt; one of her first passengers was young Samuel Holland, on his way to join his father at Ffestiniog. In the following year the service was extended to Bangor, Caernarvon and Beaumaris once a week, and soon there were three or four Liverpool steamers providing, from April to October, a daily service to the Straits. By 1850 they were running throughout the year around the coast as far as Portmadoc, performing the voyage in half the time it had taken the stage coach, and offering meals on board. In the same year a steamboat left Portmadoc itself for New York.

The steamboat was an important factor in attracting the summer visitor to Caernarvonshire, and it aided and abetted the railway in setting some of the local resorts on their feet. But in the long run all this was outweighed by the mortal blow it dealt to the local shipbuilding industry. Like the decline of the English handloom weaver, it was a long-drawn agony. Portmadoc, which came last into the field, persisted longest, because of its primacy in building the ocean-going trading schooner, which long held its own against steam; but by 1903, says the historian of the port and it shipping,[13]

> the trade of sailing vessels had fallen back to what it used to be in 1852, the competition of steamers and railways had at last beaten the little ships. At the end of the World War, 1914-18, during which losses had been considerable, they quietly passed out of being.

Portmadoc's last vessel was built in 1913; fortunately the town had by then an established reputation as a summer resort, and it switched over to this new way of life as Beaumaris and Barmouth had done at an earlier date. There is something symbolic in the fact that Caernarvon's best-known shipbuilder, Samuel Samuel, died in the very year the *Cambria* steamboat first visited North Wales; but the

[13] *Immortal Sails,* xi.

industry lingered on, although only three ships were laid down after 1878. Similarly Conway launched its last vessel in 1891. and only two others in the preceding twenty years. Pwllheli and Porthdinllaen, Bangor and Nefyn had all dropped out of the race by 1880. Even the little boats that used to sail to Liverpool from Bardsey and Llŷn with lobsters and crayfish were beaten by the railway van and the motor bus, and the fishing industry itself declined from mid-century; the census of 1861 (the first to give these statistics) records only sixty-four full-time fishermen in the shire.

The open sea was not deeply rooted in Caernarvonshire's tradition. In the days of Charles I and ship money, as we have seen, the number of men who made their living at sea was negligible, and even in Hyde Hall's day the fishing boats were all grounded at harvest time. The navy, which in (and even before) Napoleonic days — as will be shown — gave many a Caernarvonshire man his first experience of the high seas, naturally played a smaller part in the life of the shire in the long years of peace that followed; and the impulse which took the rural landlubbers and the crews of little coasting vessels of Nefyn or the Traeth on oceanic voyages, and turned them into hardy seamen talking and singing of the ocean as their home, was a revolution at least as great as the creation of the quarry villages with the Biblical names.

## BIBLIOGRAPHY

For a detailed contemporary account of Caernarvonshire see E. Hyde Hall, *Description of Caernarvonshire* (1810-11), ed. E. Gwynne Jones (*CHS* 1952). The economic development of North Wales generally from *c*. 1760-1850 is described in A. H. Dodd, *Industrial Revolution in N. Wales*. These can be supplemented from the files of the local press (*Shrewsbury Chronicle* from 1772, *Chester Chronicle* from 1775, *North Wales Gazette* from 1808, *North Wales Chronicle* from 1827, *Caernarvon [and Denbigh] Herald* from 1831).

A. Agriculture at the beginning of the 19th century is described in W. Davies, *General View of the Agriculture . . . of N. Wales* (1810); at the end in *Rept. of Royal Commission on Land in Wales and Monmouthshire* (1896, C.—8221); and the appendices to this help to fill in the intervening gap. On Madocks and Traeth Mawr see E. Beazley, *Madocks and the Wonder of Wales,* and cf. T. Morris, ' Penmorfa Panorama' (*TCHS* 1963), and ' Thomas Jones, Cefnmeusydd Ucha' (id. 1961).

B. The development of the slate industry is the subject of articles by D. Dylan Pritchard in *TCHS* 1942 and in *Quarry Manager's Jnl.* 1942-6; see also J. Griffith, *Chwarelau Dyffryn Nantlle a Chymdogaeth Moeltryfan* (written 1889, pub. posthumously, n.d.) The rise of Bethesda can be traced in UCNW, Carter Vincent MSS 2685-2781, cf. E. Roberts, *Ar Llwybrau Gynt* (1965). On W. J. Parry, see J. Roose Williams, ' Quarryman's champion' (*TCHS* 1962-7). Documents relating to the disputes of 1874-1901 are printed in W. J. Parry, *The Penrhyn Lockout* (1901), on which see also E. Roberts, *Bargen Bywyd fy Nhaid* (1963). On stone-quarrying the main sources are UCNW, Bangor, MS. 2531 (Penmaenmawr) and Samuel Holland, *Memoirs* (Merioneth Hist. and Rec. Soc., 1952) (Trevor).

C. References to woollen mills, other than Tremadoc (on which see Beazley, as above) are mainly from advertisements in the contemporary local press and from trade directories.

D. On the Holyhead road, see C. G. Harper's book with that title (1902), ii. References to coaches are mainly from the local press and trade directories. On the Caernarvonshire turnpikes see articles by R. T. Pritchard in *TCHS* 1952, 1956, 1958, 1961. A contemporary account of the rise of Llandudno is Walmesley, *Llandudno as it was, . . . as it is* (1864, repr. from *Liverpool Mercury,* 1849 and 1864); for that of Portmadoc see H. Hughes, *Immortal Sails* [1946]; of Llanfairfechan, W. Ogwen Williams, ' The Platts of Oldham' (*TCHS* 1957). On the substitution of bridges for ferries see H. R. Davies, *Menai and Conway Ferries,* 199-280. For shipping and shipbuilding, D. Thomas, *Hen Longau* (see chap. IX, above).

# XII

## SOCIAL WELFARE
### (1780-1900)

·INDUSTRIAL and agricultural progress undoubtedly increased the total wealth of the county, and in the long run improved the general standard of living. The growth of banks, and still more of savings banks, is a clear indication of this. Denbighshire and Flintshire, with their higher degree of industrialisation, had their first banks — each arising out of a local industry — during the last two decades of the eighteenth century. At Caernarvon the earliest known bank was started by Richard Roberts, a member of an ancient local family who was agent to the Coed Helen estate; he died in 1799, but the banking business was continued by his brother Robert till his death ten years later, and then by his son Richard, who died in 1828, after which it seems to have closed down. But in the main it was from Anglesey copper that Caernarvonshire's early banks were financed. The Chester and North Wales bank was founded by Owen Williams, son of the Anglesey 'copper king' Thomas Williams, in partnership with his brother-in-law Colonel Hughes of Kinmel (later Lord Dinorben), part proprietor of Mynydd Parys mines, and Pascoe Grenfell, partner with Williams in the Holywell copper-smelting works. They opened a branch at Caernarvon by 1812 (where in the absence of any nearer bank it was used for receiving subscriptions to the repair of the Traeth Mawr embankment), and within the next decade at Bangor and elsewhere.

A further step forward was taken when branches of English joint-stock banks were established at developing centres in the shire. First experiences were not happy. The Northern and Central Bank of England, a Manchester concern, set up branches at Caernarvon and Bangor within a few years of its foundation in 1833, but it came to an untimely end in the commercial crisis which marked the opening of Victoria's reign. In the preceding year, however, the North and South Wales Bank had been floated in Liverpool, and the far stronger commercial ties of North Wales with Liverpool than with Manchester enabled it rapidly to expand its business here. It took over the branches of the 'Northern and Central' at Caernarvon and Bangor and established new ones at Conway, Pwllheli and Tremadoc (hitherto without a bank, despite Madock's attempt to establish one as part of his original plan). By 1840 Portmadoc too had a branch. But the crippling financial crisis of 1847-8 led to a temporary stoppage of the 'North and South', and, after business was resumed, to a contraction of its activities by the closure of several branches. Those at Portmadoc, Pwllheli and Ffestiniog were sold to a new partnership, based this time on the slate industry. The firm was formed by William Casson, the Lancashire partner of William Turner in the Ffestiniog quarries. At Pwllheli, however, it encountered competition from the local manager of the abandoned branch, who under the name of the Pwllheli District Bank contrived to retain much of its local *clientèle.*

By the middle of the century Caernarvonshire was well covered with private banks, most of them issuing their own notes. But the closing years of the century and the early years of the next saw them swallowed up one by one by the giants of the banking world: Cassons were re-absorbed by the 'North and South' in 1875, the Pwllheli bank in 1891, and the 'North and South' itself by the Midland in 1908. Williams's bank at Bangor, which is said to have survived the panic of 1848 by the device of displaying to timid customers a barrel of sawdust topped with golden sovereigns, was taken over by Lloyds in 1897.

The spread of banking is a testimony to increasing commercial prosperity, but at the same time the halt to expansion

after 1848 demonstrates that in Caernarvonshire the Industrial Revolution — if we may call it so — was already reaching its limits. A better index to the prosperity of the wage-
earner is the spread of savings banks. Within twelve months
of the Act of 1817 which provided their legal foundation,
savings banks had been founded at the inevitable three
centres — Caernarvon, Bangor and Pwllheli. In less than a
decade deposits at the Bangor bank had grown from under
£500 to nearly £11,000, though it is significant that the
number of depositors did not increase in anything like the
same ratio, the average deposit being twice as great in 1827
as in 1823. But the increase was not maintained; at Caernarvon deposits were already falling off owing to bad trade
in 1829, and in 1844 savings bank deposits for North Wales
per head of population were not more than half the average
for the whole country. The chief depositors were obviously
to be found among the lower middle class and the more
prosperous artisans; at Caernarvon, for example, the average
amount put in annually by any one depositor was about £6
to £8, but over the years the proportion of the lowest class
of depositor tended to diminish, that of depositors of £20
and upwards to increase. It is probable that the genuine
' working-class ' contribution to savings banks came chiefly
through their Friendly Societies and Benefit Clubs, of which
no fewer than five kept their balances at the Bangor Savings
Bank in 1827.


   These are some of the signs of increasing prosperity; but
progress often meant dislocation, and dislocation brought
with it patches of extreme if temporary destitution. It was a
great misfortune that so many of the economic developments
coincided with a long-drawn period of war, entailing the
interruption of foreign markets, a halt to domestic building,
and heavy war taxation. The first process worked in two
directions. On the one hand corn prices went rocketing
because of shortage of supplies from abroad. The big landlord and the big farmer who produced for the market could

bask in the sunshine of monoply prices; not so the labourer
or the smallholder who had to pay more for his loaf. On the
other side, the interruption of foreign sales meant unemployment — as we have seen in the slate industry, which also
felt acutely the slackening of building operations. Fewer new
houses, together with a slow but steady rise in population
(most conspicuous in the poorer sector of society) which
seems to have gone on since early in the eighteenth century,
also meant higher rents; and if the cottager tried to build
for himself, Enclosure Acts stopped him from squatting on
the wastes and despoiling them of timber. Nor had wages
kept pace with rising rents and prices; on the Madrun estate,
as late as the beginning of Victoria's reign, unskilled labour
in the fields was still paid at five to seven shillings a week —
for women half-a-crown, which was what they had earned
a century earlier.

As for war taxation, the income tax imposed experiment-
ally in 1799, and permanently from 1803 for the rest of the
war, did not touch incomes under £60, which left the
working man's wages intact; nor was he affected by luxury
imposts like the window tax, or those on commodities like
tea and sugar (which did not normally enter into his budget)
or even soap (which he often made for himself). The malt
tax came rather nearer the bone, but what hit him most of
all were the duties on slate and coal carried coastwise. Of
the former we have already seen the effects; the coal duty
was a much older one, dating back to William III's wars
with France, and it had already become a source of grievance
in Caernarvonshire during the American war — another
period of financial stress — when the sheriff called a county
meeting to protest against it. For Caernarvonshire, so long
as the state of its roads debarred long overland hauls of coal,
depended wholly on the loads which sea captains carried
from the pits of the Dee estuary or from Liverpool, and
landed at one or other of the seaports, or some humbler
creek which could be reached without too great difficulty by
farm cart.

At this time the aggrieved were almost exclusively the

gentry and a few of the more substantial farmers. Twenty
years later, when we were again at war with France, the
duty was increased till it amounted to an extra four shillings
on every ton brought by sea, on top of the cost of transport.
This meant that coal sold at the Flintshire pithead for five
to ten shillings a ton might cost the Caernarvonshire householder 28s. or even up to £2. And by now a much wider
section of the community was affected: even the small
farmer was learning to lime his fields and needed coal to
burn the lime, and the cottager, so often deprived of his
customary fuels by enclosure, was struggling to afford a
bushel or so (costing him everything from twopence to
sevenpence the bushel) if he could make his way to some
*iard glo* where a sea captain had deposited his load. Fire-
grates were just beginning to come in as part of the furnishing of a small house or cottage, instead of being confined to
the mansions; Hyde Hall (much impressed by the fuel difficulties of the poor) was forever urging that closed stoves
such as the French peasant used would make their fuel go
farther. In 1808 W. A. Madocks introduced into parliament a
Bill (which was rejected by the Lords) for the exemption of
North Wales from the coal tax; at the same time the newly-
founded *North Wales Gazette* carried frequent reports of
protest meetings and attacks on the duty from angry corres-
pondents. But like the slate duty, that on coal survived all
assaults until 1831; and even after its repeal by the Whig
government in that year, the heavy costs of transport made
fuel a crippling item in the cottager's budget until the railway came to ease the situation.

Another war-time burden on the poor which particularly
affected the fisher folk of Llŷn was the salt tax. This was as
old as the coal tax, but it increased even more catastrophically during the French wars, till it reached the startling level
of £30 a ton. This was bad enough for the ordinary cottager
who needed only small quantities for seasoning his food; but
for the herring fisheries it was disastrous. No wonder salt
and coal were so often included in the cargoes brought by
smugglers to obscure creeks of the Caernarvonshire coast

(along with soap, candles and spirits), nor that smuggling
increased apace during the late eighteenth and early nineteenth centuries, especially at times when the war-time
demands on shipping forced the government to relax its
vigilance. The salt tax did not finally disappear till ten years
after the war was over.

These then were some of the causes of local destitution in
the early nineteenth century. But there is another side to the
picture. 'Improving' landlords who were waging war on
scraggy flocks, scanty crops and weedy and waterlogged
fields were equally offended by rags and hovels on their
estates, and the sort of destitution which would have been
taken for granted in an earlier generation began to offend
the aesthetic if not the charitable impulses of the leaders of
society. Until about the period of the American war, cases
of exceptional poverty had been met by Church collections,
or doles out of Church rates or the diminishing income of
ancient charitable legacies, or the bounty of the manor house
at Christmas or other hard seasons. We have seen how in
some regions parents had formed the deplorable habit of
sending their children round to beg instead of letting them
go to school. The Elizabeth Poor Law, which provided the
machinery for more organised parish relief, was not obliga-
tory, and in fact was not adopted in Caernarvonshire until
the third quarter of the eighteenth century.

By 1776, however, poor rates were being levied in all but
twenty parishes of the shire, in sums ranging from the
negligible total of five shillings in Botwnnog to nearly £30
in Llanbeblig, the parish which included Caernarvon. The
total raised from the whole shire was not much over £400,
but the mere fact that the Elizabethan Act was at last being
invoked indicates on the one hand changing standards on the
part of the squires and parsons who managed local affairs,
on the other hand war pressures which were creating problems of destitution too widespread to yield to the traditional
methods of informal and unsystematic relief. For although
Caernarvonshire was not hit by the American war in the
same way as Merioneth (which lost the principal market for

its cloth manufacture), the dislocation of trade left its mark everywhere.

This was a trifle, however, compared with what happened after the outbreak of war with France in 1793. After ten years of war, poor rates in the shire had risen from a little over £400 to over £9,000 — £3,000 more than in Anglesey, but less than a third of what was raised in the more industrialised Denbighshire. The assessments ranged from sixpence to 9s. 2d. in the pound, according to conditions in the various parishes; clearly poverty was very unevenly distributed over the shire. And the same is true of the effects of the slump which followed the conclusion of peace. As we have seen, it was the agricultural parishes that suffered most; to slate quarrying peace brought a period of progressive expansion. But over the shire as a whole the poor rate had by 1819 reached a total of £20,000 — the highest ever reached under the old dispensation. And even this was not enough. If begging was widespread in the days when Dean John Jones was trying to establish his schools, the situation was far worse in the first years after the fall of Napoleon. 'A few years ago', wrote an Anglesey farmer in 1818,[1] ' no one approached our doors for alms but the aged, the infirm, or a neighbour in case of sickness', whereas ' the distress of last year broke through every barrier', till ' Beaumaris gaol and castle together' would not have held the swarm of tramps and vagrants had the law been strictly applied. In the same year Bangor set up a nightly patrol to arrest wandering beggars.

A more constructive contribution came from public works and private charity. It was no doubt with a view to relieving distress in the coastal parishes that in 1808 — while the war was still raging — a few great houses like those of Baron Hill, Plas Newydd and Glynllifon, and the ever public-spirited W. A. Madocks, took out shares in the scheme initiated by the Caernarvon lawyer John Evans for the joint-stock purchase of trawlers and trawl nets for fishing the adjacent seas. The fish were sold mainly in the English

---

[1] *N. Wales Gazette*, 5 Feb.

market, and doubtless did something to relieve rural distress in both counties; and the trawling company lived on into the post-war years. Two years after its foundation, during a season of acute local famine, Thomas Assheton Smith and his partner William Turner bought a cargo of barley at £1,700 for distribution at cost to the neighbourhood. This was their reply to the corn riots to which reference was made in an earlier chapter. It will be remembered too that in 1817 work was pushed forward on Telford's new road partly as a measure for the relief of unemployment; in the same year Caernarvon corporation, with the aid of public subscriptions, employed the numerous poor of the town in levelling the mound of earth and rock known as the Maes, formerly the arena for cock-fighting, to create the present central square; the earth was wheeled away and thrown behind the piles which reinforced the walls of the quay. At Bangor a parish fund was built to employ the poor on improving the local roads, and a visiting theatrical company gave a benefit performance to help it on.

Alarming as the increase of pauperism and the rise of the rates must have been to contemporaries in Caernarvonshire, it was slight compared with what was experienced in other shires with more developed industries and therefore more sensitive to booms and slumps. Quarrying was Caernarvonshire's only big industry, and except for a temporary halt after the speculative boom of 1825 it was set on a steady course of expansion. In Montgomeryshire, with all the dislocation caused by the introduction of textile machinery, rates by 1821 averaged over twelve shillings a head, and in Denbighshire, the principal seat of the heavy industries of North Wales, nearly ten shillings; in Caernarvonshire at the same time they were just under six shillings — a lower quota per head than in any of the other North Wales counties. It was the phenomenal rise in the poor rates over the country as a whole that prompted the Whig government in power after the Reform Act of 1832 to appoint a commission to review the whole question of the poor laws, and on its findings to put through the Act of 1834, which remained the

basis of poor law administration till after the first World War.
The effects of the new Act in Caernarvonshire will have to
be considered later; meanwhile it will be useful to examine
the way in which the money raised for the county's poor
was actually spent under the old law, and which of the
abuses in administration denounced by the commissioners
were to be found here.

One of the evils prevalent in the agricultural south-east
of England was mercifully absent here: the so-called
'Speenhamland' system of doles out of the rates to bring
wages up to subsistence level. Grants in money or in kind
in time of sickness or in bad seasons, which had long been
feature of social life before ever the machinery of the Elizabethan Act was adopted, remained the commonest form of
expenditure. The Caerhûn vestry book records in 1785 the
payment of half-a-guinea for nursing the baby of a deserted
wife in the parish, a further eight shillings to an attendant
for looking after the mother during an illness following
childbirth, and two shillings for a warrant for the arrest of
the absconding husband at Llanrwst. Four years later a
surgeon from Conway is paid 16s. 6d. by the same parish
for setting a broken leg — unsuccessfully, it appears, for one
of the next entries is the cost of a shroud for the patient!
Sometimes the process of relief was short-circuited by a
direction from the vestry to the ratepayer to hand over part
of the rates due from him direct to a pauper named in the
order.

A more dubious practice was the payment, in part or
whole, of the house rents of paupers. This was a golden
opportunity for the speculative jerry-builder, who put up
rows of what soon became slum houses in the confident
expectation of recovering his rents from parish funds. At
Bangor, where population and housing had remained virtually static for four centuries or more, a new labouring
population flocked in from 1800 to seek work at Port Penrhyn
or in its ancillary trades. They found refuge in a maze of
narrow alleys inhabited largely by paupers — an abiding
eyesore until the slum clearances of the present century. At

European Magazine

LORD PENRYN'S SLATE QUARRY,
near Bangor, N Wales.

Published by J Asperne, at the Bible Crown & Constitution &c. until November 1808.

PLATE XIII

PLATE XIV

TRAETH MAWR AND THE EMBANKMENT IN 1806

YNYSCYNHAEARN CHURCH, BEFORE 1830

PLATE XV

Plate XVI

Capel Newydd, Nanhoron

Caernarvon the problem was older, for a seaport town naturally attracted to itself destitute immigrants from Ireland and deserters from ships, who swarmed into huddled courts and alleys, often built in the back gardens of respectable householders ready to barter amenities for spot cash. These could lie hidden and forgotten behind the façade of clean streets and well-built houses admired by fashionable visitors — until their presence was revealed, as we shall see, by deadly outbreaks of pestilence. Llanrûg parish, with a population swollen by the growth of the quarries, solved the problem by different methods but no happier results: three cottages, each measuring 15 feet by 13½ and 5 feet high, were purchased out of the rates at a cost of £27, and here the parish paupers were herded together without supervision, without any provision of work or amenities, and in conditions of the utmost squalor. In the other cases grants were made out of the rates to help cottagers to build or repair their own houses. Rather more than three per cent of the rates raised in 1776 were devoted to this purpose; Caerhûn vestry in 1789 made a grant of 3s. 6d. to a cottager to help in the thatching of his house.

Most parish authorities had by this time given up any attempt to comply with the provisions of the Elizabethan Act for ' setting the poor on work ', but occasional purchases of wool or flax, a loom or a spinning wheel, for a needy parishioner, are recorded in the vestry books; payments of this character amounting to between £12 and £13, appear in the accounts of Llanllechid and Llanaelhaearn in 1803. But it was Llanbeblig, with all the problems of a port town to face, that made the most ambitious experiment in this direction. In 1786 a house was bought for the then substantial price of £360, and in it the paupers were not only lodged but fed and (where necessary) clothed. Flax was provided for the inmates to spin, and an announcement was issued that ' such that expects to be relieved by the said parish will be received at the above house and be maintained at the expense of the parish ', but that any who refused their prescribed tasks, or absconded, forfeited all claim to relief.

The basic principle of the new Poor Law of 1834 was the gradual abolition of all outdoor relief and the adoption of a rule, like that imposed at Llanbeblig in 1786, that relief should only be given in a properly supervised institution. But in these institutions conditions were to be ' less eligible ' than those prevailing in the homes of the lowest grade of independent labourer. This was certainly not the case at Llanbeblig, where the inmates appear from time to time to have been regaled at the ratepayers' expense with meals of pork as well as more commonplace dishes like herrings, ' stirabout ' and bread-and-treacle, and to have been warmed with coal fires to the tune of three and a half tons in the year, costing nearly £3; how many Caernarvonshire labourers enjoyed such luxuries? A second principle was the grouping of parishes into Unions; the commissioners had recommended this partly with a view to making possible, by virtue of this wider area, a variety of institutions suited to the needs of different categories of pauper, but this corollary was not embodied in the Act and in fact was very seldom put into effect. Finally, the old Poor Law authorities — the parish vestry, with appeal to the nearest magistrate — were to be replaced by elective Boards of Guardians as the final court of appeal from the overseers throughout the Union; this, it was hoped, would lead to a more uniform and consistent policy and give greater power to those who paid the piper to call the tune.

Caernarvonshire was covered by two Unions and parts of three others. It was an interesting re-grouping of the ancient divisions, based primarily on economic factors. Pwllheli Union, covering the whole of Llŷn, five western parishes of Eifionydd and one of Arfon, catered for thirty-two mainly maritime parishes earning a scanty living, as we have seen, from part-time agriculture and part-time fishing, with nothing in reserve for a bad season in either. Then came Caernarvon Union, embracing twelve parishes of Arfon, from Clynnog along the coast to Bangor and inland to Llanberis, together with five Anglesey parishes of the south-west which looked to Caernarvon as their shopping centre.

This, of course, was a region largely dominated by the slate industry. East of this was the Bangor-Beaumaris Union, centred in Bangor but including fifteen parishes of south-eastern Anglesey together with the northern quarrying parishes of Arllechwedd, now closely linked with them by Telford's bridge and Bulkeley's road from it to Beaumaris. The Conway Union covered the lower Conway valley, Creuddyn and coastal parishes stretching into Denbighshire as far as Llysfaen — like Llŷn an agricultural and fishing area, but generally with less poverty and lower rates. Then came the Llanrwst Union, belonging to the upper Conway valley and mainly in Denbighshire, but including seven southern parishes of Arllechwedd; and finally the four eastern parishes of Eifionydd, forming the hinterland of the Traethau and included in the Ffestiniog Union, which was dependent economically on the slate industry of northern Merioneth.

Pwllheli Union was the first to put the Act into full operation — partly, perhaps, because of the high rates with which some of the western parishes were burdened. Its Board of Guardians was elected in 1837 and a workhouse to hold two hundred inmates was built. Ten years later all relief outside the workhouse was stopped. In accordance with the spirit of the Act, conditions were less ' eligible ' here than they appear to have been in the old Llanbeblig workhouse. Breakfast and supper consisted in porridge or gruel made of seven ounces per person of oats with buttermilk or water; for dinner, four ounces a head of meat were allowed on Sunday, on other days soup, stew or cheese, with six or seven ounces of bread per head. But the full squalor is revealed only when we learn that no knives or forks were issued until 1900, and then only under pressure from the Local Government Board! The Llanbeblig workhouse had either faded out or did not satisfy the requirements of the Act, but there was naturally opposition to the expense of building a new one, and it needed a judicial order in 1843 to compel the Guardians to act. The new workhouse was at last built in 1846, but it did not have a good name: as late as 1880 it was reported that the bedding remained unchanged for weeks on end, and that the children went about tattered and verminous.

In the Bangor-Beaumaris Union there was acute controversy about the building of a workhouse. A strong party, especially on the Bangor side, feared that such an institution would only be a further burden on the rates; they were also alarmed by reports of the mob violence provoked by attempts to enforce the 'workhouse test' in Montgomeryshire. It was chiefly the influence of Sir Richard Williams Bulkeley on the Anglesey side and of Dean Cotton in Bangor that at last in 1843 produced a resolution in favour of compliance with the Act; even then the Bangor parish vestry offered all the obstruction it could, and the workhouse was not built for another two years. Outdoor relief, however, was not abolished; instead, all able-bodied paupers were subjected to an 'outdoor labour test' before they could secure relief, half of which was to be in kind. The result was that by 1846 there were only six able-bodied inmates of the workhouse, but croakers could point in triumph to the fact that over £5,000 still went in outdoor relief and the total of paupers in the union remained as high as two thousand. Conway was happy in the possession of borough funds out of which paupers were relieved as need arose till 1798. With the Llandudno mines in a fairly flourishing condition and agriculture reasonably prosperous in the lower Conway valley, pauperism was not as acute a problem here as in the other unions. An outdoor labour test was imposed in 1847, and at last a workhouse was built in the 'sixties; a directory of 1873 describes it as providing 'more than ample accommodation for its requirements'.

The history of the workhouses of Caernarvonshire, as elsewhere, is one of a very slow improvement in general amenities, a cautious relaxation of the principle of 'deterrence' and a gradual differentiation of the various types of pauper according to age and circumstance. We learn something of early conditions from the reports of assistant commissioners and inspectors. They are not flattering documents.

In 1847 a report on the workhouses of North Wales in general condemns as 'iniquitious' the effects of the 'general mixed workhouse' on the young who were exposed there to degrading and even criminal influences. The answer to this in the following year was the institution of workhouse schools at Bangor, Caernarvon and Pwllheli. The Bangor school-master was paid £15 a year (later raised to £20), with his keep. Subsequently a schoolmistress who had previously taught at Bangor National school was added to the staff, also with a salary of £15. Bangor had a fairly favourable report; at Caernarvon, with a higher proportion of monoglot Welsh children, efforts at teaching them through the medium of English naturally did not meet with much success; Pwll-heli workhouse school was condemned root and branch. In none of the three was any effort made to replace the valuable Elizabethan provision for 'apprenticing the children of the poor to a useful trade' — now outdated by machinery — by some sort of industrial training. It was not till about twenty years later that the first schoolmistress was appointed to teach the pauper children of Conway Union. There was no differential treatment for the elderly anywhere until in 1856 the Bangor workhouse varied its dietary to the extent of allowing them such comforts as tea, sugar and butter. As for the able-bodied adults, the 'work' provided for them, as late as 1870, was undistinguishable from the penal tasks imposed in prisons.

From about 1867 the policy of the Poor Law Board (and afterwards the Local Government Board) began to veer away from the principle of 'deterrence' in the direction of improved amenities, but the Caernarvonshire Guardians were loth to embark on any scheme involving higher expen-diture and therefore higher rates. None of the three authori-ties controlling the county's older workhouses would listen to pleas for structural alterations to make possible separate treatment of the different classes of pauper, and even Conway, when at last it built its institution, followed the now outdated (but less expensive) pattern of the 'general mixed workhouse'. The Pwllheli Guardians strongly resisted suggestions for boarding the floors and installing laundry appliances (even a mangle!). Another change of policy was in the treatment of sick paupers, for whom no provision had been made in early workhouses except the ministrations of fellow-inmates in the general ward, supplemented when necessary by visits from the Poor Law doctor. By 1882, however, Bangor must have had a separate ward at least for infectious cases, for it was used (contrary to regulations) for the general public during the typhoid epidemic of that year, of which more later. But here again it was not until the turn of the century that those up-to-date workhouse infirmaries were built (notably St. David's at Bangor), which came just in time to serve as military hospitals in the first World War and then as units in the National Health service. On the other hand, the appointment of one or more medical officer in each Poor Law Union was an important step towards rescuing the poor from the ministrations of the quack and the ' wise woman ' of the village.

The obstructiveness of local Guardians was not always a disinterested protest against sentimental humanitarianism; the *Memories* of Sir Llewelyn Turner,[2] written in 1903, contain some horrifying tales of corruption on the Caernarvon Board of Guardians, on which he served. On the other hand, the relaxing of discipline did not always have happy effects: in 1904 there were allegations of promiscuity among the inmates of Conway workhouse. It was not until the inter-war period of the present century that the cumulative effect of these conditions brought about the break-up of the Poor Law of 1834 and the rise of a generation for which the once terrifying word ' workhouse ' has no longer any meaning.

Another by-product of industrial development was the incidence of disease, notably of epidemics. Epidemics were of course an all-too familiar feature of medieval life, and they continued to take their toll, though a somewhat dimin-

[2] Pp. 336-9.

ished toll, in the sixteenth and seventeenth centuries. One of the later visitations of bubonic plague was experienced over most of Wales in 1637-8, and may well have contributed to the general political restlessness of those years. The prevalent plague of the eighteenth century was smallpox, but it was much less a respecter of persons than bubonic plague, and as frequent a visitant to the courts of kings as to the courts and alleys of congested towns; William III's Queen Mary died of it in 1694 and in the course of the following century at least five other European monarchs were among its victims, while eighteenth-century portraits often reveal the ravages of the disease among the aristocracy. Why it should have caused over sixty deaths in remote Penmachno during a few months in 1705-6 remains a mystery.

Industrial development contributed to the spread of epidemics in two ways. On the one hand it created new congested areas of habitation and of work; on the other hand greater ease of communication by both land and sea were conducive to a more rapid spread of germs as well as of people. It should also be added that we know far more about the incidence of disease in more modern times, and that for that reason comparisons may often be misleading. An outbreak of typhus — notoriously an ally of malnutrition — in 1740 is known to us only from an Anglesey diary, but we learn there that the epidemic was deadlier in the other two shires of Gwynedd, with Llanrwst as a principal centre of infection through the wide resort to it for marketing. Dysentery, which often accompanied typhus, was prevalent all over North Wales in 1762, and twenty years later the incumbent of Bryncroes in Llŷn recorded the year in his parish register as *blwyddyn y farwolaeth mawr* — the year of the great mortality. The epidemic is undefined, but the symptoms suggest an acute form of influenza, which was then raging in Cheshire.

It was in the late eighteenth century that smallpox became sufficiently menacing in the area to call for energetic countermeasures. The older and not very successful preventive of innoculation had been known and used since early in the century, but North Wales was not introduced to it until the period of the American war, when an enterprising doctor at Bala took it up; the omnipotent Sir Watkin Williams Wynn subjected to it, willy nilly, the poor of his parish of Ruabon, and David Pennant, son and heir of the antiquary, performed the same service in Flintshire. The far more effective method of vaccination spread more rapidly, because by the time of its invention — soon after the Napoleonic war began — the character and dangers of smallpox had come to be more widely recognised. An outbreak in Anglesey in 1808 was met by offers of free vaccination from doctors of the district, and probably helped to stimulate the scheme for a Loyal Dispensary for Caernarvonshire and Anglesey which was put forward as part of the local celebrations of the jubilee of George III in the following year.

Rival proposals for siting the institution at Bangor or at Caernarvon obstructed progress for a time, but in the end Bangor carried the day, and the Loyal Dispensary opened its doors in 1810. Within a month it had secured supplies of vaccine, and in the course of the next seven years between two and three thousand patients from the two shires were vaccinated, and nearly ten thousand attended for treatment of one sort or another. Three years later an apothecary was appointed as secretary at a salary of £60; but it was not until 1845, after removal to a new site on Penrhyn land in the developing suburb of Upper Bangor, that the Loyal Dispensary became the Caernarvonshire and Anglesey Infirmary, providing beds and nursing on the spot for a limited number of patients either paying for themselves or provided for by the patronage of subscribers. But the staff remained small : ten years after this, the only addition to the original provision of three surgeons and a physician was a matron.

Despite all precautions, epidemics continued. Smallpox frequently broke out at Bangor and Caernarvon in the 'twenties, and on the next decade their narrow and insanitary alleys were rarely clear of smallpox or typhus or both. After vaccination became compulsory in 1853 outbreaks of smallpox became gradually less frequent and less devast-

ating: the last serious onset came in 1871. Even the country
air of Aber was no safeguard against infection: in the years
1866-8 there were nearly twenty deaths from typhoid or
similar epidemics. An outbreak of typhoid at Bangor in 1882
was attributed to defects in the water supply. It spread over
the whole town, claiming nearly five hundred victims, eighty-
nine of whom died. Pressure on hospital beds grew desperate,
for the ' C. and A.' could offer only eleven; as we have seen,
irregular use was made of workhouse accommodation, and
in addition an unoccupied house was pressed into the service, and a second to house convalescents. One consequence
of the epidemic was the temporary evacuation of Friars
school to Llanfairfechan, prior to removal to a new site in
the healthier air of Upper Bangor. It was also a powerful
stimulant to the movement for incorporation as a chartered
borough, which came a few years later.

Unhappily, as smallpox and typhus receded, a new and
even deadlier epidemic took their place. Asiatic cholera first
appeared in western Europe in 1831; in the following year
it swept through Flintshire and Denbighshire into Caernarvonshire, causing thirty deaths there. It coincided with
(and no doubt stimulated) a religious revival touched off by
a sermon of John Elias. But the heaviest incidence of the
plague was in South Wales; and this was even truer of the
second onset of cholera in 1849, when nearly seventeen
hundred deaths were recorded in Merthyr alone, while
sixteen victims in Caernarvon town were the sum total of
this county's casualties. The epidemic of 1853 was again confined in the main to South Wales, and three deaths in Bangor
are all that are recorded in the North. It was the last great
visitation in 1865-6 that hit Caernarvon hardest, for the
disease is believed to have been carried in a schooner from
Liverpool (where it was raging) which docked at the port in
November 1865. Before Christmas, 471 had been taken ill
and sixty died, to be followed by another fifteen in January.
A house had to be taken over as a cholera hospital, and
people long remembered the heroism of the vicar (James
Vincent), the mayor (Sir Llewelyn Turner) and the Baptist

minister and bard Cynddelw (Robert Ellis) in exposing themselves to infection in the worst of the plague-stricken courts
and alleys to minister to the sick.

Sir Llewelyn Turner was a son of the William Turner
whom we have met as Assheton Smith's one-time partner.
He had long agitated about the deplorable state of housing
in Caernarvon, due largely to shortage of available building
land, but he could make no headway against the obstructiveness of owners of slum property or the supineness of government departments until cholera provided him with an
unanswerable argument. Then at last a few of the more
noisome courts and alleys were got rid of, landlords were
persuaded to part with land for building, and the town began
to grow outwards on to the Twthill site; it was the first
extensive slum clearance in the county — and that even
before Disraeli's Artisans' Dwellings Act of 1875 first empowered local authorities to undertake a task which nowadays
absorbs so much of their energies. The new dwellings were
not 'council houses', of course, but privately built and
owned, nor was there any question of peopling them with
former slum dwellers; the significance lay in the breaking
of the housing deadlock and the acceptance of some measure,
however small, of public responsibility for this social service.
By 1883 it could be claimed in a trade directory that the
'new town . . . beyond the ancient precincts' was 'more than
treble the size of the old town', and that Caernarvon's 'excellent drainage' made it 'one of the most healthy towns in
the kingdom'.

Apart from such major catastrophes as pestilence, some
progress was made during the eighteenth and nineteenth
centuries towards better medical provision for more commonplace ailments. The medical history of Caernarvonshire has
yet to be written, but what Hugh Latimer in one of his
sermons said of the sixteenth century remained broadly true
of its successor: 'Physic is a remedy only for rich folks . . .
for the poor is not able to fee the physician'. A properly
qualified physician was rarely to be found outside the bigger
towns, and when by some chance he settled in the country

it was on the wealthy gentry that he depended for his living; even they preferred whenever possible to go for medical advice or treatment to a city practitioner. The surgeon's traditional task was blood-letting, which remained the sovereign remedy for fevers till the eighteenth century; and although the immemorial practice of combining the surgeon's calling with the barber's had been illegal since Henry VIII's day, it took a couple of centuries to root the anomaly out from remoter regions, and it was not till 1745 that the ancient Company of Barber Surgeons was finally dissolved and the surgeon's practice given status under the supervision of the new College (later Royal College) of Surgeons. Below the surgeons came yet another group, the apothecaries, who until the nineteenth century justified the desription[3] of ' shop-keepers who did a little doctoring'. Despite the biting satires of Elis Wynne and Twm o'r Nant, the apothecary was really the first general practitioner. He may have had little theoretical knowledge, and his remedies may have been pragmatic and not without relics of witchcraft and super-stition, but at least he had much practical experience, and the succession was kept up and the stock of medical lore gradually expanded by a system of apprenticeship which became general in the eighteenth century, till the Apothe-caries Act of 1815 placed the profession under the control of Apothecaries' Hall in London and gave it legal standing.

It was largely from the ranks of the apothecaries that the Poor Law Unions drew their medical officers and the early hospitals their permanent staff. Henry Ellis, who became medical officer to the Bangor-Beaumaris Union for the parishes of Bangor, Aber and Llanfairfechan, was a son of Ellis Parry of Llanllechid, and was apprenticed to a Bangor doctor who had been practising since at least 1828. Ellis carried on a chemist's business one or two doors away from his former master's premises until, leaving the business in charge of his wife, he went to Dublin for two years to com-plete his training, paying his way by wholesale dealings in

[3] G. Penrhyn Jones in *Denbighshire Hist. Soc. Trans.* 1959, 59-60.

potatoes, and then qualified at the Royal College of Surgeons before returning to Bangor. Two of his sons entered the same profession; one of them was a victim of the typhoid epidemic of 1882.

As a cathedral city, Bangor was probably in the van of medical provision. The death in 1772 of a man described on his tombstone in the cathedral ground as ' surgeon and man-midwife' suggests some advance in obstetrical practice more than seventy years before survivals of the old order were pilloried by Dickens in the character of Mrs. Gamp. In more general practice was a doctor living in High Street in 1786, in premises which suggest a wealthy *clientèle;* but as he was then only twenty-five it is unlikely that he was a qualified physician. Caernarvon by 1823 had at its disposal the services of a distinguished surgeon and physician in Dr. O. O. Roberts, a farmer's son from the Denbighshire side of the Conway who after education at the local grammar school qualified as a physician in Edinburgh and as a surgeon in London and acquired his hospital experience at Chester. It was after practising in an extremely busy and extensive partnership at Llanrwst that he moved to Caernarvon. During the first cholera epidemic he was instrumental in forming a local Board of Health, and during the second, in 1849, he published a pamphlet giving simple but sound advice on the avoidance of the disease. Long before this, however, he had moved his practice from Caernarvon to Bangor, where he helped to set the infirmary on its feet in its new premises, and strongly criticised the ' exclusiveness ' of Friars school and the failure of the local Guardians to provide constructive work for the inmates of the workhouse. Dr. Roberts's vitrolic pen was employed in many other political and social agitations which will concern us later.

The spread of medical practice was rapid during the first half of the nineteenth century : by mid-century Bangor had eight doctors and Caernarvon six (each including one fully-fledged M.D.), Conway two, Pwllheli four, Tremadoc, Portmadoc, Llangybi, Llanengan and Llanystumdwy one apiece. Medical practice, it will be seen, was reaching out to the smaller villages, till by the end of the century there were few (apart from those on isolated farms) that were not within easy reach of skilled medical attention — though as late as 1889 it seems that the nearest doctor to Llandudno was one living at Conway. Apart from the general public and the very poor, the quarrymen at Penrhyn had their own special arrangements. The first Lord Penrhyn formed a contributory Benefit Club, heavily subsidised by himself, with its own surgeon and subsequently its own casualty hospital; this was originally at Bangor but was removed in 1842 to the immediate neighbourhood of the quarry. The first quarry surgeon was also one of the original staff of the Loyal Dispensary and later took charge of the hospital at Bethesda, while remaining a consulting surgeon to the C. and A. Infirmary, of which his son was the first secretary. The son is also believed to have been the local pioneer of anaesthetics, which he used for an amputation at the quarry hospital in 1848, only a year after Simpson first employed them in Edinburgh. The Penrhyn Benefit Club was a bone of contention in the strike of 1874, when the contributors complained that they had no voice in its management, and investigation revealed that the official manager was unable to account of over £2,000 of the accumulated funds; Lord Penrhyn, horrified at the disclosure, made good most of the deficit, and conceded the principle of democratic control of the club.

Apart from such institutions as the Poor Law, Benefit Clubs, Friendly Societies and Savings Banks, another remedy for destitution excited such interest and produced significant results in the late eighteenth and early nineteenth centuries; this was emigration. Until after the beginning of the French Wars in 1793 Caernarvonshire had been little affected by the movement, apart from a few isolated emigrants. Nothing is known of the reasons which prompted Owen Williams, of Meillionydd in Llŷn, to go out as a planter to Virginia in 1664; he came of a famly of local eminence, descended from

Cochwillan, and his elder brother had been the sheriff who bridged the return from Commonwealth to Monarchy in Caernarvonshire. But he was the fourth of six sons, and his worldly prospects at home seemed bleak, so land hunger is the likeliest explanation; had he known that his elder brothers would die childless and that the succession would ultimately pass to the youngest, maybe he would have stayed at home! Then there was the emigration to Pennsylvania of the group of Llŷn Quakers, mentioned in an early chapter. A small trickle of Caernarvonshire emigrants followed them to Pennsylvania, but the only names that have come down to us are those of two men from the Cricieth neighbourhood who went out (for unknown reasons) just as the War of Independence was starting. Still less propitious were involuntary emigrations like those of thirty-two Caernarvonshire boys and youths of ages ranging from eleven to thirty, sent in Liverpool corporation ships in the decade 1697-1707 to be bound 'apprentices' to planters in Virginia, Maryland and Barbados; or of the sheep-stealer from Llŷn who was deported to Virginia about half-a-century later.

Interest in emigration from Caernarvonshire begins in 1792 with the romantic expedition of John Evans of Waunfawr in search of the supposed descendants of Madog ab Owain Gwynedd and his followers, believed to be living as white Indians somewhere near the sources of the Missouri. Evans was a son and grandson of Methodist ' exhorters ', and the motive behind his expedition was primarily missionary fervour — comparable to the medieval quest of Prester John, the mythical Christian emperor marooned beyond a sea of paganism. Evans found the sources of the Missouri but not the Welsh Indians; the importance at home of his quest lay in the sudden awakening of local curiosity about America. Patriotic sentiment and economic hardship came to the aid of missionary enthusiasm; for John Evans's expedition coincided with the revived feeling for Welsh culture and antiquities which will be dealt with later, and with the efforts of Morgan John Rhees and William Jones of Llangadfan to found a Welsh colony which (in Rhees's words)[4] should 'flourish under the auspices of a free and enlightened people' at a time when 'the old Cambria is neglected and despised'. Then came the distress of the early years of the war with France to add an economic spur: nor can we leave out of account the troublous times through which Methodism passed while the panic caused by the French Revolution was in full swing, and Methodist *seiadau* were lumped in the popular mind with other secret societies which might be centres of Jacobin intrigue. In fact, to many in Wales America became the goal of millenarian hopes not unlike those which had inspired the Fifth Monarchy men a century-and-a-half earlier.

The forceful appeal of William Jones of Llangadfan at the Llanrwst eisteddfod of 1791 for a group of enthusiasts ready to shake the oppressive dust of the old world from their feet and to carve out a new Wales in the backwoods of America, was backed up by persistent but unsuccessful efforts to negotiate the grant of a block of land for the purpose in upstate New York; and in a preaching tour embracing Nefyn, Garn Dolbenmaen and Llanberis, Morgan John Rhees held out the same apocalyptic hopes. But there were opposing voices. Not only were Tory and Anglican influences hostile to a republican *régime* rejecting any church establishment, but the Methodist leaders also were suspicious. The matter of emigration was discussed at the *cyfarfod misol* at Brynengan in 1794, and a resolution was passed virtually denouncing the flight to America as escapism: 'so farewell to America for now', was the rueful conclusion of Robert Jones, Rhoslan. Even Morgan Rhees's fellow-Baptists, who had no inhibitions about republics or established churches, were by no means unanimous in sharing his enthusiasm. Christmas Evans, the powerful preacher who had done so much to spread the Baptist gospel in Anglesey and Caernarvonshire, remained implacably hostile to emigration.

[4] *Nat. Lib. of Wales Jnl.* ii. (1941-2), 139.

In spite of all warning voices, the year 1794 witnessed the first extensive response in Caernarvonshire to the call of the Atlantic. Between then and 1801 nearly six hundred emigrants left the county for America, most of them for New York state and a high proportion from Llŷn — though the figure of ' twelve score ' given by the rector of Llanengan is no doubt much exaggerated. In any case it was almost exclusively an agrarian migration. What is striking is that during these years Caernarvonshire, which had been so late waking up to the possibilities of emigration, provided more than forty per cent of the total that went out from Wales. As the struggle with France intensified, numbers naturally dwindled, partly for lack of available shipping, partly through government efforts to check the drain on man power, till by 1798 they had shrunk to nothing. But the absence of Napoleon in Egypt in 1800, followed by the naval successes of Nelson, eased the pressure and led up to Britain's first breathing space, the Peace of Amiens. No sooner was the brake relased than numbers shot up again till in 1801 there were 348 from Caernarvonshire alone — almost exactly half the total for Wales. A great many came from the neighbourhood of Llangybi.

After the renewal of war in 1802 emigration died down once more, but by no means ceased. By now, as we have seen, slate boats were from time to time leaving Caernarvon or Pwllheli, Port Penrhyn or Felin Heli (or later Portmadoc), for New York, Boston or Charleston in South Carolina, and they often made room — if grossly inadequate room — for a party of emigrants; but passage by slate boats long had a bad name on both sides of the Atlantic, and emigrants from Llŷn and Eifionydd (who still formed the majority) often preferred to walk from their homes to Pwllheli for a boat which would take them to Liverpool, where they might find better accommodation on regular emigrant vessels, even if they had to wait for days with no provision for food or lodging before she sailed. Emigration was indeed a painful and perilous adventure, and only the extreme of wretchedness on the one hand or a boundless utopian faith on the other could have driven men to it. It was not for lack of warning. The Tory *North Wales Gazette*[5] in 1811 tried to frighten them off by publishing accounts of life in America which call to mind Dickens's savage picture of Eden City, a generation later; and it returned to the charge in 1817 with laments about the departure of ' some of our best artificers ... who by their situation in life might appear to have no cause whatever for quitting this country '. A few — though only a very small minority — of those who had gone out sent similar warnings home; the vast majority wrote in enthusiastic terms which probably had a greater influence on their neighbours than all the persuasions of William Jones or Morgan John Rhees.

The movement was not resumed in force till 1817, in the trough of the post-war slump. From then on the drain of Caernarvonshire men, women and children to the new world was almost continuous. Of the flotsam and jetsam of the emigrants — largely illiterates or at least unpractised pen-men — we naturally know little except for the occasional glimpses afforded by the letters of fellow-passengers; we know more about those who were not driven out by sheer hunger. The Madog legend still had a powerful attraction long after John Evans's death in 1799. It had from the beginning been taken up with enthusiasm by the London Welsh-men responsible for re-establishing the eisteddfod, and a group of Caernarvonshire bards who were in touch with these formed a plan of following him to join in the search for the Welsh Indians; but in the end the only one who went was Abraham Williams, a Llanberis man by birth who after working in the Penrhyn quarry set out in 1793, at the age of thirty-eight, for Philadelphia — the traditional goal of Welsh emigration. After many wanderings he settled down as a cabinet maker in Pennsylvania, and was still writing Welsh poetry ' in the dark forest by the banks of the Susquehanna ' a quarter of a century later. Abraham Williams is an except-ionally early example of a quarryman emigrant; and as the

[5] 25 July 1811, 20 March 1817.

quarries then offered excellent prospects and the war with
France had not yet begun to disrupt the life of the district,
we may assume his motives to have been idealistic rather
than economic.

Which motive predominated with John Williams of Plas
Llecheiddior, Dolbenmaen, is less easy to determine. He had
been an early convert of Methodist evangelism, but his conversion impelled him eventually into the ranks of the
Baptists, and in the early 1790's he became pastor of the
congregation at Garn Dolbenmaen. But in 1795 he too sailed
for New York, much to the disgust of his friend and fellow-
Baptist Christmas Evans. Although his proficiency in
English was very limited at the time of his emigration, within
three years he took charge of an English Baptist church in
New York city. Nor again can we easily distinguish the prevailing motive that determined the daughter of Charles
Mark of Bryncroes, whom we have met as the mainstay of
early Methodism in Llŷn, to leave for Trenton, New York,
with her husband and eight of their children, on her father's
death in 1795. Was it that the prospects for Methodism, in
those days of stress, seemed brighter across the Atlantic, or
the prospects for stonemasons — her husband's trade, which
provided work for him (in company with other Welsh
emigrants) in the construction of the Erie canal — or just
the prospects of keeping a large family in independence?
Something of a poetess herself, she sent versified invitations
to the three children left at home to follow her. One of them
did; another, who was a grown man at the time of the
emigration, stayed at home to become known as Ieuan Lleyn,
schoolmaster, bard and hymn-writer; we shall meet him
later. Another migration from the same neighbourhood fifty
years later, which denuded the congregation of a local
Methodist chapel by spiriting away some fifty men and
women, was preceded by a moving open-air service before
sailing, and was soon followed by the building of a new
chapel in their new home bearing the same name. It was
often noticed, indeed, that emigrants from Caernarvonshire

tended to cling together in the new world more than those from other parts of Wales.

Emigration was as brisk as ever in the 'forties and 'fifties — in fact during the decade 1841-50 the numbers from Wales reached a peak of over two thousand; but its character was changing in several respects. Partly owing to more stringent government regulations from the 'twenties, emigration by slate boat was dying out, and Liverpool became the regular port of departure; and from about 1852 the steamboat began to replace the sailing vessel. The duration of the voyage was thus drastically shortened, its miseries vastly reduced, and many of the uncertainties of sailing eliminated. Moreover the official prejudice against emigration was breaking down. It was no longer a leap in the dark now that American institutions had proved themselves in two generations of independence, and the loss of skilled man power cease to be a nightmare at home in the piping days of peace: on the contrary emigration was welcomed in many quarters as a remedy for the recurrent bouts of unemployment, and was fostered as such not only by a growing number of unofficial agencies and printed propaganda in English and Welsh, but even by official policy. The Llanllyfni vestry book records in 1832 — before the passing of the new Poor Law — a payment of over £24 for sending a family to America, and fourteen years later a much smaller sum for the same purpose. Caernarvon Guardians in 1851 more cautiously gave £5 to make up what an intending emigrant's friends had managed to scrape together to send him to Canada, and several sums ranging from £3 to £20 were granted in the same way to Clynnog emigrants in 1832 and again in 1842. Bodferin parish in 1827 found in America a useful dumping-ground for an unwanted bastard child, and paid an emigrant £2 12s. for taking the child out with him.

Another change was in the incidence of emigration. Hitherto the great bulk of the emigrants had been smallholders or labourers from Llŷn and Eifionydd; now the quarrymen of Arfon and Arllechwedd began to take the lead. The Hungry Forties, as we have seen, were bad times in the quarries, with reductions of wages and short time at Penrhyn in 1842. Four years later the local paper announces the departure of ' many scores ' of quarrymen from Llanllechid, Llandygái and Llanddeiniolen for America, and an audience of some four hundred flocked to a meeting in Bethesda to further the cause of emigration. About this time the firm of Davies of Menai Bridge (of which more later) had as many as a dozen ships lying ready to convey emigrants between Wales, Liverpool and America. The census report for 1851 records the departure overseas of five hundred souls from the area of Llanrûg, Llanberis, Llanddeiniolen, Betws Garmon and Llanfair Isgaer, and in the same year a ship from Port Penrhyn left for Boston. The years 1852-3 saw further extensive migrations from Bethesda, Dolwyddelan, Llanberis and Dinorwig. For the slate industry was now developing in America, and quarrymen dissatisfied with conditions at home could take their skills with them and find abundant scope for exercising them in newly exploited areas where all the competition was for men and not for jobs. As early as 1794 two Welsh emigrants, one from Bala, the other from Drws y coed, had done some pioneer quarrying in New York state; but it was in the 'forties and 'fifties that Caernarvonshire men began to take a significant part in the development of the industry here and in Pennsylvania, Vermont and elsewhere, often as overseers or as partners in the enterprise.

A new goal for emigration from Caernarvonshire was provided by the opening up in the 1830's of Wisconsin which with its mines and its boundless prairies was cried up as ' ideal for Welsh settlers '.[6] It is significant that a book on the new territory was written by two Bethesda men and published in Bangor in 1845. The project of a Welsh colony in America once more became a topic of discussion, with Wisconsin as its venue; one of the leading Methodist preachers — John Jones, Tal y sarn, who already had many relatives in the States — was seriously considering at this

[6] N.L.W. Cwrtmawr MS. 1044 E.

time the project of leading out to Wisconsin a party of his
fellow-Methodists, partly with a view to strengthening the
cause across the Atlantic by an accession of accredited
preachers and leaders; but in the end he was dissuaded. On
the more crudely economic plane, however, the project had
a considerable appeal in the quarrying areas, and about
1851, clubs began to appear among the quarrymen of
Dinorwic, Bethesda, Caernarvon and Llanllyfni to enable
them to hire their own shipping for the passage. The loss at
sea in 1854 of an emigrant ship with many Caernarvonshire
quarrymen aboard was a damper to this enthusiasm, but
emigration continued. It is not unlikely that the twenty
emigrants from the tip of Llŷn who left Pwllheli in 1851
on their way to Liverpool had also been attracted by the
news of Wisconsin; but migration from this region was now
slackening off — not necessarily because life was becoming
easier there, but because men with no inside knowledge of
the quarries saw in the many gaps which emigration was
leaving among the quarrymen an opportunity for moving
into what seemed a more promising economic environment,
without too great violence to their immemorial home-keeping
instincts.

After 1860 there were no more mass migrations from
Caernarvonshire. It is true that among the most ardent
backers of the plan for a Welsh colony in Patagonia in 1865
were that many-sided man Sir Love Jones Parry of Madrun
and his brother-in-law and fellow radical David Williams of
Castell Deudraeth, who wrested the Merioneth seat in parliament from the Peniarth interest the following year; but the
only known Caernarvonshire names among the original
emigrants were seven from Bangor (from two families), two
each from Caernarvon and Llanfairfechan and one (a
woman) from Bethesda. Hostility to feudal landlordism and
the Church establishment expressed itself during the following years mainly, as we shall see, in political struggles at
home, not in escape to a new land. Emigration had now
become an individual expedient for bettering one's condition,
like seeking work anywhere else, rather than a communal

quest for Utopia. There had always, of course, been sporadic emigration to other countries than the United States — Canada, South Africa, later Australia and New Zealand — but none of these aroused the millenarian fervour attached to what a Merioneth emigrant described to his young son,[7] on returning in 1799 from seven years in the States, as ' a great and good country beyond the ocean where there is no king, no tithes, and where poor people can get farms '.

## BIBLIOGRAPHY

Banking in North Wales is described in Crick and Wadsworth, *A Hundred Years of Joint Stock Banking* (1936), vi, and in A. H. Dodd, ' The beginnings of banking in North Wales' (*Economica*, 1926). On Savings Banks see Dodd, *Industrial Revolution in N. Wales*, 375-7. On the Poor Law in North Wales generally, id. in *Arch. Camb.*, 1926, and for Caernarvonshire, C. Flynn-Hughes, ' The Bangor workhouse ' (*TCHS* 1944), and ' The workhouses of Caernarvonshire ' (id. 1946). On epidemics and doctors, G. Penrhyn Jones, ' Cholera in Wales ' (*Nat. Lib. of Wales Jnl.*, x, 1957-8), and ' Aspects of the medical history of Denbighshire' (*Denb. Hist. Soc. Trans.*, 1959); and J. Ingman, ' Early days of the Caernarvonshire and Anglesey Hospital ' (*TCHS* 1950). Conditions in Caernarvon are described in Sir Llewelyn Turner's *Memories* (ed. Vincent, 1903) and in W. H. Jones, *Old Karnarvon* [1888]; for Dr. O. O. Roberts see E. H. Owen in *TCHS* 1949. There is a brief sketch of Welsh emigration in general in A. H. Dodd, *The Background of Early Welsh Emigration to the United States* (2nd ed. 1957), and an exhaustive account of Caernarvonshire emigration in Bob Owen, ' Yr ymfudo o Sir Gaernarvon i'r Unol Daleithiau ' (*TCHS* 1952-4). On Patagonia see R. Bryn Williams, *Y Wladfa* (1962), and for John Evans's explorations, D. Williams, *John Evans and the Legend of Madoc* (1963).

[7] B. Childlaw, *Story of My Life* (Philadelphia, 1890), 18.

# XIII

## POLITICS AND RELIGION
### (1780-1900)

### A. POLITICS, 1780-1850.

OUR last glimpse of Caernarvonshire politics was in 1774, when the Glynllifon interest suffered a severe blow by its defeat at the hands of Assheton Smith, and its long political monopoly was at last breached. Lord Newborough strained every nerve and spared no expense to retrieve his position. Fort Williamsburg, which he had built in his father's lifetime when there was talk of French invasion, was little more than a typical eighteenth-century ' folly '; but Fort Belan, which he now constructed to guard the western entrance to the Straits, had a serious purpose; it was in fact put into use as recently as the second World War. The danger when he built it was from American privateers co-operating with their French allies to threaten the shipping round our coasts. This became apparent when in 1777, very soon after the fort was built, two American privateers appeared off the coast of Anglesey, and captured a vessel believed to be carrying to Bangor the furniture of Bishop John Moore, who had been appointed to the see of Bangor two years earlier and was now evidently contemplating residence there. Whether the rumour was true, and if so whether the bishop ever got his furniture back, is not known. In the following year the militia was again embodied, and Newborough, as lord lieutenant of the shire, was much concerned in this; but he went farther and raised, clothed and paid a force of his own, four hundred strong, known as the Royal Carnarvon Grenadiers, presumably for the defence of Fort Belan.

In the same year 1778 another local issue arose which helped to stir the county, and indeed all North Wales, out of its apathy. This was the question of the crown lands. George III's policy of rescuing the crown from the political control of the oligarchy extended to the landed possessions of the crown, large areas of which during long years of neglect had passed into the clutches of the same dominant class. The issue was particularly acute in North Wales, where so many former manors of the Welsh princes had fallen into the hands of the crown at the conquest. Here the freeholders were in name tenants of the crown, paying quit rents that had become nominal with changes in the value of money, and which under a slack *régime* remained uncollected for years on end: Caernarvonshire, the worst defaulter of all the Welsh counties, was £6,000 in arrears by 1787. Nine years before this, Lord North appointed a new surveyor of crown lands in Wales, with a view not only to recovering arrears of rent but to reasserting crown claims in the waste lands, which developments in mining and quarrying had now revealed as potential sources of untapped wealth if they were leased at economic rents to competent adventurers. It was a case of the forest of Snowdon all over again, in a different context but with the same reactions. Under the leadership of that stout Tory Sir Watkin Williams Wynn, a series of county meetings was held in five of the North Wales counties (Montgomeryshire, where far more of the manors were in private ownership, was less interested) during the years 1778-9, and fiery resolutions were passed about 'alarming invasions . . . of our undoubted rights and liberties'. London politicians of the opposition took up the cry for party ends; a metropolitan newspaper dubbed the new crown surveyor 'Inquisitor General to the Principality of Wales'.

Government bowed to the storm, a composition was arrived at, and calm was restored. But it all forms part of the background to the general election of 1780. Newborough was in a dilemma. He was desperately anxious to recover his local prestige, but he dared not fall foul of the government, for his ability to cut a figure locally depended on his continuing to be *persona grata* in high quarters; and unhappily for him, the stock of the government had run very low in Caernarvonshire both as a result of the crown lands episode and because of North's gross mishandling of the American war, which had been brought home so sharply here by the bravado of the American privateers. In trying to run with the hare and hunt with the hounds he came to grief, and a quarrel with his more popular brother Glyn over an annuity, ending in a Chancery suit, did not help.

He claimed later that he had suffered at the government's hands for his opposition to the 'ruinous and disgraceful American war', but there is no sign of this opposition in the division lists of the House; Lord North, however, no longer regarded him as a 'a safe' man, and withdrew the support which had enabled him to be returned for a Cornish pocket borough when his county rejected him in 1774. Creditors, sensing the direction of the wind, began to close in, and his lavish scale of expenditure left him dangerously exposed to them. His brother Glyn was 'influenced' by Lord Bulkeley to desert to the opposition, but with his docile corps of out-voters, his personal popularity and his colonelcy in the regular army, his borough seat was safe enough. In the county Assheton Smith, the victor of the last election, had taken too little interest in his constituency to be acceptable for a second term; he loftily owned that he 'did not expect to have been approved of by the common freeholders', but was piqued that Bulkeley, another absentee, should have withdrawn his support on those grounds. The Bulkeley nominee, backed by Brogyntyn but spurned by Vaynol, was John Parry, a younger son of Madrun who had succeeded at the law and become attorney general for North Wales. A preliminary canvass showed that Parry had a six to one lead, and Newborough backed out at the last minute. His attempted 'come-back' had failed.

Since before the election, discontent in the country at large had been expressing itself in a succession of county

meetings at which resolutions were passed directed chiefly
at government extravagance, corruption and incompetence.
At many of these meetings Associations were set up to take
whatever action seemed possible to implement the resolutions; for the electoral machinery as an expression of the
country's will had fallen into sad disrepute, and indeed many
of the county resolutions were designed to free it from cor-
rupt control. The movement spread to Caernarvonshire in
1782, when a county meeting passed resolutions, with one
dissentient, in favour of economic reform, shorter parliaments and 'more equal' parliamentary representation, with
a rider that, failing satisfaction, their representatives should
be 'instructed' to vote against supplies. At the same time an
Association was formed (with the concurrence of the new
member, John Parry) to correspond with other county
Associations on the restoration of the 'constitutional rights'
of the electors.[1]

It was all very late in the day (Denbighshire, for example,
had had its county meeting the preceding year), and it
proved a damp squib, for only a month later there were
public rejoicings in Caernarvon over the recent change of
ministry : Lord North had resigned, in fact, only a matter of
days after the Caernarvonshire resolution. There followed
what George III had tried so hard to keep at bay — the
return to power of the Whig families. During the three short
ministries that followed, John Parry showed an independence
which Caernarvonshire had long since ceased to expect of its
representatives : he gave them a general support, and voted
(as no doubt his constituents would have wished) for the
peace with America which they concluded; but when North
tried to recover power by a not very creditable coalition
with the most destructive critic of his former ministry,
Charles James Fox, Parry's was among the votes which
brought the coalition down. Glyn Wynn had been bought
back by North before he fell, by the office of receiver-general
for North Wales, but this did not deter him from supporting

[1] Text and report in *Chester Chron.* 15 March, 1782.

each of the successive ministries that supplanted North — except that he cannily absented himself from all the more critical divisions.

The fall of the Fox-North coalition was followed by an election which stands out in the parliamentary annals of the country from the fact that it brought to an end the succession of political crises, and possibly averted revolution, by taking the form of a massive vote of confidence in the younger Pitt, ' the pilot who weathered the storm ' and guided British destinies, with one short break, for over twenty years. Pitt was the king's choice, it is true, and all the resources of royal ' influence ' were behind him in the election; but there was probably a wider display of public interest and a more decisive expression of public sentiment than at any previous election; it has been described as[2] ' the first in which the whole weight of government coincided with the whole impetus of public feeling '. In this context the Caernarvon-shire elections are a barren anti-climax, for in essence they are a reversion to the traditional idea of an election as a struggle for prestige between two rival groups of local families. In the county Lord Newborough, finally stripped of his offices, had to flee abroad from his creditors; but he still declined to accept the fact of his personal unpopularity and was optimistic enough to believe that the long sway of his family and his own lavish public expenditure would rally some sort of following in a campaign directed from abroad through his agent — especially if it were reinforced by threats of eviction should any of his tenants favour the opposing faction. He was wrong. John Parry was again returned unopposed.

Rejected by the shire, Newborough resolved to put up against his brother for the boroughs. Here the decisive factor was the determination of Lord Paget of Plas Newydd to take a personal hand in Caernarvonshire borough politics, and the equally strong determination of Lord Bulkeley to safe-guard his own newly-recovered influence on the mainland.

<hr/>

[1] Feiling, *The Second Tory Party* (1938), 14-15.

Neither could offer himself as candidate; Bulkeley in 1784 went a step up in the peerage by exchanging his Irish title (which enabled him to sit in the Commons) for a peerage of Great Britain (which disqualified him); Paget, long a member of the peerage, was promoted in the same year to a higher rank as earl of Uxbridge. Both had important possessions in Caernarvonshire, but precedence in Anglesey was the real issue. The disarray into which the Glynllifon interest had fallen made the contending brothers obvious catspaws for the real protagonists. It all had very little to do with politics, since Baron Hill and Plas Newydd were both supporters of Pitt; and it only marginally affected the interests of Caernarvonshire folk. Yet it proved to be the fiercest and most expensive contest the boroughs had yet experienced.

Both sides had been preparing the ground ever since Newborough's flight to Italy in 1782. Glyn Wynn managed to secure the office of constable of Caernarvon castle (carrying with it the mayoralty) for his nominee, and all Bulkeley's efforts failed to dislodge him; thereupon, in collusion with Paget, Wynn contrived the election of nearly seven hundred new burgesses, largely tenants of Plas Newydd. Bulkeley for his part used his old alliance with Brogyntyn to bring about over four hundred admissions to the burgess roll at Cricieth, largely from his Llanfairfechan estates. Thereupon Paget and Glyn Wynn by very dubious tactics contrived to have the borough records of Nefyn and Pwllheli secreted (after sixty new admissions had been made in the former) to forestall any further inflation of the burgess roll. To make confusion worse confounded, Newborough and his agent, owing to slow communications, were often acting at cross purposes, while his mother, who administered the estate in his absence, favoured her younger rather than her elder son. The only shred of political principle discoverable in the contest lay in Bulkeley's repudiation of Glyn Wynn because, after being bribed by him to desert Lord North, he had been coaxed back into support of the Fox-North coalition, which Bulkeley detested; but rather than become one of ' Fox's martyrs ', Wynn obligingly swung round to the support of Pitt.

The result was an election lasting ten days, dragged out by frequent legal wrangles over the qualifications of individual voters (with a flagrantly partial mayor as arbiter), and landing Lord Uxbridge in a bill of £1,150; this included 8,000 meals (at half-a-crown a head for gentlemen and eight-pence for ordinary burgesses), 900 beds, and over 3,000 gallons of porter. These may be compared with Sir John Owen's reported expenses in the election of 1666: just over five guineas for drink and a little over £16 for meals and services. Glyn Wynn carried the day by 490 votes to 410, but it was a short-lived triumph: in the following year Uxbridge got himself appointed constable and mayor of Caernarvon, thereby ensuring the return of his son for the boroughs at the next election. In this capacity the Plas Newydd family did much for the amenities of the town. We have already seen how Uxbridge and his son contributed towards giving it its brief day of glory as a place of fashion with both summer and winter seasons. The election, how-ever, left other, more dubious legacies to Caernarvon. Up to 1784 only two or three public houses in Caernarvon had taken out licences to sell spirits; the others had for the most part been content with 'home-brewed'. But the election orgy seems to have brought about a permanent change in drinking habits: henceforth spirits were obtainable every-where — as witness the 2,500 gallons that went down the throats of the borough electors when, nearly fifty years later, the last old-style election was fought there.

In parliament the county member gave solid support to Pitt's administration, but locally his most important vote was one which helped to quash, in the interests of Caernarvon's navigation, the project of an embankment and wooden bridge connecting Anglesey with the mainland. Glyn Wynn also generally supported Pitt, but voted against the adminis-tration whenever a measure came up (such at Pitt's Reform Bill of 1785) which was known to be personally distasteful to the king. Even the seemingly bottomless purse of the Pagets could not stand a repetition of the prodigal expendi-ture of 1784 at every election, still less could that of the

Bulkeleys; so the two houses formed a compact soon after the election, dividing Caernarvonshire into 'spheres of influence', the county falling to Baron Hill, the boroughs to Plas Newydd. This remained the pattern of Caernarvonshire politics for nearly half a century. For thirty-six years after 1790 the Bulkeley nominee for the shire was Sir Robert Williams of Marle and Eriannws (heir to the Penrhyn baronetcy founded by Archbishop Williams's nephew), who had married the widow of the sixth Viscount Bulkeley, and whose grandson was destined to inherit Baron Hill. The borough seat was shared between members of the Plas Newydd family. Glyn Wynn died in 1793; his elder brother had returned from abroad the preceding year with a foreign wife over whom a haze of mystery and romance still hangs, and re-entered parliament, by the grace of Lord Bulkeley, for his pocket borough of Beaumaris, which he held till his death in 1807.

The lull in parliamentary politics was prolonged by the outbreak of the French Revolution. In 1793 the main body of the Whigs formed a coalition with Pitt, leaving only a small remnant led by Charles James Fox to uphold the programme of reforms which had caused such a stir in 1778-80. In the same year England entered the war with France which absorbed all her energies till 1815. In Caernarvonshire there was almost universal support for Pitt, expressing itself in the Menai Pitt Club, which embraced Caernarvonshire and Anglesey. The only critical voices, echoing the sentiments of 1780 and joining Fox in sharp-shooting at the government, were those of two outsiders, from Denbighshire and Flintshire respectively, who had settled in Caernarvonshire but sat for English constituencies: W. A. Madocks and G. Ll. Wardle; and so far were they from representing the sentiments of the shire that in 1809 the Menai Pitt Club passed a formal resolution[3] expressing complete satisfaction with 'our glorious constitution', and adding that if any amendments to it were needed, the two

[3] *N. Wales Gazette,* 20 July, 1809.

gentlemen purporting to represent Caernarvonshire and Anglesey at a recent inflammatory meeting at the Crown and Anchor in London (presumably Madocks and Wardle) were not the men they would trust with the task.

The satisfaction with the government expressed by the gentry was not necessarily shared by the rank and file who had no part in politics. Apart from the disturbances caused by economic hardship, which have already been dealt with, balloting for the militia caused a good deal of trouble in the three counties of Caernarvon, Merioneth and Denbigh. The militia was embodied, as soon as war began, under the terms of Acts which fixed the quotas due from each county. These were to be chosen by ballot from among all able-bodied men between eighteen and fifty, unless they were specially exempted or could find a substitute. This loophole naturally gave rise to jealousies and suspicions comparable in kind if not in degree with those which had troubled wartime Britain as far back as Elizabethan days. At Caernarvon and elsewhere clubs were formed which arranged that if any member were chosen in the ballot, £5 would be provided out of club subscriptions to pay a non-member to serve as substitute. Obviously the well-to-do were placed at an advantage; when in 1795 the Act was applied in Llŷn and in the region of Penmachno, Dolwyddelan, Ysbytty Ifan and Capel Curig, there was widespread resistance, and a man at Cerrig y drudion was rescued from the military by the mob. But the militia ballot could be escaped by joining a local body of volunteers under the Act of 1794; these had rather the character of Home Guards, and were not under the discipline of the regular army. A corps of volunteers was formed at Caernarvon, and both they and the militia used to parade the streets weekly. By 1798, when Ireland was aflame, with a French force ready to land and help, opposition had died down and the country was quiet again. But the cost of the militia was still helping to swell the poor rates: in the year before Trafalgar one-fifth of those raised in the little parish of Ynyscynhaearn went in supporting the families of militiamen.

The militia ballot had its naval counterpart (but without its bolt-holes) in the press gang. It got busy round the Caernarvonshire coasts as naval warfare intensified, carrying its victims off to distant seas they had barely heard of before. Others joined the service voluntarily, some as officers, surgeons or chaplains. There was indeed something of a naval tradition along the shores of Eifionydd, going back to the earlier wars of the century; but the return of peace found local seamen back in their normal life ashore. Thomas Jones of Cefnmeusydd Uchaf (Ynyscynhaearn) returned from fighting under Hood to become an extremely active churchwarden, father of a Congregational minister — and greatgreat-grandfather to the present earl of Snowdon. Mention has previously been made of another Thomas Jones, from a humbler walk of life, who fought at Trafalgar but was perhaps better know round Pwllheli for his versatility as a blind musician.

Even parliamentary politics occasionally came to life. In 1796 there was a lively contest for the county seat, occasioned by the determination of Lord Penrhyn, who had failed to find a following in the election of 1784, to force his way into the parliamentary hierarchy of the shire. He entered the lists as a Tory, with the backing of the bishop, John Warren, who had just been translated from Llandaff on John Moore's elevation to the see of Canterbury, and like his predecessor lived in the diocese. Plas Newydd and Baron Hill as Whig houses (but of course Pittite Whigs) continued to back Sir Robert Williams. There being no national issues at stake, the election was fought on what might be called a local platform. Penrhyn's sponsor the bishop was under attack on two flanks. On the one hand there was strong (but mainly unfair and captious) opposition to the expensive reforms he had set on foot — including a new building — for Friars school, which were alleged to be fitting it for ' sons of gentlemen ' at the expense of the local ' free scholars ' for whom it was designed. On the other hand the proprietors of the Anglesey copper mines, who included Sir Robert Williams's principal backer, alleged that the bishop was not pulling his weight in the rebuilding of Amlwch church which they had undertaken.

The opposition to Penrhyn hired a vitriolic but extremely able pamphleteer, writing under the pseudonym of Shôn Gwialan, to voice these accusations in an open letter to the bishop; the author has been identified with great probability as David Williams, a protagonist of the American and French Revolutions in this country and a Deist in religion. But there is no reason to believe that those who hired his services shared his revolutionary ideas in religion or politics. There were cartoons in circulation (but with no reference to national politics), a lawsuit, and riots in the cathedral ground; but after all the sound and fury there was no change in the county representation. The most interesting feature of the election is a substantial rise in the number of votes cast : in 1774 there had been 318; there were now 1,060. One can only conclude that resort had been had to the familiar eighteenth-century electioneering device of the splitting of freeholds, the counterpart in county elections to the creation of burgesses in those of the boroughs. If so, it must have been the work of Sir Robert Williams, for there were few freeholds on the Penrhyn estate, whereas Williams, as lord of the manor of Beddgelert with wide estates in Betws Garmon and Llandwrog, was well placed for increasing his poll in this way. Another novelty was an alleged promise by the Whig candidate of land for building a chapel for the Methodists (who of course were not yet separated from the Church) at Beddgelert, to secure the support of an influential Methodist farmer of the neighbourhood.

After 1796 there was another lull in political interest, lasting some thirty years. But once the war was over and the panic caused by the French Revolution had had time to subside, politics began to take on a new face. Political parties, though still far from clear-cut in either membership or principles, were gradually re-forming, and national issues which had long been shelved obtruded themselves into local elections. Chief among these were Catholic Emancipation — promised as part of the Irish settlement after the rebellion of 1798 but firmly vetoed by George III — and parliamentary reform, which had been kept alive only by the little group of Foxite Whigs since Pitt dropped it in 1785. The first was made urgent by O'Connell's agitation in Ireland from 1823; George III was dead, but his successor took the same line, and so did a large section of the Tory party, with the result that measure after measure of Catholic relief was rejected by either Lords or Commons. Sir Robert Williams, still representing Caernarvonshire, voted for the relief proposals of 1825, but in the election of the following year he declined to explain his conduct to his constituents, appealing only to his long services to the constituency.[4] The county chose as its member Lord Newborough's son and successor in title, who opposed Emancipation, while Sir Robert was accommodated by his half-brother (of Baron Hill) with the borough seat of Beaumaris, and transferred himself to an Anglesey estate. This must have been the first time in the county's history that an electoral change was determined by a political issue. It certainly reflected the views of the unenfranchised Caernarvonshire Methodists (despite Sir Robert's friendly gesture in 1796); it also may have expressed the strong ' no-popery ' sentiments which Hyde Hall deplored as characterising the county in general, and which in 1829 found vent in petitions from Caernarvon, Bangor, Pwllheli, Cricieth and Tremadoc opposing Emancipation.

The most striking changes, however, were in the boroughs — notably in Caernarvon, by far the most populous and the most rapidly growing of the five. The parish of Llanbeblig, in which it was situated, had over 3,600 inhabitants at the first census — three times as many as Pwllheli's parish, and over four times as many as Conway. By 1841 there were over eight thousand in the town alone; none of the other boroughs increased in anything like this ratio. More important than the population at large was the composition of the burgess body. From early in the nineteenth century the pro-

4 *N. Wales Gazette*, 29 Sept., 1825.

portion of resident burgesses was increasing at the expense
of non-residents, and the residents were drawn largely from
the ranks of business and professional men with their own
approach to politics. As Sir Charles Paget, who had represented the boroughs since 1807, was warned in 1830 by a
neighbouring landowner with property in the town,
' Strangers from all parts have settled there, and the attach-
ments and opinions of its present inhabitants are much
altered since you first were elected there '. In a compact
body like this it was easier for parties and factions to form
than among the scattered squires and freeholders of the
shire; Paget himself wrote that year of a ' party spirit, exercising control in the business of the Corporation '. Leadership was provided by the arrival in 1823 of Dr. O. O. Roberts,
a man of violent Protestant and anti-clerical sentiments and
an inveterate exposer of every kind of ' abuse ', who could
well have served as the original of Dr. Bold in Trollope's
*The Warden.*

Roberts found little difficulty in rousing opposition to the
Catholic claims among the shopkeeping and professional
element in Caernarvon, where (as in modern Liverpool)
Romanism tended to be identified with the despised Irish
immigrants and where Methodism, which through its leaders
had expressed itself so emphatically against Emancipation,
had by now gained a strong foothold. Only three years after
his arrival in Caernarvon, Roberts got himself elected bailiff,
in company with George Bettis, agent to Lord Newborough,
who was of the same faction. But the borough was still under
the patronage of Plas Newydd, and Lord Uxbridge's son —
now Marquess of Anglesey since his return from serving as
second in command to Wellington at Waterloo — was a
convert to Emancipation, while his brother Sir Charles, who
held high rank in the navy, had voted in the same lobby
with Sir Robert Williams on the abortive Bill of 1825. Lord
Anglesey was naturally indignant at the suborning of Caernarvon voters from their traditional allegiance, and he was
not slow to point out what the borough would lose by the
withdrawal of his patronage. At the same time he held what

were for the time advanced views on representation, which he expressed as follows:

> The representative must act on all publick questions upon his own judgement. If that judgement coincides with the opinion of the electors, then all is . . . as it should be. But when the reverse is the case, the member is bound to withdraw.

Sir Charles took the same line, and declined to stand again on the ground that his views were in opposition to ' those of my constituents whose opinion it was my duty to respect '.

Both the Caernarvon electors (for sound material motives) and the Plas Newydd family (for reasons of prestige) were reluctant to break old ties, so a compromise was arrived at by which the seat was offered to the Marquess's second son Lord William, who was now at sea and had not had occasion to declare himself on the issue of Emancipation. He was duly elected, and — as might have been foretold in so well-disciplined a family — voted for the crucial measure when it was finally passed in 1829. The two bailiffs went so far as to call a public meeting to demand his resignation; but Paget sat tight and nothing happened. Although the Catholic question was thus settled, its shadow still hung over the election of the following year, occasioned by the death of George IV. The Act had been put through, reluctantly and under threat of rebellion in Ireland, by a Tory government, and there was widespread resentment among country Tories at this ' betrayal '. A wider franchise, it was felt, might have reflected more truly the feeling of the country, which was generally hostile to the measure. This may well have contributed to the Whig victory — the first since the war — at the election, and so have helped to bring the question of parliamentary reform back into practical politics.

As in the 1826 election, local feeling in Caernarvonshire comes out most clearly in the boroughs — a complete reversal of eighteenth-century, still more of seventeenth-century conditions. The young Lord Newborough did not again contest the shire; in fact the family from now faded out finally into the background of county politics. Sir Robert

Williams stuck to Beaumaris. For the first time in nearly a
century, Cefnamwlch reappears on the political stage. The
last of the Griffiths had died childless in 1794, leaving his
estate to his cousin Jane Wynne of Foelas, whose husband,
Charles Finch, was the younger son of an earl. Their son took
the old family name with the estate, coupling it with his
mother's, and Charles Griffith Wynne was returned unopposed for the county seat. Politics do not seem to have
entered into this election, but it was different in the boroughs.
Here the challenge to the Paget ascendancy came from the
house of Brogyntyn, whose principal footing in Caernarvonshire — the borough of Cricieth — had been irrelevant so
long as the Glynllifon interest had been able to swamp it by
mass creations of burgesses in Caernarvon. But now a strong
party in Caernarvon, under the leadership of O. O. Roberts,
was burning with indignation over Catholic Emancipation
and ready to support the candidature of William Ormsby
Gore, successor to the Owens at Brogyntyn. Gore himself
was prepared to challenge the great numerical preponderance of Caernarvon by using his powers as mayor to swell
the burgess roll at Cricieth with an adequate number of yes-
men. This was enough to frighten off the Pagets, who had
had quite enough of squandering their fortune on disputed
elections. Lord William was up to the ears in debt and
estranged from his father; Sir Charles had no money to spare
on a contest for a seat he never really wanted and only took
up out of deference to his brother; Lord Anglesey himself
was beginning to balance the cost of his patronage of the
boroughs (which he reckoned at some £5,000 between 1817
and 1821, quite apart from the actual cost of elections)
against the advantages it brought. The upshot was that Plas
Newydd retired from the field and Gore was returned
unopposed.

The whole situation was changed when in 1831 the new
Whig ministry under Grey announced the terms of its proposed Reform Bill, and on its rejection in the Commons went
to the country on this single issue — the first example of this
kind of election in British history. Lord Anglesey had not

yet finally reconciled himself to either the loss of prestige or the closing of so many avenues to place and power for his numerous family which abdication from borough patronage and membership of parliament would entail, and under strong pressure from him Sir Charles Paget offered himself once more for the boroughs as an avowed advocate of Reform. Ormsby Gore took the opposite side, and gained much kudos from his support of the recent repeal of the slate duty; this helps to account for the part taken in an extremely riotous election by gangs of quarrymen in scuffles with sailors from Paget's yacht. The poll was open for eight days, and there were many charges of intimidation on both sides. Pwllheli, where the pro-Reform Mostyn family exercised much influence, produced a majority for Paget, but in the out-boroughs as a whole he only gained fifty votes as against nearly four times as many for Gore. It was Caernarvon that decided the issue. Despite the increase over the years in resident as opposed to non-resident burgesses, there were still three times as many of the latter as the former, and it was among them rather than the residents (for all the efforts of O. O. Roberts) that Paget secured the votes which tipped the balance in his favour — by the narrow margin of ten. In the county things went much more quietly, and Griffith Wynne was again returned unopposed.

The new Act made no revolutionary change in the franchise : in the counties it meant the extension of the vote to the £10 householder and the £50 leaseholder; in the boroughs a uniform franchise vested in resident householders paying an annual rent of £10 or more, but with the addition of Bangor to the contributory boroughs of Caernarvon and the concession that those who had hitherto exercised burgess rights at elections might keep them for life. Perhaps the most startling innovation was the compilation of registers of electors in each constituency. There was a long process of trial and error before satisfactory machinery for this new procedure was arrived at; but at the worst it was better than the interminable process of settling disputed claims in the hurly-burly of an election. The Whig government very properly decided on an immediate general election to test the new electorate. This election of 1832, unlike its stormy predecessor of 1830, was not fought on any single political issue; but the Whigs, and especially their radical allies, were known to have up their sleeves a whole pro- gramme of what they believed to be overdue reforms, many of which were unacceptable to Tories. In modern terms, what the government was seeking, and what in the issue it obtained, was a mandate for its programme of reforms.

How far such considerations counted in Caernarvonshire it is hard to tell. Griffith Wynne of Cefnamwlch, who had represented the shire in the last two parliaments, did not seek re-election. His place was taken by Thomas Assheton Smith, whose father had held the seat in 1774 — before the new candidate was born. Since then the local importance of the family had increased enormously with the development of the quarries and the Enclosure Acts of 1806-8, and there could be no question of taunting the son, as the father had been taunted, with being a stranger to his constituents. He was far more interested in fox-hunting than in politics, but politics had also changed. In 1774 the government had been effectively the king's government, and the senior Assheton Smith had been prepared to join in the Whig-inspired opposition to its inefficiency and corruption. Now the govern- ment consisted of a knot of Whig politicians bent on tamper- ing with some of the historic institutions of the land, and this the revived Tory party was determined to resist. The bulk of the Caernarvonshire gentry, while still shy of party labels, no doubt shared these sentiments and found the owner of Vaynol acceptable on this as on other counts; and it was still the gentry who counted, for all the Reform Act had done was to increase the county electorate from 1,060 to 1,688 — most of them dependent in one way or another on the gentry, and none in a position to oppose an Assheton Smith. So there was again no contest.

The boroughs, led by Caernarvon (where O. O. Roberts was still a force to be reckoned with), were more politically conscious. Lord Anglesey still looked on them as his special

preserve, but shrank from facing the  prodigal outlay of
another contested election. When Ormsby Gore transferred
his candidature to his own county of Shropshire it seemed
as though this could be avoided — until another opposition
candidate appeared in the person of O. J. Ellis Nanney of
Gwynfryn (Llanystumdwy). Fearing that the boroughs also
would be delivered over to the Tories, Dr. Roberts crossed
to Dublin (where Lord Anglesey ruled as lord lieutenant) to
persuade him ' not to desert his friends '. Very reluctantly,
the Marquess consented that his even more reluctant brother
Sir Charles should stand again, merely in the hope of scaring
off the ' nanny-goat ' (as Paget privately called the inter-
loper). But although Ellis Nanney did not rank high among
the political families of the shire, he came of a house with a
long record of service to the Church, and that was an asset
in days when the Whigs were suspected of anti-clerical
leanings like those of their opposite numbers in France. The
Mostyns were still ready to back the Paget cause in Pwllheli,
and Assheton Smith promised to stay neutral if Dr. Roberts
called off his venomous press attacks; most of the other
families of consequence encouraged Ellis Nanney to persist
in his candidature.

So there was nothing for it but another contested election,
in the course of which another £1,500 of Plas Newydd money
went down the drain to pay for an orgy of food and drink
which exceeded even what had been consumed in the
memorable election of 1784. In spite of all attempts of Lord
Anglesey and his chief agent to limit expenditure, the
numerous sub-agents poured his money out so freely that if
the figures in the Plas Newydd papers may be trusted those
who voted for him must each have consumed on an average,
in the course of the eight-day poll, something like twenty
dinners and sixteen suppers, seventeen barrels of beer, four
gallons of spirit and at least five bottles of wine! Unpaid
bills from publicans at Caernarvon and Bangor kept pouring
in up to the eve of the next election. Paget, who had never
wanted the seat, was dragged in triumph on his way to the
poll through the streets of Bangor in a carriage drawn,

appropriately, by a party of sailors; and he scraped in with a majority of 47 out of 773 votes.

The defeated candidate petitioned, as usual; this time on the ground that sixty-seven votes for Paget from Pwllheli had been wrongly accepted by the returning officer, having been cast by non-burgesses who on that score had been excluded from the register. On this Paget was unseated, but his supporters counter-petitioned, alleging bribery by the other side — an outstanding case of the pot calling the kettle black! This time the whole matter was gone into thoroughly by the House of Commons committee, which decided that most of the disputed votes were after all valid, because, they adjudged, the franchise was vested not in the burgesses as such, but in resident ratepayers. The conclusion was (as we have seen) historically wrong, but it stood, and the effects were of greater moment locally than those of the Reform Act itself; henceforth there could be no influx of manufactured burgesses from outside to swamp opposition, no monster electoral sprees.

In fact the Reform Act of 1832 was important less for its actual achievement than as one stage in a long process of political evolution. Political structure was slowly changing, and for long the old and the new existed side by side. Patronage remained important, and members were still drawn, in county and boroughs alike, from the same circle of families; but elections could no longer be settled by a gentleman's agreement like that of 1708, fixing a rotation of service for years ahead, nor by an allocation of 'spheres of influence' like the compact between Baron Hill and Plas Newydd after the 1784 election; still less could a single family dominate both boroughs and shire, like Glynllifon from 1714 to 1780, or boroughs alone, like Plas Newydd from 1784 to 1830. Candidates had now at least to profess attachment to a political cause, and to seek support among groups of constituents — even those outside the county hierarchy — who shared the same sentiments. They might privately resent, as Sir Charles Paget did, having to ' go cringing down Carnarvon for their stinking votes ' instead of having the automatic support of a disciplined body of retainers, grateful for displays of public munificence and lavish hospitality; but they could no longer avoid it. Electoral corruption in its cruder forms — if not so crude as in Dickens's Eatanswill — long persisted, and members still had a considerable amount of local patronage with which they could reward their supporters, so that even minor jobs (like, for example, that of postmaster of Bangor in 1836) were the normal expectation of faithful backers if their party got into power. But candidates were also learning a subtler approach to appropriate groups of their constituents, as when Paget's agent advised him in 1832 to stress his support for the abolition of slavery, ' a question of great interest among the religious sects '. How correctly he judged will appear later.

Opinion was also expressed and moulded by agencies unknown before. There was the local press. The *North Wales Chronicle*,[5] an embodiment of Tory views on Reform, waxed indignant that ' the ignorant and easily excited mob of towns ' should be ' called in to exercise the franchise in defiance of the spirit of the constitution '; ' The Commons ', it roundly declared, ' were never meant to include the lower classes ', who ' look upon Reform as a first step towards democracy '. The opposite side was taken by the *Carnarvon* (later *Carnarvon and Denbigh*) *Herald,* the first Liberal newspaper — to use the party label then coming into currency — in North Wales. Founded in 1831 by a well-to-do local Unitarian, it served as organ for the views of O. O. Roberts, who was a frequent contributor, and from about 1840 it was under the able editorship of James Rees, who had come to Caernarvon as printer in the year the paper was founded, succeeded to the editorial chair, and in 1854 founded a companion paper in Welsh, *Yr Herald Gymreig.* Roberts also seems to have been behind the personal attacks of *Figaro in Wales* (a scurrilous paper published at Bangor in 1835-6) on the local aristocracy, clergy and Tories in general, which

[5] 3, 16 and 31 March, 1831.

landed the printer in a libel action and heavy damages and put an end to *Figaro*'s short life.

In the county constituency things changed more slowly, for so sprawling a unit did not lend itself to party organisation, and the habit of deference to the traditional circle of natural leaders, reinforced by the fact that they virtually controlled the jobs as well as the homes of most of the electors, easily survived the mild extension of the franchise in 1832. Besides, till 1888 the county's only governing body was the bench of magistrates, which meant the same circle of families, whereas boroughs had since 1835 enjoyed an elective constitution. Tory politics consisted in a determination to preserve the existing order in Church, state and society, and until the much more significant extension of the franchise in 1867 there could be no question of electing anyone but a Tory: an Assheton Smith, then an Ormsby Gore, and then for a quarter of a century a representative of the Penrhyn family. The only substantial change from late eighteenth-century conditions lay in the fact that the ruling houses of that day — Glynllifon and Baron Hill — whose preponderance had been due to the weakness or absenteeism of the other historic families of the shire — abandoned all attempt at political domination once Penrhyn and Vaynol had recovered their ancient prestige. Glynllifon was content with economic and social eminence; at Baron Hill the Bulkeley line came to an end, after four centuries of uninterrupted descent, in 1822, and the estate passed to the son of the last Viscount's half-brother, Sir Robert Williams, who founded the new line of Williams Bulkeley and gradually withdrew from Caernarvonshire politics, until in 1856 he finally disposed of the bulk of his estates on the mainland.

In the boroughs the change was masked by the alliance (once the distraction of Catholic Emancipation was over) between the radical group in Caernarvon led by O. O. Roberts and James Rees, and the Whig Pagets, the borough's traditional patrons. At the 1835 election the coalition backed the candidature for the boroughs of that rare phenomenon, a Caernarvonshire landowner of Liberal views. He was Major L. P. Jones Parry, the son of a Denbighshire landowner who had acquired by marriage the Madrun estates. With his lawyer brother Lloyd Roberts as local agent, Dr. Roberts had been busy organising his party in the borough and making every effort to ensure that his supporters were duly included in the register — the task which first brought local party organisation into existence in the country generally. As will appear later, Nonconformity had by this time become a power in the borough and it constituted the backbone of Jones Parry's supporters, who by a gigantic effort succeeded in defeating Ellis Nanney by twenty-eight votes. But at the next election — the first of Victoria's reign — Jones Parry was toying with the idea (which he eventually dropped) of contesting the shire itself, and O. O. Roberts persuaded Lord Anglesey once more to add the glamour of his name to the Liberal cause by putting up a member of his family for the boroughs, on the understanding that the Caernarvon supporters would guarantee his expenses up to £500. But the old magic failed to work; the Tory candidate (this time Bulkeley Hughes of Plas Coch in Anglesey) was backed by the strenuous campaigning at Cricieth of Ormsby Gore; 'that cursed Cricieth', was Roberts's rueful comment when the Tory victory was announced, 'has swamped us'.

The same story was repeated in 1841. This was the last occasion when a Paget put up for the boroughs. The strange alliance between the radicalism and Dissent of Caernarvon and the patrician patronage of Plas Newydd was wearing thin, if only because elections were still costing more than Lord Anglesey was prepared to keep on disbursing: even in 1841 he was faced with bills amounting to over £1,000 — twice as much as he had authorised. At the 1847 election Bulkeley Hughes went in unopposed. O. O. Roberts had now moved to Bangor, which did not offer him quite the same scope as Caernarvon. Yet even here new elements — including Methodism and Dissent — were seeping in to dilute the Toryism of cathedral society, and

Robert Pritchard the postmaster was described[6] as 'the active leader of the Reformers of Bangor', who had 'suffered so much from Mr. Assheton Smith and the Tories' that Lord Anglesey himself intervened on his behalf with the government. The defeat of 1837 and the Tory 'walk-over' of 1847 left Dr. Roberts bitterly disillusioned with the 1832 Act.

The disillusionment was shared by many left-wing elements throughout the land; in industrial areas it found vent in Chartism, which in 1839 was the cause of violent outbreaks in Monmouthshire and Montgomeryshire. There was nothing like this in Caernarvonshire, where the only formidable working-class element was in the quarries; and until well past the middle of the century, quarrymen were too completely dependent on their employers for their houses and their jobs to do other than support them politically. Besides, as we shall see shortly, Methodism was a powerful political sedative till after 1840. Roberts's efforts were confined to the formation in 1837 of the North Wales General Reform Association, which stood for a further widening of the franchise, but never cut much ice. It was not until the 1852 election that the new politico-religious forces in the boroughs were able to stand on their own feet, independent of aristocratic patronage. To see how this came about we must retrace our steps to look at some of the religious developments that had been taking place during these years.

## B.  RELIGION, 1780-1900

The most striking feature in the religious life of Caernarvonshire during the earlier part of this period is the phenomenal progress of Calvinistic Methodism and, to a lesser degree, of the older Nonconformity which benefited from the same revival. Soon after 1780 the centre of gravity of the Methodist movement began to shift. Up to now Caer-

---

[6] Quoted *TCHS* 1963, 281.

narvonshire Methodists had lived on the organisation with
which Howel Harris had endowed them and the initial
enthusiasm he had inspired in the days when he took the
whole of North Wales as his province. But Harris had been
dead since 1773, and he had ceased to direct the movement
for the last ten years of his life. Daniel Rowland was now
the acknowledged leader and Llangeitho the metropolis of
the movement. We have seen how scattered Societies had
fanned outwards from Llŷn, till it was possible to hold
periodic Assemblies or district meetings at some central
point. But none of the Caernarvonshire clergy had joined
the movement; few were even sympathetic. Local farmers,
shop-keepers, even labourers, gave what leadership they
could in local affairs, but for direction on major points of
doctrine, discipline and organisation the local *seiadau* still
looked to the South. Regular missionary journeys had long
ceased, but Rowland and Williams of Pantycelyn both
attended the Pwllheli Assembly of 1777; messages passed to
and fro, and now and then a party from Llŷn would make
the adventurous journey to Llangeitho to seek inspiration at
one of the great Assemblies there.

    The settlement of Thomas Charles at Bala in 1784 pro-
vided a new and more convenient focal point. Henceforth
North Wales had its own distinct organisation, with Charles
as the leader to whom all the local Societies could look for
guidance. The Sunday School, which he helped to establish
in North Wales, catered (like the Circulating schools before
it) at least as much for adults as for children, and drew into
the Methodist movement many who initially attended simply
to learn their letters. And his preaching tours gave new life
to what had seemed in the 'seventies a languishing cause.
Methodism now spread through the shire less by accidental
contacts than by a succession of mass ' revivals ', some localised, some widespread. The more extravagant phenomena
that had marked earler revivals (such as the ecstatic leaping
at Lon Budr in 1762 which had for a time saddled Methodists
with the nickname 'Jumpers') became rarer, but the meetings
were often marked by shouts of joy and tears of contrition

and kept whole villages at fever-heat for days on end,
service following service with barely an interval for refresh-
ment, while the concourse of horses — the counterpart of
the modern car park — was described by eye-witnesses as
' like a fair day '. Notices like the following, which appeared
in a local paper in 1809,[7] no doubt reflect an all too common
experience: ' Stolen or strayed, from Pwllheli, a mare.
Missed on the day of the Methodist Association and not
heard of since '.

To some extent, naturally, these revivals were ephemeral
in their effects, but there were also lasting and visible fruits,
such at a continuing increase in the number and membership of local Societies, the emergence of new evangelists —
some of them destined to play a critical part in the development of the movement — and during the last decade of the
century a conspicuous activity in chapel-building. Chief
among the new leaders who emerged during this period was
John Elias, son of Elias Jones of Abererch. His religious
impulses and education came from his grandfather, a pious
churchman whose name he took; but it was Thomas Charles
who started him in 1794 on his career as preacher. For five
years he exercised his remarkable gifts as a roving evangelist,
travelling through the length and breadth of Wales and
often into England; then he settled in Anglesey, and on
Charles's death in 1814 Elias virtually stepped into his shoes.
A second name, that of Evan Richards, or Richardson, brings
home the fact that this phase of the religious revival owed
as much to educational impulses as to the emotional fervour
of the mass meetings. He was a Cardiganshire man, intended
by his parents for the Anglican priesthood; but under the
influence of Daniel Rowland he joined the Methodists and
was persuaded by Robert Jones of Rhoslan to open school
on the lines of Griffith Jones at Brynengan, which now
became the centre point of a widespread revival in Eifionydd. Among his pupils and disciples at Brynengan was a
former Cilgwyn quarryman, Robert Roberts, who became a

---

[7] *N. Wales Gazette*, 5 Oct.

powerful and influential lay preacher, with Clynnog as the main centre of his activities.

From Brynengan Richardson moved to Pwllheli and Llangybi and eventually to Caernarvon. This proved an important milestone in the history of the movement for two reasons. For one thing, some of the leaders not only of Methodism, but of other national movements received their only formal education at his school there: John Elias and Sir Hugh Owen, whom we shall meet later as one of the great pioneers of popular education in Wales, are two notable examples. Richardson's settlement in Caernarvon also signalised the fact that at long last Methodism had breached this strategic but long hostile citadel. A chapel was built there in 1793, and in the following year an Assembly (the first of many) actually met in Caernarvon itself. It was during this decade that so many of the established Societies (Beddgelert, it may be remembered, was among them) built themselves permanent meeting places instead of temporary accommodation in barns, lofts or farm kitchen. Naturally the architecture followed the same unpretentious lines; it was only later that Gothic or classical examples were emulated — not always with happy results. At Bron y foel, near Portmadoc) an ancient and abandoned mansion was divided, and part of it fitted up for worship. But chapel building, on however primitive a plan, meant, in those days of widespread economic hardship, substantial sacrifices, whether in cash or in personal labour after working hours — to say nothing of the recurrent difficulty of procuring a site from unsympathetic landowners.

During the next dozen years the movement spread rapidly along the coast to Bangor, Llanfairfechan and Penmaenmawr and inland to the quarrying areas of Arllechwedd, to link up with existing groups in the Conway valley. The schools — whether day, night, or Sunday schools — that kept springing up in its wake provided a reading public for Thomas Charles's journal Y *Drysorfa,* which first appeared towards the end of the eighteenth century and created another common bond. Yet another was the publication by Robert

Jones, Rhoslan, of a collection of hymns (mainly by Panty-celyn) which was the first in common use among northern Methodists; as a result hymn-singing took an increasing part in later revivals. An accompanying book of tunes was published in 1816 by John Ellis of Llanrwst, who since the beginning of the century had made it his business to tour the neighbourhood instructing congregations in the rudiments of music.

Economic hardship was not the only war-time trouble of the Methodists; they were also subject, for reasons we have seen, to political suspicion. The ecclesiastical courts were no longer their principal bugbear, for Chancellor Owen, their ancient enemy, had been dead for a quarter of a century; it was rather the landlords, or more often their resident stewards, who invoked the law against them and threatened their farms or their livelihoods. The stewards of the absentee owners of the Brogyntyn and Rhiwlas lands in Caernarvon-shire had a bad name in this respect. On the other hand it is interesting to learn that at Nanhoron Richard Edwards, a colonel of militia and a direct descendant of his namesake of Commonwealth days, declined to interfere with Methodism that had invaded his household; but then his mother had in her widowhood been, as will appear later, a member and benefactress of the Independent congregation meeting near by at Capel Newydd. The law invoked against the Methodists was that of Charles II against unlawful conventicles, which had been repealed by the Toleration Act of 1689, but only in respect of registered and licensed congregations of Protestant Dissenters. Thomas Charles now advised his followers to register their chapels under that name — one they had hitherto studiously avoided. The Conway Methodists were already following this course in 1793, and it became common in the shire from early in the next century; sometimes they hedged by merely using the word ' Protestant ', which apparently satisfied the authorities. Sometimes they boldly called themselves ' Methodists ' (or, after Wesleyans had appeared in the county, ' Calvinistic Methodists '), and the license was allowed in that name.

Whatever the nomenclature adopted, however, it was becoming increasingly difficult for Methodists to avoid the taint of Dissent, or for their lay preachers to be satisfied with ministering in chapels where, unlike their Dissenting brethren, they might preach but not administer the sacraments. It was this sort of pressure that ultimately persuaded Thomas Charles in 1811 to confer on eight of these lay preachers what were in effect Presbyterian orders. John Elias was an obvious choice, but his work lay mainly in Anglesey. Evan Richardson was the only one assigned to Caernarvonshire; Robert Roberts had been dead since 1802, having burned himself out at forty. After some six years Richardson's health too broke down and he resigned his school to William Lloyd, an Oxford man and a regularly ordained clergyman who had served curacies in Anglesey but seceded with the Methodists — the only North Wales cleric except Charles himself to do so.

Even after the secession, Methodists fully committed to the movement remained few in comparison with those who followed the preachers ', attending the big Assemblies but retaining a shadowy allegiance to the parish church and communicating there occasionally. What gave the new denomination its hold on the county was a renewed outburst of revivalism. About 1817 there broke out over most of North Wales what has been described as the most powerful religious revival the country had yet experienced, with its centre at Beddgelert. It had spread from Llŷn, where it is believed to have doubled or trebled Methodist membership. In this atmosphere new leaders emerged. The best known is John Jones, whose name is always linked with that of the village — Tal y sarn, near Pen y groes — where he worked as quarryman and made his home. He had been brought up at Dolwyddelan, an outpost of the Beddgelert revival, and in 1820 he was working on Telford's new road between Capel Curig and Ogwen; then he turned to quarrying, and in the following year — with no formal education at all — he started preaching, and was discovered to have outstanding gifts, both musical and oratorical. After

eight years he abandoned the quarry, received ordination
and devoted the rest of his thirty-six years to the ministry,
travelling far and wide on preaching tours and resisting with
some difficulty, as we have seen, the lure of the new Welsh
settlement in Wisconsin. Soon after the Beddgelert revival,
the Calvinistic Methodists of Caernarvonshire could count
over sixty Societies, more than a third of them in Llŷn and
Eifionydd. The labours of men like John Elias, Robert
Roberts and John Jones both consolidated and extended the
hold which Howel Harris had precariously established in
one corner of the shire, over thirty years before the elder,
and fifty before the younger of these two evangelists was
born.

Revivalism was not confined to this newcomer among the
sects; the older Dissent was also caught up in it, and
expanded accordingly. The groups left behind by the Baptist
mission of 1775 were still imbued with the missionary spirit
on which they were founded; after all, a public baptism has
in itself the elements of a revival meeting. From 1783 the
Baptists began to look beyond makeshift arrangements like
open-air meetings and borrowed pulpits and to build themselves chapels, if only with mud walls and thatched roofs.
In the course of the next thirty or forty years they built over
twenty of them, widely spread over the shire excepting its
south-eastern corner. Much of their success was due to the
tireless evangelism of Christmas Evans, son of a Cardiganshire shoemaker, who had educated himself while working
as a farm labourer, and became one of the shining lights of
the Welsh pulpit. From 1789 to 1791 he served as itinerant
evangelist to the Baptists of Llŷn; then, after a quarter of a
century as overseer of the Anglesey churches (with frequent
preaching tours through Wales), and six years in South
Wales churches, he returned to minister in Caernarvon for
the rest of his life.
The Independents, as we have seen, had a far longer
history in Caernarvonshire, but revivalism was not in their
tradition, and when in the 1740's the spirit of evangelism was

abroad, the Caernarvonshire Independents were apt to rely
on their more active brethren of Montgomeryshire. But some
twenty years later — in 1769 to be precise — the little group
of Independents meeting at Lôn Dywyll in Llangian parish
took the forward step of buying a plot of land to build a
new chapel — Capel Newydd — which has in recent times
been restored and preserved as the earliest surviving Nonconformist chapel in the shire. It became the missionary
centre from which sprang a number of daughter churches
in that part of Llŷn, and it is also of interest as the chapel
where the wife of the squire of neighbouring Nanhoron
became a member till her death in 1811. Mrs. Catherine
Edwards also enters into the story of Caernarvonshire
Independency in another capacity. In Caernarvon itself the
handful of Independents who had maintained some sort of
continuity since the days of Ellis Rowland was still without
a permanent home and only occasionally under the minis-
tration of a settled pastor, till in 1785 they invited to the
pastorate a young Carmarthenshire man fresh from Carmarthen academy (after a spell at the school which Christmas
Evans had fitfully attended). This was George Lewis, who
proved to be not only an eminent theologian whose works,
written in Welsh, became standard in their field throughout
Wales, but also a man of great evangelical fervour whose
widespread preaching during his nine-year pastorate gave
new life to Independency in the shire. It was he who
persuaded Mrs. Edwards of Nanhoron to bestow a piece of
land on which the Caernarvon Independents built in 1791
their first permanent chapel.

Soon after George Lewis settled in Caernarvon he turned
his attention to the cathedral city — no easy nut to crack
in view of the complete dominance there of the cathedral
authorities. A small congregation — hardly twenty of them,
and those largely of the new ' working class ' of Bangor —
was gathered by him and kept precariously together for some
twenty years, under ministers drawn from Pwllheli and
then Pembrokeshire, until in 1805 they were able to build
themselves a chapel. But the cause made slow headway till,

five years later, a pastor of distinction was found in Arthur
Jones, a young schoolmaster (descended on his mother's side
from Bishop Morgan the translator), who had taught at
Betws Garmon and married a daughter of Twm o'r Nant. His
ministry lasted, with a five-year break when he took charge
of London Welsh congregations, till 1854, and like that of
his Caernarvon colleague it left a profound impress on the
surrounding district. Like him he was both scholar and
evangelist. In addition to his pastoral duties he took charge
of the Dr. Williams school transferred to Bangor from
Pwllheli. His theological learning — a source of many controversies — was recognised by a German doctorate; his
evangelism, built on the labours of his predecessors at
Bangor, helped to spread Independency in the Conway
valley; and the fact that the chapel that gave Bethesda its
name followed the same denominational pattern is another
testimony to the work of Arthur Jones and George Lewis.
By 1820 there were twenty-seven congregations of Independents in the shire, and their membership was greatly
increased by a revival which affected both of their main
centres of influence — Bangor and Bethesda on the one
hand, Capel Helyg and Nefyn on the other — some twenty
years later. In Caernarvonshire it was they who started the
practice — as early as 1802, if not earlier — of giving their
chapels scriptural names, a practice soon followed by the
other denominations.

At the beginning of the nineteenth century yet another
band of itinerant evangelists began to penetrate Caernarvonshire. John Wesley had early come to a tacit understanding
with Harris and Rowland under which he confined his
ministry in Wales to the English-speaking regions, leaving
them undisturbed in their own field. But after his death some
of his Welsh disciples began to chafe at this brake on their
enthusiasm and persuaded the Methodist Conference in
London to empower them to bring to Welsh-speaking Wales,
which knew Methodism only in its Calvinistic dress, Wesley's
doctrine of ' free grace '. Accordingly in 1800-1 three devoted
Wesleyans, of Swansea, Wrexham and Llanfyllin respec-

tively, turned their steps to Caernarvonshire, starting with Arllechwedd and Arfon and then proceeding to Eifionydd — the reverse order from that by which Methodism had first entered the county. By this time both popular and clerical opposition to evangelistic missions was on the wane; the novelty had worn off! The missioners reported[8] a 'very liberal disposition' on the part of the 'gentlemen and magistrates' as well as of the vicars of Caernarvon and Pwllheli. It was their fellow-Methodists of the Calvinistic persuasion and some from the older Dissenting folds, who resented these intruders even when the did not abhor their theology. In other part of Wales the Welsh-speaking Wesleyan mission succeeded, as a rule, only in regions which its Calvinistic predecessors had failed to evangelise; Caearnarvonshire was the most notable exception. Whatever the reason, the mission there had a phenomenally rapid success: within ten years there were already about a dozen parishes where both branches of Methodism were established — sometimes in unedifying hostility to each other; and by 1820 the Wesleyans had opened over twenty chapels in the shire. At this stage, however, they registered them simply as 'Wesleyan chapel', without following the scriptural fashions set by the other Nonconformist bodies. Perhaps their outstanding convert was a young weaver from Bryncroes named William Rowlands, who had been brought up a Calvinist but was won over by the Wesleyans and served in their ministry in both North and South Wales till his death in 1865; he is best known as Gwilym Lleyn — editor, Welsh prose writer and pioneer bibliographer.

The beginnings of a revival of Roman Catholicism are due to quite other causes. It was Catholic Emancipation that brought back into the religious life of the shire this element that had so long been missing; actually some quiet missionary work had been done by priests (whose calling had ceased to be illegal in 1780), even before public worship was legalised. It began in 1827 with the provision at Bangor of masses

[8] Quoted A. H. Williams, *Welsh Wesleyan Methodism*, 103.

in inconspicuous houses, primarily for Irish hawkers passing through. The normal congregation was under a dozen; but as Bangor became a popular centre among Irish visitors for sea bathing and mountaineering, numbers increased, and five years after Emancipation a chapel was built, to which was added a mission house in 1844 and then in 1847 a school. The city's population had meanwhile increased from under two thousand at the beginning of the century to over seven thousand in 1841, rising in the next decade to nearly ten thousand. Naturally the influx included many new residents with Roman Catholic backgrounds, for whom spiritual provision was needed. Bangor thus became the centre from which the long-outlawed faith was spread to other parts of the shire. Priests from Bangor visited Caernarvon and said mass in private houses till in 1866 a chapel was opened through the generosity of a lady convert. But Caernarvon had not forgotten old prejudices : it is said that the patroness had to address the assembled mob in persuasive Welsh before they could be prevailed upon to keep their hands off the building. Here too the extension of the town in the 1860's brought in an increased Roman Catholic population, and from 1872 Caernarvon had a resident priest. At Pwllheli mass had occasionally been said by priests from Bangor to a handful of the faithful from about 1860, but here also numbers increased and a chapel was consecrated for their accommodation in 1879, served initially from Caernarvon. The extension of Roman Catholicism, however, belongs chiefly to the twentieth century. On the other hand the development of Protestant Nonconformity is most conspicuous during the second half of the nineteenth, especially after what has been called[9] 'the most dramatic of all religious revivals' that of 1859, which brought a substantial increase to all the Nonconformist bodies of Wales, and in many parts relegated to the position of a minority religion the Church which had so long enjoyed an undisputed social and political as well as religious dominance.

[9] K. O. Morgan, *Wales in British Politics*, 12-13.

How did the establishment react to this formidable threat to its entrenched position? With the translation from Llandaff in 1783 of Bishop John Warren — 'a prelate of the greatest application to business, undoubted talents, candour and integrity', as his obituary notice describes him[10] — the diocese entered on what seemed a promising period in its history. He was certainly a man of drive, as witness his work for Friars school, which has already been briefly referred to and will be more fully treated in its own context. He is credited[11] with 'enforcing parochial residence among his Clergy with the most rigorous exaction'. His ordinations were more numerous and more frequent than those of any of his predecessors since early in the century, and they were more closely directed towards filling gaps in the parishes than any before John Moore's episcopate, which immediately preceded Warren's. In some ways his career resembles that of his seventeenth-century predecessor Lewes Bayly. With the same outspokenness, the same zeal for education and for Bible-reading (attested by his warm support for Thomas Charles's Bible Society) — and, it should be added to complete the picture, the same preoccupation with the advancement of his own family in the Church — he had the misfortune like Bayly (but without his toughness of fibre) to come up against the ambitions of the powerful laity of his diocese, chiefly in those petty political squabbles which have been dealt with in an earlier chapter. According to a possibly biased contemporary, he refused 'to make the patrimony of the church a treasury for election bribes'.[12]

His death in 1800 was followed by two short and undistinguished episcopates; nine years later began the long rule of Bishop Majendie, who is remembered as the last bishop of Bangor to wear the eighteenth-century wig — in some way, perhaps, a symbolic survival. The diocese had to wait till 1890 for a bishop familiar with the language of the great majority of his people; in 1800, when the preponderance of

[10] *Gentleman's Mag.*, 1800, i. 184.
[11] Evans, *Tour*, 1804, 227.
[12] id., p. 228n.

Welsh was far greater and the pulpit eloquence and hymn-singing of the revivals had given it added weight, it was much more of a limitation to be cut off in this way from so much of the daily life of the diocese — but not necessarily a fatal one, as appeared in the contemporary career of Bishop Burgess of St. David's. To some extent the deficiency was made good by a growing Welsh element on the cathedral chapter, which Warren and even Majendie had tended to treat as a family concern.

First effects of the revival on Church life had often been stimulating. In some cases, as in Llanengan as early as 1749, old Dissenters had been won back to it by the Methodist preachers. The preaching of Richard Nanney at Clynnog and of John Morgan at Llanberis had a local influence comparable with that of the first Anglican revivalists in South Wales. Evan Hughes, who is said to have come to his Bangor curacies from Llangeitho itself, befriended the Circulating schools of the district after Griffith Jones's death, and not only packed Lleniestyn church with worshippers but was ready to carry his message outside the church into private houses or the open air. In his Merioneth curacy of Llanfihangel y pennant he was able to report in 1776 seventy monthly communicants and two hundred at Easter, out of a population well under five hundred. But none of these three lived to see the great disruption. Meanwhile things had changed. The swarm of outsiders from other parishes who were drawn to church by these preachers, and their unrestrained expressions of emotion, offended old-fashioned worshippers, and Methodists began to find themselves more at home in the *seiat* than the church; the rift of 1811 had been preparing for many years.

The loss of all this zeal and fervour certainly weakened the Church, and (to quote a historian of Bangor diocese)[13] ' it was not until the third and fourth decades of the nineteenth century that decisive measures were taken to steer [it] out of the backwater '. These took several forms. First

[13] A. I. Pryce, *Diocese of Bangor during Three Centuries*, lxxviii.

there were local efforts like the Diocesan Tract Society founded at Bangor in 1804 by a member of the cathedral chapter (who incidentally was later one of the commission of four appointed to supervise the 1841 edition of the Welsh Prayer Book), for the purpose of issuing pamphlets in Welsh by competent scholars on religious topics. More fundamental reforms followed during the episcopate of Christopher Bethell, who was translated from Exeter to Bangor in 1830, and ruled for nearly thirty years. Some of these originated within the diocese, but there were others, affecting the whole Church, which arose from state action; for this was the age when a series of Acts of Parliament removed many ancient anomalies and abuses and tried to bring the administrative and financial machinery of the Church more into line with the needs of the age. A readjustment of clerical incomes paved the way for getting rid of the long-standing scandal of pluralism, and at the same time the provision of funds for building parsonages fulfilled a need which had remained a pretext for non-residence ever since clerical marriage was legalised. Again, machinery was provided to facilitate the creation of new parishes to cope with a shifting population. But the proposal in 1840 to unite the sees of Bangor and St. Asaph, and to syphon off the revenues saved by this economy for the benefit of the new diocese of Manchester, ran into strong local opposition and came to nothing.

In Caernarvonshire, from 1843 (when the process began) to the end of the century, some half-dozen new parishes were mapped out, mostly in quarrying areas where the remoteness of quarry from parish church had contributed materially towards the drift to Methodism and Dissent. There was also a regrouping of parishes (which up to now had retained their medieval pattern) to ensure that growing urban centres like Caernarvon, Pwllheli and Portmadoc were adequately served. All this meant a considerable building programme, undertaken at a time when so many decrepit churches (notably in Llŷn, with its numerous and poverty-stricken parishes) were being rebuilt and restored — sometimes more than once in the century to satisfy changing standards. Over a dozen churches were built or extensively rebuilt, and about thirty restored; few were left untouched. Partly this was accomplished by private benefactors like the Penrhyns, the Assheton Smiths, the Newboroughs and W. A. Madocks, partly by grants from central funds, partly by local effort through the Diocesan Church Building Society founded in 1838.

Nor were reforms confined to externals. An important turning point came when in 1810 Bishop Majendie brought to Bangor as vicar and precentor an energetic young clergyman named J. H. Cotton, whose quality he had discovered in his former diocese of Chester. Cotton's work for elementary education in the county will concern us later; what needs to be emphasised here is his achievement in bringing the cathedral into closer contact with the changing community around it and ultimately, when he became dean in 1838, with the diocese at large, over the whole of which he travelled every year. He was perhaps the first of the cathedral clergy to realise the extent to which the cathedral had lost touch with a city which was no longer a mere dependency of dean and chapter. In this context he came to appreciate the importance of the Welsh language and of the newly-awakened national consciousness of which it was the symbol. He taught himself the language to the point of being able to preach in it — even if with a barbarous accent! He interested himself in Welsh tradition and identified himself closely with national movements. One of his first acts after his arrival was to start a Sunday school in the nave of the cathedral, and he followed this up with an adult school conducted in Welsh in co-operation with the 'principal Shop-keepers of Bangor'.[14] Cathedral services in Welsh were revived, and Cotton carried out a minor restoration of the building by partitioning off the long disused nave and furnishing it for the use of the Welsh congregation. Even *Figaro in Wales* excepted him from its venomous attacks on the

[14] Cotton's diary, quoted W. Hughes, *Life and Speeches of . . J. H. Cotton,* 16.

clergy. Even 'Y Sgolor Mawr', who rarely praised his superiors, had a good word to say for him, while smiling at his Welsh.[15]

Another novelty fostered by Cotton was congregational hymn-singing in Welsh; for he realised how important a part the hymns of Pantycelyn had played in the revivals which had drawn so many away from the Church. In the very year (1827) when he completed his reconstruction of the cathedral, a volume of Welsh hymns was published by a Trefriw bard who, though of Methodist parentage, had just taken orders in the Church; this was Evan Evans, better known by his bardic name of Ieuan Glan Geirionydd. The hymns were soon in use at the cathedral, and before Cotton's death his co-vicar (himself a musician and composer of hymn tunes) was holding week-night practices to train the Welsh congregation in singing, much as John Ellis had done for the Methodists half a century earlier.

In the parishes the problem was different. Here there was no language barrier to separate parson from people, for the bishops of Bangor were patrons of ninety per cent of the Caernarvonshire livings, and even when they knew no Welsh themselves they generally realised that in a parish priest this could be a fatal disability. A case like that of the presentation in 1766 (by an absentee bishop) of a monoglot English rector to a monoglot Welsh Anglesey parish, which was unsuccessfully challenged at law, would not have caused the scandal it did had it been a common occurrence; in any case an Act of 1835 made it impossible for the future. Actually several of the Caernarvonshire incumbents were not only fluent in Welsh, but leaders in the national movement which we associate with the revival of the eisteddfod. David Ellis, who after serving as curate of Llanberis died vicar of Cricieth in 1795, was himself a bard; his younger contemporary Peter Bailey Williams, who became rector of Llanberis and Llanrûg in 1792, was certainly no bard, but like Ellis an assiduous collector of bardic manuscripts, as well as an

---

[15] *Figaro in Wales*, vii (Sept. 1835); *Life and Opinions*, 287-8.

antiquary and topographer who often contributed to the
literary and archaeological journals springing up like mush-
rooms in the Wales of his day. Both added substantially to
the stock of standard devotional works translated into Welsh.

The barriers in Caernarvonshire parishes were geographical rather than linguistic. On the one hand there were
the villages which had sprouted wherever quarries were
opened, often leaving the parish church high and dry and
making their own provision for public worship; on the other
hand the much older problem of the scattered population of
Llŷn, with plenty of churches built, perhaps, in more populous and prosperous days, but now without the means either
to maintain the fabric or to provide a living for the incumbent — except by giving him charge of more parishes than
he could adequately serve. It was natural that the Methodist
system and that of the early Dissenters — neither of them
tied down to parishes — should take root here; for example,
the important Methodist centre of Brynengan was set in a
wild and mountainous tract overlapping four parishes, each
with a distant parish church. Things might have turned out
differently had the reforms of the mid-nineteenth century
come half a century earlier, when the situation was still fluid.

More fundamental than all the Church reforms embodied
in Acts of Parliament was a movement that was taking place
within the Church itself, originating at Oxford and therefore
popularly known as the Oxford Movement. It aimed at
giving a more positive content to the teaching of the Church
and a stronger sense of vocation to the clergy by restoring
some of the Catholic doctrines and practices discarded at
the Reformation: in fact it might almost be called an
Anglican Counter-Reformation in reply to the challenge of
Methodism. These aims were to be promoted by greater
frequency and seemliness of services and a return to traditional forms in church architecture and furnishings, in
vestments and music. Bishop Bethell, a Cambridge man
himself, was a warm supporter of the Oxford Movement.
He brought to the diocese a number of young clerics who
had been at Oxford in the stirring days when the *Tracts for*

*the Times* were launched as manifestos of the new church-manship; and by planting them in parishes as far apart as Meyllteyrn, Clynnog and Llanllechid (while moderating the ardours of the more impatient), he not only leavened the Church with the new spirit throughout the shire, but put Bangor diocese in the van of the movement in Wales.

His boldest step was to invade the very citadel of Dissent by installing two successive ' Puseyites ' (as they were called locally) in the important parish of Llanllechid and creating a new parish for Bethesda, named Glanogwen to avoid the sectarian associations of the village name. Glanogwen church, built in 1862 (shortly after Bishop Bethell's death) by the owner of Penrhyn, was designed as a sort of shop window of the Oxford Movement. A graphic picture of the progress of the movement in Bethesda and Llanllechid, and of the controversies it aroused, is drawn in the autobiography of Robert Roberts ('Y Sgolor Mawr '). He went there to teach in 1853 and helped (against a good deal of clerical opposition) to found an association designed to give the laity something of that active share in the work of the Church which was such a source of strength to Methodism.

A distinctive feature of Tractarianism in Caernarvonshire was its close association with the Welsh cultural movement now at its height. For seven years from 1840 its chief prota-gonist in the neighbourhood was Morris Williams, best known by his pen name of Nicander. Brought up in bardic circles in Llangybi, he wrote prolifically in Welsh both prose and poetry, especially hymns. He also encouraged Robert Roberts, though still a mere tyro, to contribute to the local press on Welsh grammar and history. Nicander and his associates threw their weight into the struggle to give back to the Church in Wales something of the character of a national church which had belonged to it before the era of absentee bishops and political appointments set in in the eighteenth century; and in a county like Caernarvonshire this contributed greatly to their success.

Among Dissenters in general and Methodists in particular, however, there were strong suspicions that the Oxford Move-

ment was a device for ' bringing in Rome again by the back
door ', and these suspicions seemed to be confirmed when
David Lewis, who had been curate to Newman at St. Mary's,
Oxford, became with him a convert to Rome in 1846; this
came near home, because David Lewis's younger brother
Evan (a son-in-law of Dean Cotton) was one of the group
of Oxford men whom Bishop Bethell brought to Bangor, and
was closely associated with Nicander (whom he succeeded
at Llanllechid) in spreading the principles of the Oxford
Movement, especially in respect of the revival of traditional
church music in place of ' hearty ' hymn-singing. Evan Lewis,
however, did not follow his brother's example, but after a
long spell in South Wales he ultimately returned to Bangor
in 1884 as dean.

By this time Bishop Bethell was dead, but the movement
he had introduced into the diocese had made amazingly
rapid progress: a few years after Bethell's death it was
reckoned that nearly a third of the diocesan clergy of Bangor
had imbibed ' Tractarian ' principles, and practices which
had seemed revolutionary in the 1840's had come to be
widely accepted as normal. These men had undoubtedly put
new life into the Church, and brought it more closely into
touch with national culture than it had been for many
generations. It is true that Bishop Bethell was succeeded in
1859 by a Scot, James C. Campbell; but Campell had ministered long in South Wales and come to appreciate the needs
of Wales and the weaknesses within the Church which had
helped to bring about the Methodist secession and the
resurgence of Dissent. He even, like Dean Cotton, taught
himself enough of the language to use it, however halt-
ingly, in the pulpit as well as in the Church service. His
episcopate began in the year of the great revival which
brought Nonconformity to the peak of its influence, but
which in some parishes stimulated Church life as well, while
strengthening the wing of the Church most hostile to
' Puseyite ' influences. It was also under his rule that the
programme of Church building reached its climax in the
complete restoration of the cathedral by Sir Gilbert Scott

between 1868 and 1874. On his death in 1890 there succeeded to the see, for the first time in nearly two centuries,
a Welsh-speaking bishop — Daniel Lewis Lloyd — the last
to live in the old episcopal palace at Bangor.

Between them these religious movements brought about
substantial changes in the social and political as well as the
religious life of the shire. It is a commonplace that the succession of religious revivals took out of the life of the country
much of its carefree joyousness, and rang the death knell of
many old customs and traditions. It was not unknown for a
country fiddler to signalise his ' conversion ' by smashing his
fiddle lest he be tempted again to use it for unhallowed
roystering. John Elias certainly waged a successful war
against the *anterliwt* in Anglesey; but he did so with the
approval of many who had no love of Methodism and much
love for tradition. In fact it has been suggested[16] that the
decline and fall of the *anterliwt,* which left no basis for the
twentieth-century revival of Welsh drama, was due more to
the intellectual snobbery of scholars preoccupied with
classical Welsh than to the frowns of the Methodists. Less
is known about the status of folk drama in Caernarvonshire.
A description of an *anterliwt,* played at the Llandudno
wakes in 1760[17] on a flat rock surmounted by turf, is silent
on the play itself, and an English traveller's account of
another, performed somewhere in Snowdonia seventeen
years later, adds little to our knowledge. We do, however,
know that Twm o'r Nant and his company performed in
Llanddeiniolen in 1787, for that was what drew Dafydd Ddu
Eryri — brought up though he was in a family known as
pioneers of Methodism in Waunfawr and Llanberis — to the
village, where he opened the first of his schools. It does not
appear that the Methodists of Caernarvonshire attacked the
*anterliwt* with anything like the relentlessness of John Elias

[16] R. T. Jenkins, *Hanes Cymru yn y Ddeunawfed Ganrif* (1928), 132.
[17] *Morris Letters,* ii. 355; cf. [Cradock], *Letters from Snowdon* (1777), 64-6.

in Anglesey; was not Twm o'r Nant given an honoured place at the opening of the Calvinistic Methodist chapel at Tremadoc, and did he not marry his daughter to a distinguished Independent minister?

The wakes, or *gwylmabsantau,* where those productions were most frequently performed, were also on the decline, along with the observance of other public festivals which had survived the Reformation. According to Hyde Hall,[18] who covered the county pretty thoroughly in his travels between 1809 and 1811, they lingered longer (as one might expect) in ' the more mountainous and secluded parts of the country ' than ' along the coast ' — which again suggests that Methodism cannot be saddled with sole responsibility for the fading away of these ancient observances; Hall slyly suggests that the resentment of employers at the loss of working days was at least a contributory factor. While deploring what he calls the ' sour spirit of Methodism ', and particularly the ' advancement to high stations of fanatics themselves ', he gives the movement credit both for the spread of literacy and for a certain softening of manners, showing itself in ' more orderly behaviour at fairs and upon other occasions of assembly ' and in the absence of serious crime; but he rejoices that it has not quite succeeded in banishing some of the ' popish ' survivals at the great festivals nor even the playing of ' fives ', quoits and skittles in the churchyard.

He reserves his censures for two malpractices of great antiquity which had so far resisted these civilising influences. One was the pilfering of goods from wrecks — a practice only too prevalent all along the western coasts of Britain, but presenting a special temptation to needy villagers on the rocky coasts of Llŷn or to copper miners on the Orme; both were notorious for shipwrecks. Hyde Hall does not suggest that deliberate wrecking went on, but he more than hints that a pilot who used his skill to avert what might have been a profitable wreck was liable to be sent to

---

[18] *Description,* Appendix i.

Coventry by his neighbours. In 1824 ten men were imprisoned for this form of theft at Llandudno; a further three were acquitted.[19] Among Methodists, however, pilfering from wrecks was treated as a sin involving expulsion from the Society in the same way as any other sort of thieving. The other count in Hall's indictment is a lingering belief in witchcraft, often associated with holy wells or local characters believed to have the power of casting spells. In remoter villages such beliefs often survived both the religious revivals and the spread of education until within living memory.

Hyde Hall does not rank habitual drunkenness among the prevailing vices of Caernarvonshire; no doubt, by the time he wrote, the preaching of the revivalists was having its effects in this as in other directions. But it was not until the 1830's that campaigns began to be focused on this particular vice, which battened on the conditions produced by industrialisation and the growth of towns, and that temperance societies spread from America to England and Wales. Initially, however, they were directed only against excessive drinking. Neither Methodism nor the older Dissent had as yet committed itself to the principle of total abstinence; in fact the refreshments which had to be provided for itinerant preachers after what was often an exhausting journey normally included a pot of ale. It was in 1833 that the word 'teetotal' was coined in Lancashire, the headquarters of the temperance movement, and five years passed before the leaders of Methodism in Caernarvonshire were won over to this more extreme wing of the movement, symbolised by the substitution of the word *dirwestol*, or 'abstinent' for *cymedrol* or 'temperate' as the appropriate adjective for their temperance societies. Once John Elias and John Jones of Tal y sarn had come round to this standpoint and Christmas Evans had joined them in the campaign, it rapidly became a distinctive badge of Methodism and Nonconformity in Caernarvonshire and indeed in Wales generally. For although many Anglicans (notably Dean Cotton) had been

[19] *N.W. Gazette,* 22 Apr., 1824.

ready to co-operate with their ' separated brethren ' in the cause of *cymedroldeb,* the Church in general — especially after it had been leavened by the Oxford Movement — shrank from committing itself to whole-hogging *dirwest.*

Part of the price paid for the intellectual stimulus provided by theological exchanges in *seiat* and Sunday school was an increasing preoccupation with the finer points of dogma, causing acute divisions within the sects themselves, a multiplication of chapels and above all an increasing gulf between the Church and Dissent. This gulf was further widened by the growing influence of the Oxford Movement. On the one side there were ' Puseyites ' like Philip Constable Ellis, for nearly forty years the very successful rector of Llanfairfechan, whose principles would not allow him to co-operate with Nonconformists even on ' neutral ' ground; on the other hand the growing dominance of this school of churchmanship drew the Methodists farther away from the Church and closer to the older Nonconformist bodies. As long as John Elias lived, he had consistently refused to countenance anything that savoured of enmity towards the Church from which he had so reluctantly separated. On his deathbed in 1841 he expressed great concern about ' the pernicious doctrines which threatened to invade the Protestant world ', and welcomed as allies those who were resisting them from within the Church; but he had deep forebodings: ' The Puseyites ', he exclaimed,[20] ' are sure to do mischief! God alone knows what will be the end of these things '. When his restraining hand was removed, the atmosphere rapidly changed, especially after the publication of the Blue Books on Welsh education six years later. The indiscriminate reflections of the report on the moral effects of Dissent, which roused such emotions throughout Wales, probably did more than any other factor — despite the trenchant criticism of the commissioners' findings by so stout a churchman as Dean Cotton — to divide the county politically, educationally and socially on ' Church and Chapel ' lines.

[20] E. Morgan, *Memoir of the Reverend John Elias* (1844), 200.

## C.   POLITICS, 1850-1900

The outstanding fact of Caernarvonshire politics in the second half of the nineteenth century is the emergence of political Nonconformity. The older denominations, of course, had been politically-minded from the start, born as they were in an age when politics and religion were inseperable; but when their wealthier supporters dropped off after the Restoration, they were left with congregations of whom few if any were qualified for the vote, and who in any case had every reason for shunning publicity. Methodism, on the other hand, was born into a world where political interest was confined to a charmed circle of initiates — especially in Caernarvonshire, where (as we have seen) a single family had gathered all the strings into its hand. In the late 1820's, however, when politics began to come to life again in the shire, some of the questions at issue had a moral or religious content which neither the old Dissent nor the new Methodism could ignore, but on which they did not always see eye to eye, and which did not necessarily bind them to either of the political parties.

First of these was the question of slavery. The abolition of the slave trade in 1807 had made the slave-owners of the British plantations more determined than ever to cling on to the slaves they already had; on the other hand the new-born missionary enthusiasm which arose from the evangelical revival, of which Methodism was the offspring, stung the consciences of those who laboured among the slaves, and led to inevitable clashes with their masters. One such incident in the slave colony of British Guiana in 1824, leading to the death of a Nonconformist missionary accused of fomenting revolt among the blacks, aroused widespread concern among his co-religionists at home, and brought to an issue the demand that the institution should be stamped out in the British dominions. The agitation spread, and among the flood of petitions sent from various parts of the country from 1826 onwards urging speedy emancipation were several from Caernarvonshire, including some congregations of Independents and of both Calvinistic and Wesleyan Methodists. In 1828 an Anti-Slavery Society was formed in Caernarvon, and a public meeting held (a new phenomenon in politics) to promote the cause. At the election three years later the announcement of Sir Charles Paget's support for the abolition of slavery ensured the sympathy (as his agent had expected) of Independents in Caernarvon and Bangor. The Calvinistic Methodist Assembly at Caernarvon had already passed a resolution condemning slavery, but the sting was taken out of this by a subsequent resolution (in 1831) dissociating the connexion from all political activity.

This official repudiation of politics divided Methodism sharply from the older Dissent, now being recalled by the issues of the day to its traditional political bent. This was notably true of the Independents; the Baptist leader Christmas Evans was almost as conservative-minded as John Elias, and exercised the same restraining influence till his death in 1838. We have seen how the Methodists, however inconsistently with their political quietism, set their faces against Catholic Emancipation. Even after it had been passed, the newly-ordained John Jones, Tal y sarn, backed up the campaign against its advocate Sir Charles Paget; later, however, he was in the forefront of the revolt of the younger generation against the dead hand of John Elias in both politics and theology. The Independents of Caernarvonshire are not known to have taken any active part in this campaign on either side, but on parliamentary reform the division between the two wings of Dissent was clear and unequivocal. 'We . . . detest their political views and conduct in the present age', wrote Elias of the reformers in 1833,[21] ' therefore we do not wish to be identified with them '. To him — and to his followers as long as he lived — dissociation from politics meant dissociation from any fundamental change in the established order; in other words, an acquiescent Toryism. On the other hand a Reform meeting

[21] Quoted R. Tudur Jones, *Hanes Annibynwyr Cymru* (1966), 209n.

in Caernarvon in 1822 was packed with Dissenters (including many ministers) from the older denominations, and
the Independent chapel paid for its political bias by having
its windows broken. In 1834 O. O. Roberts started an
agitation in Llanbeblig parish vestry against payment
of church rates; the *Sentars* backed him up, but the
Methodists — who believed in the establishment if only
as a bulwark against popery — stood aloof, and he lost the
day. During these same restless years the spirit of reform
invaded also the Wesleyan body, issuing in a secession movement in Anglesey and Caernarvonshire, which maintained
itself for some years as a separate denomination (' Y Wesle
Bach '), more democratically constituted.

Soon after the death of John Elias in 1841 Methodism
began to draw nearer to the old Dissent. One of the earliest
fields of co-operation was the agitation against the Corn
Laws. In 1840 the Anti-Corn Law League appointed Walter
Griffith as its paid propagandist in North Wales. He was a
Bethesda boy, now working in Manchester, whose father
had been an Independent minister in Llŷn. His success was
immediate. Six months after John Elias's death a two-day
meeting of ministers of all denominations was held in Caernarvon in support of the cause. It had a strong material
appeal for the Caernarvonshire smallholder, who was easily
persuaded that the Corn Laws protected the landlord and
the big farmer but offered him only a dearer loaf; and the
moral appeal which Cobden and Bright infused into the
campaign went home to the Nonconformist conscience.
Another meeting was held in the Independent chapel at
Bangor, the use of the Church school having been refused.

This new sense of a distinctive Nonconformist standpoint
in politics took some time to find expression at the polls, if
only because so few Nonconformists as yet had the vote. The
Corn Laws ceased to be an electoral issue once they had
been repealed in 1846. Sir Robert Peel in taking this step
against the opposition of his rival Disraeli split his own Tory
party, and after his death his followers (including Gladstone)
drifted towards the Whigs, till they coalesced with them

and the radical 'ginger group' to form the new Liberal party. Meanwhile the controversy aroused by the Blue Books on Welsh education had given a new impetus to the political consciousness of Welsh Nonconformity, both old and new. It found its first practical expression in the borough election of 1852, when Richard Davies, the son of a Llangefni shop-keeper, who had developed a very flourishing shipping business at Menai Bridge, was adopted as Liberal candidate. He had been educated at an elementary school and was a Calvinistic Methodist elder and the son-in-law of a popular minister — a type of candidate unheard of before; and although he failed to dislodge the sitting member he secured the respectable total of 276 votes in a poll of 672. Only in Pwllheli did he gain a majority; in the cathedral city he was of course hopelessly outnumbered. Elsewhere — even in the old Brogyntyn stronghold of Cricieth — voting was fairly close. But it was not numbers that mattered; this was a completely new type of election, and it set the tone for the rest of the century. The agitation against slavery and the Corn Laws had shown the propagandist value of public meetings; now and henceforth they became part of the regular stock-in-trade of elections. There were two in Caernarvon, one in Bangor, and probably some even in Pwllheli and Nefyn.

Pulpit oratory had been developed to a fine art during the revivals and had spread to the older denominations, accustomed as they were to a quieter and more didactic style. But pulpit oratory could readily be transplanted to the political platform, and by whom better than by the ministers themselves? Caledfryn (William Williams), a Denbighshire man who now ministered to the Caernarvon Independents, was the life and soul of this election. He was a bard of some repute, a pioneer of Welsh journalism, and an impassioned radical who was suspected of having been a subscribing member of a Chartist organisation. His fellow-minister William Ambrose (the bard Emrys, a Bangor-born man who had formerly accompanied him on preaching tours) supported him, and the better-known Gwilym

Hiraethog, who was related by marriage to the candidate, came in from Denbighshire to help. Ministerial experience in open-air speaking was also called into play for one of the Caernarvon meetings when the use of the market hall was refused; the other was held in the Calvinistic Methodist chapel, which was of course well adapted as an auditorium. At Bangor John Phillips, a Methodist minister whom we shall meet again as a pioneer of Nonconformist education, was an ardent supporter, with the inevitable O. O. Roberts and Thomas Lewis, a flourishing flour merchant in the town.

From all this we can gather how completely the new Liberalism now gathering force contrasted with the older Whiggism which had so often held the boroughs. Sir Richard Williams Bulkeley, himself a good Whig, voted Tory because he believed (not without reason) that the candidate had been chosen not for his admitted personal qualities and standing but for his religion; Plas Newydd expressly denied a rumour that it too had gone Tory, but only after a friend's reassurance that men of Davies's stamp were often ' softened by being in decent company '. O. O. Roberts, on the other hand, took pride in the fact that the candidate came ' from the ranks of the long-maligned people of Wales '. There was no specific issue before the electorate. Basically it was a struggle of the under-privileged for recognition — not as yet the economically under-privileged, for Davies was a well-to-do man with a fine house on the outskirts of Bangor; moreover a contingent of Assheton Smith's by no means over-privileged quarrymen was brought into Caernarvon to give moral support to the Tory cause. It was the privilege enjoyed by the established Church in worship and in educa- tion, by the gentry and the English language they spoke, that were challenged. All were closely linked, and col- lectively they were in a position to exert a pressure on electors colloquially and opprobriously known as *y scriw*. (Tories replied — not without reason — that there was an equally potent chapel *scriw*!) One step towards reducing this pressure was a drop in the cost of elections. The last Whig election bill — itself a mere fraction of what had been spent in 1832 — had still been over £1,000; Richard Davies's was under £200. In short, the battle ground of future Caernarvonshire elections up to the end of the century was already sketched out in that of 1852; that is what gives it an importance out of proportion to the numbers involved or the immediate effects.

So far it was a flash in the pan. Richard Davies did not contest the boroughs again, but in 1868 he made history by capturing the county seat in Anglesey, this time with the full support of Sir Richard Williams Bulkeley, the retiring member. But this was after Disraeli's further and much more drastic extension of the franchise in the preceding year. The establishment of the ratepayer vote in the boroughs and the £12 householder vote in the shires brought in the small shopkeeper, the small farmer, and even the upper stratum of the wage labourers; in Caernarvonshire it meant a threefold increase in the electorate, in the boroughs nearly fourfold. In many parts of Wales besides Anglesey the result was the dethronement of the county families who had monopolised representation time out of mind. In Caernarvonshire it brought the almost equally startling result of the defeat of the Penrhyn candidate — the popular Lord Penrhyn's unpopular son — by a Liberal. The Liberal victor was, it is true, a man of very different type from Richard Davies. He was Love Jones Parry (the future Sir Love) son and heir of the victor in the borough election of 1837. He has been described[22] as 'a buccaneering landowner of unorthodox social and moral outlook', but he was warmly supported by the Nonconformist element (including the ministers), and he in turn cultivated them, and showed his attachment to 'the long maligned people of Wales' by his strenuous efforts to get the Patagonia colony on its feet. The election is also noteworthy for having for the first time brought the issue of Disestablishment to the fore in Caernarvonshire politics. The Independent minister and musician Tanymarian (Edward Stephen) was taken to task by some of his fellow-Dissenters for having opposed it; but he was a Penrhyn tenant!

[22] K. O. Morgan, *Wales in British Politics*, 23.

The county election was a riotous one. The riots were caused by the pressure on his men exercised by the manager of Nantlle quarry in the Penrhyn interest; Penrhyn himself, as lord lieutenant, had troops ready at Chester to march in should the situation get out of hand (which fortunately it did not), and he even asked the admiralty (in vain, of course) for a gunboat to stand by. As lord lieutenant he had authority over the new county police force, and he used it to swear in a thousand special constables and to borrow sixteen regulars from Merioneth, where the seat was uncontested. The borough election, apart from some street brawling in Caernarvon, went quietly, because Bulkeley Hughes, who had long had the reputation of a ' shuffler ', now came out as a Liberal, and in that character defeated a Tory Wynn of Glynllifon, belatedly returning to politics. The aftermath of the election was long and bitter. Eighty Penrhyn quarrymen lost their jobs, and they at least believed that they were penalised for supporting the Liberal candidate; some farmers lost their holdings for the same reason — nothing like the number that suffered in West Wales, but enough to bring the land question to the forefront as another plank in the Liberal platform, and to add the tenant farmer to the list of the ' under-privileged '. All this served as ammunition for Gladstone when he brought in the Ballot Act three years later.

The ballot had little effect on the elections of 1874. Farmers and quarrymen only remembered what had happened in 1868 to those who had risked voting against vested interests, and they distrusted the new machinery; so Penrhyn got his seat back. Accordingly the Liberals made a point in their election campaign of 1880 of explaining and advertising the Ballot Act. On this the county was won back, first by a Liberal lawyer from Denbighshire, and on his promotion to the bench, by the Liverpool merchant William Rathbone, who came of a family of Quaker philanthropists (now turned Unitarian), with Anglesey connections. He kept his seat till 1895, when he resigned it because there were aspects of contemporary Welsh Liberal policy he could not accept. On the death of Bulkeley Hughes in 1882 the boroughs were taken over for the next two parliaments by the more forthcoming Jones Parry. In the meantime Gladstone's Reform Act had further expanded the electorate, bringing the vote within reach of the quarryman and farm labourer, and the Redistribution Act which followed had given the county two members instead of one. Till the end of the century each of the two divisions regularly returned a Liberal member — usually a lawyer or a merchant. Then in 1888 came the County Councils Act, ending the rule of the squirearchy in local government and giving the shires the sort of political coherence the boroughs had long enjoyed. The boroughs in 1890 were captured after a furious fight by David Lloyd George, whose candidature had something of the character of that of Richard Davies forty years earlier: both militant Nonconformists with an elementary school background and an urge to fight against privilege; but with the important reservation that Davies already had an assured position, whereas Lloyd George, a rising lawyer, had his to make. How he made it is now a matter of world history. He remained member for the boroughs for nearly fifty-five years; three years after his elevation to the peerage the constituency ceased to exist.

Parliamentary representation by the country gentry, after lasting more than three hundred years, disappeared in the course of fifty; even when, four years before Lloyd George's parliamentary career began, the Caernarvon boroughs turned Tory, they were represented by a Denbighshire lawyer, not a member of one of the old county families. Parliamentary politics had been as completely transformed as religious life in the county. Ministers, journalists and lawyers had become its new political mentors; party had superseded family feud as the focus of elections, and party was the expression of ideological conflicts which would have been barely intelligible to the eighteenth-century electorate. It remains to consider the contemporary transformation in education and local government.

## BIBLIOGRAPHY

*A and C.* The sources listed under chapter IXA cover the earlier part of this period. Later elections are described in K. Evans, Eighteenth century Caernarvon' (*TCHS* 1946-8, 1950); E. G. Jones, Borough politics and electioneering' (id. 1956); Ll. Jones, ' Sir Charles Paget and the Caernarvonshire boroughs' (id. 1960); F. P. Jones, Gwleidyddiaeth Sir Gaernarfon yn y 19eg ganrif' (id. 1965); see also W. H. Jones, *Old Karnarvon,* 76. The question of the crown lands is dealt with in *Rept. on Land* 1896, 194 ff. and A. H. Dodd, *Industrial Revolution in N. Wales,* 56-8. Caernarvonshire petitions on Catholic Emancipation, slavery, etc., are listed in *Shrewsbury Chronicle* and *North Wales Chronicle,* 1826-31. There is a full account of the 1852 election by O. Parry in *Er Clod* (ed. T. Richards, 1934), 135 ff. The disorders of 1868 are described in J. O. Jones, *Hist. of the Caernarvonshire Constabulary* (1963), 37-9, 47-8. On politics generally since 1868, K. O. Morgan, *Wales in British Politics, 1868-1922* (1963).

*B.* The religious revivals are described in H. Hughes, *Hanes Diwygiadau Crefyddol Cymru* (1906). On Methodism in Bangor diocese before and after 1811, Bob Owen in *Er Clod,* 35-50 and 83-112. W. Hobley, *Methodistiaeth Arfon* (6 vol., 1910-24) traces in great detail the history of the movement in one part of Caernarvonshire, and R. Roberts, *Pengryniaid Eifionydd* (1883) preserves many local traditions for another. On the older denominations, sources listed under chap. X, and R. Tudur Jones, *Hanes Annibynwyr Cymru* (1966); lists of chapel licenses, 1793-1808, in A. I. Pryce, ' Side-lights on the rise of Nonconformity in the diocese of Bangor' (*TAAS* 1922 and 1924). A. H. Williams, *Welsh Wesleyan Methodism* (1935) covers another branch of the subject. Some details of the Roman Catholic revival appear in *Cennad Catholig Cymru,* ii (1913), 51-2. On the cathedral and diocese see W. Hughes, *Recollections of Bangor Cathedral* (1904) and *Life and Speeches of . . . Cotton* (1874); A. I. Pryce and J. W. James (see bibliography to chap. X) also cover this period. On the Oxford Movement in the diocese, D. Eifion Evans in *Jnl. of Hist. Soc. of Church in Wales,* vi (1956), and on church building, M. E. Clarke in *TCHS* 1961.

# XIV

## E D U C A T I O N  (1780-1900)

THE closing decades of the eighteenth century and the first decades of the nineteenth were a critical time for education in Caernarvonshire. In 1779 Bridget Bevan ('Madam Bevan') died at Laugharne in Pembrokeshire. During the eighteen years since Griffith Jones's death she had been the mainstay of the Circulating schools. Robert Jones of Rhoslan is said to have walked twice all the way to Laugharne to persuade her to continue the work in Caernarvonshire; she consented on condition that he taught in them himself, which he did, after only six weeks' schooling, at four centres in his own shire, one in Anglesey and one in Flintshire. The last, at Brynengan, was held in 1778. Madam Bevan left a substantial sum to continue the schools, but the will was disputed, and for over a quarter of a century the money lay idle in chancery; Caernarvonshire was thrown back on its own resources. The Circulating schools were an institution without permanent buildings or staff, and now without funds; yet everything depended on continuity, for those who had learned their letters in the schools were expected to pass their knowledge on: Robert Jones himself is a case in point. Higher education, of course, was in the much happier position of having its own endowments and its own buildings; but even the grammar schools, as will appear shortly, were for different reasons going through a time of stress. How did Caernarvonshire rise to the challenge and fill the gap before the state began to provide a more solid and permanent backing for education, first at the elementary level and then, much later, in the domain of higher education?

It has been suggested[1] that in seventeenth-century England ' basic literacy was common even among the poor ', but that then it declined; and although the decline was arrested for a time by ' the heroic efforts of the Charity Schools ', it reached rock-bottom ' between 1770 and 1820 ', largely owing to ' the understandable reluctance of clergy and schoolmasters to pursue the hordes of migrant workers into the noisome urban slums '. Clearly these conclusions cannot be applied to Caernarvonshire as they stand. The vast slum areas of industrial England had no real counterpart here : the only ' migrant workers ' to form important new centres of population were those in the quarry villages — unpleasing to the eye, perhaps, but far from being ' noisome slums ', still less (we shall see) hives of utter illiteracy; and the slums of Bangor, Caernarvon or Pwllheli were relatively small pockets which, however widely they might disseminate disease, had little bearing on the general level of literacy. Some particulars abstracted from the parish registers of Llanllyfni by a former rector (now dean of Bangor) suggest almost exactly the opposite tendency from that indicated above. The decennial average of those able to sign their names in the marriage register was not more than nine per cent in the middle of the eighteenth century, and was still only just over ten per cent thirty years later; but in 1803 it was approaching a quarter. In other words, in this particular branch of literacy the most rapid advance took place during the very years when it is believed to have reached its nadir in the country at large.

Statistically, of course, not much can be read into a sample taken from a parish with only about a thousand inhabitants, where the number of parishioners married in each decade of the period averaged only a little over 112. Moreover ability or otherwise to sign one's name is a very limited test of literacy. It would not be difficult in this or much later periods to find men and women

[1] Lawrence Stone, 'The educational revolution in England, 1560-1640' (*Past and Present*, no. 28, July 1964), 79, 69.

who read avidly but had never taken pen in hand; for there were few occasions when the property-less labourer had to sign his name, whereas he had been taught to look upon ability to read the Bible as a neecssary path to salvation. Indeed in many parts of the shire surnames were still a novelty, for it was only a generation or two back that the practice of adopting the paternal Christian name as a surname had spread downwards (under pressure from parish parson or clerk, no doubt, for convenience in registration) from the upper ranks of society, where it had become the fashion in the sixteenth and seventeenth centuries. On the other hand a man who could write could nearly always read as well. So far as this scrap of evidence goes, then, it suggests a rising rather than a declining standard of literacy. How far down in the social scale it extended we have no means of knowing, but the readiness with which weavers and small farmers turned into teachers and preachers suggests a considerable reading public at least at this level. It must have provided purchasers for the output of the local Welsh presses which became active from 1776, and for the more ambitious publications of the London Welsh societies, for which Dafydd Ddu Eryri acted as local agent when he was schoolmastering in Caernarvonshire; for there would not be much custom among the anglicised 'upper crust' of county society.

At Trefriw David Jones, himself a bard and a considerable anthologist and collector of manuscripts, acquired the wooden press first set up by Lewis Morris in Anglesey, and from 1776 he was publishing collections of Welsh verse, ballads, a translation of a religious work and another of a political pamphlet on the quarrel with the American colonies. At Caernarvon Thomas Roberts set up his press in 1797; a man of education and a Welsh scholar, he had learned his craft as a member of Howel Harris's Trevecka community. The business was carried on by his family after his death, and its output resembled that of the Trefriw press : Welsh poetry, a hymn book and a Biblical concordance, and two short-lived literary journals. A second press at Caernarvon had in the meantime been set up by Lewis E. Jones, joint publisher of the sermons of Peter Williams and publisher of an account of the work of the Bible Society. To all these we must add the growing wealth of denominational periodicals — some of them by now including material of wider interest — which circulated in the district, and the ballads, broadsheets and almanacs issuing from the same presses, which appealed to a less sophisticated public.

How was this level of literacy maintained? Small legacies for teaching the children of the poor to read had long been a common form of parochial endowment; they were usually administered by the parson or curate, and some were still in active operation. For example the tiny *enclave* of Llanbedr y cennin, in the midst of Caerhûn parish, had the benefit of what Hyde Hall somewhat grandly calls a ' chartered school ', where six boys from this and the two adjacent parishes were clothed and taught their letters by virtue of an endowment of £120 left by a former rector, early in the century. The schools endowed about the same time by Dean John Jones do not seem to have fared as well. All that Hall has to say about the one at Aber is : ' a school is occasionally kept in the church '; the Gyffin school seems to have completely disappeared; the endowments at Bangor and Llanllechid helped with the setting up of National schools in the early 'twenties, but must meanwhile have lain dormant, although we have seen that the Llanllechid school, at least, was still alive in 1754. Each of these four schools had a £100 endowment; but two generations of absentee bishops, and concurrent vacancies in the secular leadership of county society, had not made for vigilance in the use of these minor endowments, lacking as they did the prestige, the buildings and the qualified staffs of the endowed grammar schools. In any case, provision for teaching their letters to half-a-dozen boys in three parishes, and ten to a dozen in each of four others, only touched the fringe of the problem in an age of rising population. The Dr. Williams trust was also making its small contribution to literacy among Dissenting groups, mainly of the farming and shopkeeping class.

Here and there the ' circulating ' principle was kept alive by local effort, individual or collective, after the central funds had been buried in chancery. A tiny endowment of £7 from the rent of a small holding in Llŷn was left by an unknown donor at an unkown date, and used to open school every fourth year for up to twenty children in each of four parishes at the tip of the pensinsula; and there is a tradition of similar arrangements in the sprawling parish of Llanllyfni at the beginning of the nineteenth century. Seven years after the Madame Bevan fund was once more released in 1804, the rector of Llanrûg and Llanberis, Peter Bailey Williams, secured a grant from it which enabled David Thomas (Dafydd Ddu Eryri) — whose own education amounted to no more than a month's lessons from David Ellis ('Person Cricieth ') when Ellis was a curate at Llanberis — to teach forty local children for two years on end instead of the three months of Griffith Jones's original scheme; twenty years later, however, there was no school in either parish. The schools previously conducted by Dafydd Ddu — who was more interested in promoting Welsh literature than in teaching children their A B C — must have been private ventures, such as kept cropping up from time to time in the county. Some were taught by parsons — Anglican, Methodist, or from the older Dissent; some by laymen who might be only a few jumps ahead of their pupils. Some were focussed on Bible-reading, others (catering chiefly for adults) had more of the character of the long-defunct bardic schools. The schools of Evan Richardson, mentioned in another chapter, became in large measure seminaries for intending Methodist ministers. It was from Ieuan Glan Geirionydd, then a layman and unsure of his vocation, that John Jones, Tal y sarn, received as a grown man his only training, and perhaps also the theological bias which enabled him to edge the Methodism of his day away from the ultra-Calvinism of John Elias.

Another example is Ieuan Lleyn (Evan Pritchard), grandson to Charles Mark the Methodist pioneer, who from 1791 to 1799 was conducting village schools, mainly in his native Llŷn, and returned to the same work after an unhappy experience as excise officer in England. As these teachers depended on their fees, it is unlikely that their pupils were drawn from far down in the social scale. At Conway, where there was no endowed school, the corporation had since the seventeenth century been in the habit of paying a pittance to a schoolmaster for instructing the children of ' poor burgesses ', and was still doing so in 1810; but the burgesses constituted only five per cent of the total population. There were fifteen pupils in 1760. ' Private ' schools, as well as those supported by endowments like those of Madam Bevan, often used Welsh as the medium of instruction; but already there were parents in the humbler walks of life who, like their betters in Tudor and Stuart days, were anxious to give their children a good start in life by having them taught English. Bailey Williams contributed towards providing a school to meet this demand in his own parish, but by the 1830's, as education spread, he was becoming alarmed at the way the native language was being pushed into the background. At Llanllyfni a short-lived private adventure school early in the century charged a shilling a quarter for teaching Welsh but six shillings to such as wished to learn English. Others were more ambitious; the vicar of Edern in 1811 advertised a ' school for young gentlemen ' in his house, and a curate of Bailey Williams at Llanberis offered in the following year (with what response is unknown) to teach English and the classics at a guinea a quarter.

There were other and more unobtrusive services performed for local education by the educated clergy of the establishment. To those aspiring after something more than the bare rudiments of learning, the loan of books or an introduction to Welsh poetry from men like John Morgan (who tutored Abraham Williams) or David Ellis, ' person Cricieth ' (who befriended Dafydd Ddu) were a godsend; and in the maintenance of basic literacy — as the lives of such men as John Elias and Robert Jones, Rhoslan, remind us — a literate home, or a home where one of the parents or even a grandparent was a reader, might have decisive influence.

During the last decade of the eighteenth century another

educational agency began making a contribution of increasing importance to literacy in the shire; this was the Sunday school. Peter Bailey Williams was responsible for starting one of the earliest of them in his own parish in 1793; eighteen years later there were 134 in the whole diocese. Half of these were of Methodist origin, about a third were under Church auspices, and the other religious bodies supplied the rest. But in the early stages denominational differences were sometimes sunk; a Sunday school with a good reputation — especially one with plenty of teachers, so that classes were small — would attract pupils from all denominations and discourage any attempts to compete; and here the Methodists enjoyed the great advantage that their system bred a large supply of men accustomed to leadership of small groups and not expecting payment.

The weaknesses of the Sunday school as an educational instrument are obvious; Thomas Charles himself only accepted it as a *pis aller* when he had failed to get the Circulating schools on their feet again. Half a day a week (and that in some cases only spasmodic) spent partly in learning to read from scratch, partly in receiving religious instruction, under teachers who were untrained and generally unpaid, meant slow progress. On the other hand the total numbers affected were probably greater than those which any previous scheme of primary education had had to its credit; and at least books were available — Bibles primarily, but also elementary primers to help the unlettered in their uphill task. This was Thomas Charles's principal contribution to the work, for he was largely instrumental, first in procuring grants from the London Sunday School Society, then in founding the British and Foreign Bible Society, and finally in the composition and distribution of elementary text books. A Merioneth correspondent of the Bible Society claimed[2] in 1814 that by then 'a man that cannot read is ashamed of himself', whereas 'thirty years ago . . . nine out of ten peasants in the country could not read'.

[2] Quoted D. E. Jenkins, *Thomas Charles* (1908), iii, 560.

During this same period, and under the influence of some
of the same parsons and schoolmasters, there occurred a
remarkable revival of Welsh culture, in which Caernarvonshire played no small part. The cultivation of the ancient
Welsh metres in obscure farmhouses of Caernarvonshire had
never wholly ceased even when the gentry no longer patronised the craft. Sometimes (as in 1728) the local poets met to
cap verses with each other and with those of Anglesey. From
1783 there began a succession of more frequent literary
meetings in houses and taverns, organised by Dafydd Ddu
Eryri in various parts of Eifionydd and Arfon, culminating
in a far more ambitious venture in Caernarvon town hall in
1821. Meanwhile, under the patronage of the London
Gwyneddigion (who provided the medals and initially the
adjudications) the local group had adopted what they conceived to have been the procedure of the medieval eisteddfod; Iolo Morganwg himself came up to admit Dafydd Ddu
to the bardic order at Dinorwig in 1802. In this movement
Anglican, *Sentar* and Methodist were at one, although the
'pagan' element in the bardic tradition and the highly
unorthodox religious views of Iolo and some of his London
colleagues caused some heartburning. John Evans's quest in
America of the descendants of Madog will be remembered
as one of the highlights of this renaissance, even though Iolo
and several of the Caernarvonshire bardic circle backed out
of the adventure, and the quest ended in smoke.

The wealth of poetic talent evoked by these eisteddfodau
was considerable, even if not much of it has stood the test
of time; and Dafydd Ddu and his colleagues helped to
impress upon the movement the classical standards revived
by Goronwy Owen and the Morris brothers in Anglesey.
Another lasting fruit was the collection and printing (often
for the first time) of manuscripts surviving from the great
ages of bardic poetry, as well as of some contemporary verse,
with the help of the Caernarvon and Trefriw presses. For
the financial backing and the bigger undertakings the
London societies were responsible, but Dafydd Ddu and
Ieuan Lleyn took charge of the local sales and jointly edited

one of the short-lived periodicals serving as organs to the local movement, which thus contributed substantially towards the preservation and enrichment of Welsh as a literary language.

Most of the members of this literary and archaeological circle have already appeared in other contexts: William Williams of Llandygái, 'slate reeve' and antiquary; Abraham Williams (Bardd Ddu Eryri), the quarryman bard; his fellow-quarryman Griffith Williams (Gutyn Peris), to whom he taught the rules of Welsh prosody while he stayed under his roof after a quarry accident, helping him thus to win several eisteddfod medals for verse which, however, betrayed little sign of native inspiration; the group of Anglican parsons and peripatetic schoolmasters whose names have frequently recurred in these pages. Not all of them were of Caernarvonshire origin: Ieuan Brydydd Hir (Evan Evans), reputed the greatest Welsh scholar of his age, was a Cardiganshire man whose main work was done outside Caernarvonshire, but the two brief periods (both before 1772) when he held curacies here helped to prepare the way for the literary revival that followed. Bailey Williams had learned to love Welsh literature before he left his native Carmarthenshire; David Ellis brought with him to Llanberis and Cricieth the strong literary tradition of Merioneth, polished up by schooling under an eminent Welsh scholar in Cardiganshire; William Williams had come under the influence of the Morris circle while still in Anglesey. And of course there was the backing of the able if erratic Welsh circle in London; but the Caernarvonshire group had their own independent approach — for example neither Bailey Williams nor (eventually) Dafydd Ddu swallowed whole the forgeries of Iolo Morganwg or the linguistic vagaries of William Owen Pughe. A striking feature of the movement is also its tendency to shift the centre of gravity of Welsh culture in the shire from Llŷn to Eifionydd and Arfon; Cefnmeusydd in remote Ynyscynhaearn — the home of Ellis Owen (a grammar school product and a Fellow of the Society of Antiquaries) — became in the early nineteenth century 'a cultural centre where many practitioners in the literary arts were given guidance and encouragement'.[3]

In 1819 the bards of Gwynedd formed their own organisation at Caernarvon—Cymdeithas Gymroadd Gwynedd—and it was presumably under its auspices that the Caernarvon eisteddfod of 1821 was held. By this time the local renaissance of Welsh culture was arousing interest beyond the Welsh-speaking population. Hyde Hall had been much impressed by it on his travels through the shire, and devoted a couple of pages of his *Description of Caernarvonshire* to an account based on information from Bailey Williams; and the Caernarvon eisteddfod was patronised in person by some of the leading gentry of the neighbourhood. The Marquess of Anglesey took the chair and made the opening speech, followed by a summary in Welsh by Dafydd Ddu Eryri; he was supported by the bishop and dean (Majendie and Warren), by the last Viscount Bulkeley, Lord Newborough and (less surprisingly) Love Jones Parry. It was at this eisteddfod that the Independent minister William Williams was received into the bardic order under the name of Caledfryn. Here, it seemed, was a development cutting across social, denominational and linguistic frontiers. It did not last, of course, as the election of 1852 was to show. What is striking is that although the English or anglicised gentry gave their generous if belated patronage to the movement, the initiative and the creative work lay with their social inferiors. It was another premonitory sign of changing leadership in county affairs.

With the grammar schools we enter a different atmosphere. As interest in primary education developed, the extent of 'basic illiteracy' began to weigh on the minds and consciences of the liberal element in middle-class society. The grammar schools, they felt, were not serving the social stratum for which they were originally endowed, and the

[3] T. Morris in *TCHS*, 1961, 43n.

classical education they offered seemed irrelevant to contemporary needs. This restiveness was general throughout
the country in the late eighteenth and early nineteenth centuries. In Caernarvonshire it became vocal, as we have seen,
in the election of 1796. One of the charges brought by his
political foes against the Tory Bishop Warren was that he
was responsible for using endowments meant for the poor to
build a fine new school for the benefit of its wealthier
*clientèle*, and that its curriculum was slanted towards equip-
ping them for the better-paid professions rather than the
' free scholars ' from local homes for their humbler walk in
life. We have seen that actually there was no sign of any
reduction in the number of ' free scholars ' during Warren's
episcopate; what we do not know is whether the greatly
increased number of ' private ' pupils meant — as it certainly
did in some grammar schools — that attention was focussed
on them to the neglect of the foundation scholars.

During Warren's episcopate and that of his successor, at
anyrate, the school continued to flourish under a succession
of able and even distinguished masters — Oxford scholars
with a knowledge of Welsh sufficient to enable them to
preach and write in the language, to contribute to the output
of the diocesan Tract Society to which reference was made
in an earlier chapter, to participate in the revised issue of
the Welsh Prayer Book and to mingle with the literary and
antiquarian circle which was doing so much to stimulate the
cultural life of the shire. Both master and usher, of course,
were of necessity clergymen, and government was still in
the hands of the dean and chapter; it was fortunate that
during this period the chapter included, as we have seen,
so many able men with a zeal for education. The classics
remained the basis of instruction and were taught free;
writing and arithmetic were recent additions, provided
gratis to foundation scholars but charged as an ' extra ' to
others. Boarders — especially since the building of the new
school — were an increasingly important source of revenue :
by 1834 there were thirty of them to twenty day boys, and
alleged preferential treatment of them was becoming a

common target of criticism. By this time the whole face of education was changing, and the reaction of Friars to these new problems can best be considered at a later stage.

Botwnnog, as a remote country school frequented mainly by sons of farmers, was very differently placed. The office of headmaster, till 1809, was combined with that of rector; the firstfruits of the separation of the offices are seen in an advertisement in which the new headmaster (still a clergyman, but without benefice) offers to teach the classics to private pupils at forty guineas a year. It does not appear that he had any better success than the vicar of Edern or the curate of Llanberis who offered a similiar bait at about the same time, but one can appreciate the urge not only to increase his income but to use his training in the classics to better purpose than providing what was essentially an elementary education to local children. In this capacity, however, Botwnnog, even if it did not give its pupils the classical training for which their parents had little desire, was fulfilling a useful function, and was well attended except at seed and harvest time, when the children's labour was needed in the fields.

Few records have survived of the more recent foundation at Pwllheli. Under the founder's will a school house to accommodate 130 had been built, but the land which was to provide the school's revenue had never been bought. In 1773, however, William Vaughan, son and heir of the founder, provided in his will for a regular endowment; but after his death the estate devolved on the Mostyns, who discharged their obligations by paying and appointing the master out of their own income. The salary was £40; it was later alleged that had the founder's intentions been carried out the endowment should have given the school a revenue ten times as great. Disputes over this, and a deadlock over the appointment of a master, brought the school to an untimely end, as we shall see, in 1840.

.     .     .     .

In the early years of the nineteenth century the crusade against illiteracy became nation-wide. Of the two great organisation formed for the purpose, the British and Foreign School Society, established in 1808, had little or no impact on Caernarvonshire for thirty-five years. Its basis was undenominational and its support came chiefly from Nonconformists, few of whom in Caernarvonshire could give either solid financial backing or sites for schools; and both societies aimed at giving primary education a more permanent footing in the land by providing it with buildings. But the polysyllabic National Society for Promoting the Education of the Poor in the Principles of the Established Church of England, founded three years later, only took eight years to strike roots here. A branch was formed in 1819, and a few Church schools had been established even before this. In fact the movement in the Bangor area may be dated from the arrival in 1810, as vicar and precentor, of the Rev. J. H. Cotton, who was tireless in his efforts, first to establish new schools, and then to satisfy himself on their progress by frequent rounds of visits as ' unpaid inspector '. Teaching proved easier to provide than buildings, for both societies, in order to reach the maximum number at a minimum cost, adopted a variant of the Griffith Jones principle: instead of sending schoolmasters to make a limited stay in a succession of centres, and expecting those who had learned their letters to pass on their skills until provision could be made for another visit, they fixed their schools permanently in one place but relied on those who had advanced further in their studies to repeat the lessons, as ' monitors ', to the beginners. Most of the schools started in temporary premises, and only acquired buildings as money came in either from local benefactors or in grants from the parent societies.

For example, at Bangor a small house was rented as a Church school about 1810, then an abandoned Wesleyan chapel was taken over until in 1822 a new building was erected and opened with much pomp and ceremony. Meanwhile, monitors from the Bangor school were sent to help in starting another outside the city near Vaynol, for which a building was put up in 1816 by means of local subscriptions and a grant from the National Society. Another had been built in the old parish of Pentir (now annexed to Bangor) in 1814. The National school at Caernarvon began life in 1820 in a vacant building, and had to wait over twenty years for premises of its own. Cotton was presented to the rectory of Llanllechid in 1821, and within seven years he had re-established Dean Jones's school in a permanent building. By 1833 there were nine National schools in Caernarvonshire, all but one of them in Arfon or Arllechwedd. The one exception was at Llanystumdwy — a school to become famous as the place where the youthful Lloyd George obtained his only formal schooling. With the cathedral as their source of inspiration, the National schools, like the S.P.C.K. schools a century earlier, naturally arose first in that area of the county — in contrast with the Griffith Jones schools, which reached it last.

The new zeal for education of 'the poor' also stimulated some of the local gentry and clergy to endow Church schools in their neighbourhood: the first Lady Penrhyn established one for girls at Llandygái shortly after her husband's death, and another for boys was set up in 1884 by one of her successors at Penrhyn. In the same neighbourhood an unsectarian school was founded in 1830, on land given by the quarry owner and with financial support from Lord Willoughby (of Gwydir) and the quarrymen themselves. The quarry owners at Penmaenmawr and (later) Trevor were also generous in their support of elementary education. Lord Newborough too built and endowed a school at Llandwrog in 1833, and the rector of Llangybi was about the same time maintaining a parish school at his own expense; but as there was apparently no endowment it did not survive his incumbency. At Clynnog in 1827 a school was conducted in Capel Beuno, adjoining the church, by the bard Ebenezer Thomas (Eben Fardd) under the auspices of the National Society; but a dozen years later he rejoined the Methodists (among whom he had been brought up), broke off his connection with the

National Society, and carried on the school on his own account first in his house and then in the Methodist chapel.

In the early days of the National schools, Nonconformist parents not infrequently sent their children there. Methodists at least had no objections to their being taught the Church catechism, nor even to their being taken to service in the parish church, so long as they could also go with their families to their own chapel; this was not difficult (even if hard on the children!), since Methodists still generally timed their meetings to avoid a clash with Church services. Sometimes they even helped to support the local National school: Bangor Methodists took up a collection for it, in recognition of the benefit they received from the new road leading to it past their chapel door; at Waunfawr the Independents helped establish a National school in 1839. The only substantial endowment from which Nonconformist education benefited, the Daniel Williams trust, was apparently now confined, in Caernarvonshire, to a grant of £20 under which thirty boys were educated free at Bangor in a very inadequate building; the school was undenominational but conducted by the Independent minister, Arthur Jones. The sister institution at Caernarvon appears to have petered out, and nothing is known of the school there which as early as 1816 received a grant from the British and Foreign Society; it was not until 1846 that a British school was permanently established at Caernarvon. Otherwise the earliest school in the county known to have received grants from the British and Foreign Society was at Tremadoc in 1839. But, as we have seen, Nonconformist ministers frequently held day schools as well as Sunday schools in their chapels; and at Beddgelert in 1831 a group of Dissenters guaranteed a salary of £20 to a schoolmaster using the chapel building.

Such arrangements as these were bound to be ephemeral. The early Church schools were often in the same difficulty when parents or subscribers lost interest or teachers left the district and could not be replaced. At Abererch a school house was built in 1834 by means of guinea subscriptions from the small freeholders and farmers of the parish; Lord

Newborough, the principal landowner and tithe owner, was (as we have seen) supporting another school at his sole expense, and declined to contribute. Till about 1840 a schoolmaster was maintained by the Madam Bevan trust, but when he left, it was taken over by a completely untrained ex-sailor, who emptied the school and left the building derelict. At Nefyn the total amount subscribed towards the upkeep of the school in 1847 was £5, and here again the three principal landowners deriving a substantial income from the parish had all backed out, making it impossible to procure any but the most incompetent teacher. Moreover, local parents were by this time objecting to the Church catechism and to compulsory attendance at the parish church.

For by now the restraining hand of John Elias had been removed from Methodism and the spread of 'Puseyism' was scaring away all sections of Dissenters from Church teaching; nor did local vicars and Church schoolmasters always handle the children of Dissenters with tact. A new phase in the history of Welsh education opened with the publication in 1843 of Hugh Owen's open *Letter to the Welsh People.* Owen was an Anglesey lad educated at Evan Richardson's school in Caernarvon and then apprenticed to the law, by means of which he rose to a position in the civil service in London. This gave him sufficient pull to enable him to procure the appointment of a local representative in North Wales of the British and Foreign School Society, and the aim of his letter was to arouse his fellow-Nonconformists to their educational responsibilities towards their own children and to push the claims of their distinctive Society. The representative appointed by the Society, on Owen's advice, was a Cardiganshire man named John Phillips, who had been converted in the course of one of the South Wales revivals, and after supplementing his early education in a local Sunday school by a short spell at a day school, went on revivalistic tours through the counties of Radnor, Merioneth and Caernarvon. Then he managed to scrape up enough money to go to Edinburgh university, and in 1837 he was

ordained to the Calvinistic Methodist ministry and posted
to Bangor. Within a couple of years of his appointment by
the British and Foreign Society, he had been instrumental
in establishing British schools at Dinorwig, at the old
Puritan centre of Llanengan, and what was still the little
copper-mining village of Llandudno, where the allotment of
the old common lands abutting on the shore, opening the
way for its development as a resort, was only just getting
under way. He did not shrink even from competing with
existing National schools, as at Caernarvon, Bangor and
Penmachno.

Phillips's campaign received support from high quarters
outside the shire. Jones Parry (senior) of Madrun, the Liberal
landowner who captured Caernarvon boroughs in 1835,
made a powerful plea in the House for Welsh education;
in 1844 the Rebecca riots in west Wales resulted in a comprehensive and not altogether unsympathetic report in the
*Times* on the conditions which had provoked the riot, and
in the same year a report by the National Society on the
state of education in Wales was the cause of widespread
alarm and despondency. Meanwhile the state had embarked
cautiously on the policy of granting small subsidies to the
voluntary societies to help them in putting up school buildings. Here was a powerful argument for John Phillips: why
should the Church schools monopolise the state subsidies?
Then in 1846 William Williams, a Cardiganshire boy,
educated at a local Church school, who had succeeded
brilliantly in business in London and become radical M.P.
for Coventry, persuaded the House of Commons to set up
a commission of enquiry into the state of education in Wales,
' especially into the means afforded to the labouring classes
of acquiring a knowledge of English '.

This was a new approach to primary education in Wales:
hitherto, as we have seen, the chief objective had been
ability to read the Bible in the common tongue; Williams,
as a successful business man, saw the problem from another
angle, and in this he probably represented the views of a
growing number of ambitious parents in Wales. So it was

natural that the commissioners' report, which was presented
to the Committee of Council on Education (the predecessor
of the present Department of Education and Science) in the
following year, should make this the criterion of literacy.
But it was unfortunate that the three commissioners chosen
should have been young and aspiring barristers with no
knowledge of Wales, of Welsh literature or of Welsh Nonconformity, and still more unfortunate that they should have
felt called upon to dogmatise, in terms bound to cause
offence, on matters neither within their competence nor
within their terms of reference. It is not surprising that Welsh
patriots, calling to mind the legendary episode known in
Welsh history as *Brad y cylleill hirion* (' The treachery of
the long knives '), dubbed the report ' The treachery of the
Blue Books ' (*Brad y llyfrau gleision*).

It was a pity, because the commissioners were able and
conscientious men, and their report, based on interviews and
investigations through the length and breadth of Wales in
the course of the year, was within its limits a pioneer factual
study of Welsh schools. Its revelations were a powerful
stimulant and irritant in their day, and they remain a valuable source of knowledge for posterity. The tragedy is that
it should have deepened existing divisions in local society
and perpetuated them by extending them to the field of
education, which they continued to bedevil till after the
end of the century. Equally disastrous were the assumptions
underlying the report, arising from its limiting terms of
reference; for these were destined to impoverish the content
of subsidised education for a critical half-century, by exclud-
ing from it the rich heritage of native culture which a century
of voluntary effort had been bringing back to life — in the
sphere of religion through the medium of Griffith Jones and
Thomas Charles, and in the secular sphere through that of
Dafydd Ddu and his circle.

What sort of picture of education in Caernarvonshire do
the *llyfrau gleision* present? The commissioners visited
something like seventy schools in the shire; the few coaching

and finishing establishments kept by clergy and gentle-women in Bangor and Caernarvon, as well as in remoter country vicarages, were of course excluded since they did not provide for the ' poor ' and were mostly boarding schools which made no impact on the shire. There were nearly fifty Church schools, some supported by the National Society, some solely by local funds; just over a dozen Nonconformist or unsectarian schools, five of them receiving grants from the British and Foreign School Society. In addition the commissioners reported on four ' dame ' schools (two in Bangor, two in Caernarvon and one in Nefyn), and about twice that number labelled ' private ' schools, situated in Caernarvon, Conway, Tremadoc, Llandwrog and Abererch. Three of the schools reported on were bilingual, the rest monoglot English. As examples of the way the native tongue was being ousted from the schools the following may be cited. The master and mistress of Caernarvon National school were both ignorant of Welsh, and the report notes with satisfaction that the children had started school young enough to make English virtually their first language, so that they were able to act as interpreters to their monoglot parents. A few years later Robert Roberts, ' y sgolor mawr ', as a student at the training school in the same town, was forbidden to attend the Welsh services at St. Mary's church; while at Cricieth a tiny endowment of £8 for teaching Welsh to children of the three adjacent parishes in rotation was now being used to teach English as well — even though the master, it was reported, had little understanding of the language. This complaint about the teachers is frequently reiterated in the report; Caernarvonshire was by way of making the worst of both worlds by raising up a generation of children without adequate training in either tongue.

What saved the situation, up to a point, was the Sunday school. There were now over 250 of these in the shire — nearly twice as many as there had been in the whole diocese thirty years earlier. About half of them were still provided by the Calvinistic Methodists; the Anglican contribution — seventeen — had not kept pace with the general increase,

probably because of the growing unwillingness of Dissenting
parents to submit their children to the teaching of the
Church catechism. In Sunday school the teaching was almost
universally Welsh, and so could not be examined by the
visiting commissioners; but from what they saw and heard
they concluded that these had become ' the main instrument
of civilization in North Wales', adding this generous
tribute : [4]

> . . . it is impossible not to admire the vast number of schools
> which they have established, the frequency of the attendance,
> the number, energy and devotion of the teachers, the regularity
> and decorum of the proceedings, and the permanent and striking
> effects which they have produced upon society.

On the day schools, where the children were instructed in
a language only half-understood by themselves and often far
from familiar to their teachers, and then examined by
strangers with unaccustomed accents, the report is naturally
couched in very different terms. The apparent stupidity of
some of the answers quoted in it cannot be taken as a
measure of the quality of the education provided: sometimes, as Dean Cotton observed in his devastating reply to
the report,[5] the examiners themselves needed reminding of
the counsel of the son of Sirach in the Apocrypha: ' First
understand, and then rebuke . . . If thou hast understanding,
answer thy neighbour; if not, lay thy hand to thy mouth '.
    Leaving this aside, the factual evidence itself reveals
glaring deficiencies. Only six of the teachers had had any
training, and that varied from two weeks to six months at the
' model schools' at Caernarvon, Chester or Borough Road.
Of the rest, seventeen were former craftsmen, a couple of
dozen had been sailors or fishermen, farmers, drovers or
gardeners, or else shopkeepers; they also included a miller,
a quarryman and a labourer. The outstanding exception was
the headmistress of Caernarvon infant school (almost the

---

[4] *Rept. on Education,* 1847, iii. 59.
[5] Hughes, *Life and Speeches,* 64-96 (*Ecclus.* xi. 7, v. 12).

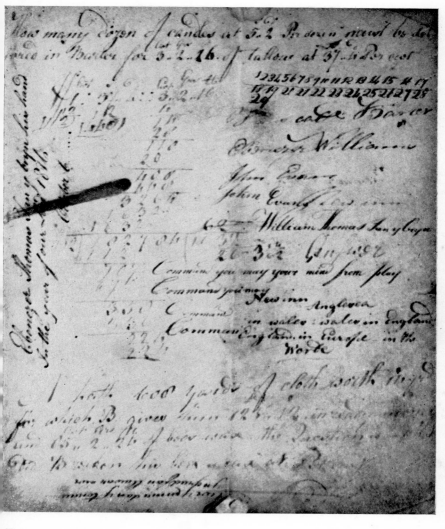

PLATE XVII

SCHOOL EXERCISE BOOK OF EBEN FARDD

only institution to receive unstinting praise), who had trained at Dublin for four years. But then, she had a salary of £40, as against the far more usual figure of £25. Some teachers were paid as little as £8, and had to combine their teaching with some other occupation: as many as thirteen Caernarvonshire teachers were in this category. Under the master or mistress was a variable number of monitors who at the age of twelve were expected (if they stayed on at school at all) to pass on their lessons to the beginners. Their quota of ' pupils ' ranged from upwards of twenty each at Bangor or Caernarvon to the more manageable number of four or five at Llandygái.

The proportion in the shire of children under fifteeen who were under regular instruction was barely twenty per cent; in this Caernarvonshire stood fourth of the six North Wales counties. What was worse, nearly half of these were in school for less than a year, and not much more than six per cent stayed for more than three years. The number on the school books could be as small as twenty (at Llandwrog) or as high as 310 (at Bangor infant school). Average attendance was naturally higher in the towns than in country villages, where weather conditions and the call for harvest labour counted so much. At Bangor it was said to be as high as 225 out of 248 on the books, and at Caernarvon 320 out of 364 — a remarkable figure in the absence of any means of compulsion. On the other hand, premises and equipment were almost universally condemned as defective.

In addition to day schools for children and Sunday schools for all ages, there were eight night schools, employed from two to five nights a week in teaching the three R's to adult pupils. The teachers included a bookseller a shoemaker, a wheelwright, two farmers, a sailor and a ' gentleman's gentleman '. Two of these schools were held at Caernarvon, and attended in the winter months by seamen to the number of a couple of dozen; two more were in the parish of Llandwrog and one each in those of Llanllechid, Llanddeiniolen, Llandudno and Aber. The numbers attending ranged from eight to fifty-five. The report deplores the absence of any form of technical instruction. At Caernarvon, Caledfryn told the investigator that children went to sea as cabin boys before they had learned to read, and often by sheer rule of thumb managed to acquire enough experience to rise to be captains of boats trading with the continent; he added that almanacs and the Bible were the only reading of most of the small-holders of the district, as distinct from the more literate quarrymen. An attempt to establish a school of navigation at Caernarvon towards the close of the Napoleonic war[6] had apparently come to nothing, but by 1846 the headmaster of the National school was adding to his many other commit-ments private lessons in navigation.

The whole work of elementary education was, of course, conducted on a shoestring budget. The total amount of endowments earmarked for this purpose came to some £350, divided between fifteen schools. Subscriptions brought in another £350, from which 46 schools benefited to the tune of a little over £20 each, and further small sums were raised in church collections and by tea meetings and the like, but these did not produce much more than £100. Few of the schools were entirely free: fees ranging from a penny a week to half-a-crown a quarter were charged, but these were generally remitted for the very poor — sometimes under an arrangement, somewhat after the fashion of voluntary hos-pitals before the National Health Service, or (earlier still) of the chartered companies for colonising North America, by which subscribers could procure free entry for their *protégés* in proportion to the size of the subscription. The ' children's pence ' brought in much the same total as the subscriptions, but it averaged out at under £20 per school. Grants from the National and British Societies were allotted only when local support was also forthcoming, and were generally confined to meeting the cost of building. Sites were often given free by landowners, but it was estimated that two-thirds of the school buildings in North Wales were held on

---

[6] *N.W. Gazette*, 29 Dec. 1814, 12 Jan. 1815.

precarious tenure. This was of course especially true of the
Nonconformist schools, which had such difficulty in finding
a friendly landlord. During the decade following the publi-
cation of the report, however — maybe in consequence of
the rude jolt it gave to public complacency — even staunch
Anglican landlords like the Penrhyn family (at Bangor), the
Bulkeleys (at Beddgelert) and the Assheton Smiths (at
Deiniolen and Nant Peris) came to the aid of the local
British school with the land it needed for building.

It is urged in the report, not without justification, that the
admittedly inadequate funds available — under £3,000 in
all for the shire — could have been used to far better effect.
The most pungent criticism is directed against the misuse
of endowments; some, as we have seen, had just disappeared
or been misapplied to other uses or were lying in abeyance;
and the commissioners reported that even where the
founders' wishes were observed, the education in these
schools was in most cases ' of little practical value '. They
are particularly hard on the few surviving schools supported
by the Madam Bevan trust, maintaining that the absence of
permanent buildings, the limitation to two years' instruction,
and the allowance of £25 for the teacher's salary, made them
educationally useless. The method was certainly outdated,
yet the salary and the length of school life were about the
average for the shire, and permanent buildings were still a
rarity. More pertinent are their conclusions on the ill effects
of social and religious divisions:[7]

> The wealthy classes who contribute towards education belong to
> the Established Church; the poor who are to be educated are
> Dissenters. The former will not aid in supporting neutral schools;
> the latter withhold their children from such as require conformity
> to the Established Church. The effects are seen in the co-exis-
> tence of two classes of schools, both of which are rendered
> futile — the Church schools supported by the rich, which are
> thinly attended, and that by the extreme poor; and private-
> adventure schools supported by the mass of the poorer classes

[7] *Report*, iii. 48-54, esp. 53-4.

at an exorbitant expense, and so utterly useless that nothing can account for their existence except the unhealthy division of society, which prevents the rich and poor from co-operating. The Church schools, too feebly supported by the rich to give useful education, are deprived of the support of the poor, which would have sufficed to render them efficient. Thus situated, the promoters are driven to establish premiums, clothing-clubs, and other collateral inducements, in order to overcome the scruples and reluctance of Dissenting parents.

In estimating the financial resources of the schools, however, the report takes no account of the parliamentary grants which many of them were now receiving through the British and National Societies — some of them since 1835, within a year or two of the initiation of public grants. The bulk of these grants, of course, were earmarked for building, and so did not help with the cost of upkeep; they ranged from £40 for a small school at Llaniestyn in 1853 to over £470 for Llandwrog in 1844. The buildings — such as have survived modernisation — often bear the stamp of an age which still bracketed elementary education with poor relief as a public charity, and recall only too vividly the ' deterrent ' aspect of the workhouse. A number of small grants — rarely more than a couple of pounds — were from time to time allotted for the purchase of maps and books, and occasionally from 1840 we find sums varying from £16 to £40 allocated to teachers' wages. From this time too experiments were being made in the use of pupil teachers as a more satisfactory expedient than the original monitorial system, though this did not become general for another six years. Grants for the training and payment of pupil teachers amounted to nearly £80 at Tremadoc in 1840, and two other schools received smaller grants for the same purpose during the next decade. In other words, the educational system was already in process of being put on a more satisfactory footing at the very time when the commissioners were writing their Jeremiad.

Most important of all, perhaps, were the steps now being taken towards the training of teachers. As early as 1837 the energetic master of the National school at Caernarvon (then the largest elementary school in North Wales) was conducting on the premises a ' model school ' where intending teachers could try out their paces under his supervision and receive from him such additional instruction as he could give out of class hours; a government grant of £200 in respect of this was paid through the National Society. Starting as a purely local effort with the backing of the vicar and a town committee, it had developed by 1849 into a separate training institution with its own principal and its own hired lecture room, still using the school as a practising ground and its head as ' master of method '. Between 1842 and 1848 it was given grants amounting to nearly £1,000 for buildings and equipment. Here some score of young men aged from sixteen upwards were trained free, normally for a period of a year, living at their own very meagre charges in lodgings in the town. It is said to have been the only institution in the country where the training college grew out of the practising school instead of the other way round. For by 1855 it had secured recognition as the North Wales Training College, having acquired the site of the old baths and adapted them to the needs of a residential college for about forty students. The official adoption in 1846 of the pupil teacher system and its corollary the Queen's scholarships enabled the college to extend its courses to two years and to adapt them to the needs of a more advanced type of student. After a disastrous fire in 1891 it was removed to Bangor.

Five years before this, the British Society had opened in Swansea the first training college for women; an attempt at Caernarvon to provide women teachers with a Church training college had broken down nearly thirty years earlier. In the interval the British and Foreign Society had established its Normal College at Bangor, with its North Wales representative, John Phillips, as first principal, and the Calvinistic Methodist body as its main supporters. Like its predecessor at Caernarvon, it started in temporary premises and with only a dozen students, but in 1862 new buildings were put up, with accommodation for forty. Almost half a century passed, however, before women were admitted as students; but the North Wales Training College — which came to be known as St. Mary's from its close association, since its inception, with the church of that name at Caernarvon — filled the gap by turning itself into a women's college after removal to Bangor.

The Education Act of 1870, by throwing responsibility on to the state, opened another era in primary education; it was followed naturally by the establishment of compulsory education in 1880 and of free education eleven years later. The greatly increased demand for teachers now filled the training colleges and soon called for further extensions. Local interest in the schools was maintained under the 1870 Act by the institution of elective school boards in each of the Poor Law areas. These had power to build their own schools and to put them on the rates along with any existing schools willing to conform to the standards in buildings, equipment and staffing laid down by the state, which also excluded ' denominational ' teaching during school hours.

The first school board elections in Caernarvonshire, as elsewhere, were exciting local events. For one thing, they gave the electorate its first taste of the ballot, for it was not until the following year that it was applied to general elections. And in the heated political and sectarian atmosphere of the time party strife was inevitable, with Anglicans and Tories on the one side and Liberals and Nonconformists on the other striving for preponderance on the body which was to determine the complexion of education in the area at a critical stage. At Bangor, for example, an angry broadsheet warfare raged round the fight for places on the board between Lord Penrhyn and Thomas Lewis the Liberal merchant, and between the new principal of the Normal College (like his predecessor a Calvinistic Methodist minister) and the ' Puseyite ' vicar of Bangor. Nevertheless, with the Act of 1870 elementary education ceased to be primarily a local concern; here then we may appropriately leave this branch of the subject.

Secondary education took a different course. The commissioners of 1846, charged as they were with the task of enquiring into ' the means afforded to the labouring classes of acquiring a knowledge of English ', felt bound to find out how far the grammar schools were contributing towards this end. Friars they described as ' exclusively a classical school, for the benefit of boarders and of a few town boys, sons of the most respectable tradesmen of Bangor '; ' the poor ', they added, ' are not admitted, the trustees being of opinion that the National School is better suited to their requirements '. Boarding fees were from £30 to £40 a year; day boys naturally paid less — and were made to feel their inferiority; and the foundation met its obligation to the ' free scholars ' by paying their modest pence to the National school — on condition of their singing in the cathedral choir. The pertinacious Dr. O. O. Roberts had presented a petition to parliament in 1844 against this diversion of the endowments, and was supported by W. O. Stanley (M.P. for Anglesey). but opposed by Douglas Pennant (the future Lord Penrhyn), who sat for Caernarvonshire. Even the Bangor-Beaumaris board of guardians felt impelled to pass a resolution to the same effect in 1849. Nonconformist and middle-class opinion in Bangor and district was generally behind Dr. Roberts, both because of the clerical government of the school and because of its classical bias.

Some concessions were made. In 1856 a few ' modern ' subjects were introduced; as we were then fighting (not too successfully) the Crimean war, they included navigation and fortification. The ' Glyn scholars ' were now selected for their academic attainments among fee-payers already in the school, instead of being hustled off to the National school. Five years later the charity commissioners drew up a new scheme of government under which five laymen (all Anglican landowners) were added to the dean and chapter. None of this went very far towards disarming criticism, and in the meantime the controversies had gravely damaged the school. Some good private schools in the neighbourhood drew away pupils, especially under the *régime* of an unpopular ' flogging' head; and in 1866 Friars closed down. This was just three years before the Gladstone ministry attempted a mild measure of reform in secondary education (hitherto completely outside the purview of the state) in the Endowed Schools Act of 1869, under which yet another new scheme of government for Friars finally removed it from clerical control. A proposal for amalgamating the school with the David Hughes foundation at Beaumaris came to nothing; so did another project for a technical school at Bangor. But in 1873 Friars reopened its doors with a new headmaster — Glyn Williams, the brilliant son of the famous Nicander.

Botwnnog came under the lash of the 1846 commissioners for opposite reasons. It was admitted to be faithful to its trust of providing free education for the poor, but at an extravagant cost. The master, who was incumbent of two neighbouring parishes, appropriated the endowment of £120 and a house, delegating his teaching duties to an usher (who was also a small farmer) at £40, while all that remained of its pretension as a 'free grammar school' was tuition in Latin for one lone pupil, as against eight a dozen years earlier. One of the trustees assured the commissioners that the endowment did little more than provide 'a sinecure maintenance for the nominal master'. Even the elementary instruction it provided was declared to rank below that of 'many schools taught by one master, and supported by the children's pence', but this was indignantly denied by Dean Cotton, who knew the school well. After the issue of the report, however, the governing body was strengthened by the addition of the bishop and dean of Bangor and several of the local gentry, and under an active head the school increased in numbers and became 'semi-classical'; but it still had no boarding house, the boys being boarded out in farms. The Endowed Schools Act did not interfere with it, and in 1881 its chief function was still to provide elementary education for the neighbourhood.

The worst case of a misused endowment was at Pwllheli. In 1840 Sir E. Ll. Mostyn, as trustee, appointed to the vacant headship the local curate. There were violent opposition among Dissenting parents, who in any case wanted a commercial school, not a classical school. They urged that the headship should be given to the Welsh poet Eben Fardd, who had just re-joined the Methodists after teaching successfully in a Church school for a dozen years. He in turn was unacceptable under the terms of the trust as a Dissenter. Deadlock ensued and the school closed. The commissioners of 1846 found the schoolroom filled with lumber and the tattered remnants of a classical library; they even discovered in a drawer of a table ' part of a human body in a state of putrefaction '. The loss of the school was bitterly deplored in the town, for most of the local tradesmen sent their children there, to the number of fifty or sixty a year. It also drew pupils from farther afield : within forty years of its foundation the Anglesey poet Goronwy Owen had a year's schooling there before going on to Friars and Oxford, and he returned ten years later for a short spell as usher. But now shipbuilders were complaining that Pwllheli could not provide men fitted to be master or mates, and that mechanics of all sorts, while generally able to read the Welsh Bible, could neither read English nor write nor do a simple sum. The incumbent spoke of hooliganism among the young, and declared that the town was fifty years behind Caernarvon — though it appears from Robert Roberts's biography that in this respect there was not much to choose between the two! The building was pulled down in 1851 and a new British school built on the site; but Pwllheli had to wait till nearly the end of the century for a revival of the secondary education it had once enjoyed.

During the last quarter of the century secondary education in Wales occupied something like the place in public attention that primary education had occupied in the 'forties. The elementary schools themselves, now rapidly becoming ubiquitous, helped to create this demand, which was particularly active in the quarrying areas. Here it found vent in attendance at popular lectures and at chapel literary societies where members wrote essays for submission to outside adjudicators; in the throngs that took up courses in evening classes (as many as 120 at Carneddi chapel in Llanllechid); and in the high tone of the lunch-hour discussions in the quarry ' cabins '. But this was not enough. The foundation of the university college at Aberystwyth in 1872 (followed a dozen years later by the sister institution at Bangor) revealed a missing link in the educational system, for these colleges found themselves faced with the task of preparing for degree courses young people often equipped with nothing beyond an elementary education, since Friars school at Bangor was now the only institution offering the necessary preparation, and it had become beyond the reach of most poor boys. It was for this reason that the North Wales Scholarship Association was formed in 1879 to help promising elementary children to enter the grammar school. In the following year three Caernarvonshire boys — from Conway National school and the Board schools at Pen y groes and Carneddi — were among those who gained the awards.

A departmental committee appointed under the chairmanship of Lord Aberdare in Gladstone's second ministry (in 1882) reported on the poverty of grammar school endowments in Wales and their strong Anglican bias — in a country which had become predominantly Nonconformist — and recommended public grants to build new and ' neutral ' schools. A proposal made to a committee which met at Bangor to discuss the best way of putting the scheme into effect revealed the only too familiar divisions over educational policy. It was suggested that Friars should become a central boarding school for North Wales and that grants should be made to support a number of ' higher elementary ' schools in the rest of the county. But the strongly Anglican and English tone of Friars (even under a master like Nicander's son, who felt strongly the need to break down ' provincialism ' in Caernarvonshire boys) alienated many, and opposition was strengthened by fears of the cost and by parochial rivalries. Since these doubts were widespread through the land, and no impartial body existed to administer the grants, action was postponed till after the setting up of elective county councils in 1888. This was rapidly followed

by the Welsh Intermediate Education Act, which empowered the county councils to levy rates (to be supplemented
from the Treasury) for secondary education, and to set up
committees to draw up and administer the necessary
schemes.

The Caernarvonshire scheme left Friars with its old name
and something of its old standing, but depleted its endowments to provide for the new ' county ' schools. At a public
meeting at Botwnnog in 1891 Thomas Ellis, M.P. for
Merioneth, revived the old seventeenth-century proposal
that the local school should be transferred to Pwllheli, but
he was successfully opposed by Jones Parry; by 1913
Botwnnog had 68 pupils, and had recovered its grammar
school status. Seven new schools were planned to supplement
the old foundations. The intention of the Act had been that
these should be ' modern ' schools, not attempting the more
' academic ' education of the old grammar schools; but local
opinion had veered round since the days when this was
attacked as pandering to a privileged class and neglecting
chartered obligations to the ' under-privileged '. Now that
basic education was provided for all, there seemed no reason
why the ' academic ' subjects should not be available to any
who had shown themselves capable of proceeding beyond
primary education. So the new schools were planned on
grammar school lines (with the addition of natural science),
and it was left to later generations to tackle the problems of
technical and commercial education.

The first of these new ' County ' schools in Caernarvonshire — indeed the first school under the new Act in all
Wales — was housed in the gloomy remains of the old
training college at Caernarvon. Pwllheli soon followed,
recovering what it had lost half a century earlier; then
Portmadoc, Pen y groes and Bethesda. The intention to
build one at Conway was abandoned in favour of Llandudno, where the school was not opened till 1907. Meanwhile a successful private school for girls at Bangor had in
1898 been adopted as Caernarvonshire's first girls' county
school under the new Act; after the pattern of the elementary

schools, both sexes had been admitted to the others, but Friars had remained exclusively a boy's school. Apart from government and county council grants, money was raised by local effort, and financial support from outside came from men like William Rathbone, the ex-M.P., and his friend Henry Tate — better known for the Tate Gallery — while Vaynol and Penrhyn gave sites for Bryn'refail and Bethesda schools. Nearly all of them opened in temporary premises : a café, a hotel, an abandoned mansion, a chapel schoolroom. When new buildings were put up, while they avoided the forbidding exteriors of the early elementary schools, they reflected, with a somewhat depressing uniformity, the taste of a generation not rich in architectural ideas. Now that so many have been replaced, they have acquired the character of ' period pieces '.

With the decision in 1884 to accommodate the new University College of North Wales in a former coaching inn at Bangor, the county had been provided with something that could fairly be called an educational ladder; what had not yet been provided was an effective link between the vernacular culture that flourished outside the schools and the pattern of education inside. It was assumed both locally and centrally that the obvious need for a thorough grounding in English precluded serious attention to Welsh in the schools. In the elementary schools the Revised Code of 1861 sounded the death-knell of Welsh teaching, since it was not a grant-earning subject; in the very next year it ceased for a whole generation to be an examination subject at Bangor Normal. There had been some bilingual teaching at the Caernarvon training school (from sheer practical necessity) in its earliest days, but as it ceased to be a local concern and attracted students from across the border, this too vanished. When schemes of work were drawn up for the new Caernarvonshire county schools, the only one which included Welsh was Caernarvon itself, and here it occupied only a subsidiary place. Yet the idea of ' peaceful co-existtence ' between the two languages had been forcefully put as early as 1821 in a sermon preached in the cathedral by the warden of Ruthin on behalf of Bangor National school,[8] when he raised the question whether ' a better grammatical knowledge of the native tongue may not be made concur-rent ' with the acquistion of English, and whether ' the use of two languages presents not an advantage in proving the intelligence of a learner '. Here was another issue which the nineteenth century left the twentieth to face — under less favourable conditions.

## BIBLIOGRAPHY

G. Richards, ' The early story of the schools of Dyffryn Nantlle ' (*TCHS* 1963) gives a sample of schooling in a quarry area from mid-eighteenth century. On Caernarvonshire printers see J. I. Jones, *History of Printers and Printing in Wales* (1925). On Bayley Williams, see G. T. Roberts in *TCHS* 1948, and on Ieuan Lleyn, T. Parry in *id.* 1965. On early Sunday schools, Bob Owen in *Er Clod* (see biblio-graphy to ch. XIIIB), 101 ff. On the revival of Welsh culture, T. Parry in *Hanes Llenyddiaeth Cymraeg*, xi (i), and *The Eisteddfod of Wales* (1943); R. T. Jenkins and Helen Ramage, *Hist. of the Hon. Society of Cymmrodorion* (1951), 39 ff; and B. L. Jones, *Yr Hen Bersoniaid Llengar* (1963). The history of the endowed grammar schools is given in *The Dominican* (Friars schools), quatercentenary number 1957, and in G. Parry, ' Hanes Ysgol Botwnnog ' (*Trans. Cymmr. Soc.*, 1957); the early activities of the ' British ' and ' National ' Societies in Hughes, *Cotton* (see ch. XIIIB, bibliography) and H. Lewis, ' Ysgolion Brutanaidd Arfon ' (*Cymru*, xxxii, 1912). The basic authority on conditions in 1847 is *Report of Commissioners of Inquiry into the State of Education in Wales*, 1847, iii; and on state grants, 1833-52, *Minutes of Committee of Council on Education*, 1853, i. 167. There is also much information on schools and educational endow-ments in Lewis, *Topographical Dictionary of Wales* (1833 ff). School board election literature, 1870, is filed in U.C.N.W. Library, Bangor. Accounts of the training colleges are given in R. Meredith, ' Early history of the North Wales Training College ' (*TCHS* 1946), and in R. Thomas (ed.), *Bangor Normal College* (1958). On the county schools see *Report on Intermediate and Higher Education in Wales*, 1881; P. T. Owen, ' The beginnings of the county schools in Caernarvon-shire ' (*TCHS* 1957); and S. A. Claridge, ' The first of the county schools ' (*id.* 1958). On industrialists and education, L. W. Evans, ' Schools established by industrial undertakings ' (*id.* 1954)

---

[8] Quoted *Welsh in Education and Life* (Board of Education Rept., 1927), 52.

# XV

## LOCAL GOVERNMENT IN THE
## NINETEENTH CENTURY

AMONG the many institutions which the reformers responsible for the Reform Act of 1832 were itching to 'tidy-up' were the municipal corporations. 'I augur no great political progress in this country', wrote one of them (Joseph Parkes)[1] to a colleague shortly after the Act was passed, 'till we do obtain a popular elective municipal system'. The Reform Act had defined the boundaries of the parliamentary boroughs and regulated their parliamentary franchise, but left their internal government untouched. In Caernarvonshire it had added Bangor to the five contributory boroughs, but the only organ of government there, apart from the county justices, was still the bishop's manorial court, which was thinly attended and little heeded. In the ancient boroughs the machinery of government set up in their medieval or Elizabethan charters lumbered on, with much creaking and groaning, as they were confronted with problems and situations undreamt of when the charters were sealed. In 1833 the Reform Parliament appointed one of its many royal commissions 'to inquire into the existing state of the Municipal Corporations in England and Wales and to collect information respecting the defects in their constitution'; Joseph Parkes was secretary. They were given eighteen months in which to scour the country and discover which towns claimed to be boroughs and under what warrant, what powers they had and how they used them. It is

---

[1] Quoted S. and B. Webb, *English Local Government: the Manor and the Borough* (1980), ii. 714*n.*

not surprising that some of the reports on individual boroughs were never completed, and others not until after the Act had been drafted and passed.

What is unfortunate for us is that T. J. Hogg, the friend and future biographer of Shelley and the commissioner to whom Caernarvonshire boroughs were entrusted, was one of the defaulters. He never reported on Caernarvon at all, and his other reports were received only after parliament, without waiting for fuller information, had resolved to include Caernarvon and Pwllheli in the new Act and to exclude the rest. Hogg, like most of his fellow-commissioners, had strong prejudices against the existing corporations and a strong belief in the virtues of government by elected representatives; but it is in any case clear from surviving records that Caernarvon was the only one of the five boroughs where the corporate machinery was really working. They all had their borough officials, of course — mayor, bailiffs, recorder, petty constables and a few minor functionaries; the offices, except that of mayor, were generally filled by local tradesmen. In the castellated boroughs of Caernarvon, Conway and Cricieth the constable of the castle, who was *ex-officio* mayor, was appointed by the crown. This, however, had little to do with the internal management of borough affairs, except that the office of constable became a prize for political factions among the neighbouring gentry and a means of swamping the electorate with imported burgesses, and so weakening the sense of civic responsibility among the residents.

Conway was saved from much of this by the absence of a dominating family; on the other hand during the long periods when the crown appointed no constable the burgesses had usurped the power of electing their own alderman to manage routine borough business, and when in 1769 the newly appointed constable, John Parry (who later represented the shire in two parliaments) claimed to be sworn in as mayor, the burgesses stalled. The issue remained unsettled in Parry's lifetime and indeed for more than thirty years after his death; at last in 1831 the burgesses had to cave in and accept as mayor the constable nominated twenty years earlier. At Cricieth, as an earlier chapter has shown, the Brogyntyn family had acquired the hereditary constableship and mayoralty; but Brogyntyn was far away, and Cricieth rarely saw its mayor except at election time; meanwhile the affairs of the borough, such as they were, were managed by the two bailiffs. The borough seal had been lost, and the inhabitants were completely ignorant of the contents of their charters. 'The Ruling Body in practice', reported Hogg 'is chosen simply and absolutely by Mr. Ormsby Gore'. The two 'civil' boroughs, Pwllheli and Nefyn, had no castles and therefore no constables. At Nefyn the mayoralty had become hereditary in the Glynllifon family, who took as little interest in the management of the town as the heredi-tary or nominated constables of the castellated boroughs,. and to all intents and purposes borough life was extinct well before the end of the eighteenth century; indeed several of the burgesses expressed themselves in 1838 as perfectly willing to surrender their corporate rights if their lands could be used to found schools or to support the poor. 'They considered the corporation of little use, because the out-burgesses came and out-voted them on all municipal occas-ions'. It will be remembered how nonchalantly these two boroughs signed away their valuable common lands to enclosure commissioners in 1811-12. At Pwllheli the mayor-alty remained elective, but civic interest was at just as low an ebb. A town with cheap living and good markets, it attracted residents of limited means, with no gentry and few substantial merchants; it was said that the nearest two resident magistrates were not on speaking terms! Rates, at 4s. 8d. in the £, brought in about £800, of which between £50 and £60 went to the county. The streets were neither effectively paved nor patrolled nor lighted, although there was a project of installing oil lamps.

In all four boroughs local government differed little save in name from that of Bangor, which had no municipal status. All were for most practical purposes under the rule of the county justices, who held monthly petty sessions at Conway and Cricieth (for geographical convenience rather than in recognition of any special status), but dealt with major offences from all four in their quarter sessions. Conway and Pwllheli had local courts meeting every two or three weeks under the recorder (usually a nominee of the mayor) for the collection of petty debts; Nefyn was entitled by charter to such a court but had allowed it to lapse. Conway originally had its own commission of the peace but that too was a thing of the past, and the quarter sessions had been removed from it to Caernarvon about 1793. The petty constables arrested and took to the lock-up brawlers, pilferers and drunks (remitting all serious cases to quarter sessions) and spent much time driving to the pound pigs and other stray animals that swarmed in the streets. In this the smaller boroughs were on a par with any other village; in fact a village manorial court was often a more active body than these borough courts with high-sounding names.

Caernarvon, with a population more than three times that of Pwllheli (the next most populous borough), and a still greater preponderance in the number of its resident burgesses, had more of the character of a genuine borough, though even here the separate commission of the peace conceded in the charter had fallen into disuse. From about 1800 increasing population and increasing traffic forced the corporation to undertake some improvements in the lay-out of the town, such as the removal (not always with discretion) of ancient buildings which had become insanitary with disuse, and the provision of more openings through the town walls for the convenience of traffic to the town centre. The gentry, or most of them, had long since ceased to live in the town houses they had built from Tudor times onwards, and all but a few of these had either become derelict or were being converted into shops and offices, while building societies were helping the better paid artisans to build small houses in the town centre or out beyond the walls. Caernarvon was losing the dignified air it had presented in earlier engravings. About 1816 the streets were paved with cobbles; the first water supply was brought by the corporation from

Llyn Cwellyn in 1829, and a private company added a supplementary reservoir. In the next decade the corporation also built new markets and installed gas lighting, but the gasworks were later leased out to private contractors. The corporation was able to meet some of this outlay from properties which brought in about £800 a year, but many of the bigger operations were covered wholly or in part by private benevolence or public subscription. The conversion of the old exchequer office for North Wales into a town hall in 1767 was due to the generosity of Glynllifon, the erection of the public baths fifty-six years later to that of Plas Newydd; the baths — claimed (incredibly) to have cost £10,000 — were in use for not much more than a quarter of a century. The levelling of the Maes in 1817, by way of ' relief works ', was carried out by public subscription, as was also the rebuilding of the town church (St. Mary's), where the curious arrangement prevailed that the corporation received the pew rents but paid the organist. The new pier built in 1827 was another gift to the borough.

Yet the business of running the town was obviously becoming more expensive. The total expenditure of the corporation during the two years 1821-3 only came to about half the annual revenue from corporation property. With one exception the payments were all small and of a routine character; the biggest item was £47 for new robes to be worn when George IV, on his return from a visit to Ireland, was greeted by the councillors at the Marquess of Anglesey's, where he was staying. We have only to pass on another five years to see a big change: the expenditure for 1828-9 amounted to £1,400, including £240 for drains and over £500 in legal costs. This could not be met out of revenue and the corporation was uncertain of its power to meet the deficit by levying a rate, so resort was had to the policy of borrowing from local tradesmen. By 1830-1 mortgage interest amounted to £270, and a further £375 had been laid out on the market.

In 1827 a Bill was promoted for ' paving, lighting and

improving the town of Carnarvon'. This landed the corporation in further expense; £234 were raised towards the
costs by subscription, but the town clerk's expenses alone
came to nearly twice as much. The Bill involved departures
from the terms of the charter, and this roused the combative
instincts of Dr. O. O. Roberts. He maintained that the effect
was to turn Caernarvon into a ' closed corporation ', and in
order to remind his fellow-burgesses of their rights he printed
and published the text of the charter. He also attended the
House of Commons as a hostile witness, and was backed by
Sir Robert Williams, M.P. for the shire — who was soon,
as we have seen, to become Dr. Roberts's political *bête noire*.
From the borough member, Paget (whom he also opposed
politically) he received no support. Nevertheless the Bill was
defeated, and on his triumphal return Roberts was fêted at
a public dinner by his grateful backers.

The defeat was a severe blow to the finances of the corporation. By 1831 its debts amounted to £14,000, and investigation revealed that its annual income was entirely swallowed up in mortgage interest. In 1834 an official receiver
was appointed by the court of chancery for the mortgagees
in possession. This was the situation when in the following
year the Municipal Corporations Act was passed, based on
the findings and proposals of the commissioners of 1833. The
Act was applied, somewhat arbitrarily, to 183 boroughs out
of the 285 investigated; in each of these the old corporation
was dissolved and a new one substituted, with all the
familiar modern paraphernalia of a town council elected by
the whole body of male ratepayers of three years' residence,
and empowered to choose its own mayor and aldermen, to
impose rates and to formulate bye-laws. Some boroughs
were given their own commission of the peace, some
remained judically subject to quarter sessions. Here the Act
was applied only to the two largest boroughs, Caernarvon
and Pwllheli; the other three were left over for future consideration (which as it turned out was shelved for nearly half
a century) — the theory being that however badly they were
run, numbers affected were too small to matter greatly.

Caernarvon recovered its commission of the peace; Pwllheli
was left under the jurisdiction of the county bench.

The new corporation at Caernarvon made a bad start by
inheriting its predecessor's debts and a lawsuit provoked by
them, in which collusion at the public expense between the
opposing lawyers was shrewdly suspected. A finance committee was set up in 1837 to examine the accounts, and
eventually the town's affairs were untangled; but naturally
the new governing body was reluctant to burn its fingers
with any expensive improvements. Nor did the Act encourage them to do so. The assumption that the work of
governing a borough meant primarily the maintenance of
law and order, the abatement of nuisances and the protection
of property — in other words a mainly negative view of
government — was carried forward from the old corporations to the new; developments and amenities remained
primarily a matter for private benevolence, and until after
1870 no central body was set up (despite the example set by
the new Poor Law in 1834) to hold a watching brief over
the new corporations and to make recommendations. Even
law and order were maintained on a shoestring: Caernarvon's police force under the Act consisted of three
completely ineffective constables. So it is not surprising that
the council minutes so often amounted to little but the
laconic entry:[2] ' There being no business the meeting was
adjourned ', and that a much-needed clean-up of the town
was also adjourned — till after 1860, in the mayoralty of
Sir Llewelyn Turner, after a sharp lesson had been learned
from the cholera outbreak, and a local Improvement Board
had been set up. The increasing powers with which local
authorities were invested by the sanitary and housing legislation of the last quarter of the century — to say nothing of
the still heavier responsibilites with which they have been
saddled in our own time — have made lack of time rather
than lack of business the bugbear of local councils.

The belief of the radical reformers that democratic insti-

'Ll. Turner, *Memories*, ch. viii.

tutions were the sovereign remedy for the ills of local government was nowhere more strikingly refuted than at Pwllheli.
'Between 1847 and 1856', says the historian of the Caernarvonshire police,[3] 'the corporation . . . lapsed into decay;
no mayor was elected and there is no record of any borough
council meeting'. Nor, as we have seen, was there any
central authority to force the local guardians of the law to
obey it themselves. Any outside intrusion into the town's
'private affairs', whether on the part of excise officers or of
a government inspector of police, was stoutly resisted. From
1857 the borough tried to safeguard its isolationist policy
(which was made easier by the fact that the railway did not
reach it for another decade) by a succession of petitions for
the separate commission of the peace which had been withheld in the Act of 1835. At the same time the council tried
to justify itself by appointing a borough police force consisting of one man (a tailor) with a salary of £40 and a
uniform, on the strength of which he was expected to patrol
the streets, serve as inspector of lodging houses and of
weights and measures (the latter by guess work), and as town
crier — and indeed to carry out any other municipal odd
jobs that were called for. In emergencies he could call on
the help of a few middle-aged special constables at half-a-
crown a day. The town council resisted with equal tenacity
attempts to merge its one-man borough force into the new
county police. But the arrival of the railway in 1867 made
it impossible any longer for Pwllheli to trade on its seclusion.
A dozen years later it came into line with the rest of the
county, and put its house in order.

At Conway the old corporation continued to operate, with
a virtually permanent mayor chosen from among the neighbouring gentry, for more than forty years after the Act. It
was in the fortunate position of having conserved much of
its extensive borough property; moreover population was
only slowly rising, and there were no acute problems of
poverty or housing to contend with. It was stated that a

[3] J. O. Jones, *History of the Caernarvonshire Constabulary*, iv.

new lock-up built in 1827 had scarcely been used in the
ensuing ten years, and that there had been no fines at court
leet within living memory. As we have seen, it was not till
the 'sixties that Conway found it necessary to build a workhouse, and even then it was rarely filled. To meet expanding
trade, a new quay had been opened in 1833, at a cost of
£1,260, of which the corporation had to borrow £400. But
it was the arrival of the railway in 1848 that changed the
face of things. As trade and traffic increased, the corporation
grew disenchanted with its antiquated machinery of government, and in 1875 it applied for a new charter under the
Act of 1835. This came into force the following year, and a
third Caernarvonshire borough exchanged its medieval constitution for an up-to-date one. Not so the other two.
Cricieth, with a population of under four hundred at the
beginning of the century and only twice as many in mid-
century, found it increasingly difficult to fill its borough
offices, and in 1873 the Cricieth Improvement Act passed
through parliament, exchanging the ancient borough machinery for that of a local Board of Health, which in turn gave
place to an Urban District Council under the Act of 1894.
At Nefyn, after the Reform Act of 1832 had rescued the
borough from the fate which had so long stifled collective
life — that of serving as a pawn in political manoeuvres of
the neighbouring gentry — a gallant attempt was made to
make its decrepit institutions work, but the struggle had to
be abandoned when a new Municipal Corporations Act in
1882 deprived it of borough status, along with some thirty
other small corporations. A dozen years later it sank its
identity (except as a parish) in the newly-created Llŷn
Rural District. On the other hand Bangor, having secured
a local Board of Health in 1859, abandoned it just under a
quarter of a century later for a charter of the usual pattern
under the Municipal Corporation Act.

While local government was thus modernised in the
larger boroughs by the Act of 1835, in the county itself the
antiquated Tudor machinery remained essentially unchanged

for a further half-century. The reason for this is no doubt
that the county justices, as their name indicates, were in
origin a judicial body, and had by no means ceased to have
this character even when the administrative duties growing
out of it came to absorb more and more of their attention.
The quarter sessions were a court of law, but a court which
in the course of its duties found itself having to issue
administrative orders; it has been shown in an earlier
chapter, for example, how urgent road repairs were sometimes effected by having a peculiarly bad patch ' presented '
before the justices (whether by a private citizen or by the
General Post Office), and using the fine imposed on the
defaulting parish to pay for having the job done. The radical
group which was behind the Municipal Corporations Act,
with all its faith in the principle of election as the panacea
for all ills, shrank from emulating the not very encouraging
American example of elected judges, so they left the quarter
sessions alone, little as they loved the Tory landlords who sat
there. It is true that a new Highways Act took away from the
J.P.'s in this same year their authority over roads, but they
were still left in control of bridges. The Poor Law of 1834,
had tranferred to a new elected authority their power over
poor relief (and at the same times placed on a more professional footing the lower stratum of local government in the
parishes); but it was still under their jurisdiction, through
the petty constables, that lawbreakers were arrested, and
they were responsible for the county gaols. Moreover it was
difficult to impose any rates in the shire, other than the poor
rate and the Church rate, without their sanction.

What modernisation was carried out in county government
was the work of the justices themselves. Gradually the
practice spread of employing salaried officials instead of men
who depended on their fees. By 1840 the Caernarvonshire
clerk of the peace was receiving £220 in salary and expenses,
and the county surveyor about half as much. They were no
doubt professional men to whom the shire paid a retaining
fee for part-time services. A more striking example is the
management of the county gaol at Caernarvon. This was

given a conspicuously bad mark in John Howard's famous report on the condition of prisons, of which the third and enlarged edition came out in 1784. It appears that in spite of legislation which Howard himself had put through nearly ten years earlier, the Caernarvon gaoler still lived entirely on fees for admission and discharge of prisoners, together with what could be extorted from the inmates themselves. The premises (apparently a former chapel of the garrison) were ruinous and insanitary. Even before the report was published, the magistrates, stirred by the widespread concern which Howard's propaganda had aroused throughout the country, held a special meeting in 1783 and resolved to build a new prison, for which they now took full responsibility, although hitherto this had been in the sheriff's province. In 1823 they installed in it a treadmill — then, strangely enough, looked on as a progressive and humane measure. By 1840 the gaol was costing the justices over £600 in maintenance, repairs and salaries: to offset this there were occasional returns (£254, for example, in 1867-8) on the produce of convict labour. Yet another new prison had to be built in 1867, at a cost of over £1,000.

These mounting expenses had, of course, to be met by the imposition of rates. In 1840 the cost of administering the county stood at over £5,000, of which nearly £2,000 went in bridge repairs made necessary by the increase of traffic, and about £2,500 in the administration of justice in its various branches. To meet all this, the rates came to a little more than £4,000, the balance being met by fines and licences. By the standards then prevailing, this was big business, and an official was needed to keep the books. Since the eighteenth century some of the larger English shires were meeting this problem by appointing one of their own number as honorary treasurer, but towards the end of the century the great increase in county business was calling for the employment of a salaried official from outside. Caernarvonshire had a treasurer, but not a professional one, by 1815; but by 1840 the office had been conferred on a Caernarvon lawyer with considerable (if not very successful) experience in handling the borough finances. From that year he and his successors issued regular printed accounts for the benefit of the magistrates, and circulated a summary of them for the ratepayers at large in the local press. But what the treasurer was paid was by way of retaining fee or honorarium rather than salary: it came to a little over £60 in 1840 and only about twice as much a quarter of a century later. By that time the treasurer of the West Riding had a salary of £600; some English shires had been paying as much as that for thirty or forty years.

In 1856 the county justices were saddled with fresh responsibilities and expenditure under the County Police Act. Up to then, while the Act of 1835 had provided for some sort of professional policing of the boroughs — however inefficient this proved in practice — the countryside was left to the tender mercies of the unpaid parish constable, with only the mild reform of 1830 which permitted the payment of substitute constables and the building of new lock-ups out of the county rates. In practice the onus of protecting property and chasing criminals was thrown on to the private householder, and all that the parish could provide if the culprit was caught was a filthy and insecure lock-up; one of the many petitions with which Dr. O. O. Roberts was wont to bombard the government was a complaint to the Home Office in 1842 about the condition of the Bangor lock-up. On the other hand, Bangor had at least set up, under the permissive Lighting and Watching Act of 1833, a patrol of three or four paid constables, even if they were a constant butt of correspondence in the local press. The wave of crimes against property, in the country generally, which followed in the wake of the Napoleonic wars and the Industrial Revolution, was met by the formation among the local gentry of Associations for the Prosecution of Felons. Such Associations were organised, from 1808 onwards, in Llŷn and Eifionydd, at Bangor and Caernarvon, and eventually at Portmadoc, Pwllheli and Llandudno. Support for them ebbed and flowed in response to the movements of the crime wave. At best they were no more than organisations of property owners to protect their possessions by the offer of premiums, on a sliding scale, for the capture of thieves and *saboteurs,* and there is no evidence that even within these limits they were conspicuously successful. Crimes of violence did not come within their scope, but such crimes — so far as the evidence of the lawcourts goes — were rare in the county.

Indeed these sketchy police arrangements could never have stood up to crime on any extensive scale; but owing largely to the religious revivals ('the distribution of Welsh Bibles by London and other Societies' was the artless explanation of one contemporary),[4] law-abiding habits were pretty general in the shire. There were 'white glove' assizes at Caernarvon in 1808, 1809 and 1814, and very few cases in the intervening and following years until the general distress which began with the slump of 1817 brought its crop of thefts, burglaries and plundering of wrecks; an outstanding example of this last crime at Llandudno in 1824 was cited in an earlier context. Between 1822 and 1830 there were at least five executions at Caernarvon, mostly for sheep stealing or burglary. Both of these ceased to be capital offences while Peel was at the Home Office during this period. In 1823, on what must have been one of the last occasions when a sheep-stealer was hanged at Caernarvon (or anywhere else), the local paper commented:[5] 'As it is not a crime now prevalent in the country, we trust our county may be spared . . . another public execution'. The wish was premature; it is true that sheep stealers during the following years were transported instead of hanged, but a burglar was condemned to death as late as 1830, though it is doubtful whether the sentence was carried out, since that crime too had just been expunged from the list of capital offences. Actually the last execution at Caernarvon (for murder) did not take place till 1910; it is believed to have been the last occasion in the country when the black flag was hoisted and the press invited to witness the execution.

[4] *Imperial and County Register,* 1810, pt. v.
[5] *N. Wales Gazette,* 3 Apr., 1823.

There was a recrudescence of crime throughout the land from 1828, but Caernarvonshire participated only to the extent of an increase in commitments in that year from fourteen to twenty-two. What we do not know, of course, is how many criminals escaped the law altogether. By 1856 it was estimated that a fifteenth part of the population of the whole kingdom lived by crime, and it was now that the government resolved to make compulsory the raising of a paid and uniformed police force in every county; this had been tried out on a voluntary basis seventeen years earlier, without much success. Under the new Act the Caernarvonshire justices appointed a chief constable at a salary of £250, with £50 for expenses. The post was given to a Welsh-speaking member of the country gentry with militia experience — T. P. Williams Ellis of Glasfryn, Llangybi. It was he who licked into shape a force consisting, initially, of four inspectors at £65 a year, four sergeants on a weekly wage of 23s. (rather less than a quarryman's wage of the time) and twenty-eight constables at 16s. to 19s., which was substantially above a farm labourer's pay. It was not a large force to keep order among a population approaching 100,000, but at least it was a disciplined, organised and well-deployed force, for under the Act the justices had to provide new lock-ups dotted over the county to serve as police stations. Half the cost was borne by the Treasury, subject to a satisfactory report from the Home Office, which exercised a general supervision.

Even so, it meant a substantial increase in county expenditure, and a new police rate to meet it. Before the rule of the justices came to an end, the police rate was heavier than the general county rate, though today both would be objects of envy : a penny in the pound for the one (bringing in about £1,400), and a penny farthing for the other (about £1,750). Further responsibilities were heaped on to the counties during the following years. After the Crimean war, thanks to Florence Nightingale's agitation about the wretched condition of soldiers' quarters, they had to provide barracks for the county militia; they also had to share in the cost of the new North Wales asylum, built at Denbigh in 1848. Then there was the heavy cost of the new gaol and the new county hall at Caernarvon. By 1875 the justices were borrowing, on the security of the county rates, to the extent of some £30,000.

It was not only the growing complexity and financial commitments of local government that were now making the rule of the justices seem an outdated survival; the control of the county police by a body of big employers and land-owners, who in Caernarvonshire were almost exclusively Tory in politics, was bound to incur suspicions of partiality whenever the force was called out to deal with riots with possible political undertones. It happened during the troubles over the Caerhûn enclosure in 1858; it happened again ten years later over the Nantlle election disturbances. It is incidents of this sort that form the background to the County Councils Act of 1888, in which a Tory government extended to the shires the electoral system that had been applied to the boroughs by a Whig ministry fifty-three years earlier. In Caernarvonshire the elections were fought from the first on party lines, and this helped to consolidate the hold which the Liberals had been gaining on the county since the Ballot Act and Gladstone's Reform Bill of 1884. It is significant that W. J. Parry, the quarryman's leader, and an ardent Liberal, was made vice-chairman of the first county council, and David Lloyd George an alderman. But there was not a complete breach of continuity, for eighteen of the magistrates were candidates at the first election, and ten of them were returned.

Encouraged by the ambitious dreams of T. E. Ellis, the early councils thought of themselves as miniature local Westminsters, and debated such national issues as leasehold reform, Sunday closing and sweated labour. But the members soon found themselves with quite enough local issues on their plates without straying far into national politics. The rising expenditure of the justices had not extended to matters like education, roads and public health, and the care of the poor had remained in the hands of the Poor Law

Unions; before long all these were added to the commitments of the new county councils. On the other hand, an offer in 1891 to hand over the suspension bridge across the Straits from the bridge commissioners to the county council was turned down. The difficulty of transferring control of the police to a body even more avowedly (if differently) partisan in its political complexion than the justices had been, was got over by the compromise of control by a joint committee drawn from the two bodies. Apart from this and their licensing duties, the magistrates reverted to their original function as a judicial body, and the Act of 1889 was the death-knell of a system of county government which had persisted from the time of the Tudors. The long rule of the gentry, which in national affairs had been ended by the Reform Acts, was now driven from its last refuge in local government.

## BIBLIOGRAPHY

Sources for the history of the ancient boroughs of Pwllheli, Cricieth and Nefyn are listed in bibliography to chap. I; on Conway see N. Tucker, *Conway and its Story* (1960), and on Caernarvon, works by W. H. Jones and K. Evans listed in bibliography to ch. XIII A. T. J. Hogg's report on the four boroughs is in *Reports upon Certain Boroughs (Parl. Papers* 1837-8, xxxv). The printed financial accounts of the last years of the old corporation of Caernarvon and the first years of the new, and also of the county treasurers from 1840, are filed in U.C.N.W. library, Bangor. Particulars of criminal prosecutions are from the local press, and of the police force from J. O. Jones (see ch. XIII A). The early years of the county council are described in *County Councils Jubilee Handbook (Caernarvonshire),* 1938.

# INDEX

Bulkeley, Richard (3rd Vsct.), 188, 209-10
„ Richard (4th Vsct.), 188-90, 193
„ James (6th Vsct), 318
„ T. J. (7th Vsct), 210-11, 313, 315-6, 322, 374
Bulkeley Hughes, 332, 362-3
Burgess, Bp., 345
Bwlch y ddeufaen, 124, 210, 268
Byng, 199
Byron, 108, 115, 117-8, 120-6, 131
Cadiz, 27
Caerhûn, 50, 240, 288, 289, 368, 412
Caernarvon: (See also Llanbeblig)
  Borough: Politics and government, 12, 16, 33, 44, 69, 71, 73, 78, 79, 95, 162, 166, 190, 200, 237, 319, 332-3, 399, 401, 403, 408, 409, 410; county hall, 412; exchequer office, 402; town hall, 150, 193, 360, 372, 402
  Education and culture, 158, 173, 221, 227, 336, 367-8, 372, 374, 378-9, 383-6, 389, 393, 395-6
  Religion, 37, 143, 170, 172, 219-20, 222, 225, 227, 253, 340, 342-3, 346, 358-9, 383.
  Families, 77-8, 98
  Social life, 249, 285, 287, 289, 296-8, 300, 309, 317, 366
  Maes, 287, 402
  Morfa Seiont, 239
  Plas Mawr, 28, 34, 77
  Twthill, 298
  Castle, military affairs, 14, 19, 26, 70, 78, 118, 122-8, 131, 133-4, 143, 151-2, 154, 156, 160, 192-3, 316, 319

Harbour, trade and communications, 34-5, 94, 198, 202-3, 205, 211-13, 245, 247, 251, 256, 268, 271, 274, 276-7, 280-2, 287, 304, 402
Caernarvon Union, 290, 293, 307
Caernarvon and Denbigh Herald, 330
Caernarvonshire and Anglesey Infirmary, 296-7, 300, 301
Caerwys, 29, 32
Caledfryn, 359, 374, 386
Cambria, 277
Cambridge, 50, 53, 55, 82, 137, 142, 349
Cambridgeshire, 100
Campbell, Bp, 351
Canada, 307, 310
Candles, 283, 285
Cantrefi, 11, 13
Canwyll y Cymru, 143
Capel Curig, 92, 264, 266-7, 269, 338
„ Helyg. (See Ty Helyg)
„ Newydd, 337, 340
Capell, 108, 110
Capon (See Salcot)
Carbery, Earl of, 160
Cardiganshire, 222, 335, 339, 373, 380, 381
Carding, 259, 261
Carmarthen, 340
Carmarthenshire, 29, 142, 220, 221, 340, 373
Carn Fadrun, 238
Carriers, 269
Carter, Col. J., 127, 131, 132, 134, 139, 151, 154
Casson, 281
Castellmarch, 30, 69, 79, 82, 91, 97, 103, 130, 134, 144, 153, 154, 184. (See also Jones)
Castellmarch Ucha. (See Ty'n y Coed)
Catechising, catechism, 40, 47, 61, 217, 221, 379, 380, 384

Flintshire, 35, 69, 96, 103, 111,
128, 148, 165, 168, 187, 205,
207, 208, 212, 259, 270, 280,
284, 297, 318, 365
Foelas, 61
Fort Belan, 311-12
„ Williamsburg, 194, 311
Foryd Bay, 251
Fox, Charles Jas., 314-6, 318, 322
„ George, 172
Foxe, 85
Foxwist, 129-30, 145, 148, 150,
151, 153
France, French, 18, 19, 27, 57,
103, 128, 130, 167, 168, 187,
194, 236, 242, 244, 260, 283,
311, 328
French Revolution, 318, 321
„ Wars: Creçy and Poitiers,
17; Revolutionary and
Napoleonic, 234, 286, 296,
301, 303-4, 306, 318-9, 409
Freeholders, 65-7, 70, 72, 313,
321
Friendly Societies, 282, 301
Friends, Society of. (See Quakers)
Fulling, fulling mills, 257-8, 261

G

Gaols, 407-8, 412. (See also Lock-
ups)
Garn Dolbenmaen, 303, 306
Garrisons, 110, 113, 116, 118,
122, 123, 127, 131, 133, 146
Gas, 402
Gaskell, Mrs. Elizabeth, 256
Gavelkind, 66
Gentry, rise of, 21
George I, 188, 191
„ III, 192, 194, 196, 237, 296,
312, 314, 317, 322
„ IV, 322, 324
Gerard, 27
Germany, 229, 264, 341

Gladstone, 358, 362-3, 392, 394
412
Glamorgan, Earl of, 120-1. (See
also Worcester)
Glanogwen, 350
Glasdŵr, 103, 144
Glasfryn, 222-3, 229, 411
Glaslyn, R., 275
Gloddaeth, 60, 137, 168, 182, 208,
273
Gloucester, 39
Glyn Cywarch, 180
Glyn Dŵr, 16, 18-21, 24, 26, 37,
44, 156
Glyn, Geoffrey, 31, 46
Glynne (Glynllifon), 29, 38, 86;
Edmund, 129, 149, 153, 160;
John, 91, 97-8, 128-32, 145,
147, 148, 153, 157, 165, 177;
Thomas, 76, 93, 97-8, 101-3,
109, 112, 114, 125, 128-9, 131,
132, 138, 157; William (arch-
deacon), 42, 76; William (2),
76; William (3), 76, 153, 160
Glynne, William (Bp.), 50-1
„ (Lleuar), 135, 149, 164
Glynllifon, 42, 43-4, 84, 104, 186,
191-6, 200, 205, 247, 259, 261,
286, 311, 316, 325, 329, 331,
362, 400, 402. (See also Glynne)
Gogarth, 156
Goldwell, T., 51
Gouge, 173-4
Grasmere, 241
Great Sessions, 58, 79, 145, 166,
208, 223
Greenfield, 246, 249, 254
Grenfell, 280
Grey, Lord, 325
Griffith ap John, 30
Griffith (Cefnamwlch), 31, 71, 75,
325; Edmund (Bp.), 88, 89,
163; Hugh, 31; John, (1), 70,
73, 77-8; John (2), 59, 81, 82,
85, 98, 102, 103, 105, 107, 110;